RARE WILD FLOWERS
OF
NORTH AMERICA

RARE WILD FLOWERS
OF
NORTH AMERICA

by

Leonard Wiley

Photographic Illustrations
by the Author
except where credited

Published by the Author
at
2927 Southeast 75th Avenue
Portland, Oregon
1968

Member of the Authors Guild of the Authors League of America

Library of Congress Catalog Card Number: 68-18618

First Edition

Published January 2, 1968

Previous Book By Leonard Wiley

Wild Harvest

Printed in the United States of America
Typography and printing by Western Lithograph
Portland, Oregon

Wayne
and
Mildred Olsson
R.M.

CONTENTS

CONTENTS

CONTENTS

INTRODUCTION

The first wild flower I ever saw was a buttercup growing in a small meadow. I picked it and took it with me to school. Although more than half a century has elapsed since that morning I remember as clearly as though it were yesterday how disappointed I was that it withered before I arrived there.

It was the first of my floral failures, and while there have been many others, there have been more successes. Since that first neighborhood excursion at the age of six or seven I have wandered farther afield. The intervening years have seen me at the seaside meadows, on the alpine slopes of the mountains and on the open prairies stretching into far distances. On these meanderings, covering untold miles and more than 50 years, it was inevitable that I should discover plants so rare that not many have seen them. These unscheduled events have been among my greatest pleasures. And they have been among my greatest disappointments too for I have never had anyone with me to share the rarities I have blundered upon. There are many people throughout the land whose interests parallel mine but who have had fewer opportunities and fewer privileges than I have enjoyed. Why not share what I have learned about the rarest wild flowers in all America? That is why I decided to write this book.

What is a wild flower? It is simply a plant that has not been domesticated at all, or to a limited extent, or for only a comparatively short period of time. Directly or indirectly our garden flowers came from the wild. Plant breeders have altered the appearance of many of them so that they have little resemblance to their wild ancestors.

To be accepted in the ordinary home garden a plant must be tolerant of different kinds of soils and watering varying with the vagaries of the owners. They have to be able to adapt to unfamiliar climates and above all, they must be easy to grow. Plants that cannot meet these requirements usually remain wild. An Iris with a fleshy rhizome or a bulb, for instance, will endure much more abuse and neglect than some of our wire rooted species that are a little fussy about the treatment they get, especially when it comes to transplanting. Nevertheless, with a little study and a little attention to their special needs many of them can be happy around our homes. And a small amount of extra care is rewarded with an abundance of beauty.

I have never thought of wild flowers as ordinary plants. To me they are living individuals with a simple beauty that is theirs alone. A plant must have a great deal of character to thrive in a cliff side crevice narrower than the thickness of a thumb nail where soil and moisture for survival approach the non-existent. They can endure the blasting heat of mid summer and the below zero chills of winter gales. In spite of these severe conditions personality expresses itself during flowering time with a shower of blossoms. Is it any wonder that the best of wild flowers are very much like the best of people?

A common native plant isn't necessarily lacking in beauty nor is a rare one inevitably possessed with great charm. These circumstances are totally unrelated.

There is no nomenclature indicating the rarity of plants. I have chosen the following words to serve that purpose:

1. **Common**
2. **Unusual.**
3. **Scarce.**
4. **Rare.**
5. **Very Rare.**
6. **Extremely Rare.**

1. **Common**. One that has a wide distribution and is relatively abundant within that range. *Trillium grandiflorum,* well known in the middlewestern, northeastern states and Canada, comes within this category.

2. **Unusual.** It may be common in a more limited range or be less abundant within a wide range. *Iris tenax* of the West Coast satisfies the first half of this definition and some of the *Cypripediums* take care of the last.

3. **Scarce**. Either hard to find if widely distributed or more abundant in small areas. *Calypso borealis*, the Deer Head Orchid, generally fits into this classification.

4. **Rare**. May have only an occasional plant here and there over a wide range or more readily found in a very limited area. The Green Spleenwort, *Asplenium viride,* usually difficult to find but covers the northern half of North America as well as parts of Europe and Asia, for the first part of the definition.

Campanula piperi of the high Olympics of northwestern Washington belongs in the last part.

5. Very Rare. Usually limited to a small area and often not at all abundant within its range. Oconee Bells, *Shortia galacifolia,* found in only a few places in the mountains of the Carolinas, certainly is a very rare plant.

6. Extremely Rare. This is the most exclusive classification of all. It includes such species as the Phantom Orchid, *Cephalanthera austinae,* which, though it grows from Washington to central California, is so rare that one may search for years without finding it. This group also includes mutations of color or form. *Campanula piperi 'White'* is only known in two or three places in the Olympics with only a few plants in each location. For these reasons it is included in this group. So does the multipetaled *Trillium grandiflorum* whose stamens and pistils have modified into petals, making a flower of two dozen petals, more or less. Fortunate indeed is the person who ever finds such a plant or knows someone who has.

Complete detailed information upon the distribution of wild plants in North America has never been compiled and probably never will be. Texts usually tell that plants are found in various states and occasionally the particular counties in the states will be mentioned. Only in a few cases will more particularized locations be given.

Some of the rare plants can be obtained from nurseries or by trading with individuals who grow them in their gardens. A number of them are surprisingly easy to grow for those who have only a smattering of horticultural knowledge. Others require special conditions and skilled knowledge. A few can be grown by some individuals where most fail. And, according to our present knowledge, occasional species are well nigh impossible to do anything with at all. No plant, however, should be considered totally impossible. If it grows unattended in nature it can be grown in the garden too. This philosophy at least is not one of failure and, in some cases, has been attended with unexpected and surprising success. It must be remembered that nature may send out thousands of seeds to produce a single plant. Naturally enough we want a better percentage of success than that and I think there is a reasonable possibility of getting it.

Before starting to dig there are a few restrictions to observe:

All property belongs to someone. If it isn't yours, permission should be obtained. This applies to privately owned lands as well as state and federal holdings. An irate rancher who catches you invading his property may be a very friendly person if you go to his home first and ask permission.

Collecting permits are usually comparatively easy to get in United States National Forests from the District Rangers whose words are authoritative and final. Permits from United States National Parks are virtually impossible to get. One of the five requirements is that you must belong to a recognized scientific body. That eliminates most people. State Park regulations vary considerably, all the way from the rigidity of the U.S. National Parks to no written permits required at all. Restrictions vary in state and county lands.

I have always requested permission from private land holders and have been refused only once. And numerous times the owners have gone out of their way to show me exactly where I could find what I wanted on their ranches. If you ignore the rights of others you can be arrested, fined, jailed and sued. Triple damages can be collected.

On public lands permits are intended to keep supplies from being exhausted and from removing plants from near roads, trails, forest camps and botanical areas where they can be enjoyed by all.

Wild flowers are found in much greater variety in the western third of North America from the Rockies to the Pacific than in the eastern two-thirds of the continent. The reasons are easy to understand. The marked variations in climate: high mountains, lowland valleys, seaside meadows with heavy rains, deserts, bitter winters of timberline and balmy Decembers near the beaches have all combined to produce a varied flora adapted to the radical conditions in which they must live. The middle west is largely prairie country and the eastern sea coast mountains are nowhere near as lofty as the Rockies, the Wallowas, Cascades, the Siskiyous, and the other ranges that have transformed much of this country into lofty peaks, terrifying cliffs and a multitude of gorges, coves and canyons.

PLANT COLLECTING

Wild flowers purchased from nurseries usually cost less than collected wild plants and they should have stronger root systems and more vigor. But collected plants offer an opportunity to observe the conditions under which they live in their native habitats. This is a very real advantage and there is no substitute for knowledge obtained in this way – knowledge that can be truly useful in making them happy in your gardens. The extra cost in time and traveling expenses is well spent.

If you are fortunate enough to have a friend who knows wild flowers, take him along. He can teach you more in a single day than you could learn by yourself in weeks.

When I start on a field trip I wear a woolen shirt with the pockets full of pill bottles or tiny envelopes for seed. In one of my front overalls pockets I have a stub of a pencil and a small note book. In a back pocket I have a ball of heavy string. The other is crammed full of plastic bags, plastic sheets, and aluminum foil. I carry a peach or tomato box under one arm. It contains a stout trowel and a large amount of damp moss taken from tree trunks or the gound. Sad experience has taught me moss isn't often available when you want it on a collecting site. This box can be shifted from hip to hip without much fatigue. I have carried such a box for over nine miles, part of it where there were no trails. I can get more plants into it than in a pack sack and the specimens are not crushed. If small plants and bulbs are the object a back pack is more desirable. Over one shoulder I carry a clam shovel. It has a long, narrow, very strong blade and a short handle – ideal for larger plants. I carry a few candy bars and a couple or so sandwiches in plastic bags. When the sandwiches are gone the bags are used for plants. A quart canteen is carried on each hip – not to quench my thirst but to moisten the plants until I can get to a stream to give them a good soaking.

I adopt a slow steady pace and never stop except to make observations and to collect. At the end of the day I return to camp with all the plants I can carry, only comfortably tired, with a good appetite and a lot of satisfaction for a successful day's effort.

Transplanting wild plants from their native haunts to the home gardens involves very different problems than moving a domesticated plant from one part of the grounds to another. By learning how to bring home wild treasures successfully you will likewise learn, to a large degree, how to make them thrive. Double value for a single effort.

Many domesticated plants have become so accustomed to being moved that they no longer resent it greatly. Often they have compact root systems. Ordinarily they are planted in soils that are easy to work.

Wild plants often have weak, sprawling roots, which, when damaged, easily shock the plant to death. Our wild treasures are found in all types of soils – sticky clays, the muck of bogs, humus, in desert sands, and in the loose broken rock of the alpine talus slopes.

When domesticated shrubs are transplanted balling the roots is usually easy. And there isn't much to worry about the roots drying out or the foliage withering.

The plants brought in from the wild often cannot be balled in their own soil and they may be out of the ground for hours or even many days. I have brought plants home, successfully, that had been dug for as long as 11 days. It is very important to ball annual plants if the seed hasn't ripened. Otherwise the chance of maturing the seed is very poor.

Biennials present a special problem. It is better to get the first year plants as a rule. They can be expected to flower the next season and supply seed for the following year. But, to prevent a non-flowering season, try to bring back the second year, flowering ones too. Carefully balled they can often be induced to ripen seed, thusly insuring an uninterrupted yearly succession of bloom.

Perennials are the most important of the three groups. They come in numerous forms and sizes. Those which have bulbs, corms, tubers or rhizomes are quite easy to handle. If they are still actively growing they should be balled, the balls covered with thick layers of damp moss and placed in plastic bags or wrapped in aluminum foil. Then tie the wrappings snugly where the tops protrude. This effectively prevents the evaporation of moisture from the balls. Such treatment should be effective for at least a week without further attention. Larger plants may have to be balled with burlap. Plants growing in sandy or rocky soil may be difficult or impossible to ball. Usually a firmer soil can be found in the vicinity which will hold the roots together more compactly and retain moisture well.

If the bulbs, corms, etc., are dormant they should be packed in plastic bags containing peat, humus, or moss that has the barest trace of moisture. Anything more than a tiny amount of moisture may cause them to rot. This material should be so dry that the dampness can scarcely be detected at all. The purpose is merely to keep them from drying. These directions apply to scaly bulbs such as the true lilies, the coated bulbs such as *Brodiaeas, Alliums, Calochorti* and *Fritillarias.* Camas bulbs, being wet soil lovers, can be packed quite wet although this isn't necessary.

Species with massive or wire roots should have large balls of earth, covered with heavy layers of moss and packed in plastic bags or metal foil as with the annuals and biennials.

Bog plants require special treatment. They often have extensive root systems that go deeply and spread extensively. With few exceptions the crowns are out of the wet and the entire root systems feed on soil that has drainage. Few can tolerate stagnant water. These plants should be taken with a great deal of soil. Even then they will probably wither badly. Keep them as wet as you can. And protect the foliage with a covering of wet moss. It is amazing how rapidly these sturdy looking bog dwellers will droop.

The rock plants require extraordinary consideration too. I have yet to find a dweller of the natural rock gardens that didn't have either a very deep, a fleshy or an extensive root system.

Remove the soil carefully, if you can call this mass of broken rock soil, until you have exposed the entire root system. As fast as it is exposed cover it with wet soil or moss. These tiny roots are delicate and full of moisture to hold them over the dry season. The plants may be badly shocked if you break the tiny roots or let them dry out.

It is astonishing how deeply the roots of tiny plants will go in their search for moisture. It is just as astonishing how much of this rubble you will have to remove to get a single plant. But it is much wiser to gather a few plants carefully than to collect a large number haphazardly and wonder why they all die. The roots go down until they find moisture. And they always find it, for death is the price of failure.

When you finally get your plant – at the cost of a quart of mixed perspiration and blood, – ball the roots carefully in a good loam or humus soil. This should be on hand ready to use before you start digging. The material may be found along the edge of a stream or beneath forest trees.

Plants growing in crevices on cliff faces call for a cold chisel, hammer, muscle, and a good deal of patience. Start half a foot or so from the plant and split the rock away, working from all sides and closer and closer to the root system until it is completely exposed. Lift out the plant and pack immediately in damp soil before the tiny roots can dry out – this on a hot day, may be only a minute or less. If the rock is cut away too close to the plant at the start, the roots may be badly damaged as there is no certain way of determining in which direction the roots travel below the surface.

Desert plants may have roots so dry that the shock of transplanting may kill them. The answer to this problem is simple but time consuming. Soak the ground thoroughly and deeply before digging. If the soil is heavy clay it may take an hour or so to get the moisture deep enough to reach all the roots. It is no fun to stand dripping water on soil that is reluctant to take it when the sun is blazing down upon your head.

As you collect you will be constantly making observations of conditions under which you find plants. Temperature, sun, sand, drainage, acidity or alkalinity of soil, looseness of soil, rainfall, ground cover, fogs, humidity, protection from cold or drying winds, freedom of competition from other plants are all important. You will try to discover if the plant is growing under conditions best suited to its welfare or whether adverse conditions have crowded it out of its favorite haunts.

You will have to consider how to utilize these observations when you bring these plants to the very different conditions of your own gardens if you expect them to do well. Many of our wildlings have an amazing adaptability. Plants growing in full sun at high altitudes require a little shade at low elevations in order to balance the temperature.

Seeds may be collected in very small envelopes. But if the seeds are tiny they may sift out of the corners of the envelopes which are poorly sealed. Pill bottles with labels glued on before departing from home are excellent. A roll of scotch tape should be included in your equipment for the stoppers will sometimes come out and spill your seeds. When the bottle is filled, taping the stopper in place will prevent such losses. I make no attempt to clean seed as it is collected. This takes too much valuable field time for a task that can be done more efficiently during leisure hours at home.

The best time to collect deciduous plants is in the fall when they are dormant. Evergreens should be dug in early spring before top growth begins. These are ideal times but seldom practical. I do my collecting whenever I have the opportunity. If color forms are important – and they often are – the plants must be taken when they are in full flower. This is often the worst possible time of the year. If it can be done, stake these choice color forms and return when they are dormant. Usually this is not practical. As I often travel several hundreds of miles on collecting trips, a return for staked plants is hardly worthwhile.

I can bring these plants through successfully in my gardens regardless of the time of the year they are collected. I have made up a number of jets so fine that the water comes out of them in such a tiny stream that, when it strikes a baffle it is reduced to a mist so fine that it looks like smoke. I turn these jets on first thing in the morning and leave them on until sunset. This mist keeps the entire plant wet and cool all day and uses so little water that the ground underneath is kept only nicely moist without soaking. I use these jets every day until the cool, rainy days render them unnecessary. No losses occur from this method. Companies that supply spray equipment usually stock these jets. Made up with garden hose attachments they cost about two dollars each and may be set up in series with connections of short lengths of hose, all supplied from a single faucet. Each jet will cover a circle of about two feet in diameter, sufficient to protect several small plants.

Winter is also an excellent time to collect if the ground isn't frozen. At this time of the year the roots are full of moisture, do not break easily and withstand shock very well. And there are no hot drying winds to contend with. Ample humidity reduces the necessity of careful packing which results in precious field time saving. But sharp eyesight and careful observing become increasingly important. Often a few dried leaves are the only signs that a plant you want is sleeping underground. Or an occasional dried flowering stem will be a good indication. The evergreens can be spotted easily from their leaves but are nowhere as easy to locate as when in flower.

Once you have your collections home they should be placed in their permanent locations as soon as possible. At the end of a long hard excursion lasting, perhaps, for a week or so, when you want nothing so much as a substantial dinner and a good sleep it is no joke to force yourself to plant at once.

If an expedition lasts for a number of days I make a base camp. When I come in from the day's collection I check the specimens at once for ample moisture in the soil. If the trip was one of many miles and the plants were packed with a meager amount of soil to save weight I immediately repack the roots more generously. Then I cover the foliage with wet moss to keep out drying winds and heat and place the entire collection in the coolest place I can find where it will be out of the sun. Sometimes the only shaded place will be under the car.

An hour in a hot car will do more damage to plants than a week in the shade. For this reason I start the homeward trip late at night or before sun up. If the entire job has been well done the plants will arrive as fresh as they were the moment they were removed from the ground.

Linear leaf

Adiantum jordanii California Maiden Hair Fern

ADIANTUM JORDANII Carl Mueller
California Maidenhair Fern

A good way to become acquainted with our wild plants is to read about them. This is especially true when the weather is too miserable to wander the forest looking for them. It was in this way many years ago, that I first became aware of the California Maidenhair Fern. Only comparatively recently did I actually find it and bring it into my gardens.

Hell Gate Canyon is a narrow section of the Rogue River Gorge 15 or 20 miles down stream from Grants Pass in southwestern Oregon. The trail I was following in that area led along a hillside. Suddenly, under the shade of some overhanging native shrubs, in light shade, I saw a half dozen of the plants. They had the delicate texture and the dainty loveliness I had been led to believe they possessed.

They were growing in a well drained, loose soil, well enriched with leaf mold. Although the mild days of spring had swept over that craggy area the soil already had lost most of its moisture. Mellow but quite dry. It was very easy to ball four of the shallow rooted plants. I added a bit of water to each plant and they were safe – I thought.

It is always helpful to study the conditions under which the wildlings grow so that they can be better adapted to our gardens. With this thought in mind I looked around further. There was a mighty boulder, taller than a house, on that steep hillside. At its base on the north side where the direct rays of the sun never reached and the gloom of dense forest shade was unknown were several dozen more of this most delightful of ferns that my eyes have ever been privileged to see. The light, rich soil was shallow with an underlayer of solid rock. Every plant of this species I saw on that north facing hillside was thriving nicely under virtually identical conditions. Our common but uncommonly beautiful Western Maiden Hair Fern, *Adiantum pedatum,* and the equally lovely but more diminutive Maidenhair Spleenwort, *Asplenium trichomanes,* thrive both in the wild and in the garden under similar circumstances. It was only natural that I assumed this new found friend would be just as happy as its two relatives at my home. I was never more botanically mistaken in my life and I still don't quite know why.

All plants belong to one of the four great divisions of plants called *Phylla.* The lowest, the *Thallophytes,* include the lichens, mushrooms, algae, and other primitive forms. Next up the scale come the liverworts and true mosses. These are known as the *Bryophytes.* The *Pteridophytes,* are in the next step up the evolutionary ladder. This phylum consists of the club mosses, the horsetails, and the ferns. They are immediately below the true flowering plants, the *Spermatophytes.*

Ferns do not bear flowers. They reproduce by means of spores. They are primitive and ancient plants, having first appeared in the early part of the Palaeozoic Era, and attaining their greatest development in the Carboniferous Period. It was during this time that they were the dominating type of vegetation. Some of the tree forms still exist. In addition to extinct species there are about 7,000 living ones. More than three-quarters of them dwell in the tropics. On our continent some of them go as far north as Alaska. They are used as food, medicine, forage, and industrial fibers. They are better known as ornamentals and as such occupy a valued position in horticulture.

History: Carl Von Linneaus named the genus *Adiantum* and described it in 1753 in his *Species Plantarum.* Although the French botanist Joseph Pitton de Tournefort, 1656-1708, described it at an earlier date his nomenclature is not officially accepted. *Adiantum* is an ancient name and refers to the leaflets repelling rain drops. There are about 200 species in the genus, most of which are tropical Americans. Seven of them occur in the United States and Canada, three on the West Coast.

Carl Mueller, 1817-1870, gave *A. Jordanii* its name in 1864. Daniel C. Eaton called it *A. emarginatum* when he gave an account of it in *Ferns of North America* in 1879. Eaton's name is more descriptive (*emarginate* means shallowly notched at the apex and refers to the leaflets) but Mueller's, having priority, is official.

Description: The root system consists of a slender, creeping rhizome, quite densely thin scaled. The scales are large, rigid, with unsymmetrical sides, dark brown, lance shaped with a very slender prolongation at the tip. The margins are entire.

The several fronds to the plant are rather close, largely erect and from eight to 20 inches long. The stems are dark brown, slender and nearly as long as the blades which are from five to 12 inches long and three to five inches wide, triangular or egg shaped in outline. The ultimate segments are roundish to transversely oval or semicircular, from a quarter to one inch broad. The lower parts of the margins are entire, the outer edge shallowly two to five lobed, and broken by irregular sharply projecting points if sterile. These terminal leaflets are a soft, delicate green unsurpassed in any fern of my acquaintance. This description, as simple and devoid of technical terminology as I can give it, tells virtually nothing of the very real beauty of a primitive and obscure plant that deserves a much better fate.

Rarity: Rare.

Distribution: It prefers rocky canyons, mostly at low elevations in the coastal ranges of California, ranging from San Diego County northward to Oregon's Curry County, Grants Pass, the lower Rogue River Valley and the Umpqua Valley. Rare in the Sierra Nevadas of central California and, seemingly, not particularly abundant anywhere in its range.

Propagation: The quickest method of increasing is by divisions made in the spring or early fall. Growing from spores is satisfactory but very slow. Spores less than three weeks old should be used. Start them on bricks or the outside of clay pots. These should be sterilized by heating or boiling, then dipped in a clay mud. The bricks should be placed in water so that the moisture will come from the bottom. Watering from the top will wash away the spores. Growth varies considerably with the different species. Usually the *prothallium* – a flat green, rootless, stemless, leafless, plant body – appears in about a week. The primary frond comes in about three months, followed by the secondary frond in another three months. About two years are required to produce a new plant with a crown half an inch in diameter and six or seven inches high, and twice that long or more for the fern to reach maturity.

Ferns started on the sides of the clay pots or bricks are difficult to transplant as the roots penetrate the surfaces and break off when they are removed. A better process is to pack soil on stainless steel wire mesh sitting in a plastic plate filled with water for bottom moisture. Tiny ferns can be removed from this medium without serious root damage. Whichever method is used the plants should be covered to prevent excessive dryness and the temperature should be maintained at between 45 and 50 degrees F.

Culture: I placed three of my collected plants on the cool north side of our home in a soil consisting of half leaf mold, one quarter rich top soil and one quarter sand. Most of my ferns have thrived splendidly there. *A. jordanii* remained green for the rest of the season, came up very weakly the next year and the following season were gone. The fourth plant I gave to a friend who put it into a flower pot which is kept in a cool greenhouse. It has thrived ever since. Two people who live in Medford near where these plants make their native home have had radically different experiences. One of them, an expert fern grower, has planted his among other ferns but *A. jordanii* has consistently died while other species are strong and vigorous. The other Medford horticulturist has her *A. jordanii* in flower pots in which they do exceedingly well. It seems that there is something about the flower pots that contributes to this success. Possibly they need the lime in the pots. A Portland expert has had this fern growing from under a rock for years. It may be that this stone is alkaline. The fact that it is growing exposed to our climate without damage negates the suggestion that our Portland climate is too severe. A report has been made that this fern will not stand the winters of the Puget Sound region in Washington. It is true that this area has something about it that will destroy plants that will thrive both to the south and north. I am confident that this fussy little beauty can be grown in gardens and that the solution to the problem is simple. I intend to keep trying until I get the answer.

One might be justified in believing that plants which have made so little evolutionary progress over the millions of years of their history would have similar requirements. It is surprising to learn that they are as variable, easy, difficult and delightful as people.

Flowering Time: Ferns do not produce flowers. *A. jordanii* is a deciduous perennial. The new shoots appear in the spring, last all summer and go to sleep in the fall.

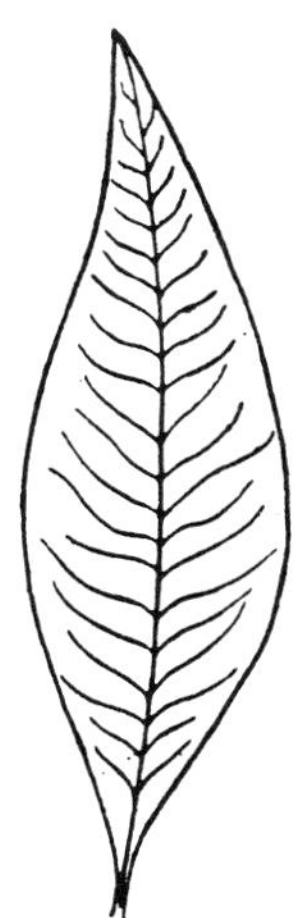

Lanceolate leaf

Aquilegia flavescens Yellow Columbine

AQUILEGIA FLAVESCENS S. Watson
Yellow Columbine

Whether this columbine is a distinct species in its own right or a variety of the common Western Columbine, *Aquilegia formosa,* is a question that has been discussed for quite some years. From a gardener's point of view, however, there is no question that there are some real differences.

The Western Columbine, with its red and yellow flowers, does well in my Portland, Oregon, gardens in ordinary well drained soil. But the Yellow Columbine is a little more fussy. Its native habitat in the mountainous regions where the rainfall is more limited and the rocky soil better drained may provide the key to its lowland needs in wetter lands. Some of mine are doing quite well. Others have passed out of the floral scene.

History: The name *Aquilegia,* is from the Latin, meaning *eagle,* the spurs of the flowers suggesting the claws of that bird. Some people may need a little imagination to see the resemblance. Others, myself included, may require a great deal. *Columbine* refers to a dove from the alleged resemblance of the spurred blossom to four doves around a shallow dish. While this also requires a certain amount of vision it is more sensible and certainly more beautiful than the eagle business.

The plants belong to the Buttercup Family, *Ranunculaceae,* of about 35 genera and 1100 species, which are among our more primitive flowers from the evolutionary point of view. This does not necessarily have anything to do with their beauty. The Iris, lilies and orchids are likewise pretty well down the ladder in development but I have never heard of anyone who challenges their loveliness.

The columbines comprise about 40 species and are native to the north temperate zone of both the old and new world. As might be expected of plants, some of which are native to Europe, the genus has been known for a long time. Carl Von Linnaeus, the great scientist and the father of modern botany, named the genus and described it in his famous *Species Plantarum* in 1753. *A. flavescens* was named in 1871 by Sereno Watson, 1826-1892, of Harvard University. Because of the confusion in the genus due to the close resemblance of some of the species to others a number of them have been given different names by various authors. *A. flavescens* has had at least seven. Botanists are concerned, and correctly so, with placing each plant in its rightful place in relationship to all others. The purpose is to clarify identification and end confusion. But sometimes, among laymen, the result has an opposite effect.

A. flavescens is certainly closely related to *A. formosa,* and may even be the parent of the latter species. *Flavescens* refers to the yellow color of the blossom which usually has no other color in it. *Formosa* has no such definitive derivation. It simply means *beautiful,* and the flowers of this species are red and yellow in the same blossom. In areas where each is entirely alone the plants retain their distinctive characteristics but where they come closer and closer the colors tend to merge and salmons and pinks are found. In the mountains of Custer County, Idaho, great patches of salmon colored flowers have entirely replaced the reds of *A. formosa* and the yellows of *A. flavescens.* This is a clear instance of natural hybridization which is a common occurrence among the various species which are planted together in gardens. Seedlings of such plants can not be depended upon to come true.

Description: The Yellow Columbine grows from eight inches to as much as four feet high, depending upon soil conditions and rainfall. Stems are smooth or sparsely adorned with soft, appressed hairs. The leaves are delicate and lacy; the basal ones have three divisions, are long stemmed, densely tufted, and each of which is again divided into three. The upper are divided into threes without the sub-division of the lower. The leaflets are thin, smooth or sparsely hairy, glaucous beneath, from three-quarters to one and a half inches long, wedge or somewhat heart shaped at the base. The columbines are worthy of a place in the gardens for the graceful shape and texture of the ground hugging foliage alone. The leaves have some of the same daintiness and appeal of the Meadow Rues, *Thalictrums,* to which they are related.

The showy nodding flowers are light yellow and are borne at the tips of the open branches. The egg or lance shaped sepals resemble petals and are from one-quarter to three-quarters of an inch long. The petal blades are from a quarter to three-eighths of an inch in length. The flowers are an inch to an inch and a half long and somewhat wider, with short, stout spurs usually more or less hooked at the apex.

Rarity: Rare. *A. flavescens* forma *minor* Tidestrom is a smaller, more hairy subalpine of the Wasatch Plateau. Very Rare. Described in 1910.

Distribution: Generally a mountain plant, often on high peaks, but may sometimes be found in foot hill areas. In the Blue Mountains and the Rockies. By states: British Columbia eastward to Alberta, eastern Washington, eastern Oregon, Idaho, Montana, Utah, Wyoming and Nevada.

Propagation: The only certain way to get additional plants that are true to type is by root divisions made in late fall, winter or early spring. There is a wide variation in the degree of success of growing *Aquilegias* from seed. Some are very easy, others discouragingly difficult. I have had good success with the Yellow Columbine. Stale seed is one of the most common reasons for failure. Sow as soon as ripe even if the weather is very warm. Year old plants may flower but more generally two or even three years may be needed to produce blossoms. Seed flats should have a rich, well drained soil and need the protection of light shade. Seeds should be taken only from isolated species plants if true to type progeny are wanted.

Culture: These are very popular garden plants and most are of easy culture, although some present real problems. A loose, sandy soil, well drained in light shade or, in cooler climates, full sun will satisfy most species. Most are too tall for rock gardens but make good background plants. Mixed with some of the ferns or *Thalictrums,* set not too closely together they are a delightful sight. The alpine species are more particular than the others, and require sharper drainage, and may be shorter lived.

Many lovely hybrids have been developed and some of them exceed the wild ones in their beauty. Colorado has chosen *A. coerulea,* for its state flower.

Once established in the garden under the right conditions they and their progeny can live for many years. The heavy, fleshy tap roots go down deeply to seek a reliable source of moisture which they can store with a goodly supply of food. The roots are said to have been an Indian food plant. I have never tried them and suggest caution along such edible lines.

Flowering Time: June to August for the Yellow Columbine, depending upon altitude.

Oblanceolate leaf

Aquilegia jonesii

No Common Name

AQUILEGIA JONESII Parry
No Common Name

Of all the Columbines, with their many hybrids, in the world the one I want most of all in my gardens I cannot have. This is the rare *A. jonesii.* The tiniest dwarf of them all it lives in the greatest of our American mountains, the Rockies. What a remarkable contrast! After the flowers have died away and the leaves have gone it would be virtually impossible to find it even though it were inches from your feet. In full foliage one might easily stand beside it and never know that it existed. Not much has been written about this obscure dweller of tremendous peaks.

If it even possesses a common name I have never heard of it although some of its larger brothers have a confusingly large number of them.

I received a shipment of a dozen plants. The package was small and I held it in the palm of my hand while I examined them. They were packed in sphagnum moss which was thoroughly dried out as were the two or three inch long roots. They appeared to be dead and at first I thought they were. Then I remembered that the collector who sent them to me simply does not supply anything but living specimens. I planted them in cracks and crevices in various spots in my alpine garden. It wasn't long before the tiny leaves began to appear and by mid summer every one, while tiny, was strong, vigorous and healthy. This was a delightful thing and I was as happy as I have ever been with any wild plant I have ever grown.

The days slipped away and in the fall the plants went into their long winter sleep. It took a sharp eye to see them even though I knew exactly where they were. The next spring I had another surprise of an entirely different sort. Only one survived. In the high altitudes of their native home they had successfully endured temperatures far below freezing and were deeply buried under tons of snow. But in the benign climate of my Portland home they could not endure the friendly weather. We have about 44 inches of rain a year and most of this falls during the dormant season. Freezing alternates with thawing and this condition is deadly to many alpines. In their mountain homes the soil is frozen in the winter and therefore dry. Under such conditions the roots cannot rot. I was well aware of this, of course, but had no idea that these miniatures were so temperamental. They were planted near the fussy *Lewisia cotyledon* which has the discouraging habit of rotting its crown in the middle of the summer if it gets even a very little moisture. They were also near that most diffiuclt of all *Lewisias, tweedyi,* which will give up the ghost with no discernible reason at all shortly after flowering. But these two species were thriving while *A. jonesii,* with one solitary exception, was only a memory.

History: Charles Christopher Parry, 1823-1890, described and named this plant in 1874 in honor of Marcus Eugene Jones who was born in 1852. Like the flower itself neither of these men are particularly prominent among American botanists. The rare but much larger *A. flavescens* was named only three years earlier, 1871, by Sereno Watson.

The beauty of flowers is often compared with the beauty of women and yet how rarely is a genus or species named by a man for the love of a woman! At the moment I can think of only one but surely there must be others. Among the 40 some species of *Aquilegias* surely there is none more worthy of such a distinction, and yet this honor has been denied this columbine. It has all the charms and graces we associate with the other sex, diminutive daintiness, delicacy of foliage, beauty of blossom out of all proportion to the size of the plant. Along with these feminine delights it has endurance and hardiness to withstand weather so severe and a climate so harsh that few of our hardiest pioneers dared attempt to live the year around in such surroundings under such conditions.

Description: One of its secrets of healthful living at high altitudes is its flat, earth hugging habit, or its protected home in the crevice of a rock. Taller plants could be twisted and torn by the violent storms that often rage among our highest mountain ranges.

To say that it has a fleshy root will give the wrong impression when compared with the feeding systems of other larger species. Nevertheless these slender roots grow deeply enough to find a little moisture and are able to store enough food to support the tiny plant until the dense clump of silvery green leaves are able to manufacture enough food to last another year. The leaves are minutely softly hairy from less than an inch up to an infrequent four inches long, with very short stems or none, divided into three principal divisions each with three broadly shaped divisions. The whole effect is one of fine laciness, of miniature beauty.

Some of our dwarf alpines offer a veritable shower of flowers but this columbine is not among their number. Each little plant has but a single comparatively enormous dark blue or lavender wide open blossom with a short spur. The flowers are turned upward, facing the sky which seems only a wind whisper away from its lofty home. The entire plant, foliage and flower, is only two or three inches high. The rich blue flowers above the silvery leaves growing on an alpine scree is a sight the mountain climber will remember – always.

Rarity: Rare.

Distribution: At alpine elevations in Montana, summit of Phlox Mountain in Wyoming, and Alberta, Canada.

Propagation: Some of the larger plants can be divided in late fall, winter or early spring. This is one of the most difficult of columbines to raise from seed. The seedlings will appear anywhere from a few weeks to a couple of years, or not at all. Good results have been obtained by sowing direct in a cold frame. Better germination can be expected if the seeds are planted in pots and left in the cold frame. Rather poor results have been experienced by freezing the pots containing the seeds and put in the greenhouse. In my climate seeds in pots left outdoors did not germinate. Fresh seed is much better than old ones. In some areas cultivated plants do not flower or if they do may not set seed.

Culture: In the right climate this is not too difficult. But it is a no nonsense plant. Perfect drainage is essential although other species may not be so demanding. In wet winter climates it may be necessary to cover it with glass or bring it into the alpine house where it will do well. The roots require winter freezing or dryness which, as far as results are concerned, amounts to much the same thing. In warm climates it should be planted in light shade so as to be kept as cool as possible. Slugs take a culinary delight in the flowers but are not interested in the foliage.

This is one of the most challenging of all *Aquilegias* and it can be one of the most rewarding.

Flowering Time: June and July.

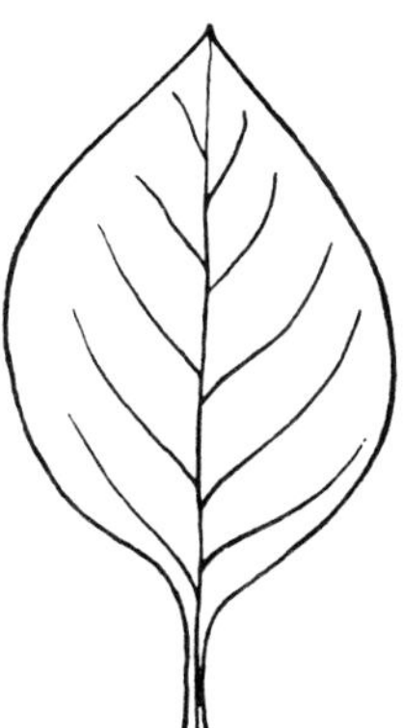

Ovate leaf

Boschniakia species Ground Cone

BOSCHNIAKIA HOOKERI Walpers
BOSCHNIAKIA STROBILACEA A. Gray
BOSCHNIAKIA GLABRA C. A. Meyer
Small Ground-Cone
Ground Cone

These peculiar plants belong to the Broom Rape Family, *Orobanchaceae,* brownish or yellowish rooted parasites without chlorophyll. The genus was named for Boschniak, a Russian botanist who, apparently, was as obscure as the plants that honor his name. This is an extremely small genus, limited as far as I have been able to determine, to four species, three of which are native to North America.

I was looking for *Lewisias* on a trip to southern Oregon when I saw my first ground cone. It was growing vertically out of the soil in the shade of some medium sized oak trees, *Quercus garryana.* It was an astonishing sight to see what appeared to be a slender pine cone growing all alone where there were no pine trees. I had never heard of the plant before and had no idea what it was except that it was obviously a saprophyte or parasite – the latter proved to be the correct guess. I picked it and added it to my collection. Then I went further south into California. At the inspection station at the state boundary I stopped for an hour or so and talked with Mr. A. L. Hobart, one of the inspectors who is also a botanist. It was he who identified my find.

After returning to Oregon I found a dozen more of these strange creatures growing under some coniferous trees between Wilderville and Merlin a few miles west of Grants Pass. Very little has been written about these plants but most authorities agree that they are parasitic on ericaceous plants such as Salal, *Gaultheria shallon;* Madrona, *Arbutus menziesii;* and the Manzanitas, *Arctostaphylos.* While this claim is undoubtedly true it is likewise true that none of these plants were growing anywhere near the ground cones that I discovered under coniferous trees in the one instance and oak trees in the other. If these plants are parasitic as they must be it must also be true that their host plants include others than the *ericaceae.* This is a matter for the botanists to worry about if there is any worrying done, for these queer forest dwellers are not at all important either as pests or beautiful flowers. They are oddities, curiosities, interesting to students perhaps or for casual glances from the occasional passer-by.

If the cone-like plants were lying flat on the ground it isn't likely that they would be seen at all by the person wandering idly through the woods for they would be mistaken for cones fallen from trees. It is their erect position that at once catches the eye, and not the colors which are dark reddish brown or yellowish. There is nothing attractive about them but they are distinctive enough to arouse curiosity in those people who want to know more about the world in which we live.

History: *B. strobilacea* is the species I discovered. It was first described officially, by the great American botanist, Dr. Asa Gray in the *Pacific Railroad Reports* published in 1856. This species was eaten by the Indians who called it Poque.

B. hookeri was discovered by Archibald Menzies, the botanist with the Lord Vancouver Expedition, at Nootka Sound. This expedition visited the Northwestern Pacific Coast during the early 1790's.

Description: The stems are thick and arise from large globose tubers which are developed at the point of attachment of the parasite to the root of the host plant. When I dug down around one of the plants and uncovered the rounded tuber I was puzzled for I had never seen anything like it before. The individdual flowers are sessile or with very short stems and are more or less concealed by scaly subtending bracts, the whole forming a dense compact strobile-like spike before maturing. In later stages the cone-like structure opens a little and loses some of its compactness. The corolla is tubular, the upper lip is entire or two cleft and the lower three parted.

Rarity: Scarce to rare, depending upon the species. Never abundant.

Distribution: *B. himalaica* is the only one of the four species that is limited to the old world. It is found in the Himalaya Mountains. *B. glabra* is located in Japan, Siberia, Asia, Alaska and south to Vancouver Island, British Columbia in Canada. *B. hookeri* may be found all the way from Vancouver Island into

Washington, Oregon and as far south as Del Norte and Marin Counties in California. This species seems to prefer the lower elevations in the coastal areas. *B. strobilacea* somewhat overlaps *B. hookeri* but the former prefers drier places. It is found as far north as British Columbia, the Olympic Peninsula in Washington, Oregon, Nevada, and into southern California at elevations from a few hundred feet up to nine thousand.

Propagation: Unknown. On this trip I brought two of the "cones" home. Several hundred granular-like particles fell from them. They may or may not have been seeds. At any rate I planted them in a rich humus soil in shade. Some I scratched into the soil lightly. Others I scattered on the surface. None germinated. Like so many parasitic plants this one seems virtually impossible to grow from seed.

Culture: Unknown. On a later trip I dug two of these plants, going down over a foot and well below the globose tubers. There were no feedings roots at all as far down as I went. The roots where I cut them off were thick. I planted them in my gardens in the hope that feeding roots would develop. The "cones" looked healthy for a number of weeks, then slowly disintegrated. It might be possible to bring in both the parasite and host plant with the point of attachment of the two plants intact and get it to grow. But this would be a doubtful undertaking and hardly worthwhile considering the large amount of work involved for so little reward. The only exception would be a person with an enormous amount of enthusiasm and muscle to match.

Flowering Time: May to August depending upon species, climate and elevation.

Brodiaea ida-maia Fire Cracker Flower

BRODIAEA IDA-MAIA Greene
Fire Cracker Flower

It is strange, and a little sad too, that over a quarter of a century flew out of my life from the time I first heard of this wonderful flower until my eyes first gazed upon it. When I was finally shown a few dozen in a wild flower nursery my first thought was, "more than 25 years wasted."

The explanation is simple, however. Its home is several hundred miles south from mine and it is a scarce plant indeed. Fortunate is the wild flower hunter who is able to visit it in its wild home.

The early pioneers of the Far West were much too busy struggling to survive and build their homes in this distant and virgin land to pay much attention to the floral beauties surrounding them on every side. But there were a few men and women here and there who did appreciate the wilds for more than the food they could wrest from it.

History: One of these was a stage driver in the Trinity Mountains of California. This patron of botany had a love of beauty and an even greater love for his little daughter. Doubtless numerous other passers-by had also seen the Fire Cracker Flower but it was the stage driver, J. Carson Brevoort, who did something about it. He pointed it out to Alphonso Wood in 1867. Dr. Wood realized that this plant was unknown to science and he believed it represented a new genus. He honored the stage driver by naming it *Brevoortia* and gave it the specific name *Ida-Maia* for the little girl and the fact that the plant had been collected on the *ides of May* (15th). It is rarely that the exact date of a new floral discovery is known.

This is a pretty little story, one of parental love, wild beauty, and a trace of romance. But it didn't last. Alphonso Wood Ph.D., 1810-1881, was a competent botanist, the author of at least six botanies, one of which, *The Class Book of Botany* sold a hundred thousand copies. Dr. Wood was the first to name the new plant and his work merited more credit than some other taxonomists have been willing to give it. According to Dr.

Wood's determination this single species comprised the entire genus. But the great Dr. Asa Gray and the equally renowned Sereno Watson changed it to *Brodiaea coccinea.* Finally Edward L. Greene gave it the now generally established designation, *Brodiaea ida-maia.* Dr. Wood was quite well known in his day but is now largely forgotten except in limited botanical circles. Brevoort and the daughter he loved so well are totally obscure today. But the flower named for them, while becoming ever scarcer, still inhabits its wild home. Whether *Brodiaea* or *Brevoortia,* it has an honored and distinctive position in the large lily family which includes some of our most beautiful flowers.

Description: The plants usually have three linear, grass-like leaves 12 to 18 inches long and three to five-sixteenths of an inch wide, each with a prominent ridge. The leafless stems, one to the plant are from one to three feet tall, but averaging about 18 inches or less. They are so slender that they dance in the slightest breeze making them difficult to photograph but delightful to look at. The entire plant arises from a reticulated fibrous coated corm one-half to three-quarters of an inch in diameter.

But it is the flowers that once seen can never be forgotten. They are borne at the top of the stems in loose pendent umbels. They may be as few as half a dozen or as many as 24 to each stem with an average of about a dozen. Each flower has a stem (pedicel) from three-quarters to one and a half inches long allowing the showy blossoms to droop gracefully until after flowering when they become erect. The floral tubes are slender giving the impression that they are more than their inch to an inch and a half long. They are a bright red and the trumpets terminate in very short, rounded slightly expanding lobes which are bright, vivid green. The whole effect is one of startling contrast and ineffable beauty, quite unlike any other *Brodiaea* or any other flower I have ever seen. There are any number of strange appearing flowers in the world, many of which are either ordinary or down right ugly. *B. Ida-maia,* peculiar though it may be at first glance, has everything. Fire Cracker Flower is an excellent choice of a common name. The loose cluster of blossoms look very much like a bunch of Chinese Firecrackers with green bands around the ends.

Rarity: Rare. This has never been a common plant and it is becoming increasingly scarce due to collecting.

Distribution: In open woods in southwestern Curry County, Oregon. In California on grassy hillsides and open forests in the Siskiyou Mountains to Marin and the Contra Costa Mountains. First discovered in the Trinity Mountains, Shasta County, near the old stage coach road from Shasta City to Yreka. At elevations from one to four thousand feet.

Propagation: From seeds and offsets. Seedling propagation, like that of the other *Brodiaeas,* may be a slow process, requireing several years from the time the black seeds are planted until the first flowers appear. They should be planted in the fall. Germination, under the right conditions is good. Offsets produce results much sooner. All the way from none to six are produced from each corm, depending upon soil and weather. In wet climates fewer offsets are produced. Richer soils produce greater vigor and more offsets can be expected under these more favorable conditions. They should be removed and planted in the fall.

Culture: Plant about two inches deep and not more than three inches. *Brodiaeas* growing in the wild are often much deeper than this but in gardens the shallower depths produce more satisfactory results. Freedom from competition with other plants, weeding, cultivation and moisture control are among the reasons shallower planting, not only of *Brodiaeas* but of many other wild plants, is more desirable. *B. ida-maia* makes a much more striking appearance when planted in clumps of half a dozen or so. They may be planted among some of the smaller ferns or with other *Brodiaeas* of lighter colors such as the yellow *B. ixiodes* or the pale blue *B. douglasii.* Contrasts obtained in this way can be outstandingly satisfactory as with all other *Brodiaeas.* I had a vase of them that remained fresh for three weeks in a cool room. In a heated atmosphere they might not last more than half that long. This is a half hardy species. Not a great deal is known how adaptable it is to various parts of the United States. It should do well on the Pacific Coast states as well as in the southern and eastern states and as far north as Virginia. It will probably stand temperatures as low as zero Fahrenheit if given a mulch of leaf mold, straw or some other protective material. It prefers partial shade and a deep loose well drained soil rich in humus. The amount of shade depends upon the climate. In Portland it can tolerate sun virtually all day. As it is native to a comparatively dry climate watering should be done sparingly.

Like so many of our lovely wildlings it is better known in the British Isles than in its native western home. I have never seen it in a garden and the nurseries that handle it are exceedingly few indeed and their stocks are small. This plant, as obscure as Mr. J. Carson Brevoort, deserves a better fate.

Flowering Time: In Portland, Oregon it blossoms in late June and July. In parts of California, and other warmer regions the bright red umbels appear as early as May.

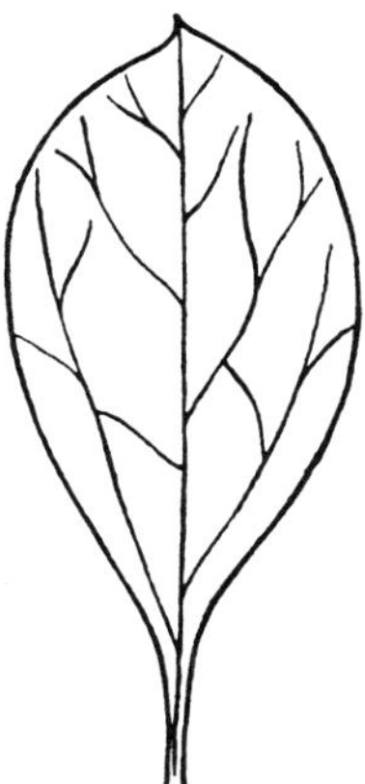

Obovate leaf

Calypso bulbosa Calypso

CALYPSO BULBOSA (L) Oakes
Calypso

A friend who lives in the upper Willamette Valley of Oregon proudly displayed a huge bouquet of Deer Head Orchids in a vase. It was truly a gorgeous sight, one that I had never seen before in such quantity for there were several dozen of the slipper shaped blossoms. These tiny flowers with rich rose and lavender and golden yellow colors had a fresh and spicy fragrance all of their own, quite unlike the perfume of other blossoms of field or forest.

Every year he made a pilgrimage to a wooded area a few miles away to bring home this floral tribute to his wife whom he loved more than anything else in all the world. He was very careful how he picked these flowers for he knew that the stems were more securely attached to the tiny bulbs than the roots were to the moss in which they spend their lives. It is so easy, under these circumstances to destroy the bulbs while picking the stems. All he did was prevent any ripening of seed and the growing of new plants from them for destroying the flower does not injure the plant in the least.

Many people who collect these flowers do not know this or don't care and many a plant is destroyed every year by these thoughtless forest wanderers. It is the most natural thing in the world to reach for something rare, something beautiful. Careless people are only one of the enemies this forest orchid has to face in a desperate and losing battle for survival. Logging operations destroy them by the thousands for wherever the trees are destroyed the *Calypsos* perish too. They are absolutely dependent upon the shade of forest trees for their survival. The steady encroachment of civilization is responsible for their destruction too. Homer D. House in his *Wild Flowers of New York* reports having found it in a tamarack swamp near Syracuse, "but the place has since been obliterated by the growth of the city." This little incident Mr. House reported is going on year after year across the land from ocean to ocean.

A few years ago I used to visit a colony no larger than an ordinary living room. It was in an isolated spot deep in a wooded area. There were 30 some odd plants there. But I no longer make such visits. A house is sitting where they used to grow.

This sad destruction of our woodland beauties can neither be slowed nor stopped. It is a sorry thing, indeed, that our civilization which is so necessary for progress, must be paid for at the cost of so much natural beauty that can never be replaced. It has been reported too that thousands of these plants are shipped across the waters every year to Oriental peoples who use them for medicine. What afflictions they treat I do not know but I do know that this bulb has no place in modern therapy. Pheasants and robins pull the plants out of the moss too and slugs will devour the entire plant, leaf, bud and bulb. Is it any wonder that this diminutive flower, along with many of its orchid bretheren, is vanishing from the face of the earth?

I no longer look for them in the forests surrounding my Portland home for it is only occasionally that one or two can be found. Searching an entire hillside will usually yield not a single blossom.

History: It was those two great botanists, Bentham and Hooker, who named the Orchid Family, *Orchidaceae,* which is composed of about 430 genera and over 5,000 species! They are widely distributed, mostly in the tropics but some, including this one, in the temperate regions. In this huge family with such a large membership is one plant that has an entire genus all to itself, The Deer Head Orchid, *Calypso.* Both the genus and species were described and named at the same time, in 1807, by Richard Anthony Salisbury, 1761-1829 who named it *Calypso borealis.* As might be expected in those early botanical days there was a certain amount of disagreement among the taxonomists where to place this singular orchid with so many relatives. It has had half a dozen different names, the most common of which is *Cytherea bulbosa. Calypso* was well chosen, taken from the Greek goddess, whose name means *concealment,* in reference to its rarity and beauty. The now generally recognized name is *Calypso bulbosa* (L.) Oakes.

Description: The leafless flowering stem, sheathed by two or three loose scales rises two to six inches above its mossy home and terminates usually in a single nodding blossom. Rarely two flowers will share the one stem. They are as strangely different from most flowers as they are dainty and infinitely lovely – the most colorful blossom you can find on the moss covered floor of an American forest. It resembles an exotic slipper, ornamented and decorated up to the limits of Mother Nature's ability and imagination. They are from three-quarters to over an inch long. The rich colors fade with age until, finally the blossoms loose all their distinctive richness. Each plant has only one leaf with paralleled veins typical of the *monocotyledons.* After the flowers have become only a memory the leaves disappear. In late summer or fall they return and remain hugging the earth all winter – quite an opposite habit from most plants which either keep their leaves year round or lose them during the dormant season. They are round egg-shaped, one to two inches long, blunt or pointed at the tip and rounded or heart shaped at the base with stems equaling the leaves in length. The entire plant is nourished by a bulbous dilation at the base of the stems. The leaf is attached to the bulb separately from the flowering stem. This solid bulb, about half an inch in diameter, replaces itself annually. In the summer you can find the new one growing smooth and plump beside the shriveled one. Apparently the new takes all the food from the old, a phenomenon entirely novel to my experience.

Rarity: Scarce to very rare depending upon the part of the world where it lives. The white form is extremely rare. I have never been fortunate enough to find one and know of only two people who have. One of these friends who lives in a forested area has seen only one in a lifetime. The other, who is a plant collector and grower, has found two or three. The next he locates he has promised to sell to me for ten dollars – a cheap enough price considering the staggering odds against success. A few of these whites were found near Eugene, Oregon until a superhighway destroyed the lot.

Distribution: From Alaska, to Labrador in Canada, the New England states, across the nation in the northern states. In the Rockies and on the West Coast from Alaska to northern California. Also in Europe. Probably most abundant in Oregon and Washington west of the Cascades.

Propagation: Unknown. I do not know of anyone who has had any success propagating his plant. Vegetative methods would seem quite impossible. They multiply by seeds in the forest. One might try scattering the tiny seeds, as soon as ripe, on the same kind of moss that the parents must have. This is the only suggestion I can offer and it is far fetched. But nature can do it and I am sure we can too if the secret, whatever it may be, can be discovered. Once this is accomplished some of the threat of extinction can be removed.

Culture: Most of the garden failures with this orchid are due to ignorance of its requirements. It must be planted, not in soil, but in moss, where the coral-like roots can be happy. First the *Hypnum* mosses must be established in the garden and this often takes a lot of doing. A rich leaf mold soil is good. Also well rotted logs. After the moss bed is growing the bulbs can be planted. If both moss and plants are placed in the garden at the same time failure will be likely. Then the bed should be covered with a screen to protect from birds and slug bait is generally required to destroy these pests before they can devour the orchids. Many gardeners feel all this is too difficult and too much trouble. I am one of those who disagree. In nature they grow in bogs, but above the soaking wet soil and also under coniferous trees. In either situation moderate moisture but sharp drainage is essential. Good luck – and you are going to need it, for this orchid belongs to the expert gardener.

Flowering Time: April to June, depending upon climate and altitude.

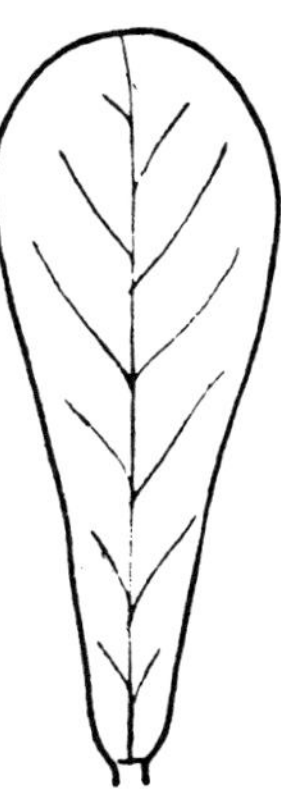

Spatulate leaf

Left to right: *Camassia leichtlinii; C. cusickii,* Cusick's Camas; *C. leichtlinii* subsp. *suksdorfii*

CAMASSIA CUSICKII S. Watson
Cusick's Camas

It was my good fortune to be born within a day's driving time of all but one of the species of Camas, two of which are found almost within the city limits of my Portland, Oregon home. I have photographed, studied, eaten them – flowers, leaves, stems and bulbs – grown them in my gardens and admired them for ever so many years. I have been somewhat frustrated too in my attempts to bring order to this rather badly confused little genus of lovely flowers.

I obtained my first supply of Cusick's Camas bulbs from a nursery on the east coast of America. I know of only one other American dealer. Commercial supplies are usually obtained from Holland. The frugal and efficient Dutch can grow them profitably for less than an American can afford to dig them. It is rather strange that one of our beautiful natives has to be imported from a foreign country across the seas.

History: They are members of the Lily Family, *Liliaceae,* comprising over 200 genera and about 2,600 species distributed widely throughout many parts of the world. Many are grown for their ornamental value, such as the lilies themselves. Others are vegetables – onions, and some have medicinal value. The family was named by George Bentham, 1800-1884, and Joseph Dalton Hooker, 1817-1911, but another name must have been used prior to their time for the true lilies, *Liliums,* were known and described by Carl Von Linnaeus in the first edition of his *Genera Plantarum* dated 1737.

The officially recognized name of the genus, *Camassia,* was given by John Lindley, 1799-1865, in 1832 although five other names or spellings were proposed by various authors between 1811 and 1866. It was taken from a phonetic Indian name variously spelled *camas, camass, quamash.*

There are five or six species and a number of subspecies and varieties confined to the temperate regions of the United States and Canada's British Columbia. They are scattered from coast to coast but are far more numerous in the northwestern states.

In 1887 the well known American botanist, Sereno Watson, 1826-1892, named Cusick's Camas in honor of W. C. Cusick, a miner and botanist of the small town of Union which is located in northeastern Oregon between the Wallowa and Blue Mountains. Cusick originally collected it in the Powder River Mountains at between 4,000 and 6,000 feet. The location was not far from his home. Apparently Mr. Cusick combined botany with his mining ventures, for a number of plants have been named for him.

Description: His camas grows from an ovoid coated bulb – in layers like an onion. Its bulbs are the largest of the genus – up to two inches or more in diameter, and according to one authority, they weigh from a quarter to half a pound. Those in my garden have the size but certainly not this remarkable weight. It is also the only one that is inedible with a pungent and nauseous flavor – an unusual peculiarity in a genus noted for its food value.

The numerous leaves are from three-quarters to one and a half inches wide and about 15 inches long, powdery above and with a deep, prominent longitudinal ridge.

The scapes, leafless stems, are stout, up to three feet high or more and bear as many as 100, six-petaled, soft, delicate powdery blue flowers, quite close together and the petals wither separately. The lower buds open first while the uppermost are still very tiny. Before the last bud opens the first will have the seed capsules well developed. This gives a delightfully long flowering season but towards the end when only a few blossoms are still offering their spectacular beauty they lose much of their appeal.

The petals are very slender – more so than any of the other species. This difference, noticeable at once, with the broader and more numerous leaves and very large bulbs, makes *C. cusickii* easy to identify.

Rarity: Very rare due to its limited range.

Distribution: In the Canadian Life Zone, usually between 4,000 and 6,000 feet where it prefers damp meadows. Stations have been located in the Eagle Creek Mountains, Powder River Mountains and Blue Mountains of northeastern Oregon.

Propagation: Camas seeds germinate easily and commercial producers use this method. In my gardens I make no effort to plant them. They self seed abundantly and there is a continuing crop of youngsters around the parents. This is a slow process, however, as four to six years are required from seed to blossom, depending upon cultural conditions. Seed should be sown as soon as ripe, either in their permanent positions or in flats. A rich, moist, well drained soil makes a good mixture. Cusick's Camas grows in clusters due to the fact that they produce offsets from the bulbs and it is the only one that does. This is a certain method but not practical in commercial quantities as too few are produced each year. Nicking or notching the side of a bulb will often result in a bulb or two. This too is slow. No other vegetative methods of propagating bulbous plants are successful with camas.

Culture: So simple as to be almost fool proof. Camas are hardy plants and can be grown from coast to coast just as they do in the wild. They should be planted in late summer or very early fall. They are ready as soon as the seed has ripened and leaves have died. Late planting is successful too as they can endure quite a lot of abuse. I dug down to some of my Cusick's bulbs in mid November. The new shoots were an inch long and the roots were making an active growth. I have also planted camas when in full flower and they don't seem to suffer to amount to anything. For this species six inches deep and the same distance for spacing is about right. The offsets should be removed and replanted every few years to prevent crowding. Other species can be spaced three or four inches apart but this one needs more room to accommodate the offsets. While Cusick's comes from subalpine and alpine elevations it adapts very well to sea level climates.

It prefers a fertile soil with more than average moisture during flowering and likes complete dryness later in the season. But in my gardens it thrives in a half leaf mold and half sand mixture that is well drained but has only average or less moisture. Either light afternoon shade and morning sun or full sunshine all day long seem to be equally suitable.

Bulbs planted one year will flower the next because the embryonic blossoms have been produced in the bulbs. But the following season flowering may be sparse or absent. They cannot adapt to their new homes, produce flowers that were already set in the bulbs and prepare for another crop the next year. That is asking too much. The gardener may think his plants are diseased when he observes this phenomenon but there is nothing unusual about it. The same thing happens to many other plants.

The larger species of camas, including this one, appear to good advantage when planted between rhododendrons or other large shrubs or as background material to help conceal fences, walls and hedges. The taller species are out of place in all but big rockeries although they grow well there.

Flowering Time: With *C. leichtlinii* and one or two weeks later than *C. quamash*. April to June. Because the basal buds open first, and work on up the stems, the season is extended.

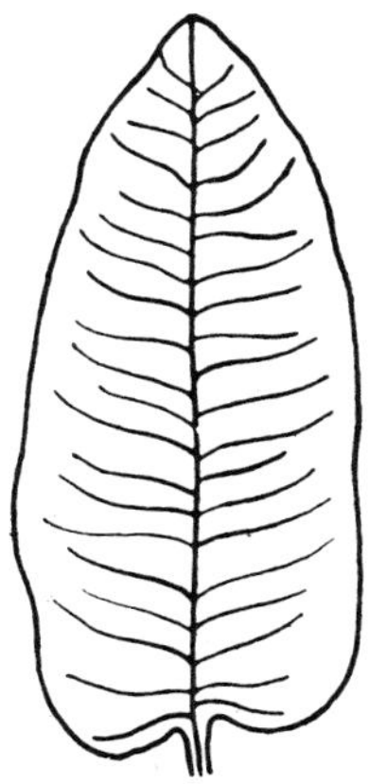

Oblong leaf

Camassia leichtlinii Leichtlin's Camas

CAMASSIA LEICHTLINII (Baker) S. Watson

CAMASSIA LEICHTLINII subsp. **SUKSDORFII** (Greenman) Gould
Leichtlin's Camas

The camas is one of my favorite flowers both in the wild and at home. *Leichtlin's* is more beautiful to look at than fun to dig. It prefers wet, even mucky soils when in blossom. They are the most difficult and exasperating plants I have ever collected. The bulbs, in favorable conditions are down about nine inches but in many places they are 12 and 14 inches. I use a very strong clam shovel with a narrow 11 inch blade. I have either damaged or lost half of the bulbs of this species that I have attempted to remove from their oozy homes. It is extremely hard work to dig them and 50 are as many as I have ever collected before exhaustion overwhelmed my enthusiasm. I simply do not understand how nurseries can afford to sell them at the prices they ask considering the toil required for their collecting. I wouldn't do it unless starvation was at my side.

When I go on study, photographic or collecting expeditions to areas where edible plants are available I take little or no food, preferring to save weight and live off the land. Half a dozen *C. leichtlinii* bulbs or twice as many of the smaller *C. quamash* make a full meal. They are rich in starch, somewhat mucilaginous and very nourishing. I have been able to detect no difference in flavor between the two bulbs but have almost always eaten the bulbs of the latter species as they are much less difficult to dig.

On the hypothesis that if the bulbs are edible the rest of the plant is too – a theory that can result in poisoning I have since learned with other genera – I tried eating the flowers of both *C. quamash* and *C. leichtlinii.* They are grass-like and slightly sweet. I also sampled the flowering stem of *C. leichtlinii.* The middle of the stalk was sweet, grassy flavored, tender and quite tasty. The extreme tip of the shoot, after removing the small flower buds was slightly bitter. The basal part of the stem was generally tough and unpalatable. The leaves were tough, fibrous, not sweet or particularly tasty.

Few of our wild plants have had so much written about them. In preparing this article I have used more than 24 botany books and by no means exhausted my library. Few western plants are so rich in legend and tradition and no other has been the direct cause of a major war between the Indians and whites. It is a sad thing that these wonder flowers are not more often grown in our gardens.

History: *C. leichtlinii* was first named in 1874 by John Gilbert Baker, who was born in 1834. He called it *Chlorogalum leichtlinii.* Sereno Watson, 1826-1892, gave it the now officially recognized *Camassia leichtlinii* in 1885. There have been three others given since, all of which are in synonomy.

Description: The flowers of one type are light to deep purplish blue and another type has cream colored blossoms. I have never seen any indications of hybridizing between these two types although they are sometimes seen in close proximity. The blue flowered petals twist together strongly when they wither. The petals of the cream colored ones fold together in withering and twist only slightly or in many cases they are only clasped without any twisting. Because of these clear differences I have believed for many years that they are two different species. It was only recently that this conviction has been justified. Watson's *C. leichtlinii* is now limited to the cream type while the purplish blue was designated subspecies *suksdorfii* by Frank W. Gould. Wilhelm Nikolaus Suksdorf was a prominent northwestern botanist who lived in the Bingen-White Salmon area of the Columbia Gorge. He was born in 1850 and was killed at an advanced age when he was struck by a train near his home.

For garden purposes both the species and subspecies are much alike except for their colors. The edible coated bulb two inches in diameter is broadly egg-shaped, smaller than Cusick's but much larger than the one inch diameter of *C. quamash.* The leaves are all basal, which characterize the genus, shorter than the scape, one half to three-quarters of an inch wide, paler on the upper surface, with a longitudinal ridge. The scapes are from a foot and a half tall to more than four feet with an average of two and one half to three. The six slender petals are broadly lance-shaped and evenly spaced. The blossoms are up to three inches in diameter and far enough apart on the stem to enhance their individual beauty. The number of flowers varies considerably. I counted one stem that had 205 buds. This of course was exceptional. Another had 50. Like all other members of the genus the lowest blossoms open first.

Rarity: The purplish blue subspecies *suksdorfii* is common. A pure white flowering one is said to exist but, although I have searched many years and examined thousands of plants I have never seen it. If there is such a mutant, and I am sure there is, it is extremely rare.

The cream colored type species, *C. leichtlinii,* is very rare. It is common enough within its range where I have seen fields numbering untold thousands but its area is very limited. It is sometimes referred to as the "White" camas but it is never white – always cream or yellowish tinged.

Distribution: The cream colored type, *C. leichtlinii:* For a number of miles in all directions from Roseburg in southwestern Oregon. At low elevations in open meadows, usually where there is more than average moisture during flowering although these places often become extremely dry during the warm parts of summer.

The purplish blue subspecies *suksdorfii:* From Vancouver Island, British Columbia, where Luther Burbank found it growing in crevices in rocks, (This was chance seeding as it prefers moist meadows) through Washington and Oregon, mainly west of the Cascades, to the northern Coast Ranges in California. Also in Utah. From near sea level to several thousand feet.

Either the species or subspecies, within the range of the former, may be associated with each other and with *C. quamash.* Or all three may grow in close proximity. Outside of the range of the cream colored species the blue *C. suksdorfii* may be living happily near *C. quamash.*

Propagation: By seeds or nicking the side of the bulb. The same as for *C. cusickii,* except that there are no offsets from the bulbs.

Culture: Although wild plants are from nine to 14 inches deep half a foot is sufficient in the garden. Because extra spacing is not needed due to the absence of offsets three or four inches apart will give the roots enough room and result in a massed floral effect that is beyond delight. Some of mine are planted in the extra room between medium sized rhododendrons. They live and do well in this dry and impoverished basement soil – as poor a growth medium as one could imagine. Weeding around the parents calls for concentrated attention. The young seedlings of various ages are so numerous that they can be mistaken for grasses and destroyed. For this reason I like to weed the beds very early in the spring before the shoots appear above ground. But this isn't always practical for the volunteers like to get out of the ground as soon as a little warm weather arrives. Cultural requirements are the same as for *C. cusickii* except for bulb spacing. Some authorities have called *C. leichtlinii* the most beautiful of all the species. Certainly it is worthy of all the garden space you care to give it.

Flowering Time: April to June, with *C. cusickii* and one or two weeks later than *C. quamash.* But due to the long flowering period there is an overlap.

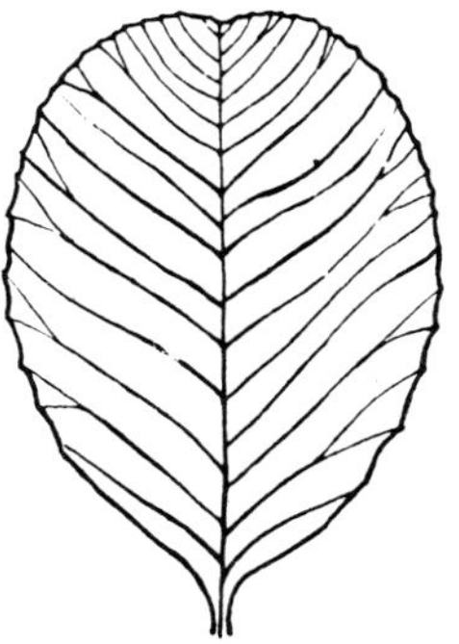

Elliptic leaf

Camassia quamash Common Camas

CAMASSIA QUAMASH (Pursh) Greene
Common Camas

There is nothing that thrills me in quite the same way as a field of bright blue camas mixed with the rich yellow of buttercups. Truly this is a wonderful sight becoming scarcer every year as the plow destroys the vast beds. For 20 or 30 miles south of Olympia, the capitol of Washington, hundreds of prairie acres are so thick with camas blossoms in the spring that they look like clear blue lakes of pure water.

This is the most abundant of all camas and is the one that the Indians used most for food. It was in 1805 that the plant first came to the attention of white men. In September of that year the Lewis and Clark Expedition descended the western slope of the Bitter Root Mountains to a beautiful open plain upon which was encamped a band of Nez Perce Indians who treated the weary travelers to a feast consisting of buffalo meat, dried salmon and a number of roots which included camas. On the following June the returning expedition passed through what is now known as the Weippe Valley in northern Idaho. The level prairies presented a perfect appearance of a blue water lake much like that of the plains of Olympia today. Yes, it was the camas in bloom.

A Nez Perce girl gave the following account of how the Indians prepared the bulbs: "We make a hole in the ground, line it with flat stones, and build a fire upon them. When the stones are red hot we rake out the coals, and cover the hot stones with a certain kind of wild grass found only in the mountains. Then upon the grass we place the camas, and over this place another layer of grass. We then cover all, first with gunnysacks, and then with dirt, and over all we build a fire which is kept burning for two nights and a day. The pit must not be opened or poked into during this time or the camas will be spoiled."

Camas was one of the most important foods of some of the western Indians. Because of their dependence upon it, it was inevitable that trouble would come over the ownership of the great beds. The Indians sometimes fought intertribal battles for possession of favorite locations but the cruelest and bitterest fights were between the native tribes and the white settlers. The Indians' rights were sometimes recognized by the federal government. But the government was in Washington – too far away to worry the pioneers who neither knew nor cared about such matters.

In the late 1870's a band of half starved Bannocks came down to Big Camas Prairie to fill up on their bulbs. They found droves of hogs belonging to the ranchers rooting up and devouring the bulbs. A fight started and some of the white herders were shot.

Soon the Nez Perce war under Chief Joseph was under way – a final, desperate protest against white trespasses upon the vitally important camas bed which they and their ancestors for untold centuries had depended upon for food.

Chief Joseph's men were heavily outnumbered, poorly armed, starving and burdened with the responsibility of saving their women and children. Nevertheless, they fought skilfully and courageously for three and a half months in 1877. The Indians realized that they could not win and so they headed for refuge in Canada. After fighting a continuous running battle for more than a thousand miles they were finally forced to surrender not far from the Canadian border. 300 warriors fought off a United States army that varied between 30 and 40 companies with supplementary volunteers and Indian scouts. The cost to the federal government was enormous for defeating such a small band. Chief Joseph has since been acclaimed one of the great military geniuses of all time. He is buried in the Wallowa Mountains of northeastern Oregon, honored and respected by the descendants of the whites who robbed his people of their homes and destroyed their way of life.

While all the species of Camassia except *C. cusickii* are edible care should be taken not to confuse them with the poisonous Death Camas, *Zygadenus,* the flowers of which are smaller and greenish or yellowish white. The leaves are stiffer and more upright and the capsules are distinctly different but the bulbs themselves are much alike. During the flowering season no difficulty should be had distinguishing the two. But *Zygadenus* plants are sometimes found intermingled with true camas and I would not care to eat bulbs dug during the dormant season unless I was certain, from previous examination of the beds, that no *Zygadenus* were there.

History: Frederick Pursh first described this species as *Phalangium quamash* in his two volume, *Flora Americae Septentrionalis*, published in 1814. Evidently, from the text in his book, Pursh made his identification from specimens collected by Meriwether Lewis of the Lewis and Clark Expedition. At least four other names have been given it since, including the one now recognized as official, *Camassia quamash,* described by Edward Lee Greene, 1842-1915, in 1894. Various subspecies have been described but these differ little from the type and, in my opinion, are no more than varieties or forms.

Description: The bulbs of mature plants are about an inch in diameter and spherical or egg shaped. The outer layers of the coated bulbs usually dry and turn black if the plants are old. They are from three to seven inches deep, averaging about five and sometimes grow in rocky soil where they are difficult to dig. The leaves are basal, linear, three-eighths to three-quarters of an inch wide, somewhat powdery above and much shorter than the flowering scape. The stems are from less than six inches to two and a half feet tall, depending upon the amount of moisture and the depth and fertility of the soil. In my rock gardens they are a foot and a half high, which is about average.

Due, presumably, to the much smaller bulbs and shorter scapes the blossoms are not as numerous as those of Leichtlin's or Cusick's. They have the usual six petals. The spacing is uneven, the lower petal being more separated from the other five and they wither separately in age, unlike the twisting together of *C. leichtlinii.* This can be confusing, however, as at least one *C. quamash* subspecies has the petals twisting together as they wither so that this characteristic alone is not sufficient for differential identification. The blossoms vary from one to three inches in diameter, the smaller ones in some areas are much denser on the stems and lack the appeal of those with larger flowers which have wider spacing on the scapes.

As with the other species the flowers open upwards from the base of the cluster. But when the petals open they separate from the base and bow outward. The tips remain adhering to each other until one or more suddenly breaks loose and springs open within less than a second. The colors vary from extremely light, pale blue to deep and rich purples.

Rarity: The blue type, very common. The whites with small, densely crowded flowers are rare. I have frequently searched all day in large fields containing a great many plants without finding a single one that had pure white blossoms. Sometimes a blossom would appear to be white but comparing it with a calling card would quickly display the very faint blue that it really was. On one occasion, near The Dalles, Oregon, I found over a dozen pure whites in less than half a day, but these all had the small, closely crowded blossoms that weren't quite what I wanted. The whites with the large, well spaced flowers are extremely rare. I have likewise searched diligently for this form and in all the years have discovered only one. It is living happily in my gardens among its less distinguished but no less beautiful, blue bretheren.

Distribution: From British Columbia southward through Washington, Oregon, and into northern California's Coastal Ranges. Eastward into Idaho, Utah and Montana. From sea level to several thousand feet in the Canadian Life Zone. There is a sheer cliff rising 75 feet above the ocean at Oregon's Cape Foulweather. Within ten feet of the edge of this precipice where the breakers dashing against it in the winter gales splash salt water over them there is a patch of *Camassia quamash*. It would be easy to pick a camas flower and, from where it is growing, toss it into the sea as a peace offering to the god of storms. It is a far cry from this very rainy climate to the arid stretches east of the Cascades and into the Rockies but *C. quamash* adapts well to these radical extremes.

Propagation: By seeds or nicking the sides of the bulbs. The same as for *C. cusickii,* except that there are no offsets from the bulbs.

Culture: Plant three or four inches deep and two or three inches apart. These bulbs are only half the size of Leichtlin's and can be planted closer together for this reason. Camas make a more colorful display when in clumps and solitary plantings generally should be avoided. It is better to plant them when they are completely dormant in late summer or early fall but they are sturdy creatures and I have planted them at all times of the year with no permanent damage. They are usually found in full sun but in a tiny meadow on top of a cliff in the Columbia Gorge there are a few growing in the light shade of adjacent fir trees where they are perfectly happy. And I am happy too whenever I visit this grassy spot with its view of the great River flowering through its majestic Gorge.

At the ocean beaches they are in deep, very fertile leaf mold soil with good drainage and abundant moisture. There is a rocky bank in the Columbia Gorge topped with only three or four inches of soil. It is never a wet spot and the most unlikely place for camas to grow that one could imagine. When I first drove past it during the flowering season I saw a flash of dark blue and stopped to see what it was. Dwarfed by these harsh conditions, nevertheless it was camas.

There is a small seasonal pond on a high plateau not far from Oregon's Hood River that I have often visited. Early in spring when the pond is full, camas plants send their leaves and flowers out of the ground around the margins. As the water recedes with the drying weather the plants appear closer and closer to the middle until finally, when the water is all gone the entire area is densely covered with the gay blue flowers. Being under water for much of the winter and early months of spring didn't hurt them at all. I have used this knowledge to advantage when collecting. I simply put the bulbs, especially when they are in flower, in a bucket of water to keep them fresh. I know better than to try this with *Brodiaeas, Fritillarias* and other bulbous plants. They would quickly rot. Near this same place is a camas bed of many acres where the plants grow in a heavy clay loam. After the blooming season is over this soil bakes so hard that digging them with a shovel is virtually out of the question, and with a pick is very hard work. The Indians must have dug them when the soil was moist during the flowering season or in the fall after the rains came. Even then they must have had a difficult time harvesting enough to eat with their crude pointed sticks.

These observations I made in their native habitat told me a great deal of what I needed to know about their garden requirements. Most any soil will do but the richer and wetter, within reasonable limits, the better. I have this species, because of its low stature, in my rock garden in soil that is half crushed porous lava and half leaf mold. I tuck them in alongside fairly large boulders for background effects.

Flowering Time: April to June, varying with the climate, season and altitude. About two weeks before *C. cusickii* and *C. leichtlinii* but with an overlap.

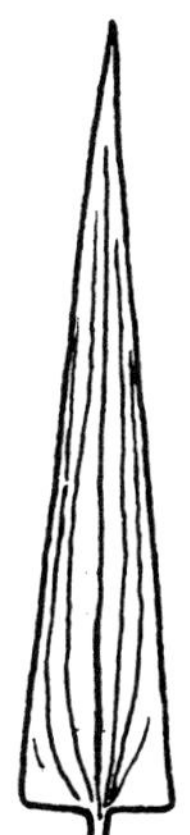

Subulate leaf

Campanula piperi U.S. Dept. of the Interior — National Park Service Photo The Olympic Blue Bell

CAMPANULA PIPERI Howell
The Olympic Blue Bell

The rarest and by far the most beautiful of the western campanulas grows only in the Olympic Mountains of northwestern Washington.

We drove from our home in Portland, Oregon to Port Angeles, Washington on the Straits of Juan de Fuca. From that pleasant little town a paved road took us to the timberline heights of Hurricane Ridge in the Olympic National Park. From there an eight mile, one way mountain road led us in a southeasterly direction to Prospect Point. My first trip on this twisting, narrow lane was a nerve shattering experience for the drop-offs are abrupt and incredibly deep. At the end of the road I took a side trail for a quarter of a mile or so, then climbed down a rugged basaltic slope to where, in tiny crevices in the hard rock I discovered the Olympic Blue Bell I had traveled so far to see.

I used a cold chisel and sledge hammer to break up the rock before I could lift the undamaged plants out of their forbidding home. A much more difficult problem had to be resolved, however, before I was allowed to collect the plants. A permit had to be obtained and this is not easy in a National Park. Five conditions had to be met before I was allowed to proceed and a guard was assigned to observe my activities. When my few plants were safely packed we drove off this awesome ridge and returned to Portland.

History: Thomas Howell was Oregon's first great resident botanist and it was he who named this lovely rarity for Charles V. Piper, professor of botany at the State College of Washington, 1893-1903. The first official description of the plant appears in the 1901 edition of Mr. Howell's *A Flora Of Northwest America* on page 409.

Description: It is a tiny plant and not at all easy to find. The leaves are only about a quarter of an inch wide and twice that long. The whole plant, except when it is in flower, is no more than an inch tall. Nestling in the protected places in the rock it is able to withstand the violent winds that rage at this 6,000 foot height. And the heavy snows of the long winter protect it until the summer sun brings new life to the shiny, toothed foliage and the blossoms that follow soon after.

The open flowers, no more than an inch wide, lift their faces up to and match the color of the clear blue Olympian skies. Many blue blossoms are tainted with purples and lavenders but not this one. It is a pure, clean and bright blue with a splendid richness unsurpassed in any campanula I have ever seen. The blossoms are only a couple of inches above the stony soil making them a miniature delight in the rock garden.

Rarity: Rare.

Distribution: Found only in the High Olympics of northwestern Washington at altitudes around six thousand feet. Plants are scattered and never abundant in any one station.

Propagation: Purchased seed has germinated poorly in my Portland, Oregon gardens. Our wet winters with alternate freezing and thawing may cause it to rot out. Seed should germinate in climates with consistently freezing winters. I have a report of a gardener in Scotland who was able to germinate seeds in three months after planting on the first of February. Well rooted plants go down a full six inches. Single stems with a few adhering roots can be established in well drained soils rich in humus. Generous sized clumps come through nicely. I have had better success transplanting in the spring than at any other time.

Artificial pollination with both finger tips and camels hair brushes was a failure and I have never been able to obtain seed from those in my garden. Wild plants must produce seed or there would be no likelihood that the species could survive.

In nature they could hardly be expected to increase by underground rootstocks due to lack of both soil and room. But in the garden roots branch out in all directions and send out new shoots in the spring. By this means nature doubles and triples the number of plants in a single season.

Culture: Field observations, of course, are very important if wild plants are to be grown successfully in the garden. And this is especially vital when moving them from six thousand feet altitude to near sea level.

Their home in extremely fine crevices calls for the sharpest kind of drainage and this is easy to provide in rock gardens. Use half crushed rock and half leaf mold and they will be happy. I prefer crushed lava as it holds moisture better than broken basalt but still maintains good drainage. The wild plants often had their roots in less than a teaspoon of soil. I drilled holes in lava boulders – an inch in diameter and six inches deep. *C. piperi* plants placed in these holes with a correct soil mixture rarely survived. They seem to want more room.

The ones I found in the Olympics were growing with a north or east exposure to protect them from the sun. In our gardens they likewise prefer this shade. In warmer parts of the country cooler places in the garden should be chosen. Moderate watering until they are well established is all that is necessary and no added moisture at all in the winter. Slugs love these plants as much as I do but in a different way. Baiting is essential.

If you can't go to the Olympics or get a collecting permit when you arrive, there are a few nurseries – I know of three – that can supply you.

Rare as it is the blue type has an even more precious form – the white, of the same purity as the snow that blankets it all winter long. Some day I hope to have it growing alongside the blue that now graces my rockery.

Flowering Time: The blossoms start to appear in late June in Portland. In a favorable year the flowers are produced so luxuriously that they virtually obscure the gay leaves of July. Flowering time is later in the high Olympics. Then, it is time for the long winter sleep again to prepare for the lavish blue and green beauty of the coming spring and summer – in my gardens; in our Olympics.

Campanula piperi 'White' The White Olympic Bluebell

CAMPANULA PIPERI 'White'
The White Olympic Bluebell

The green leaves and the size and shape of the blossoms are the same as in the blue type. The flowers themselves are a startling white of a purity and clarity seldom found in any plant, domestic or wild.

Rarity: Extremely rare.

Distribution: This rare mutation is known in only two or three stations in the Olympics and three or four plants in each location are all that have been found. A few, a very few people are fortunate enough to have it in their gardens and it is extremely difficult to get starts from them.

Propagation: Same as for the blue type. White is recessive to blue so that only a few if any seedlings could be expected to come true from the parent white unless self pollenized.

Culture: Same as for the blue type.

Flowering Time: Late June, July and August in the home garden. July, August and early September in the High Olympics.

Cephalanthera austinae Phantom Orchid

CEPHALANTHERA AUSTINAE Heller
Phantom Orchid

The narrow trail led through the deep woods. Suddenly I stopped, for there at my feet was a Phantom Orchid. I gasped with astonishment for I had never expected to find this rare and beautiful plant.

Realizing that the plant would be destroyed because it grew on the trail, I dug it as carefully as I could. The soil was broken rock and loose humus, so that balling the roots was impossible. Although it was planted carefully in a friend's garden, it disappeared the following year after blossoming weakly.

One might spend a lifetime in the woods and never see this orchid, *Cephalanthera austinae,* for it is a phantom indeed, one of the rarest of our natives. The entire plant is waxy white, except for a golden throat in the flower.

The cold language of botany cannot describe the ineffable beauty of the delicate petals and the graceful flowers. In fact, it cannot be described at all.

It was merely by chance that I stumbled upon it. Although I had never seen it before I recognized it at once from the excellent photograph in Leslie Haskin's *Wild Flowers of the Pacific Coast*. I had looked for it often without any real hope of success, but always with the thought that some day Nature might be kind and lead me, unknowingly, to her diminutive white altar in the deep forest where this lovely orchid is an elusive dweller.

This chance meeting was the peak of my botanical career in the outdoors up to that time. As the years went by, I had asked various wild flower fans and botanists about it, but no one was able to help my painstaking and aimless search.

One day, however, a friend told me his wife had brought home a white flower. It was *all* white, I thought, of course, it must be an Indian Pipe but his lay description did not fit that plant. So I hurried to his home where I saw my second Phantom Orchid in a glass on a window sill. It had been found a short distance from Gresham, Oregon. In a space no larger than half an acre in the shade of a grove of Douglas Fir trees, to my utter amazement, I found 70 by actual count. I spent most of that Sunday morning there photographing and studying them.

The Sunday I located the 70 plants held other surprises. On a hill in a dense forest of second growth Douglas Firs, were growing the Striped Coral Root, the Spotted Coral Root, the Leafless Wintergreen, and nearly a dozen plants of the Indian Pipe – saprophytes all. Among them, in an area of less than five acres, bringing life and beauty and a marvelous richness to the deep shade. I gazed in wonder upon no less than 865 more Phantom Orchids!

The trees have been since logged off. Then a fire raced over the denuded land, leaving no trace of my saprophytic friends. But I shall never forget that quiet Sunday morning of long ago when, on a lonely hill top, I found my Botanical Holy Grail, my New Jerusalem of Flowers.

History: There are about a dozen species in the genus, found around the world, but this is the only one native to America and it is restricted to the Pacific Northwest. Others are found in Japan, the Caucasus, the Himalayas, temperate Asia, Greece, Mesopotamia, Persia, Sicily, Asia Minor, Europe, and North Africa. It was named *C. austinae* in 1900 by A. A. Heller, 1867-1944. Heller renamed it in 1904 *Eburophyton austinae,* a monotypic western species. But I prefer the older, better known name, much easier to pronounce.

Description: This orchid is entirely lacking in green leaves, which have been reduced to white sheathing scales. It is a true saprophyte, one of several such plants found in the Pacific Northwest. Its perfume is as delicate and rare as the blossom itself. If you are a flower lover, and are fortunate enough to discover this plant, you will never forget it. Usually there are a half a dozen or so blossoms upon each stem, although they may number up to 40. The lower blossoms open first, assuring a succession of bloom. They are herbaceous perennials. I dug around one plant with my trowel and found the stump of the previous year's flowering stem. Two inches below the surface of the ground the heavy, fleshy roots spread out and downward for a considerable distance in their search for food. The roots are white, the same color as the stem, and the outside has a thin layer of light brown skin with the white heart showing through. The stems vary in height from six to 20 inches, the shorter ones having fewer blossoms.

As a cut flower it remains fresh fairly well, but the buds do not open. The stems bend toward the light indoors. This is a surprising quality in a plant that is wholly without chlorophyll, and presumably lives entirely independently of light. The flower seems to remember vaguely that, somewhere in its misty past, like all normal plants, it too had green leaves and looked to the sun for nourishment. But when it became a dweller of the deep shade where there was not enough light for survival the Phantom Orchid did the only thing possible under the circumstances. It went to the soil for pre-digested food.

The only plant likely to be confused with it in our territory is the Indian Pipe, but the two are easily distinguished. The Phantom Orchid turns brown when it is dying, while the Indian Pipe becomes almost black. While the Phantom Orchid appears to be snow-white, beside a piece of white paper or cloth it is seen to be slightly cream-colored. The Indian Pipe is pure white. *Cephalanthera* blossoms a full two weeks ahead of the Indian Pipe, although both can be seen in flower at the same time as there is an overlap. The Phantom Orchid appears in clumps of two or three occasionally, but usually it is alone. The Indian Pipe, however, flowers in clusters of from two to 150 stems and rarely occurs with only one stem.

Rarity: Extremely rare.

Distribution: It is very difficult to establish the exact range of so rare a plant. It favors mountains at low altitudes although it can be found in the valleys all the way from the Olympic Peninsula of extreme northwestern Washington, through Oregon to Mariposa and Monterey Counties in central California and eastward to Idaho. Portland, Oregon is particularly fortunate in that a few of them are growing in the deep shade in the Hoyt Arboretum. There are a few up Oneonta Gorge, about 35 miles east of Portland, if you know where to look.

Propagation: Observations made of several dozen plants after they had matured showed little indication of seed. I found only two that had enlarged ovaries, and of those only one on each plant was swelling. The scarcity of seed may be one of the reasons for the extreme rarity of this plant. There is so little food in each tiny seed, although a great number may be borne in an ovary, that few indeed are able to germinate and produce mature plants. I do not know of anyone who has succeeded in growing it from seed. But it can be done. Nature can do it and so can we. Perhaps the best suggestion is to broadcast the seeds as soon as they ripen, on a rich, leaf mold soil in deep shade. Wild plants, even when dug with large balls of earth, are almost certain to perish in the garden. It does not seem to make any difference how much thought and care is given them, the results are inevitably the same. It may be that the shock of transplanting is too much for them. Soil conditions do not seem to be a determining factor for most any well drained soil in their native habitat seems to be satisfactory. Some day we may learn the secret of growing this beautiful but difficult orchid.

Culture: Unknown. In the wild state it receives no artificial help of any kind, neither extra food nor water. Once established in the garden it should be left alone.

Flowering Time: Mid June and July. It is possible to see it as early as the middle of May but three weeks later will generally find them at their prime.

Cordate leaf

Claytonia nivalis Wenatchee Claytonia

CLAYTONIA NIVALIS English
Wenatchee Claytonia

It was merely by chance that I encountered *Claytonia nivalis.* I was going through a recently arrived wild flower catalogue and saw it listed as "One of the loveliest and most elusive of alpines from high barren ridges, with deep green rosettes of meaty foliage and deep pink flowers peeking out between the leaves."

Acting upon the assumption that the description was reasonably accurate and that an expensive plant ought to be a good one, I sent in an order. I wasn't too impressed with them when they arrived but planted them carefully nevertheless. When they attained adult size and blossomed next year I knew I had made one of my better horticultural investments.

History: The *Claytonias,* which have been freely confused with the *Montias,* belong to the Purslane Family, *Portulacaceae,* in such distinguished company, besides the *Montias,* as *Talinums, Calandrinias, Spragueas, Calyptridiums, Lewisias* and, of course, *Portulacas.*

The family was named by that well known botanical team, George Bentham, 1800-1884, and Joseph Dalton Hooker, 1817-1911. It comprises about 20 genera and 220 species, distributed throughout the world – in Asia, Europe, Africa, Australia, North and South America, the tropics and arctic regions.

The genus *Claytonia* was named and given its official description by Carl von Linneaus in 1753 in his famous *Species Plantarum.* (Another source suggests the date 1737 and the first edition of Linnaeus *Genera Plantarum* but this discrepancy, more than two centuries later, is of little consequence.) It honors the American botanist, John Clayton, 1685-1773. There are about 15 species, natives of North America and the arctic regions. There is so much difference of opinion among systematic botanists as to whether a plant should be a *Claytonia* or a *Montia* that the exact number of species, and therefore the range, is still under question and, no doubt, will be for a considerable time.

C. nivalis was late coming into its own. It was listed in *Flora of the State of Washington,* by Charles Vancouver Piper, who was born in 1867, as *Claytonia megarrhiza,* a Rocky Mountain species. The variety *arctica* of this species was named by Asa Gray in 1862, and the type species itself was named by Parry in 1878. The specimen upon which Piper made his identification was collected on Mt. Stuart in the Wenatchees by Adolph Daniel Edward Elmer, born in 1870.

Carl S. English Jr., a Seattle, Washington botanist, was not satisfied with this identification. He found this plant on a mountain not very far from Mt. Stuart and compared it with plants obtained from the Rockies. After growing them side by side his observations led him to conclude that they were two different species. He therefore raised the Wenatchee Mountains plant to specific standing by naming it *Claytonia nivalis* and published his findings in 1934. Mr. English's designation is still recognized as authoritative today. But why he decided upon *nivalis* is a little difficult to understand. The word means *snowy* or pertaining to *snow.* No part of the plant fits that description although it lives where the annual fall of snow is from 50 to 100 inches. This may have been the reason for Mr. English's choice.

Description: It is a perennial with a stout taproot and a thick, sometimes branched base, one-half to one inch in diameter. It has numerous very fleshy rich green leaves arranged in a compact basal rosette. They are from one to three inches long, including the stems, averaging about one and a half. The blades are strongly spatulate, a half an inch or more long and nearly as wide, rounded or less often slightly pointed at the apex. They taper gently into slender petioles (leaf stems) which are from less than an inch to two and a half inches long. The petioles become enlarged as they approach the base so that only in the middle are they gracefully slender. The change from blade to stem is so gradual that it is difficult to say where one ends and the other begins.

It is a lovely plant for its evergreen rosettes alone. It may have several flowering stems which peep out from between the leaves. They do not always appear at the same time and each will have from one or two to as many as ten flowers but this latter number is rarely seen, at least in my gardens. The five rose colored petals are about half an inch long and the blossoms themselves, because the petals do not spread out flat, are only slightly larger. Two or three rather large shiny black seeds are produced in each capsule.

Rarity: Extremely rare.

Distribution: Limited to the Wenatchee Mountains of Central Washington State. Mt. Stuart, 9470 feet altitude, (also spelled Stewart), Fish Lake, Ingalls Peak, and a few other stations are known. It prefers cracks in boulders, loose rock and talus slopes in the Hudsonian to Arctic-Alpine Life Zones. This high altitude alpine does not like crowding.

Propagation: Seeds should be planted as soon as they ripen, which begins in June in my gardens. Crownal offsets are produced fairly freely but are difficult to root. The problem is to strike a balance between sufficient moisture to allow the cuttings to strike but not enough to let them rot. Failure to achieve this balance is fatal – and a common experience.

Culture: The fact that this *Claytonia* inhabits rock crevices might indicate that it requires good drainage. My experience has been that not only is this true but that even a *little* extra moisture can rot the entire root system and destroy the plant. The rare *Lewisia tweedyi,* from the same mountains, is notoriously fussy about water. *C. nivalis* is even more so. I have lost *C. nivalis* under identical conditions that *L. tweedyi* thrives on. I use a mixture of crushed lava rock with equal parts of leaf mold. *C. nivalis'* fleshy leaves and thick roots can hold a surprisingly large amount of water and it will, therefore, tolerate substantial droughts. I give them morning sun and afternoon shade. They are planted in holes I have drilled in very porous lava boulders and in holes I have cut into the sides of pumice block walls with loose cap stones for servicing.

While slugs have not attacked my *Lewisia tweedyis* they will devour *C. nivalis* and constant baiting is necessary to save them. All this may seem hardly worth the effort but such is not the case. The picture that accompanies this article does not and cannot do justice to the remarkably beautiful rose colored flowers. It is one of my outstanding floral treasures. It is difficult to acquire. I know of only one nursery that handles it and it is grown in very few gardens.

Flowering Time: July and August in its native Wenatchee

home. Somewhat earlier at lower elevations. May in my gardens. From two to four blossoms appear at one time and continue for about a month.

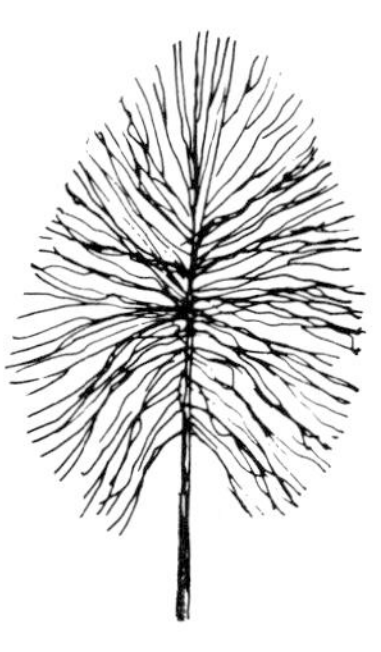

Obcordate leaf

Corallorhiza striata Coral Root

CORALLORHIZA SPECIES
Coral Root

History: American species include *bigelovii, corallorhiza, innata, maculata, mertensiana, multiflora, neottia, ochroleuca, odontorhiza, striata, trifida,* and *vreelandii.* The genus was named in 1760 by J. J. Chatelain of France.

The name of this genus of plants, *Corallorhiza,* comes from the Greek meaning *coral* and *root.* The reference is a good one for the massive, branched roots resemble coral as nearly as one could expect from any living plant. The genus comprises about 15 species and at least 12 of them live in North America. They are members of the Orchid Family and, like other members of this family, they range from truly beautiful to rather ordinarily attractive, depending partly upon individual taste and partly upon the plants themselves. All are either saprophytic or parasitic, being completely destitute of green foliage. As might be expected they are dwellers of shady forests where they live upon decayed vegetable matter or on roots of living plants.

Description: They may be divided, in a general way, into two groups, those with striped petals and those that are spotted. Colors range from brownish, yellowish, red, purple and various combinations. None of them have gay, vivid blossoms and may generally be regarded as curiosities. But a few have a waxy gloss and enough contrasting colorations to be truly charming in a subdued way.

Corallorhiza striata has flowers of red and white stripes somewhat reminiscent of peppermint candy sticks of childhood days. This striped effect, of course is not confined to the coral root, being quite common in chlorophyll bearing plants. To me this is one of the most attractive plants in the entire genus. Other people of good judgment, disagree and consider some of the spotted species more desirable.

The leaves have all been reduced to sheathing scales and the flowers are in terminal racemes, subtended by minute bracts. The sepals are about as long as the petals, and there are three of each as with other orchids. Both are from a quarter to half an inch long, depending upon individual specimens and species. Some have short spurs entirely attached to the ovary, others are free of the ovary for half the length or the spur may be entirely lacking.

At first glance some of the coral roots might be mistaken for the leafless Wintergreen *Pyrola aphylla,* in areas where both are found. But the distinction is easy. The *Pyrolas* have five petals and the *Corallorhizas* only three. And the spots and stripes of the coral root flowers are not found on the winter-greens.

The stems are from six to 20 inches long, depending upon the species and the numerous flowers on the solitary scapes will number up to 30 or more in some of the taller growing plants, fewer in the shorter ones. They are borne in terminal racemes. The capsules, the seed bearing organs, are oblong, ovoid or oblong-ovate, and drooping. These plump, hanging organs are very prominent when the seeds, hundreds of them and as fine as dust, are ripening. A casual glance immediately identifies them.

These plants are not as noticeable in the somber forests they prefer as most of the other species of plants that have lost their green leaves. Their duller colors tend to blend them with their surroundings.

I have sometimes seen dead stalks of last year's blossoms with no new flowers of the season's growth, while only a few feet away other coral roots were in blossom along side the dried stalks of the previous season's plants. This is because they sometimes rest for a year. A few inches below the surface of the soil the massive coral-like lumps will be discovered, alive and healthy, while they rest before sending forth flowers the next year.

Rarity: Scarce to rare according to the species. But not as difficult to find as many people think for few flower hunters penetrate the deep forests where they live.

Distribution: In the north temperate regions in parts of Europe and Asia. In North America from southeastern Alaska across the continent to Nova Scotia. Southward on the West Coast in British Columbia, Washington, Oregon, California and Utah. In the middle states in Colorado, Michigan, New Mexico,

Ohio, Nebraska, Missouri. On the East Coast, New York, other New England states, and southward to Georgia and Florida. In North America this is a very widely distributed genus considering the few species that grow in our country and in view of the remarkably varying climatic conditions in which they live it is a highly adaptable one.

Propagation: Like most all of our native parasitic and saprophytic plants the coral roots are exasperatingly difficult to grow. Seed is produced in great abundance but they are so small that each has only minute amounts of food to give it a start until it can establish roots to draw food from the soil. Undoubtedly many thousands of seed ripen and fall to the ground, only to perish, for every one that produces a living, healthy plant. No greater success can be expected in the garden. The seed should be scattered on the surface of the soil consisting of rich leaf mold. A light covering of finely ground peat will help hold the moisture. It might be even more advantageous to dust the seed on top of the peat. The planting area should be in moderate to deep shade. Neither I nor anyone of my acquaintance has ever succeeded in growing any of the coral roots from seed. Someday, it is reasonable to believe, that the secret will be wrested from Mother Nature and we shall be able to have these in our gardens.

Culture: Unknown. Considering the large amounts of food that must be stored in the compact massive coral-like roots one would expect them to be easy to transplant from the forests into the gardens and that they would thrive in their new homes. Such is not the case. I have dug them carefully several times and planted them just as carefully in a rich and deep leaf mold soil in my gardens. Sometimes they never came up the following year. Others would flower feebly the next season and then completely and permanently vanish. The reason must be that the tiny feeding roots so necessary for life among the higher plants refuse to re-establish themselves. In such an event the plant can live only until it has exhausted all the food it has stored in its root system.

Flowering Time: From April to September, depending upon the species and climate.

Cypripedium candidum Adams Studio Photo Small White Lady's Slipper

CYPRIPEDIUM CANDIDUM Willdenow
Small White Lady's Slipper

On the north side of my house in a bed of very rich, moist leaf mold is a colony of Lady Slippers. Strange bedfellows these for, of the more than half a dozen species growing there, no two are alike and none is in its native home. They came to me across the nation, from coast to coast.

I like to think they have forgotten their journeys, some from far away, and as with our early pioneers, are happy in mixed company in a new land. Apparently there is more than wishful thinking in this horticultural philosophy for they give their varying distinctive blossoms freely in the abundant days of spring.

Among them are four of the Small White Lady's Slippers that a Michigan friend – and a real friend he must be – gave me. We have been exchanging floral gems back and forth for some years and when he promised me a start of *C. candidum* I expected just that. But when I opened the package there before my astonished eyes were four, fresh, mature plants, for these are rarities among the American *Cypripediums,* one of the most costly, and difficult to get at any price.

History: These strangely exciting and wonderfully beautiful flowers, modest though they may be in numbers, belong to the great Orchid Family, *Orchidaceae,* originally spelled *Orchideae* by Bentham and Hooker and slightly modified by John Lindley, 1799-1865, in 1836. No one seems to know how big it is. Some authorities suggest 430 genera and over 5,000 species. Others claim 450 genera and at least 7,500 species, widely distributed but mostly of the tropics.

Most botanists agree that all of our flowers are descended from the buttercup. This primitive flower developed a number of branches going in different evolutionary directions. One of the most fascinating of these became the arrowheads which, in the course of time, produced our lilies. Some of the lilies went a step higher and created the Irises. Those Irises which had to struggle to adapt themselves to a changing environment were transformed into orchids.

The lilies and Iris belong to the great *order Liliales* and the orchids are in the significant *order Orchidales.* These three flowers in their two closely allied *orders* have vastly enriched the earth with their variety and beauty.

The *Cypripediums* are but a minute speck in this enormous group. There are between 20 and 30 species, all of the north temperate zone, about ten of which are claimed by North America. The name originates from two Greek words meaning *Venus* and *shoe, sock* or *buskin* from the shape of the blossom. Little imagination is needed to recognize this resemblance which accounts for the various common appellations: Moccasin Flower, Lady's Slipper, Shoe of Venus, Partridge Moccasin, Noah's Ark – this is getting far out, – Whip-poor-Will's Shoe and a few others.

One authority claims the name was given by Linneaus in 1735. Others say he described it first in 1753 in his *Species Plantarum.* At least ten other generic names have been announced at various times but *Cypripedium* is still official and authoritative.

Description: *C. candidum* is one of the smaller species, the stiffly erect stems being from six to 12 inches high from short rootstocks which produce numerous thick feeders. The three to five parallel veined leaves are three to five inches long, tapering abruptly or gradually to a sharp point. They are two-thirds to one and a half inches wide and from lance shaped to two or three times as long as wide and with a uniform curvature nearly throughout. The uppermost leaves are narrower and shorter. Each stem usually bears but a single flower and only rarely two.

The lance-like sepals are greenish, spotted with purple. The petals are somewhat longer and narrower than the sepals, greenish and wavy twisted. The lip or 'shoe' is an unbelievably pure white (*candidum* means *pure white*), purple striped inside, and an inch or slightly less in length. It is this snowy structure that accounts for startling beauty of this otherwise, not very imposing plant.

The abundantly produced seeds are very tiny – and this

leads to complications, frustrations and horticultural despair.

Rarity: Very Rare. It was the misfortune of this dainty *Cypripedium* to have its home where people liked to build theirs. Vandalism, indiscriminate collecting, and the encroachment of the multitudinous needs of civilization have all contributed to the increasing rarity of this once not too uncommon orchid. Most of those that are left are in alkaline bogs in Michigan and Wisconsin.

Distribution: From New York, New Jersey and Pennsylvania southward to Kentucky and Missouri. Westward into Michigan, Wisconsin, Minnesota and Nebraska where it prefers marly (lime containing) bogs, sphagnum bogs and moist meadows. This is a lowland species.

Propagation: Nature grows and distributes them by seed but I have yet to learn of a man who has had any real success competing with that Greatest of all Propagators. There is so little food locked in each seed that it cannot establish feeding roots before the nourishment is exhausted. It takes thousands, hundreds of thousands, perhaps millions, of seeds to produce a single plant under natural conditions. That may be good enough for nature with plenty of time and plenty of patience. But horticulturists either can't or won't wait. I have scattered the seeds around parent plants in the remote hope that the impossible would occur. No such luck. One of my friends was able to germinate the seeds in agar solution. The minute creatures turned green – a sure sign of life – then perished.

The practical method – and this is as delightfully successful as the other is dismally frustrating – is by division. The roots should be worked carefully apart until they are free, with one or more dormant growth buds to each section. Late summer or early fall when the foliage has died but before new growth has begun is best although early spring divisions can be made too. As soon as they are dug they should be nestled in their new locations. No other means of propagation are known at the present time but I am tempted to try the Thwing Method used for *Trilliums*. For instructions on this system see under *Propagation* section of article on *Trillium grandiflorum*.

Culture: Amateurs often regard these strange, awesomely beautiful flowers with some trepidation, as being as difficult as they are distinctively spectacular. One of my friends has put it bluntly in his catalogue: "They are easily grown, long lived and multiply readily into beautiful clumps if cared for properly. If the right conditions cannot be provided, don't buy them. These are not plants for indifferent gardeners."

My experience with them might be considered typical. It is a great advantage to be able to study wild plants in their native homes so that the conditions can be approximated in the garden. I have searched throughout the years but I have yet to see a *Cypripedium* where nature grew it. I simply have never been in the right place at the right time. While I have been deprived of this advantage, nevertheless, by observing their few essential needs, mine are healthy, happy and floriferous. I removed the basement dirt to a depth of 18 inches from a stretch on the north side of the house and replaced it with one-half leaf mold, one-quarter rich black top soil and one quarter coarse sand. This gave them the food, loose soil, moisture retention, and drainage they need. All has been well since.

Once established they should be left alone. If undisturbed they will increase readily and soon form nice clumps. The most common cause of failure is too deep planting which is absolutely fatal. Scoop out a shallow hole, spread the roots out flat with the new growth buds not more than an inch below the surface. This seems like an invitation to trouble during severe freezes but these are hardy plants frostwise and won't mind at all.

C. candidum is one of the most adaptable of them all. It has been sold from coast to coast and grown in the British Isles for more than a third of a century. The biggest problem in growing this species is getting the plants. I know of only one grower and his supply is small. He obtained his start of 11 plants during the middle of the Second World War and has so few to sell that he rarely lists it in his catalogue. He has grown them in a mixture of subsoil and peat, and in very sandy soil mixed with rotten wood and decayed leaves. This indicates an acid condition. One of his neighbors has them in an alkaline bog with a fixed water table. In the middle west they can be grown in full sun except during the hot summer months of July and August when grass should be allowed to grow tall about them for the considerable shade it provides. Another *C. candidum* fan has his in a bog of black soil mixed with decaying vegetation but with no peat. The crowns must be kept above the water table but with the roots in the wet soil. This gives the plants a cool root run and always ample moisture. A top dressing in autumn of leaf mold or compost will give them a little extra food and this is all the attention they need.

These practical experiences indicate that the White Lady's Slipper will thrive in either a mildly acid or alkaline medium. The other conditions, however, are important: a loose soil rich in leaf mold, good drainage, shallow planting and no disturbance once established. If there is an *abundance* of moisture during the growing period they can stand full sun in the milder climates, and sun with shade during mid summer months and warm part of the day in the hotter part of the country. If this extra moisture is not available light shade all day during the growing season will be necessary.

As indoor vase flowers the *Cypripediums* are excellent. Cut them when approaching full blossom and be sure their stems are in water. They will remain as fresh and lovely as long as their more exotic cousins, the tropical orchids. When making the cuts include as few of the leaves as possible so that those remaining will be able to manufacture enough food to store in the roots for next year's growth.

Flowering Time: May, June and into July.

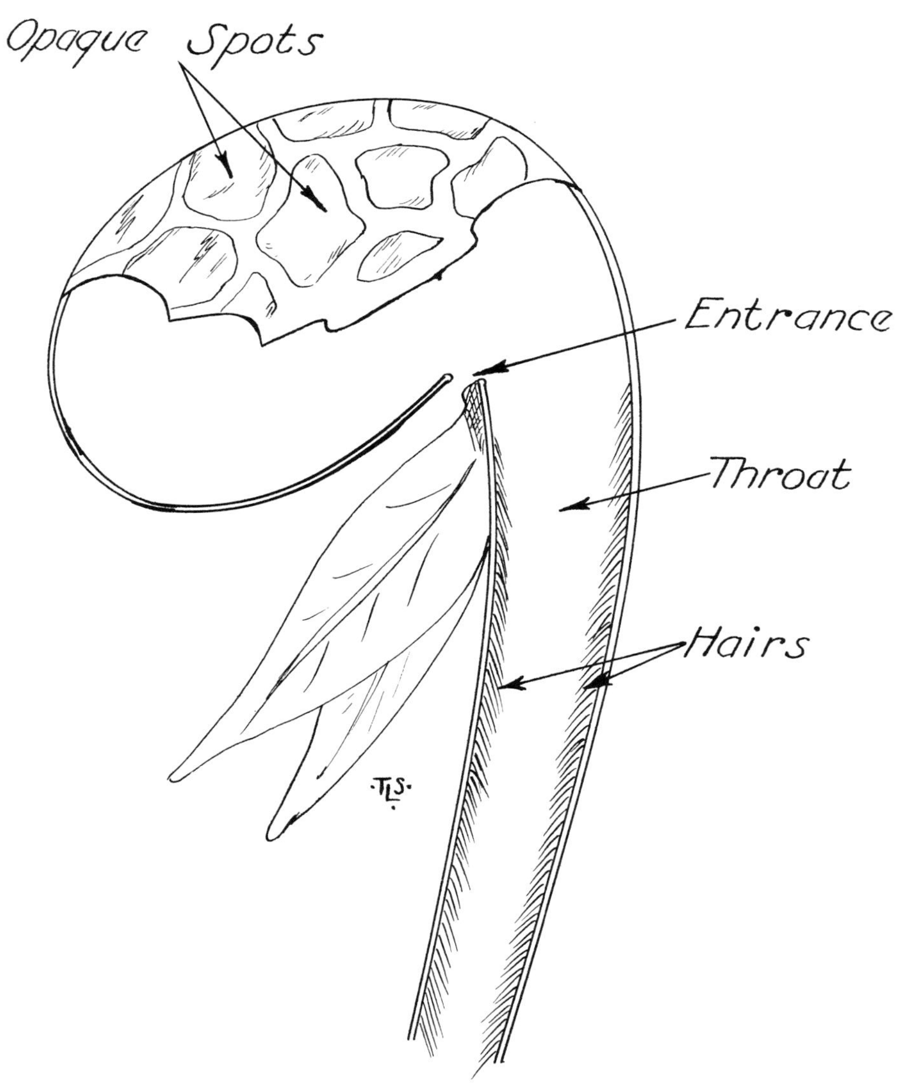

Darlingtonia californica Wayne Olsson Illustration Pitcher-Plant

DARLINGTONIA CALIFORNICA Torrey
Pitcher-plant

After having spent a lifetime in the wilds, grown hundreds upon hundreds of native plants in my own gardens and seen and studied untold thousands in their natural haunts none has impressed me in quite the same way as the perennial greenish yellow Pitcher plant, *Darlingtonia californica.* It is the strangest and one of the most fascinating creatures I have ever known. It might be called odd, peculiar, unbelievable. It has even been described as beautiful but this calls for an imagination as extraordinary as the plant itself.

I first encountered it more or less by chance many years ago. I was driving on a one way mountain road deep in the Siskiyou National Forest of southern Oregon. There was a small alpine swamp near the narrow lane I was following. Growing out of the oozy muck were literally many hundreds of these startling plants. They gripped my attention at once as they do virtually everyone who ever sees them. They looked like weird aquatic birds from a different age and another world, with only their nodding heads and long, slender necks above water. They might almost as well be compared with that East Indian snake, the king cobra, rearing its deadly hooded head into the air looking for a victim. There would be some truth in this analogy for the *Darlingtonia* has its lethal qualities too.

They were close together, some in the rich black soil, others in shallow water. Having a written permit from the forest service to gather a few plants I removed three of them.

They have extensive, creeping rootstocks, and like so many swamp plants, were difficult to dig. I saw a great many bogs, small and large on that trip, and all were heavily stocked with these fascinating creatures.

History: The unusual generic name is in honor of William Darlington, 1782-1863, a well known botanist and writer of West Chester, Pennsylvania. In 1854 the plant was given its first official description and named by John Torrey, 1796-1873, who was one of the most distinguished of the earlier American bot-

Darlingtonia californica Pitcher-plant

anists. Torrey's name and work is well known today among those who are engaged in the field of plant science.

The specimens were not collected by Torrey, but by W.D. Brackenridge of the Wilkes Exploring Expedition, on the southern slopes of Mount Shasta in California. Mr. Brackenridge gathered these plants in something of a hurry when the expedition was retreating from attacking Indians. This gives an idea of the botanical zeal that characterized some of the early far western adventurers.

There is only one species in this western genus of the Pitcher Plant Family, *Sarraceniaceae* which comprises three genera and about ten species. One genus of one species is native to Venezuela, the third, *Sarracenia* of eight species inhabits eastern North America.

A new name, *Chrysamphora californica,* given by Greene in 1891, is now official but little used as the older one is so well established. All of these plants have characteristics in common as they belong to the same small family. They are not related to the Venus Fly Trap, *Dionaea muscipula,* which belongs to the Sundew family, *Droseraceae,* found in a very limited area on the coast of the Carolinas. Besides Pitcher Plant, Calf's Head is sometimes applied to it by local residents.

Description: The tubular stalk, ending in a hood, is really a modified leaf structure, adapted to capturing and assimilating insects. This part of the plant is not a flower as many people believe. The blossom, not particularly appealing, is on a separate stalk which grows, leafless, from the ground to a height of two or three feet. It terminates in a single dark purplish nodding flower with heavily veined petals. The capsule is obovate-oblong and contains numerous small seeds. The mature leaves are one to two feet or more high making the taller flowering stems conspicuous.

At first sight the hoods are very impressive and on closer examination they are charming and intriguing, but somewhat offensive from the faint odor of decaying flesh – a device intended to attract insects which it does quite successfully. The translucent hood, with opaque spots, transmits a filtered light to the interior of the plant. This, with the foul fragrance which is enticing only to insects, lure many of them to their deaths.

Darlingtonia californica Pitcher-plant

Once inside the hood the insect is usually doomed. Attracted by the light and the honey glands interspersed with down growing hairs the insects step on to the upper interior of the tube. This is extremely smooth and affords no foothold whatever. The bug soon tumbles down the tube into the lower part. The downward directed hairs prevent the insect from climbing out. It finally lands in a pool of liquid at the bottom which is excreted by the pitcher wall. The insect disintegrates and its products are absorbed through the thin areas of the lower cavity, and the plant has its carnivorous meal. This is a radical reversal of nature's scheme wherein it is customary for the animals to devour the plants. These carnivorous plants are not the aggressors, however, except to the extent that their odor is intended to attract.

Insect catching is most active during May and June. By midsummer the tube may have an accumulation of decaying insect remains to a depth of as much as eight inches although two or three inches is more common.

A friend, with his family, gathered around me while I cut open one of the stalks. In the liquid at the bottom we counted one yellow wasp, or what was left of it, three or four large flies, over a dozen gnats, and about a cubic inch of miscellaneous insect remains too far gone to identify. Observations have indicated that more species of flies are caught than of other insects. But bees, butterflies, dragon flies, beetles, grasshoppers, snails, and centipedes are found. If this swamp dweller isn't a botanical fly swatter at least it has the same effect as far as the insects may be concerned.

While the *Darlingtonia* is a small bug destroyer it also has at least two enemies that prey upon it. One is the larva of a moth. And the larva of a two-winged insect feeds upon the insects the plant has captured for itself. There is an old adage that you have to pay a price for everything you get and even this aquatic oddity cannot get something entirely for nothing.

A popular fallacy is that these plants depend completely upon the insects they capture for their sustenance. Insects are no more important to the *Darlingtonia* than orange marmalade is to you – nice, but you can get along without it. Like all other chlorophyll bearing plants it gets most of its nourishment from the soil and air.

The short rhizomes annually produce a terminal rosette of leaves, all of which are modified into upright pitchers when they are quite small. The top part of the tube curves over in a rounded manner and forms a down directed orifice through which the insects enter and from which depends a bilobed crimson and green appendage which is as distinctive as it is attractive.

It always grows in very wet places and seems to prefer full sun but I have found it in moderately deep shade doing very well. The water may be ponds without current or along slow moving streams. I once found it alongside a fast tumbling little stream on a very steep hillside where it was close enough to the water to keep the roots continually wet.

Rarity: Rare. Often abundant in various swamps and bogs but strictly limited in its range where it has attracted a great deal of attention and is mentioned in numerous wild flower books.

Distribution: From sea level in sphagnum bogs along the coast to 8,000 feet in the mountains. Its northern limits are from near Florence in Lane County, Oregon and southward across southern Curry County to western Josephine County in the same state. In California in the Siskiyou and Sierra Nevada Mountains to Nevada County and the headwaters of the Sacramento River in northern California.

Propagation: Growing bog plants from seed is often considerably more difficult than from ordinary plants. Sow in live sphagnum moss in pans placed under bell jars or glass in an atmosphere that is both cool and moist. The sphagnum should be of uniform texture and not too loose.

Entire plants dug in the wild, even when supplied with a large ball of rich, wet soil, are almost certain to perish. Of the first three I mentioned earlier in this article one was given to a bio-chemist on the staff of a Portland college. In spite of his brilliant background and great care the plant died. I planted mine in a wooden lard tub with an abundance of leaf mold soil and set it in shallow water where it could have a constant and adequate supply of moisture. It lingered along for a month or so and perished. The same thing happened to the third plant given to another competent gardener. These plants are occasionally advertised for sale in garden magazines. These dealers are usually either ignorant or avaricious for such starts are no more likely to live than did my three originals.

Divisions are sometimes recommended but these are almost always failures too. But there is one vegetative method that *does* work. This I discovered after a multitude of failures. Take the tiny shoots that grow from the outside of the base of the plant. These should be as small as can be found – an inch to three or four inches high – and get as much of the roots as possible. Pot in their own soil or one composed of sphagnum moss, leaf mold and sand with a preponderance of the last two materials. The pots should have the lower parts immersed in water to furnish a steady and abundant supply of moisture. They will take hold slowly and produce good plants.

Culture: A friend has several dozen *Darlingtonias* growing on an upright artificial log made of concrete. The plants have an amazingly little amount of soil to each plant. There is a constant flow of water trickling down the sides of this rough concrete surface supplying all their heavy needs for moisture. This friend has decided that the running water is the secret of her success. But this method is not the only one that can be used. Another friend has a healthy clump growing in a flower pot set in an old wash basin which is in the ground up to the rim. The soil is three parts ordinary garden soil, sifted, and one part fine peat moss. The flower pot is set above the rim of the basin so that the crown of the plant is always above water. The basin holds enough water to keep the plant steadily supplied. The old leaves live through the winter and disintegrate when the new ones appear in the spring. The flowering stem appears before the new leaves. In the garden, slugs and cut worms have to be fought off.

This is a worthy plant for the bog garden and its scarcity in our home plantings must be due, in part at least, to ignorance of its requirements. Amazingly enough, however, it was first introduced into cultivation in 1861. A horticultural variety, *rubra,* is known and differs from the type in being of a reddish hue.

It has been grown outdoors the year around in a few places on the east coast such as in Massachusetts and Vermont. As a greenhouse plant it requires a little shade in the warmer parts of the nation and should never be allowed to dry out. A cool, moist, even temperature of forty to fifty degrees in the winter is about right with a gradual rise as the season advances. A good potting mixture is two-thirds fern root fiber and one-third chopped sphagnum moss and coarse sand. Protection is necessary in summer from hot, drying winds. Once well established it should be repotted every other year. Around the first of July is a good time but the condition of the plants should be considered, choosing a time when they are least active. This is not too difficult a plant to grow once its requirements are met and the little effort is well rewarded.

Flowering Time: April, May, June, and July, depending upon the altitude.

Orbicular leaf

Dicentra formosa 'White' 'Sweetheart' Bleeding Heart

DICENTRA FORMOSA (Andrews) Walpers
Dicentra formosa 'Sweetheart'
Bleeding Heart

It was my good fortune to be born in a land of floral beauty. It was my bad fortune not to realize it until my childhood years were well behind me. From the time when I was a very young boy I wandered in the woods. Among the first wild flowers I saw on these early pre-juvenile expeditions was the Bleeding Heart, *Dicentra formosa.* It was beautiful. Of course it was beautiful. I didn't know that flowers could be anything else. Under the right conditions it grew so abundantly that it wasn't possible to keep from seeing it or, indeed, from stepping upon it.

I found it growing in light to moderately deep shade, sometimes along streams but more usually under the filtered light of Dogwoods, Alders and Maples. Its earth borne companions were such delights as the now rare Calypso, the common Star Flower, Trilliums, Solomon Seals, Anemones and numerous other treasures.

History: As my knowledge grew with the passing years I finally realized that the Bleeding Heart,. which I had come to know so well, was one of the best of the genus of about 16 North American and Asiatic species ranging in color from golds, yellows, purplish, lavenders, to pinks and pure whites. Like a good many of the other species *D. formosa* has had numerous names, all seven of them being generic. The specific name, *formosa,* meaning beautiful, has remained the same, however, and rightly so, throughout all the muddling years – nearly a hundred of them in fact. It was given its first name in 1800 when it was described by Henry C. Andrews, a botanical artist and engraver. Dr. Frederick Vernon Coville, (1867-January 9, 1937) assistant botanist and principal botanist with the United States Department of Agriculture, gave it a last designation of *Bikukulla formosa* in 1893. But it was Wilhelm Gerhard Walpers (1816-1853) who, in 1842, gave it the now officially accepted name.

Description: The *Dicentras* are herbaceous perennials, that is they die down to the roots during the dormant season. *D.*

formosa's leaf stems are from 12 to 20 inches long, nearer the former than the latter length, and rise from the stout creeping rootstocks. They are smooth, very faintly glaucous beneath, that is, powdery, and divided into three segments, each of which is then again divided with the ultimate parts variously toothed and deeply cleft. Sounds dull, but this repeated process gives a delicacy and laciness of texture that is surprisingly charming and makes the plant desirable for the foliage alone which is produced luxuriously.

The flowering stems are leafless or with a much reduced leaf, and rise from the rootstocks as do the leaves, and to about the same height or slightly taller, making them as prominent as they are daintily lovely. Up to a dozen and a half heart shaped flowers are borne in succession at the end of the stems in loose or often close clusters. Each blossom is half an inch to three-quarters of an inch long. They are variously described as rose purple, lavender or pink. My eyes tell me they are mostly a soft pink with a daintiness that surpasses the foliage. The rootstocks are all that can be seen of the plants in the winter. They are either on top of or close to the surface and make dense mats.

Rarity: The type, very common within its range. The variety *breviflora* with smaller flowers, very rare due to its limited range. The white form, extremely rare. I have traveled the woods for a lifetime among uncounted thousands of plants and never seen it. A few nurseries stock it.

Distribution: It inhabits moist, more or less open woods made up mostly of deciduous trees, rarely under pure stands of conifers. From Vancouver Island and western British Columbia, through the Cascades and Coast Ranges of Oregon and Washington and into western California to the central part of that state. It prefers sea level and middle altitudes within its range and is never an alpine. The variety *breviflora:* Mirror Lake, south of Mt. Hood in Clackamas County, Oregon. The white form, with the type, if you can find it.

Propagation: Seed can be sown in February or as soon as the frost is out of the ground. The young seedlings can be potted up in a peaty soil or one rich in leaf mold during mid-spring. In early fall or spring they should be ready for placing in their permanent homes. This method is not commonly used, however, as increase is ever so much easier and faster with divisions of the clumps in spring or early summer. In my mild Portland climate and with this species, divisions can be made most any time when the ground isn't frozen. It isn't likely that the white form would come true from seed.

Culture: Bleeding hearts were in herbariums for many years before they were introduced to western civilization from Japan in the late 1840's. They were first flowered in England in May of 1847. They became very popular and were soon in many gardens. This was undoubtedly *D. spectabilis* which is native to Japan and is the one commonly cultivated in ordinary gardens. My first encounter with this oriental was in one of my mother's flower beds when I was a child. The fact that I remember it clearly for so many years speaks well for this species as well as for the genus as a whole.

Many wild flowers are difficult to adapt to home plantings but *D. formosa* presents no such problems. Quite the opposite. If fast ground coverage is wanted this is the species to use. In loose soils rich in humus, if only an inch or so deep, it spreads with remarkable rapidity from the eager rootstocks. It prefers light to moderate shade but I have a nice clump growing in full sun all day long where it does very well. But the soil is rich, loose, deep, and kept constantly moist. These conditions are the secrets to success where it is not protected from heat. In cool spots it will grow in ordinary garden soils if well drained, and it will not spread as rapidly as it does under the ideal surroundings it enjoys in the wild. If you have the woodsy earth it likes and you want to limit the speedy growth it would be wise to confine it to pots set flush with the surface of the ground so the lips will not show. Otherwise the chore of removing the excess roots will quickly become tiresome and something of a nuisance when the time so spent could be used to better advantage. Heavy clay soils are to be avoided.

The white form is the reason, of course, for including this common species in a book that is limited to rare flowers. It has been in a few distinctive gardens for at least 23 years and it is quite likely for somewhat longer than that. It was found growing wild in southwestern Oregon in Camas Valley between Roseburg and Myrtle Point presumably in the late 1930's. It was discovered by a Mrs. Brown and introduced into horticulture by the Pearce Seed Company of Moorestown, New Jersey. The rest of its history has vanished into the floral mists of time. Other whites have been found since that time. Its pure white flowers, produced abundantly, are too prominent to be easily overlooked. It has quite appropriately been given the horticultural name "Sweetheart." So often white mutations are small flowered, sparse, pale, weak, muddy or otherwise impure so that they lack garden appeal. Not so with "Sweetheart." It has all the qualities the name implies and, in my opinion, is a very choice addition to any wild garden. A common complaint is "What can I plant in the shade?" There are many answers to that question but *formosa* is one of the best.

Flowering Time: From April to June or July in the wild. Moisture is an important factor in determining the length of the season. In the forests when the warm days of summer dry out the earth the blossoms cease to exist. I am writing these lines during the fore part of November. Outside my office window in the shade of the north side of the house "Sweetheart" is still flowering and shows no sign of quitting. I am sure it will last another two or three weeks unless frost destroys it. A little water and a little love is better than mink to keep my "Sweetheart" happy.

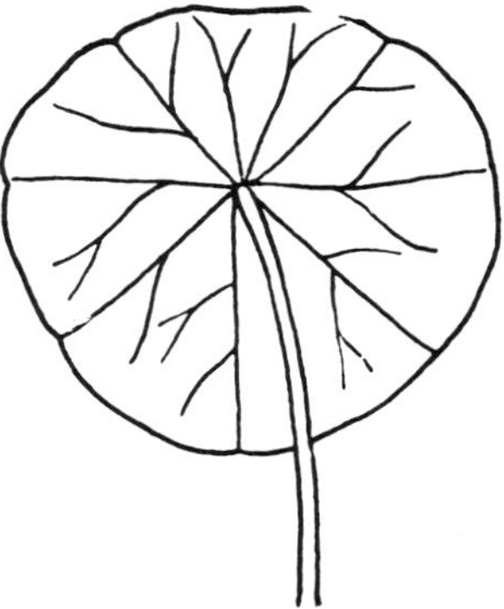

Peltate leaf

Dicentra oregona Oregon Dicentra

DICENTRA OREGONA Eastwood
Oregon Dicentra

It was a warm spring day in the foothills of the Oregon Siskiyous – a splendid time to hunt wild flowers in that fascinating region of the Far West. I was wandering along a dry creek bed searching for that rare and tiny gem, *Trillium rivale.* Suddenly, half in shade and half in sunshine near the top of the stream bank I found a wild bleeding heart I had never seen before. I searched the area and found a few more. It was the rare *D. oregona.* (Sometimes spelled oregana, take your choice). I dug three of them and added a little moisture to the balled earth around the roots. Outside of being sandy and, therefore, well drained, the soil had little to recommend it, being as poor and impoverished as any one could expect to find. Certainly it was not the place to expect to find *Dicentras,* or *Trilliums* either, for that matter. But both were there in limited numbers where neither really belonged, a circumstance not particularly unusual. The *T. rivale* prefers a little more shade, moisture and better food. This *Dicentra,* however, likes conditions quite different from its close and more common relative, *D. formosa.* It is a rock plant and is usually found more readily on north facing talus slopes and other similar stony areas.

History: The Bleeding Hearts belong to the Fumewort Family, *Fumariaceae,* comprising five genera and about 170 species of the north temperate zone and southern Africa. There are about 16 species of *Dicentras,* mostly of North America, although, one, *D. spectabilis,* the most popular of them all as a garden plant, is native to Japan. It grows two or three feet tall, is somewhat coarse in foliage, and in my estimation does not merit its wide popularity. There are others much more delicate in overall appearance though of lesser stature.

The genus was given it first official description and named in 1833 by the German botanist, Johann Jacob Bernhardi, 1774-1850. These plants have lived miserable lives, botanically speaking, and if they were capable of thinking no doubt would be utterly confused. They have been described by no less than 11 authorities as belonging to at least 13 different genera or spellings of the same genus. And one botanist even placed them in an entirely different family, among the poppies. Six of the western species have had from four to seven names each. The seventh, *D. Oregona,* has been more fortunate, having had only two, the one given here and *D. glauca,* which is no longer used. But even with this plant the differences of opinion are not entirely resolved. *D. nevadensis* is listed as closely resembling Oregona and possibly not specifically distinct.

While the genus was given its now generally accepted name in 1833, it was almost a hundred years later before *D. oregona,* was recognized botanically and described. More surprises. It was a woman botanist, Alice Eastwood, born in 1859, who performed this service in 1931 when she was in her seventies. This species must have been seen and admired many years before this lovely flower received its well merited recognition. And it is entirely appropriate it came through the efforts of one of America's few women botanists.

Description: It grows from half a foot to a foot high from long stemmed basal leaves which are divided into three parts each segment of which is repeatedly branched. This gives a lacy effect which in itself is thoroughly charming outside of any consideration of blossoms. The leaves are silvery green which accounts for much that distinguishes this species from some of the others. Prolonged wet spells tend to obscure this powdery effect and leaves that open during these rainy days may have none of this quality. As soon as dry weather takes over the silvery leaves promptly return. The Siskiyous are mountains of less rainfall than in Portland and it is likely that in their native habitat they retain the glaucous effect the greater part of the season. The nodding blossoms are truly heart shaped and are borne in several flowered clusters at the ends of the branched and generally naked stems. They are usually creamy white or sometimes tinged with yellow and have more or less rosy tips. The entire plant arises from a very stout and woody rootstock. It is a perennial with deciduous foliage. The entire plant in the cold weather is limited to the underground parts which have ample food stored for next season's combined loveliness of leaf and blossom.

Rarity: Very Rare. The range is limited and it does not seem to be abundant in any one place. It deserves a better fate than its present obscurity. I do not know of any dealers that handle it although surely some nursery must have a few plants tucked away in an out of the way corner.

Distribution: Siskiyou Mountains of southwestern Josephine County in extreme southern Oregon and Del Norte County of California. Telephone Point near the Oregon-California state line on the Waldo-Crescent City highway. It was near Waldo that I stumbled upon them.

Propagation: By division of the clumps in spring or early summer. They can be potted up or planted in their permanent positions. I don't know of any reason why they cannot be grown from seed. Divisions are so much easier that I have had no occasion to use any other method.

Culture: The Dicentras are among the easiest of plants to adapt to the garden. Mine are growing in humus 18 inches deep on the north side of the house where the shade is light but sun never strikes. A friend has one in a pot in partial sun. It is growing in the poorest of garden soil and doesn't seem to mind at all. Its main requirement is good drainage. Nothing else seems to make a great deal of difference. As might be expected it does nicely in the rockery especially if the roots are tucked under a stone where they can be sheltered from the sun. *D. formosa* has somewhat more finely dissected foliage and could be considered superior to *D. oregona* in that respect. But in rich, loose soil *D. formosa* spreads from creeping rootstocks to such an extent that it can become a beautiful pest. In the woods it often makes large colonies due to this habit. *Oregona* has no such disagreeable tendency. For this reason it is ever so much more welcome in my gardens than its more common and more delicate close relative.

Flowering Time: April to June depending upon altitude mostly but also amount of moisture and shade. In my gardens, where moisture can be supplied, it flowers well into August.

Dionaea muscipula Hugh Morton Photo Venus Fly Trap

DIONAEA MUSCIPULA Ellis
Venus Fly Trap

This is one of the most remarkable plants in the nation, and perhaps in the world. It occupies only a comparatively tiny space on the Atlantic coast and yet it is known by both scientists and ordinary gardeners 3,000 miles across the country to the shores of the Pacific. In the other direction its fame has leaped the Atlantic to the British Isles where it is as well known among those islanders as it is to Americans.

History: It is the only member of its genus, *Dionaea,* from a Greek word for Venus, which accounts for its common name. It belongs to the Sundew Family, *Droseraceae,* comprising four genera of about 90 species of wide distribution, the largest of which is the genus *Drosera* of about 85 species most abundant in Australia, but also well known in America. The *Droseras* and the *Dionaea* are closely related, the differences being mostly technical. The *Droseras* have four to eight stamens and three to five styles deeply parted while *Dionaea* usually has 15 stamens and the styles united into one.

This monotypic genus of insectivorous plants, in spite of its close relationship to the numerous *Droseras* has attracted far more enthusiasm than any other members of the family. It has been known for a very long time. John Ellis, 1711-1776, of England gave the first official description of the genus – and therefore the species also as there is only one – in Carl Von Linnaeus' work, *The Mantissae Plantarum* published in the latter half of the 1700s. Even at that early date the common name was likewise established. It has had at least four different specific names, all of which have been discarded in favor of *muscipula.* Thomas Nuttall, the prominent North American botanist, described the plant in considerable detail in his *The Genera of North American Plants,* published in 1818 and Charles Darwin devoted an entire chapter to it in his *Insectivorous Plants.*

Description: There are four to eight herbaceous leaves from one to five inches long in a spreading basal rosette. Each leaf consists of a flat expanded stem which terminates in a two lobed blade, the midrib of which acts as a hinge although the lobes themselves bend inward too. The leaf margins are prolonged into bristles that interlock when the halves close, making a very effective prison. They have been described as somewhat resembling a rat trap. Each half bears three-jointed and highly sensitive hairs arranged in a triangular manner over its upper surface. There are an abundance of stemless glands, usually crimson in color in the sun, that cover this surface and render it attractive to insects. But in shady places the glands and the leaves are green.

When one of these highly irritable hairs is touched once it does not cause the lobes to close. But if two adjacent hairs are touched once each at short intervals the halves quickly close, and whatever has caused the disturbance is caught so securely that escape is almost out of the question. The more the insect struggles the tighter it is held.

Continued and repeated stimulation caused by a struggling insect or to chemical reaction to the insect's tissues causes the glands to exude an acid and peptonizing digestive fluid that starts the disintegration of the insect's tissues and the dissolved products are absorbed by the plant's leaves. Then the leaves open again and are ready for another victim. The fate of the insects is the same as those that enter the *Darlingtonia* of the West Coast. *Dionaea* snaps the trap tightly while *Darlingtonia's* downward bristles do not allow the insect to escape. The digestive juices of the plants are likely very similar.

Among the insects captured are earwigs, millipedes, flies, ants, wood lice, dragon flies and numerous other species. Darwin mentioned four instances in which the leaves, after catching insects, never reopened but began to wither. Another observer noted that on cultivated plants five leaves digested three flies each and closed over the fourth but died soon after the fourth was taken. The Venus Fly Trap has a more limited power of digestion than that of the Sun Dews, *Droseras,* which have been known to capture and assimilate many insects in shorter periods of time. The digestive juices have been discovered to resemble the pepsin and gastric fluids of man.

Asa Gray, one-time professor of natural history at Harvard University, and perhaps the most distinguished of American botanists, became so alarmed at the possibility of extinction of this rarity that he attempted to induce the government to purchase a strip of land upon which the plant grows. But nothing came of this effort.

The flowering scape, growing from the middle of the plant, arises in May to eight or ten inches and bears four to ten white flowers in terminal umbels, which expand in June. Cross pollination is necessary to produce the twenty to thirty small black seeds in each one celled roundish capsule.

The plant grows in sandy bogs in pine forests but does well only when the tips of the small roots reach a moist substratum and when active transpiration of moisture proceeds. The perennial underground part is a bulbous swelling. It prefers plenty of sunshine and humid atmosphere.

The lobes are remarkably selective. If bits of stone, glass, cork, wood, moss and like materials, if completely dry, are left on the lobes they will not contract but let a bug land and action is speedy.

As the Venus Fly Trap is a chlorophyll bearing plant it is not dependent upon insect food for its survival. Bugs of one kind or another are simply extra snacks to liven the diet.

Dionaea has no known medicinal properties but its close relatives, the Sun Dews, have been powdered and used in treating whooping cough and other pectoral complaints but it is probably of little or no value in therapeutic practices even though it is listed in the United States Dispensatory.

Rarity: Very rare and increasingly so due to its limited range and the encroachments of civilization.

Distribution: About 50 miles north of Wilmington, North Carolina and about the same distance south of that city, carrying it into the extreme northern border of South Carolina. A coastal plant extending inland about ten miles.

Propagation: Comparatively easy. The black, shiny seeds germinate freely under a bell jar or glass that will keep a relatively high humidity. The seed bed should be moist sandy soil mixed with finely ground peat. Each seedling forms two lanceolate cotyledons then tiny fly trapping leaves appear that are much like the adult ones.

Culture: Wild plants can be dug successfully from November to March. It is seldom that the plant is seen in good health for any great length of time after being removed from its wild home. It will not tolerate too much dry air, shade or unsuitable soil. When wild plants can be dug with good sized balls of soil in which they are found growing they can be kept healthy for many years if humidity and sun can also be provided.

Seedlings thrive in three to five inch pots in a mixture of sand and soil rich in leaf mold with a light top dressing of sphagnum. The bottom inch of the pots should be kept immersed in water. If grown in a greenhouse keep near the glass on the south side. Plants grown in the sun have a reddish cast; in the shade they are green.

It is possible to grow them in the house, using a somewhat different method. Plant in a wide, shallow pan, without drainage, in loose, live sphagnum moss. Use a glass covering to maintain a humid atmosphere. This last is vitally important. The air in the average home is almost as dry as that of a desert. Water every other day until the dish is filled, then drain it off. This provides permanent moisture but never allows the potting material to become sour.

The Venus Fly Trap has only a few requirements for good health. If these are provided there is no reason it can not be grown successfully indefinitely.

Flowering Time: June.

Reniform leaf

Dodecatheon dentatum White Shooting Star

DODECATHEON DENTATUM Hooker
White Shooting Star

Some authorities have grouped the *Dodecatheons* as being all much alike. Others do not agree with this opinion. At any rate there is at least one that is so distinctive that it stands well alone – in diminutive charm, in daintiness and in startling whiteness – the White Shooting Star.

I have had this plant in my yard for a number of years where it seems to be contented in rich leaf mold and protected by light shade. It is slightly less pleased with the stony soil of my rock garden and exposure to sunshine for most of the day. I did not collect my original small start of this plant from its wild home as I do with most of my natives. It was given to me by Dr. Matthew Riddle who has grown it, quite undisturbed, in his flower beds for a great many years. Dr. Riddle is world renowned for his work with Iris, especially the Pacific Northwestern species. His source was the cliffs of Oneonta Gorge, a small and only locally known side canyon in the vast Columbia Gorge. The sheer cliffs at the mouth of Oneonta are so close together that one can easily get the illusion that they could be touched with the outstretched finger tips. This is one of the most awe inspiring and lonely places I have ever known – towering cliffs, tumbling waters, numerous cascades and falls in the rippling stream, vasty mountain slopes and a silence in the deep forests such as I have never known elsewhere. It has been my favorite hiking place for fully 45 years. And while this is the home of *Dodecatheon dentatum* I have never seen it there during my wanderings over its steep and rugged slopes in all this time. Few people go there and few know what they are missing. This gorge is scarcely more than half an hour's drive from Portland, Oregon and the White Shooting Star is one of the few rarities that can be found so close to a large city.

History: Modern botany is over 200 years old and there is still a vasty confusion in this fascinating science in spite of the many intervening years. But even I was astonished by the amount of it in this really small genus of strangely beautiful flowers.

They belong in the Primrose Family, *Primulaceae* which comprises about 25 genera and 600 species of Africa, Europe, Asia, Australia, some of the islands of the Pacific and both Americas.

The genus *Dodecatheon* was named by Carl Von Linnaeus in 1751 and also in his significant *Species Plantarum* in 1753. It is a Greek name, referring to 12 Gods, that was used by Pliny, the Roman naturalist, 23-79 A. D., and Theophrastus, a Greek philosopher and naturalist who died about 287 B. C. These two men used the name *Dodecatheon* for a different plant as the Shooting Stars were unknown to civilization at that time. In fact botany as a systematic science didn't even exist 2,000 years ago. I wonder why Linnaeus chose this name instead of creating a new one? There was quite a squabble about this name at the time. The English naturalist, Mark Catesby, 1679?-1749, established a new genus, which was published in 1752, after his death, for a plant which was discovered in America. He called it *Meadia* in honor of Dr. R. Mead, 1673-1754, a celebrated physician. Linnaeus rechristened it in his authoritative work, published a year later, because he was unwilling for any genus to honor a person little skilled in botanical knowledge. This arbitrary decision, whether justified or not, caused English tempers to flare. After Linnaeus' death this ruling was relaxed and remains so to this day. But the English physician has not been forgotten. The first discovered species, native to the middle western states, and some of the eastern and southern ones is known today as *D. meadia.*

This did not end the confusion however. Rather it was the beginning. No less a person than the distinguished and respected American botanist, Dr. Asa Gray, once thought the genus comprised only the one species *D. meadia.* Today it is generally agreed that there are about 30 species although taxonomists are still fighting this botanical war and it isn't likely that there will be complete agreement in the near future.

The distribution of the *Dodecatheons* is also controversial. Most of them are concentrated in western North America. One authority confines all of them except *meadia* to this part of the continent. Another lists them from "Maine to Texas, from the Atlantic to the Pacific, from the islands of Lower California to

Bering Strait." Also in Asia, especially in the northeastern part of that continent.

Some of the common names are particularly appropriate. *Shooting Star* is one of them. The stamens come to a sharp point and seem to be shooting through the sky while the sharply reflexed petals fall behind like a comet. The beak-like cluster of stamens and pistil account for the term *Bird Bill.* Less desirable and adding to the turmoil is *Cowslip.* This word is applied equally freely to a *Buttercup* and an *Erythronium* – three different plants in three unrelated families!

When we get down to our present species, *D. dentatum* the troubles begin to disappear. It is true that it was once considered synonymous with *D. meadia* and it has been placed in two other species. But *D. dentatum* was given it by William J. Hooker in 1838 and is now official, the others coming later, are placed in synonomy.

David Douglas visited the Pacific Northwest in the mid 1820s, discovered the plant, and was sufficiently impressed with it to include it in his collections.

Description: The *Dodecatheons* are deciduous perennials. *D. dentatum* grows from a short and slender rootstock. The leaves are in basal rosettes, unevenly and sharply toothed. Being a shade lover it is quite natural that it should be thin in contrast to the often thick, leathery leaves of the sun dwelling members of the genus. They are from one to four inches long and one and a half to two and three-fourths of an inch wide, more or less egg shaped in outline, sharp pointed or blunt, with the leaf stems as long as, to twice as long as the blades. One recent authority describes the leaves, including the stems, as from two to 20 inches long. This last dimension must be erroneous. I have never seen or heard of a *dodecatheon* leaf 20 inches long, or anywhere near it. The comparatively slender leaf stems, petioles, are winged above and the leaves themselves are wedge shaped or somewhat heart-shaped at the base. The plant is smooth throughout.

The slender scapes are from three to 16 inches tall, terminating in a one to six flowered umbel. The flowering stems in my gardens and in those of two of my friends are from three to five inches tall and give a much better balance between blossoms and foliage than the alleged 16 inch height which I have never seen. This earth-hugging compactness accounts for much of the distinctive charm of this species and makes it particularly welcome in my floral home. Unfortunately all plants in a clump do not flower every year. The blossoms are more scattered than those of some other species. This is the only fault it has. There are five reflexed calyx lobes and the same number of white corolla lobes which are bent backwards very sharply, with one, or more usually, two purple dots at the base of each. The stamens are likewise five, not united, with dark, very short filaments. The anthers are very dark purple, tapering from the base to a sharp double toothed apex. The contrast between the lovely white petals and the royal purple anthers is very pronounced and immediately catches the eye. The identification of *Dodecatheons* often is not easy but *D. dentatum* is the only white species within its range and a single glance is enough to establish its identity. The only exception would be a single white flowering mutation of some other species – an all too rare occurrence and a real delight when encountered. All other species in its area will be lilacs, rose, purples, pinks and an occasional flaming red. As the nodding blossoms fade and the seed begins to ripen the capsule slowly turns upward until it is completely erect as though offering its harvest to the Twelve Immortal Gods for whom the plants were named.

Rarity: Rare. While it has a considerable range it is nowhere common.

Distribution: On moist cliffs and stream banks from near sea level to several thousand feet in British Columbia, Washington, Oregon, Idaho and Utah. It is quite possible to blunder upon it unexpectedly or to wander the shaded places it likes for years without seeing it.

Propagation: There are only two ways of making increase, by divisions and seed. This second method is not often used as seedlings do not come true to type and are likely to be generally inferior to a choice parent. Quarantine restrictions and fumigating requirements to and from foreign lands often make delivery of live plants difficult or impossible. Seeds, however, can be mailed freely and many people use this system to acquire new species. That is how many *Dodecatheons* as well as numerous other genera of American plants have been established in British gardens. From seed to flower is much slower than by division and in many species is uncertain. From two to four years are required depending upon cultural conditions and species. Seed should be planted as soon as ripe in a rich, well drained, moist soil out of the sun. *D. meadia* seed germinates almost 100 per cent. Some of the other species sprout less freely and can be disappointing.

I like to take my divisions in the spring when the fleshy roots are swollen with moisture. The plants die down after the seed ripens. When the flowering stems break off and blow away it takes an exceedingly sharp eye to discover the tiny crowns. If these are dug up with a few dead looking broken roots attached the inexperienced gardener may throw them away in disgust. Quite a mistake for these hopeless remnants will swell up with the rains and produce healthy plants. And the tiny, brittle roots often callous over and make new crowns. This tenacity can be disappointing for the first season or so because these root-produced crowns do not flower as readily as the parent plants. That is why I prefer to make divisions in the spring when the roots are beginning to grow and are almost as pliable as rubber bands.

Culture: *D. dentatum* likes shade although it will survive in light sun in moderate climates. Rock dwelling plants often require the sharpest kind of drainage but *D. dentatum* isn't that fussy in the garden. Any reasonably well drained, fertile soil will do very nicely. It resents crowding and a plant as delightful as this should not have to fight for elbow room. Even mosses will inhibit growth. Clean cultivation and moderate moisture during flowering time is all it asks to be happy in its adopted home.

Flowering Time: April or May in the lowlands and June and July at the higher elevations, with seasonal variations altering the floral display from year to year.

Dodecatheon poeticum Poet's Shooting Star

DODECATHEON POETICUM Henderson
Poet's Shooting Star

When I walked into a high school science classroom on a spring day of 1920 my eyes first gazed upon a girl I had never seen before. Within three days my life was completely changed for I had discovered the only girl I have ever loved. It was in that same school during that same year that I met W.W. Rodwell, a botany teacher who owned an apple orchard in Hood River Valley about 70 miles east of my Portland birthplace. I spent many week-ends working on Mr. Rodwell's ranch. On our rides through the Columbia Gorge we talked of the legends and traditions of that great land, and of the flowers that grew there in such magnificent profusion.

One sunny day early in that year I had a few hours away from my pomaceous duties and wandered a mile or so to the banks of the river. It was there, in an open meadow, that I first saw *Dodecatheon poeticum.* I was just sprouting my botanical wings and only knew it as a shooting star. Indeed it was the only name I could have given it for it was ten years later before the systematic botanists finally described it.

I have Mr. Rodwell's copy of *Gray's Lessons and Manual of Botany* but he is no longer here. And it has been 39 years since I last spent a few fleeting hours with Ruth. Much has happened since. Only two of my friends of those days are left. Some have passed away. The vanishing years have scattered the rest throughout the land. But it was my love for this obscure girl that has sustained me until this very minute through many a desperate hour and numerous crises. And it was Mr. Rodwell himself, now half forgotten, who lighted the botanical fires that were just beginning to glow within me. 1920! The coming of my very human love, my entrance into the world of wild flowers. Truly a very wonderful year – the greatest of the many I have known.

Ruth lives in my heart and *poeticum* in my gardens. They will be there always.

History: The history of the Poet's Shooting Star, *D. poeticum* is so illogical that it simply couldn't happen – but it did. It was 92 years after *D. dentatum* was officially described before Dr. Louis F. Henderson of the University of Oregon named it *D. poeticum* in 1930! This is simply an incredible circumstance for both these plants grow in the same general area and their ranges overlap. Furthermore, while *D. dentatum* is by no means common in the Columbia Gorge, *D. poeticum* sets the open meadows aglow within sight of the majestic river. It doesn't seem possible that David Douglas could have found the scarce white flowers of *D. dentatum* in the mid 1820's and totally overlooked the abundant pink *D. poeticum.* While I knew it well ten years before Dr. Henderson introduced it to the world of science I make no claims of discovery. Hundreds, yes, thousands of ranchers, farmers, settlers and travelers had enjoyed its delights decades before I was born.

In doing the research on the article for *D. dentatum* I used 16 books from my extensive botanical library. *D. poeticum* presented no such voluminous problems. Only two of my texts dealing with the flora of northwestern America even mention it. Even the nurseries do not stock it. Most of the other species for this part of our nation have had several – up to five – different names each. But the taxonomists have left Henderson's *poeticum* alone and it is well that they did. I can imagine no other name quite so appropriate for such a beautiful and almost wholly neglected flower.

It may be unwise for a researcher to make extravagant statements. Nevertheless, of the *Dodecatheons* I have seen – and I cannot claim all of the 30 odd species – *poeticum* is my favorite. It may be partly memories of the past but I am sure it is mostly its present living beauty that has so much appeal.

Description: The plant arises from an erect root-crown producing many elongated fibrous roots which become quite fleshy during flowering time. All the parts above ground except the corolla are glandular and clothed with very fine short hairs including even the calyx and seed-bearing capsule. Like all other members of the genus the root crowns and roots are perennial while the leaves and floral parts vanish with the coming of dry weather. The leaf margins are more finely toothed than *D. dentatum.* The leaves, including the petioles, are from two to five inches long with the shorter length more typical. The leaf stems are from the same length as the blades to very much shorter.

The leaves vary from narrowly egg shaped with the widest part below the middle to broadly or narrowly lance shaped with the widest part above the middle with blunt or short rounded tips. The slender scapes, flowering stems, grow from three to 12 inches tall with an average of about six and terminate in a one to ten flowered umbel. The scapes are more numerous and have more flowers on each than *D. dentatum* and are, therefore, much showier. The corolla is five lobed like *D. dentatum* although some of the other species have only four. The beak, composed of the stamens and pistil, is deep purple. The corolla tube is light yellow at the base. Above is a wavy line of purple followed by a broad band of rich yellow which quickly changes into rose-purple, rose-pink or a rare bright red. The flowers solemnly nod their heads as though in prayer. As they fade away the many seeded capsules turn completely erect, ripen and discharge their seeds hopefully for new plants the next season.

Rarity: Rare. Abundant within its limited range.

Distribution: In the Gorge of the Columbia River five or ten miles west of Hood River and eastward in Hood River, Wasco, Sherman and Wallowa Counties of Oregon and in Skamania, Klickitat and Yakima Counties in Washington. It is pretty much limited to the Arid Transition Zone from close to sea level to 1,000 feet or so higher. Occasionally I have found a few under the light shade of stunted ponderosa pines but generally it prefers open meadows with full sunshine all day long. It does better in oozy places during the blossoming period although it grows quite well on the open prairies where the soil content is only normally moist. I have found it mostly in earth composed of the rich humus and fine sand that has been deposited by the winds that have blown through the Columbia Gorge for untold centuries. These soils are usually very shallow and are underlaid with solid basaltic rock. Its companions and close neighbors are the Bitter Root, *Lewisia rediviva;* the rosy flowered *Pentstemon rupicola;* the rare and light purple *P. barrettae;* the diminutive early spring Gold Star, *Crocidium multicaule;* the dainty Yellow Bells, *Fritillaria pudica;* the hosts of Grass Widows, *Sisyrinchium grandiflorum;* the rich yellow blossoms of the Dogtooth Violet, *Erythronium parviflorum;* and the many other earth-born floral treasures that make the majestic Gorge of the Columbia River such a paradise of flowers.

Propagation: See article on *D. dentatum*

Culture: Full sun and sharp drainage are the two basic requirements of this species. It should be allowed to dry out completely after flowering. The only moisture it gets in my gardens is that provided by nature. And that is ample. Good results cannot be expected in the ordinary garden soils that are suitable to *D. dentatum*. This plant belongs in the rockery. The soil I use for it is composed of one-half crushed lava rock and one-half leaf mold. This combination provides the essential drainage and sufficient nourishment for abundant flowering. Too much food might encourage vegetative growth at the expense of blossoms as often happens with other species of wildlings. In its native home it gets from 30 inches of precipitation yearly to less than half that much. Portland has 44 inches and this does not seem too much but I doubt if it would survive the coastal climates where rainfall is often more than 100 inches. It doesn't like crowding. I have never seen it in competition with other plants except stunted wild grasses.

In collecting wild specimens for the garden a good deal of attention should be given to color selection. Most are attractive rose-pinks or rose-purples but occasionally a clear bright red of magnificent beauty will be found. These rare specimens are very much worth the considerable searching required to find them. I have collected *poeticum* in early spring when only the first few leaves have been showing. At this stage it is difficult to tell from one of the Saxifrages with which it is associated. A short time later the pink buds appear and doubt is eliminated. But to get the truly bright, vivid colors the meadows must be visited when the flowers are in full blossom.

Flowering Time: Generally March and April. In the Columbia Gorge, however, the season can vary as much as a month or more. The fact that you have seen the Poet's Shooting Star on a certain day of the month one year is no guarantee that you can find it on the same date the next. I do not know any way that this seasonal change can be determined in advance. All my predictions over the years have been wrong. But an excursion to this plant's home is never wasted. If one flower isn't in blossom another, perhaps equally choice, will be.

Palmately veined leaf

Douglasia laevigata Columbia River Douglasia

DOUGLASIA LAEVIGATA variety CILIOLATA Constance
Columbia River Form

I have known this plant for many years, for the greater part of my adult life in fact. And for years I have worked with it, hoping to find some way to make it happy in the garden. It is a story of hard work, some danger, frustration and almost despair. But in the process I have unlocked some of its secrets. Only recently, however, I believe I have learned why it grows so luxuriantly on its sheer basaltic cliffs and almost invariably perishes in the garden.

It is best known at Mitchell's Point, a rocky crag jutting out close to the river in the Columbia Gorge. When the Columbia River Highway was first built a ledge was blasted out of the side of the cliff about 125 feet above the river, and the road built on that narrow shelf. In the spring the pastel shades of pinks, purples and lavenders, splashed the cliffs with these small plants in such profusion that the automotive passerby could almost reach and touch some of them.

These flowers were so extraordinary and so delightful that groups of people have made annual spring pilgrimages to this place for no other purpose than to photograph and admire the flowers. It was inevitable that others with less commendable purposes should likewise visit the site. In the course of years all the easily accessible plants disappeared. Then the Oregon State Highway Commission decided to move the road to the base of the cliff and the old road was blocked off to traffic. In the last few years the decision was made to widen the new road. This means that a 100,000 yards of the cliff face between the old and new highways was blasted away to provide the necessary room. The cliff extends about 150 feet above the old highway and the plants that are dotted upon this part of the promontory are reasonably safe from destruction. The rock is badly faulted basalt, checked and weathered to such an extent that I am sure attempts to climb the sheer face with its overhangs would likely end in disaster. The entire surface is a mass of cracked rock so loose that much of it can be pried out with a screw driver or a cold chisel. Pitons, used by rock climbers, could not be depended upon to hold under such conditions if they could be used at all.

When I heard that nearly half the *Douglasias* at this site were to be blasted out of existence I wrote to the State Superintendent of Parks and asked permission to remove all the plants that were to be destroyed. This was granted. I used a ladder to work from the base of the cliff and collected all I could get up to about 30 feet. Then working from the old road I lowered myself over the cliff and gathered what I could get from this position. Using a cold chisel and hammer I carefully cut away the rock until the roots were exposed, lifted them out, and immediately wrapped them in damp moss. I took from a quarter to half an hour of hard work to release each plant and there was some danger involved as my safety line, rubbing against the loose rock above sent occasional boulders down upon me. A sharp lookout and quick dodging brought the project to a safe conclusion. I obtained 50 plants. There was one, a pure white, the only one I have ever seen, that could not be reached and the DuPont boys ended its existence.

History: The *Douglasias* belong to the Primrose Family, *Primulaceae,* comprising 25 genera and about 600 species. But the *Douglasias* themselves are limited to seven species, one from Europe, *D. vitaliana,* two native to Alaska, *arctica* and *gormani* and the others *nivalis, dentata, montana* and *laevigata* with its variety *ciliolata.* They are closely related to the primulas and androsaces.

The genus was named in 1827 by the illustrious English horticulturist John Lindley, 1799-1865, in honor of the even more illustrious Scotch botanist David Douglas who collected in northwestern America in the mid 1820's. The species we are concerned with was described by the American botanist Asa Gray in 1881.

Description: The type plant, *D. laevigata* which is fairly common in the Olympics, has rose colored flowers and is not particularly difficult to grow. It seems to be a short lived plant, lasting about five years, and under good conditions will readily self seed so that the usual tedious propagating methods are unnecessary. But its variety from the Columbia Gorge is quite different. The colors are all soft pastels of delicate beauty and the various tones and hues on the cliff sides are a striking sight.

Mature plants average about three or four inches in diameter and an inch high but I have seen some as large as eight inches across and larger ones have been reported. The growth is very compact from an abundance of closely clustered stems produced from short basal offsets. It has a short woody base. The slender somewhat spreading stems are crowded at the summit with leaves either smooth or with long hairs on the margins. They vary in shape but are usually long and narrow with the width about the same until it narrows to a point and are from a quarter to a half inch long. The flowers are borne profusely on very short slender stems and blossom just above the green perennial leaves. The floral tube terminates in five wide spreading lobes in masses so dense that they often threaten to obscure the foliage.

Rarity: Extremely Rare.

Distribution: Cliffs and mountains in the Columbia River Gorge. The common opinion for many years was that it was limited to Mitchell's Point and one other station on the opposite side of the river in the state of Washington. However, a few years ago there was a rock slide at Crown Point – near the western portals of the Gorge. This massive rock movement wrecked a train. A reporter from one of the Portland newspapers sent to the scene found a huge boulder beside the tracks with five of the plants growing on it. It has also been reported from a few other places and it is likely that still others exist. I have attempted to locate such sites with binoculars but the cliffs are so inaccessible that the effort was wasted.

Propagation: My efforts to germinate seed have been total failures. I sent about a dozen seeds to a friend in Scotland. He was able to germinate five and bring them into flower. Other successes may have been achieved but none have been brought to my attention.

The under sides of the stems sometimes show evidences of roots having been produced and dried due to lack of earth in which to grow. The indication is that cuttings would be an easy method of propagation. Such is not the case. I have obtained about a dozen in this way from several dozen placed in a sand box.

But the roots were weak and only one or two survived transplanting. Cuttings should be taken with old and new wood after the cool weather arrives in the fall. Temperatures should be kept below 50 degrees but not freezing. In some parts of the country this calls for greenhouses. They should be rooted by spring.

Culture: Altogether I have had about 75 collected plants. Less than a dozen remain alive and only four or five of these are in good health. I have planted them in holes drilled in porous lava rock using a mixture of half leaf mold and half crushed rock, assuring excellent drainage. Others have been placed in crevices between stones, using the same mixture. Some were placed in level soil, facing upwards, others were partially on their sides and some were completely at right angles to the ground. These were conditions closely approximating those under which they thrive on sheer cliffs. For years I puzzled why my efforts were such dismal failures. It wasn't a question of rain for there is very little difference in this regard between the amount that falls in their part of the Columbia Gorge and what we get in Portland. And winter snow protection isn't the answer either. I was on the cliff face at Mitchell's Point during a snow storm and noticed that very little clung to the plants due to the near vertical rock face.

I have long believed that many of our horticultural problems have logical and simple explanations. Success eludes us because there are so many factors involved that it is difficult to find the right ones.

Nursery trees two or three years old, when planted in soil that has a hard pan a foot or two below the surface, will grow until the roots strike this unyielding material. Then, unable to penetrate deeper, they die because there is not enough root to support the top. But when a tree seed is planted in such soil, the root and top develop together, so that neither is out of balance, and in the course of time a large tree will be produced. It is this principle which is the key to our failures with this particular Douglasia.

This is a tap root plant which often penetrates the tiny crevices in the cliff face to a depth of six inches or more. I cut the stone away from one such plant that was living on less than half a teaspoon of soil. The entire root system was as large as my hand with spread fingers but was so fine and frail that it was like the most delicate spider's web imaginable. When I tried to lift it, the roots, less than a thousandth of an inch in diameter, collapsed. Transplanted into the garden these plants require several years to reestablish their slow growing roots. This they cannot do and they die for just the same reasons that trees planted over hard pan perish.

On the cliffs hundreds, perhaps thousands of seed drop out of their capsules for every one that is able to fall into a tiny crevice where there is a little soil and a little moisture for it to germinate. Then the roots slowly work their way into the crevice and the stems develop in proportion until, ultimately, a full sized mature *Douglasia* is growing and flowering on the perpendicular cliff.

If we can find some way to germinate the seed in the places where we want the plants to grow permanently I feel this can be a successful garden plant.

At Mitchell's Point the leaves take on a yellowish green appearance in the summer from lack of water. While they prefer the shady sides of the cliffs even these protected locations are hot during July and August. But they are able to live through the drought until fall rain revives them. The same thing happens in the garden and if you become soft hearted as I did once, and attempt to revive them with a liberal drink, disaster will be certain. The leaves will take on their vivid, robust green. Then the crowns will rot and the plants will be dead.

Flowering Time: Usually in April but I have seen them as early as February. The weather is variable in the Columbia Gorge and there is no way to predict the progress of each season. They remain in blossom as long as two months or more.

Dudleya farinosa Sea Cliff Stonecrop

DUDLEYA FARINOSA (Lindley) Britton and Rose
Sea Cliff Stonecrop

Much of my knowledge of native plants has come from studying them in the wild and growing them in the garden. When not engaged in these activities I am in my botanical library pouring over books in the endless search for knowledge and truth. And so it was from the printed page that I first met this remarkable member of a fascinating family. The scientific descriptions from the limited amount of available literature indicated that it would be a valuable addition to the rockery. When I first saw the living plant many years later this opinion was amply confirmed.

The nurseryman who owned a few plants gave me two of the offsets. I scraped the dead leaves from the bottoms of the rosettes and planted them in separate places, expecting that they would root easily like almost all other members of the Stonecrop Family. But they slowly became smaller and smaller and finally disappeared. The rooted plant, consisting of the parent and two offsets that I obtained from another grower, developed nicely until a six degree above zero storm destroyed it.

History: For the history of the Stonecrop Family, *Crassulaceae,* to which the *Dudleyas* belong, see under *Sedum spathulifolium pruinosa.*

Nathaniel Lord Britton, 1858-1934, Director of the New York Botanical Garden, New York City, and Joseph Nelson Rose, 1862-1928, Assistant Curator with the United States National Herbarium, Smithsonian Institution, examined these plants which were variously listed as *Sedums, Cotyledons* and *Echeverias,* and decided that they merited a genus of their own. So it was that in 1903 they established the genus *Dudleya* in honor of the late William Russel Dudley, professor of botany at Stanford University, and published their findings in the *Bulletin of the New York Botanical Garden.* It was at this same time in 1903 that they named *D. farinosa* along with all the other species. Britton and Rose did not discover these plants of course. At least one of them was known as early as 1803. They simply made their en masse transplantation into the new genus. Botany is replete with these differences of opinion and in this instance the confusion is understandable for the *Dudleyas* closely resemble the Mexican *Echeverias.*

There are anywhere from about 30 species to at least twice that many, depending upon whose authority you care to adopt. Britton and Rose published at least 60, most if not all of which grow in California although some of them are not confined to that state, nor to the United States. But it is a strictly Far Western North American genus.

D. farinosa has had at least two other designations. John Lindley, 1799-1865, described it as *Echeveria farinosa* in 1849, and John Gilbert Baker, 1834-1920, keeper of the Herbarium of the Royal Gardens, Kew, England, decided, in 1869, that it should be *Cotyledon farinosa.* It will be noted that all three authors kept the specific name, *farinosa* in reference to the heavy mealy or powdery coating of the leaves – an exquisitely beautiful effect which accounts for much of the startling loveliness of the plant.

Description: The short, stout base supports the single or several rosettes of closely tufted, perennial, very glaucous, basal leaves. They are numerous, exceedingly fleshy, broadly triangular-egg shaped in outline, three or four times as long as the greatest width which is below the middle and tapering to a point. From one to two inches long and both a little more and less than three-quarters of an inch wide they are flat on the upper surface and slightly rounded on the back. Perhaps a more understandable description would be to say that they are somewhat tongue-shaped.

The flowering stems are stout, upright or slightly leaning, four to 20 inches high, coated a wonderous powdery pink that is beyond all imagination, with many small, alternate leaves, triangular egg-shaped, three-eighths to three-quarters of an inch long, more numerous and somewhat larger on the upper part of the stem. These stem leaves are just as richly powdered as the basal rosettes and the lower ones have the same unbelievable soft ruby purity as the stems. They are slightly concave, sessile with the basal lobes often turned upward – a leaf character a bit rare.

The main stem divides near the top into several branches

which rise from the leaf axils. The light lemon yellow flowers are borne in dense terminal clusters, the uppermost opening first. While these are beautiful blossoms, in gross appearance much like those of the sedums, they do not equal the loveliness of the plant – a reversal of what we generally expect from wildlings.

The erect fruits bear many seeds.

Rarity: Rare.

Distribution: Bluffs and cliffs along the ocean. This is the northernmost growing *Dudleya* and the only one that extends into Oregon. From Coos County, Oregon in the vicinity of Bandon, where the excellent *pruinosa* variety of *Sedum spathulifolium* also lives, about 80 miles north of the California border, southward to central California. Limited to the Upper Sonoran and Humid Transition Life Zones which means this is a low elevation plant. To the best of my knowledge this species is found only near the seashore.

Propagation: I do not understand why so little has been written about *D. farinosa* for it has been known for well over a hundred years. There is nothing in my extensive botanical library which even mentions the propagation of this species or any other member of the genus. Only three people of my acquaintance have it in their gardens and none of them have made any attempt at its propagation. It should come easily from seed but this is only an unsubstantiated opinion based upon its close relationship with the *Sedums*.

One or two side rosettes are produced each year. If these rosettes are pulled gently apart they will split down into the main root, leaving part of it attached to each offset. Then they can be planted separately and make good plants. My attempts to root the leaves in water and in sand indoors did not succeed.

Culture: They are found on rocks and cliffs at the ocean edge where they often form tremendous colonies, clinging and rooting in any crevice they can find. They are easy to collect although it is sometimes necessary to climb the cliffs or pry them loose with long sticks. Apparently part of a cliff collapsed at one time for one of my friends found some of the plants floating in the ocean. When they washed ashore they were picked up, rinsed in a fresh water stream, brought home and planted. They grew. These are the only terrestrial plants I ever heard of that were collected in the ocean.

While they are rock plants in their native habitat they will do well in ordinary gardens if good drainage is provided. In the rockery they can be tucked into cracks between boulders or any other place where they are not crowded. The side of a rock wall is an excellent place for them. They should have a fair amount of water. In the northern part of their range the annual rainfall is around a hundred inches. Except in the very mildest of climates they do best in partial shade. This is not a hardy plant. In its wild home freezing weather is virtually unknown. Although one of my plants in the open could not endure six degrees above zero another belonging to a friend survived two degrees above zero but this was protected from too much moisture by an overhang. In the colder parts of the country it can be handled nicely in the alpine or greenhouse.

Tenderness is one of the few faults it has. It never wanders in unwanted places in the garden as some of its close relatives, the *Sedums,* do. Wherever the leaves are touched the glaucous covering will be desecrated. Its light green foliage showing delicately through the frosty whiteness is of such extreme loveliness that any effort to make it happy will be very much worthwhile. *Dudleya farinosa* is the gem of the Stonecrops, a plant beyond compare.

Flowering Time: Late spring.

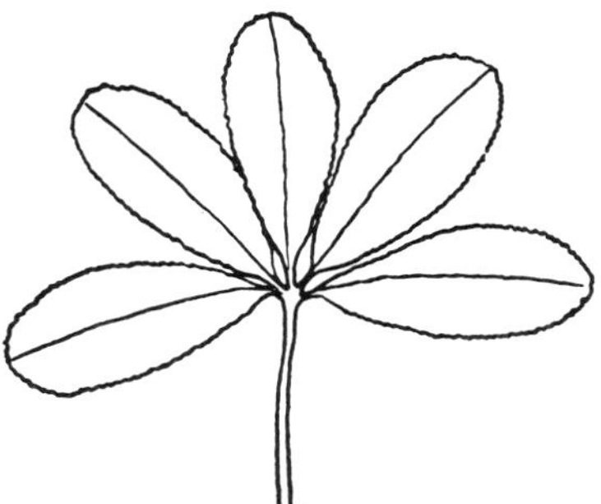

Palmately compound leaf

Fritillaria recurva Scarlet Fritillaria

FRITILLARIA RECURVA Bentham
FRITILLARIA RECURVA COCCINEA Greene
Scarlet Fritillaria

Hell Gate Canyon is on the Rogue River, 15 or 20 miles downstream from Grants Pass near the southwestern corner of Oregon. A friend and I were searching the rugged hillsides looking for Howell's Lewisia which we knew was there. We didn't find it and were discussing our disappointment while walking along an abandoned logging road. Suddenly, at the top of a ten foot bank in the underbrush I saw the bright red trumpets of the Scarlet Fritillaria. I had never seen it before although I had listened to its praises sung for many years. There wasn't the slightest doubt about what it was. No other plant in that entire Siskiyou-Rogue River area could boast of such a magnificent flower in such a splendid color.

I crawled to the top of the embankment and scouted around. There were several others scattered among the native shrubs. I dug three or four of them carefully and balled them. This was difficult as the soil was slightly of a humusy nature, very loose and just barely damp although it was still spring when most of the other coastal areas of Oregon are quite wet.

We continued our drive down the river in a northwesterly direction towards the ocean. The paved highway gave way to a rock road with sharp blind curves. It was very narrow. In most places there was room for only one car for the right of way was carved out of the cliffs – straight up on one side and straight down on the other. My pal was an excellent driver and, being on the uphill side wasn't concerned at all. But when I looked out my side and saw drop offs within, seemingly, inches of the wheels I was half terrified. Lack of adequate sleep, long hours searching hills and gullies for plants – the usual thing in botanical field trips – had put my nerves on a fine edge and this wacky road hadn't done me any good at all. (The driver laughed at me. But, on the return trip, he was on the drop off side and it was my turn to snicker at his suddenly pale face.) At the extreme edge of the road at the base of the cliffs in the shallow rocky soil here and there we saw two or three dozen more *Fritillarias* scattered along five or ten miles. I wanted to get out and look at them but there wasn't a chance. I knew if some nut came whizzing around one of those abrupt corners there would be just as many *Fritillarias* left in the world but two or three less people.

Nowhere did we see more than three or four plants close together. It is doubtful if they are ever found in dense colonies.

History: They belong to the Lily Family, *Liliaceae,* which consists of about 120 genera and 1,250 species widely distributed in the old and new worlds. Some of these genera are of such markedly different appearance that one would need to be a botanist to know that they are related. There are about 50 species of *Fritillarias* of the North Temperate Zone in both worlds. They are very closely allied to the lilies. Some of them are so strikingly like the *Liliums* in both flower and foliage that a thoughtful examination is necessary to determine the difference. I was once sent a *Lilium bolanderi* in full flower. At first I thought it was a *Fritillaria* until a close inspection proved I was wrong – and not for the first time either in a long and happy career.

The differences in the two genera are not difficult to tell however. Most of the old world *Fritillarias* have coated bulbs like the tulips. The American species have scaly bulbs as do the true lilies. But these scales are plump, rice grain-like and are so loosely attached to the parent bulb that many of them break off when they are dug. These scales make new plants close to the old ones. Lily scales are strongly attached and do not resemble rice at all. *Fritillarias* are usually only two to four inches deep while I have had to go as deep as 14 inches to get some of our native lily bulbs.

The mature lily plants usually have their leaves arranged in whorls. So do some of the *Fritillarias* and the similarity can be so close that it is very difficult to detect the difference without examining the flowers and bulbs. Lilies almost always have much larger flowers than the smaller and often less colorful Frits.

The genus was named and described by Carl Von Linneaus in 1735 in one of his classic works. As might be expected when a plant was named in the days when taxonomy was still in its childhood there was a good deal of uncertainty what to call this genus. Besides the one now fully established, as it was originally designated by the father of modern botany, no less than 13 other generic names have been presented in the intervening 138 years. The last was offered in 1873 and all has been quiet on this botanical front ever since. George Bentham, 1800-1884, published the specific name in 1857. *Recurva* means curved back.

Scarlet Fritillarias is a good common name and is the only one I have found in the numerous botanical reference books I have used as an aid in preparing this article. But I have never heard it anywhere else. Gardeners, settlers living near its native habitat, and flower lovers generally, in their conversations with me, have always referred to it as Red Bells. This appeals to me as being just as good as the other and perhaps a little more distinctive.

Description: Mature stems are rather stout and grow from six to 30 inches with the average about halfway in between. The leaves are usually in two whorls of four or five leaves each near the middle of the stem with several individuallv scattered. They are narrow, blunt, and from two to four inches long. Below ground – just a few inches – is the bulb with a broad fleshy base, three-quarters to an inch in diameter, which is shaped remarkably like the well-known summer squash. It is surrounded with numerous, lightly attached, rice grain scales, with an occasional one that has separated and sent up a slender leaf or two of its own. Time to be weaned and make your own home even if it is only a tiny distance from Mom.

While the foliage is pleasing enough it isn't sufficiently outstanding to have any garden value. It is the strikingly bright red trumpet-like flower that catches the eye at once and holds it in the mind forever. Its bell shaped blossom widens towards the outer end where the six perianth segments are strongly curved outward and backward. The flowers are from an inch to an inch and a half long, bright scarlet lightly tinged with purple on the outside and scarlet spotted with yellow within. (I was amused to find some botanies describe the inside as yellow spotted with scarlet. If the preponderance of color is scarlet then the spots, I suppose, would be yellow. If yellow predominates one could say that the spotting is scarlet. Hair splitting – and side splitting too.)

In the wild state from one to half a dozen flowers are borne from the axils of the upper usually solitary leaves on short erect or upward growing stems. But the flowers themselves are gracefully nodding. Erect pedicels and blossoms bowing as though giving thanks for their beauty is a combination of great loveliness. *F. recurva,* the showiest of all the *Fritillarias* has been known to have as many as 35 blossoms! This I never expect to see but if I do I'll spend the rest of my days talking about it.

F. recurva coccinea named by Edward Lee Greene, 1843-1915, in 1892, is very similar to the type and possibly not even a variety though some botanists consider it a distinct species. The floral segments at the tip are generally not recurved and the flowers are said to be more brilliantly scarlet.

Rarity: Rare, the type. The variety *coccinea,* very rare. Both are becoming increasingly rare due largely to the activities of both commercial collectors and casual woods wanderers.

Distribution: Dry open woods and brush lands. The type in western Douglas County through Josephine and Jackson Counties in southern Oregon. In California to Mendocino County in the Coast Ranges and to Placer County in the Sierra Nevadas. Variety *coccinea* more restricted. Hoods Peak and Napa Ranges.

Propagation: Rarely grown from seed. It can be done but there is a long time from seed to seedling to flowering plant. Dealers sometimes offer seed but it is hard to come by. The usual method is from offsets as this is a comparatively rapid process. Lift, divide and replant every three years in the fall so the offsets will not rob the old bulbs and vice versa.

Culture: If I could have only one genus of plants in my gardens it would not be the *Fritillarias.* The *Erythroniums* are universally beautiful and all have much the same horticultural requirements as do the *Trilliums* – and many other kinds of plants too. But the Frits. are in a class by themselves. Some are easy to grow. Others, and *F. recurva* is among them, are difficult. There is a great deal of difference in garden value among them. Reginald Farrer in his *The English Rock Garden* says "that an enormous number of *Fritillarias* have more of less stinking bells of dingy chocolate and greenish tones –." One of our western species, *F. agrestis* has two common names which are revealing: Ill-scented Fritillary and Stink Bells. Yellow Bells, *F. pudica* is a very choice semi-dwarf of real beauty and does fairly well in my damp climate. But, *F. recurva* is near the top of the floral ladder in color, in form, and in loveliness. In comparatively dry climates that are not too cold it can be handled without too much trouble. The bulbs should be planted two to four inches deep, depending upon the character of the soil which must be very well drained.

I bought some from a nursery a few years ago and planted them in the light shade of a small cherry tree where I had a small rock garden. The soil was half crushed lava rock and half leaf mold. That was the last I saw of them. I planted the few I collected on my trip to southern Oregon. Same conditions but in two different places. They sent out a few weak leaves the following spring, then disappeared. It was merely by chance that I found the secret of success with this plant. Take some of the soil in which they are growing. Apparently there is a bacteria, fungus or some other symbiotic relationship necessary for their survival. Once I made this discovery through a friend who had them growing beautifully in his gardens, I had no more trouble.

Flowering Time: April and May.

Gilia aggregata Scarlet Gilia

GILIA AGGREGATA (Pursh) Sprengel
Scarlet Gilia

While driving up a steep one way mountain road six inches deep in dust I saw a small red flower on top of a bank through the tightly closed windows. I stopped, walked through the stifling cloud I had stirred up and knelt beside the little plant. This was the Scarlet Gilia and the first time I had ever seen it. I dug three of the foot high plants, packed them carefully in some of their own soil, added a little water and brought them home in excellent condition. They were planted in a sunny spot and appeared to like their new home. But in a couple of weeks or so, in spite of my devoted attention, they were nearly dead.

After a lifetime of collecting, growing and studying wild plants I consider myself fairly competent in this field. While this first experience with the *Gilias* was during the early years of my studies I was well enough informed to know that lack of care was not the reason for their early demise. I have never been a successful quitter so back I went for more plants even though this involved a round trip of around 150 miles. There was less dust this time but still plenty of plants – far more than I had noticed the first time. For among the flowering ones was a considerable number of others with finely dissected leaves parted into seven to 13 linear, pointed divisions. They were a rich glossy deep green and quite flat so that numerous as they were they made a compact basal rosette that had a special charm of its own sufficiently lovely to merit a place in any rock garden. On my first trip to this area my delight with the flowers had caused me to completely overlook the flowerless rosettes and this was the wholly obvious reason for my failure for these were biennials. The first year the seedlings make these tight, earth-hugging clusters. The second year the flowering stems shoot up, send out their scarlet trumpets and die. I was a little ashamed of my blunder – and still am – but I learned a lesson that I have never forgotten – study the plants and surrounding conditions. This is a big help in understanding how to make them grow at home, and in some cases including this one, is vital to success. I ignored the flowering ones on this second trip and took only the year old seedlings. They blossomed nicely for me next year.

I collected some of their seeds and grew new plants which I placed in a circle for use as a border. In the wild the rosettes were about three inches in diameter. Mine at home were a little larger and had a slightly better green. I decided that the richer soil had something to do with it as well as a little more moisture than they had in their native volcanic pumice mixed with a little humus. I wanted even better growth so I watered lightly but frequently and the leaves became beautifully green, larger and much healthier appearing. Then, one morning, the shock came. The crowns of nearly half the plants had rotted off and they were dead. Another blunder and another costly lesson that I have since applied to rock and alpine dwellers to good advantage.

Observing how the plants grow in their natural habitat makes wild plant collecting much more instructive then buying from nurseries even though stock purchased from dealers may be much less costly than the time, gas and labor spent in going after the wild ones.

History: The Gilias were named in 1794 in honor of Filipe Luis Gil, a Spanish botanist, by Hipolito Ruiz Lopez, 1764 - 1815, and Jose Pavon, likewise botanists of Spain, authors of a *Flora of Peru and Chile.* These two scientists found a single species, *Gilia laciniata,* in South America, and a new genus was born. Other members have been found on that continent since then. There are about 40 species and all are confined to the New World. About 28 of these are found on the west coast of North America with more of them in California, perhaps, than in any other state. The *Gilias* belong to the Phlox Family, *Polemoniaceae,* of about 15 genera and over 200 species.

Gilia aggregata was first described by Frederick Pursh, the Polish Botanist, as *Cantua aggregata,* in his *Flora Americae Septentrionalis* published in 1814. He left Dresden in 1799 where he had received his education, for Baltimore, Maryland, to study the American flora. He returned to Europe in 1811, after spending nearly 12 years in our country. The name was changed in 1825 to its present one by the German botanist Kurt Sprengel, 1766 - 1833. It has been a confused species, having had at least 19 different scientific names at one time or another, seven of which were generic. If plants could think this kicked around species no doubt would be in a state of shock. David Douglas, the great Scottish botanist, who must have been a busy man indeed on his expeditions to the west coast of North America in the 1820's, sent several species to Europe where they became garden favorites even in the days when California was still part of Mexico.

Description: In the wild state I have seen it growing on an average from six inches to a foot and a half high. At 6,000 feet a short distance from a tiny spring in crushed basaltic rock and very little soil and not much more moisture I once found a few that were only about three inches tall. These miniatures, these incredible dwarfs were perfectly happy in their harsh habitat and produced a shower of crimson trumpets. Friends of mine have found others that were four feet tall, fiery torches, in the region of Washington State's Mount Adams. A correspondent in northern Scotland has been able to grow them just as tall in his gardens but this takes some doing.

The plants usually have minute woolly hairs and are sticky to handle. The flowering stems are erect, simple in small plants, and branched in the larger ones. The leaves are numerous, finely pinnately dissected, one to two inches long, the lobes from a quarter to three-quarters of an inch long, smaller and farther apart upwards. The flower is tubular-funnelform, from one to two inches long and bright red. The slender tube ends abruptly in five wide spreading petals – truly a living trumpet of remarkable beauty. The entire plant depends upon a deep tap root with rootlets spreading for food and moisture.

Rarity: Scarce. Although this plant is widely distributed a lovely little colony may be found in a particular spot and then many miles may have to be traveled before it is encountered again. Pink and golden yellow forms have been described which must be considered rare. Whites too are known and these must be very rare. My experience has been limited entirely to the incredibly rich crimsons.

Distribution: Generally a sub-alpine to alpine, occurring from below 4,000 feet up to 10,000 feet, in drier climates. Cascade and Rocky Mountains. British Columbia, Washington, Oregon, California, Montana, Colorado, Utah, Nevada, New Mexico, Idaho, Arizona, western Texas, western Nebraska and likely in other states too.

Propagation: While this is a biennial in a genus that includes annuals and perennials, occasionally a flowering plant will blossom the third season but will not survive longer. Seeds are produced freely as might be expected from a plant that cannot live more than two years, or three at the most. As the flowering buds open from the bottom of the stems upwards all seeds do not ripen at the same time. I wait until nearly all the blossoms have faded away, then shake the stems vigorously over newspapers and get a small shower of fully mature ones. If I need more I cut the stems close to the ground and spread them on papers in a cool but dry room where they will obtain additional food from the still green stems. When thoroughly dry I shake out the additional seeds.

When sown in seed flats with a rich but well drained soil they germinate well and can be set out in the fall. The plants come so readily, however, that I have discontinued this practice. I simply let them drop from their ovoid capsules onto the ground where their parents spent the two years of their lives. I get an abundance of new plants the following spring to perpetuate my garden stock.

Reproduction from seed is the only method I know for this particular species of a widely varying genus of fascinating plants.

Culture: Plenty of sunshine although they will do well with a little light shade in some of the warmer parts of the country. Soil should be very well drained and on the dry side. I use one-half crushed lava rock from pea size up to as large as my fist mixed with an equal part of humus. Don't get soft hearted on a hot day and turn the hose on them. The crowns will rot if they get very much of this misguided treatment.

Flowering Time: May to October, depending upon altitude and climate. They are at their best when the spring flowers are all gone and few other desirable wildlings can be found to take their places. Blossoms appear for a considerable length of time. The first one or two that open at the beginning of the season are a promise of crimson showers to come. Near the end of the summer when only a few are left at the top of the stems raggedness begins to take over. But when the plants are a mass of color during the middle of the season they are truly a gardener's delight.

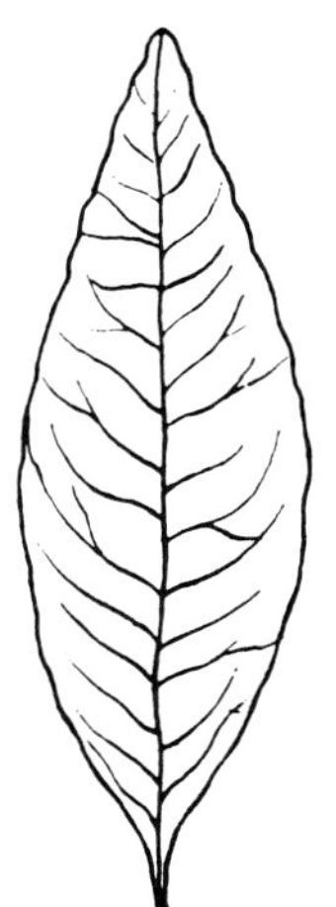

Pinnately veined leaf

Hypopitys species Pine Sap

HYPOPITYS LANUGINOSA (Michaux) Nuttall
Monotropa lanuginosa Michaux
Hypopitys latisquama Rydberg
Hypopitys brevis Small

HYPOPITYS FIMBRIATA (Gray) Howell
Monotropa fimbriata Gray

HYPOPITYS AMERICANA (DeCandolle) Small
Hypopitys multiflora americana De Candolle
Pine Sap

History: These interesting saprophytic plants of the north temperate regions have been known for a long time. Carl Von Linnaeus, the father of modern botany, described them in the first edition of his *Genera Plantarum,* published in 1737. Since that time, more than 200 years ago, there has been confusion and disagreement among botanists as to exactly what they are. And the end is not yet. Some authorities place them in the Wintergreen Family, *Pyrolaceae.* But these people are in the minority. Others consider them members of the Heath Family, *Ericaceae.* Other authorities, who are recognized as competent botanists of excellent reputation, consider them in the Indian Pipe Family, *Monotropaceae.* To further complicate an already difficult problem each species has at least one synonym, and various authors have placed them in two different genera. And all this muddled botanical picture is over a genus comprising no more than half a dozen species at the most.

The fact that some of them have been called *Monotropas,* the genus to which the Indian Pipe belongs, is undoubtedly due to the marked resemblance to that strikingly beautiful plant. Both species nod their heads during the earlier stages of their flowering and when the seeds begin to ripen they straighten their stems and look straight up into the sky as though praying that a few of their multitudes of minute seeds might produce another generation of ghostly plants.

While the botanists may squabble about the correct

nomenclature of these greenless plants there are no such differences among ordinary people who simply love beautiful flowers. This is an extraordinary reversal of the common experiences associated with plants. Often there may be so many common names applied to a single plant or the same name may be given to several totally different flowers that a discussion using these accepted non-scientific terms may terminate in the wildest imaginable confusion. But Pine Sap is the common name associated with this particular genus although such others as Bird's Nest and Beech Drops may be used occasionally. *Hypopitys* is a Greek name referring to its growth under fir trees. This is somewhat misleading too because it also grows under pines.

Description: While wandering along a pleasant trail through a coniferous forest on the lower slopes of Mount Hood in northwestern Oregon, at an altitude of 4,000 – 5,000 feet, I chanced upon these plants for the first time. Although I had never seen them before a single glance told me what they were for their resemblance to the Indian Pipe was pronounced. The only striking difference was in the color. The Indian Pipe, of course, is a waxy, snowy white. These particular Pine Saps were reddish brown in their entirety. Like the Indian Pipes the stems were numerous – a dozen or so from a single plant, closely clustered, and arising from a dense mass of fleshy roots. Sometimes the flowers have the delicate fragrance of violets according to some people whose olfactory organs are more sensitive than mine.

The flowers range from pinks, reds, yellows and whites, varying from plant to plant and from species to species, but none of the colors are bright and vivid as in the Indian Pipe or the Snow Plant, *Sarcodes.* Nor do they have any degree of purity. I have never seen a pure white. Rather they tend to a certain drabness which greatly detracts from their charm.

They do have a modest attraction and a quiet beauty, however, that make them truly worthy of attention from the forest wanderer. The flowers are irregularly vase-shaped, somewhat small in a simple, nodding terminal raceme. The terminal flowers are usually five parted while the lateral ones have three or four petals, each with a nectary on either side. These nectaries, surprisingly enough, would indicate that bees and other insects are welcome in the deep forests for their pollinizing activities. I have never seen insects visiting either the Pines Saps or any other saprophytes but this is pretty much what one might expect. However, my visits to these peculiarly attractive plants have been neither frequent enough nor long enough at any one time to prove anything.

The leaves have been reduced to scales. The plants are pubescent and usually very short or long ciliate, (hairy.) The stems are from two to 16 inches tall with the average about half-way between. The many-seeded capsules vary from nearly globose, broadly ovoid, oblong-oval to ovate.

While both the Pine Sap and its closest generic relative, the Indian Pipe can sometimes be found in the same general area the *Hypopitys* seem to prefer somewhat drier places. While the snowy Indian Pipe attracts immediate attention its lesser brother deserves consideration too and it never fails to get it from me whenever I am fortunate enough to find it in my wanderings through the deep evergreen forests.

Rarity: Rare in various degrees depending upon the species.

Distribution: *H. lanuginosa,* in the Coast and Cascade Mountains from southeastern Alaska to British Columbia, California, eastward to the Atlantic Coast and southward to Florida. Also in Mexico, Japan, and Europe. *H. fimbriata,* Coast and Cascade Mountains from British Columbia, Oregon, to Northwestern California. *H. americana,* Ontario in Canada to New York and North Carolina. Also in the mountainous regions of Tripoli. The genus is distributed around the world in the north temperate zone but nowhere common.

Propagation: Unknown. The seeds are very fine, and like other closely related saprophytes, are difficult to germinate. Scatter on top of a soil rich in decayed vegetable material in the shade. It is doubtful if many people will attempt to propagate this plant when other close relatives, such as the Indian Pipe and the brilliant Snow Plant, might, theoretically at least, return a much greater floral reward for the same effort.

Culture: Unknown. Plant divisions would be even more impossible than attempting to transplant entire plants. If this is attempted as large a ball of earth as possible should be taken and planted, undisturbed, in a well shaded spot in the garden. Likelihood of success beyond the first year or two is remote indeed.

Flowering Time: June, July, August and September, depending upon species, climate, and altitude.

Note: Names in italics at the head of this article are synonyms.

Pinnately compound leaf

Iris chrysophylla 'Yellow' Slender Tubed Iris

THE IRISES (Tournefort) Linnaeus

History: *Liliales* is a large order of monocotyledonous plants comprising 11 families, two of the most important of which are *Liliaceae* and *Iridaceae.* In the evolutionary family tree of plants the *Iridaceae* are just immediately above the lilies and just below the orchids.

The Iris family, *Iridaceae,* (originally spelled Irideae) was named by George Bentham and Joseph Dalton Hooker. It contains about 57 genera and 1,000 species of the temperate and tropical regions of both hemispheres.

The best known among the 57 are the Iris which are planted in thousands upon thousands of gardens in many parts of the world. Over a hundred species with innumerable varieties are offered by American dealers. The genus was named by Linneaus in his *Species Plantarum* dated 1753 although Tournefort, in 1735, gave it a name which is no longer considered official. *Iris* comes from a Greek word meaning *rainbow* in reference to the many colored flowers. At least 26 other generic names have been published since then, the last appearing in 1869. Few gardeners have ever heard of any of these synonyms and not many botanists are familiar with them. Perhaps it is just as well that they have slipped into obscurity for there is enough confusion within the genus itself to satisfy anyone.

Distribution: There are anywhere from 100 to 170 species, depending upon whose authority, if any, you care to take, distributed very widely but mostly confined to the North Temperate Zone. Over 700 synonyms exist – something of a horticultural madhouse. Approximately two and a half dozen species are native to North America, distributed all the way from Alaska to Florida and from the Atlantic to the Pacific. They inhabit dry soils and bogs. Some live in the mountains, others at the seashores. There are enough variations in size to please anyone – from a few inches to several feet – and the colors range from dull, drab, thoroughly uninteresting to the exquisite hues of the rainbow. Pure, snowy whites, yellows, oranges, near reds, blues, lavenders, violets to almost black.

Description: All are perennial, some being deciduous and others evergreen, with creeping, often woody, usually stout or sometimes slender rhizomes or bulb-like root-stocks. In hardiness they run all the way from scarcely freeze tolerant to subzero indifference. Most of them are easy to handle in the garden when once established and need little care. Wild transplants of some species are often difficult for the first year.

Somewhere there is an Iris with the right color, size and garden adaptability to suit every taste.

The western part of America is rich in Irises of great beauty. Most of them are of the wire rooted group and present more difficulty in bringing from the wild to the garden than those with heavy rhizomes or bulbs. But their striking colors are so delightful that almost any effort to make them happy in their new homes is entirely worthwhile. But the Far West has no monopoly on Iris loveliness. The middle west and east has its charmers too.

The astonishing thing about this wondrous genus is that, while we are surrounded with their glorious wild blossoms we go to foreign lands for other species which may be of lesser worth. Within half a dozen miles of my Portland, Oregon home are wild Irises equal to any but none of my neighbors possess them or hardly know they exist. A gardener once sent for a *Spiraea* that was enticingly described in a nursery catalogue. It was a beauty all right – and it was also growing wild in his own meadow.

Complete leaf

Iris bracteata Siskiyou Iris

IRIS BRACTEATA Watson
Siskiyou Iris

The sunlight filtered through the scattered Jeffrey Pines in the Illinois River Valley in extreme southwestern Oregon. As I wandered along a dirt road in the shade of the trees I saw two or three dark shiny green grass-like leaves on top of a two foot bank. It was a lonely little plant struggling to survive in the dry red clay loam. This was the first time I had ever seen *Iris bracteata* and I was a little excited, and disappointed too, because I could not take it with me. There were no others in the vicinity and my collecting permit would not allow me to dig isolated specimens.

It was quite a number of years later, on another trip to the same vicinity, that I stopped to get a drink from a wayside fountain. On the other side of the road there was a ten foot bank of the same hard, dry, red earth that I had seen on the other expedition. I took a run for the steep bank and made the top, hoping but not expecting, to find anything of interest. The land stretched away for quite a distance in front of my eyes. It was a logged off and burned over region of desolation with charred stumps and a few manzanitas here and there. And among them were quite a number of *Iris bracteata.* Getting back from the road I dug a few, wrapped the roots in wet moss and tucked them into my collecting box. They were past the flowering stage and I had yet to see their blossoms. I was inclined to think they liked those harsh living conditions. But I was wrong. It was one of nature's vagaries that they were growing there where extreme dryness had forced them into early flowering. Quite a number of miles farther south I found more in a slightly moist grassy meadow. The soil was better in this place and the plants were much more vigorous – and joy of joys, in blossom. The blossoms were creamy, light and moderate yellows of good color, but none with the deep lemons I was hoping for and, of course, none of the very rare pure whites. But I was happy with my find for *I. bracteata* is one of our excellent yellow natives. The specimens I collected that day occupy a special place in my gardens, in splendid isolation from all my other wild Iris.

History: It was Sereno Watson, 1826-1892, of far away Harvard University who first published the still officially recognized name, *Iris bracteata,* in 1885. The specific name, meaning *bearing bracts,* in reference to the bract-like stem leaves, was an excellent choice and seems to have gone unchallenged throughout the intervening years. Something of a phenomenon considering how botanists often squabble about such things. Thomas Howell, Oregon's first resident botanist, likewise discovered it at about the same time near Waldo, in the extreme southwestern part of Oregon. One authority gives the date as 1884, another, 1887. Traveling in those days was a bit primitive and Mr. Howell, who lived in Portland, did much of his botanical exploring with horse and wagon. *I. bracteata* was introduced into cultivation in 1888. It is well known in the British Isles where it has been grown for more than half a century.

Description: This is a curious Iris to the extent that it has a more scanty growth perhaps than any other known species. Its slender rhizome creeps widely but has few branches so that the growths are at some distance from each other. Furthermore usually only solitary leaves grow from each point. These and the flower stems appear together in the early part of the growing season an inch or more in front of the previous season's growth, which then withers away. It never makes the dense clusters of leaves that are so typical of some of the other western species such as *I. tenax* and *I. douglasiana.* The evergreen basal leaves are from ten inches to two feet long, a quarter to three-quarters of an inch wide, stiff, leathery, a deep rich green above and much lighter beneath, erect or curving gracefully outward. The simple, flattened stems are eight to 12 inches high and usually bear two flowers which appear in succession on one to two inch slender pedicels. The stem leaves, two or three, are bract-like, often reddish, distended and from two to six inches long. The comparatively large light yellow blossoms are delicately netted and veined with brown. While I have yet to see an *I. bracteata* with the deep yellows of *I. innominata* the colors are clear and very lovely. The capsules are about an inch long and in my gardens seed is produced sparingly. Some very beautiful natural hybrids appear in gardens where *I. bracteata* is associated with other west coast species.

Rarity: Very rare, the type, partly due to its restricted range, and partly due to its seemingly lack of abundance anywhere. The white form, extremely rare. A friend has an "egg shell" white. Those with the purity of snow must exist but I have yet to see one.

Distribution: In the Arid Transition Life Zone, commonly at low altitudes. In the Siskiyou Mountains of southwestern Oregon and northwestern California. In Josephine County in southwestern Oregon. I saw my first few plants near O'Brien not far north of the California border. A few miles further south they were more abundant on both sides of the highway. I found some a mile or so west of Cave Junction where they were growing and flowering beautifully on a hillside in the filtered shade of conifers. Other stations are near Waldo and on Oregon Mountain.

Propagation: From seed and divisions. Plant the seed as soon as it is ripe in a loose, well drained, rich, moisture retaining soil. They may be scattered on the surface of the earth or planted shallowly. Many people experience complete failure in their seed flats but find numerous volunteers around the parent plants. The secret is simple. Leaves and other debris keep the seeds permanently moist. If they are allowed to become dry on the under side they will not germinate. During wet springs germination is often much better than in dry ones. Often the seed will not germinate for two or three years if they are too dry. Humidity and moisture can be controlled better in cold frames or greenhouses. Outdoor flats should be shaded and kept constantly damp on the surface. Flowering may be expected in the second or third season.

Divisions may be made in the fall after the rains have started or in the spring after the danger of severe frosts is over. Fall divisions make a better growth but are something of a gamble. Unseasonal cold spells have cost me a good many plants. They will often kill transplants but not injure established stock. I generally make a few divisions in the autumn but wait until very early spring for the main part of the work.

Culture: In mild climates such as my Willamette Valley home it does equally well in full sun and light shade. In warmer areas it should have a little protection. Its native home, largely away from the gentle coastal regions, is in an area of 100 degree summers and cold winters. In my gardens it survived a zero winter without damage. It requires good drainage but otherwise tolerates most any acid or neutral soil. Healthier and more vigorous plants may be expected if it is provided with an abundance of sand and leaf mold so that the rhizomes can enjoy their vagrant inclinations. Some of mine are in an unprotected rockery. Others open their yellow buds after the apple blossoms over their heads have disappeared. *Bracteata* is an easy *Iris* to grow and a beautiful one to own.

Flowering Time: During the last half of May in my gardens. A little later in the wild at higher altitudes. While other native Iris may blossom longer *bracteata* makes joyful the third and fourth weeks of May.

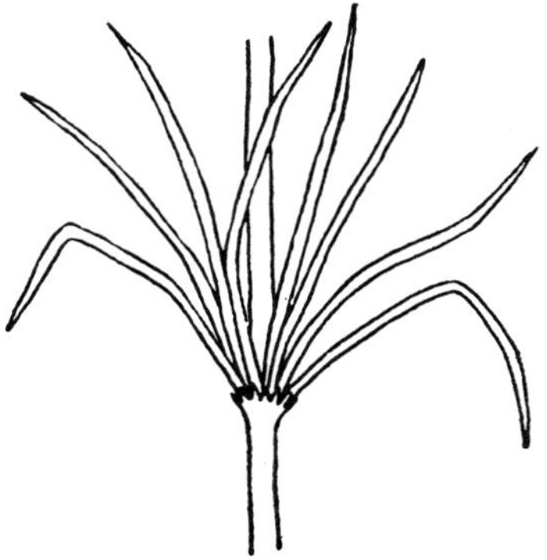

Whorled leaves

Iris chrysophylla Slender Tubed Iris

IRIS CHRYSOPHYLLA Howell
Slender Tubed Iris

Throughout the years of my woods wanderings there have been many frustrating experiences, temporary as a rule, in the search for rare wild flowers. Time after time I have asked people about plants that I knew were growing in their neighborhoods – and about which they were totally ignorant. Finally I hit upon a workable device. Ask the children. They are often more observing than their parents and are almost always not only willing, but eager, to help.

This was my experience with *Iris chrysophylla.* Culp Creek is a small logging community on the Row River about 15 miles east of Cottage Grove which is located on Oregon's Upper Willamette Valley. After knocking on various Culp Creek doors and being told in friendly words that, no they knew nothing of any wild Iris, white or any other kind, I finally asked a couple of small boys. Sure, they had seen them. Come with us mister. Less than 100 yards away we found them, scattered under some young fir trees where they were fully protected by poison oak. This robbed me of some of my enthusiasm. I asked if they didn't know where we could find others. In the pasture, back of the school house, they said. The cattle had cropped away the grass and the creamy blossoms dotted the meadow in bold relief. There were several dozen clumps among the wild rose bushes. The owner didn't care how many I dug – in fact he thought I was a bit peculiar to have traveled all the way from Portland for plants that, to him, were only weeds. But I had my reward and I saw to it that the boys received theirs.

There were no yellows among them so I spent another two days exploring little traveled mountain side roads. I wandered through the open fir forests examining countless plants – but they were all much the same. The yellows had eluded me so I headed south towards the Rogue River. On the 13 mile stretch between the tiny villages of Merlin and Wilderville I suddenly came upon them. They were scattered here and there on both sides of the road for a distance of no more than a hundred yards. Most of them were the usual creams. Only a few were yellow and most of these were in very light shades. But I managed to select a few good colors far enough from the right of way to salve my conscience.

History: Thomas Howell, 1842-1912, named this plant in 1901 in his *A Flora of Northwest America.* He was the first botanist to call Oregon his home – a competent and respected scientist. His rare book is still useful to those who are fortunate enough to possess it. Why he chose *chrysophylla* for the specific name eludes my understanding. The word means *golden-leaved* and there is nothing golden about it. The extreme base is reddish and the next inch or two is a pale yellowish green – far from golden – and the remainder of the blade is the ordinary green common to many irises.

A good deal of confusion still exists about the exact identification of the plant. Some authorities suggest that it may be only a form of *I. californica,* while others say that *chrysophylla, californica* and *macrosiphon* are the same plant or so much alike that, for garden purposes they are identical. It is probable that the first mentioned concept is the accurate one but I am going to enjoy their beauty and let others worry about the details.

Description: From the slender or stoutish rhizomes rise the more or less evergreen leaves, either in masses or somewhat scattered. They are stiff and leathery but less so than those of *I. bracteata,* slightly thicker in the middle and thinned to almost knife-edged margins, from a sixteenth to three-eighths of an inch wide and from six inches to fully two feet long – the latter length being quite common under good cultural conditions. They grow directly out of the ground, are deep green above and lighter beneath, sometimes a bit glaucous and finely grooved and ridged on both sides.

The flower stems are low and slender, from two to eight inches high but the much longer leaves are spreading for the most part and do not hide the blossoms. The lance-shaped floral bracts are two to four inches long and gradually taper to the apex. Each stem bears usually one but up to three, stemless, or nearly so, comparatively huge blossoms, creamy white, or rarely varying shades of light or medium yellow. Dainty and delicate blue or brown lines proceed from the clear yellow spotted falls. It is one of the most compact and low flowering species on the west coast and the overall effect of the fragile blossoms with their delicate coloring makes it as desirable as it is beautiful.

Rarity: The cream colored type, scarce; the yellow, very rare.

Distribution: The type species: From Marion and Polk Counties in northwestern Oregon south to California. I have never seen this iris north of Cottage Grove which is about mid way between the Washington and California borders. The yellow variety: Between Merlin and Wilderville in southwestern Oregon and on the north side of the road on the three mile stretch between Mill City and Gates near the North Santiam River in western Oregon. This species prefers meadows, open woods and thickets generally at moderate altitudes in the Arid Transition Zone. Where it overlaps with *I. tenax* lovely natural hybrids have been found which exceed either species in beauty. Color patterns such as bicolors are produced which are not usual for either parent.

Propagation: Same as for *I. bracteata.* During favorable seasons in my gardens seed is produced sparingly. Most years none.

Culture: The allegation that this is a short lived species has not been proven in my gardens. Its life tenure seems to be much the same as its western brothers. Its preference is for loose, well drained soils rich in leaf mold but it isn't overly fussy. Its native home is a bit on the dry side and overly moist garden conditions are to be avoided. I have found it under fir trees in moderately deep shade where it flowered but not as abundantly nor with the growth vigor of those in open meadows where sunlight dominates them all day. In warmer climates a little shade will be beneficial. The type species is not at all difficult to grow and spreads rather slowly. My success with the yellow forms has been disappointing. For some reason that I do not understand they do not like captivity and both leaf and blossom are meager – quite unlike their robustness in the wild.

Flowering Time: One typical year in my gardens *chrysophylla* blossomed from May 19th to June 11th. Somewhat later in its wild habitat where altitudes are usually greater.

Crested Dwarf Iris

Iris cristata

IRIS CRISTATA Aiton
Crested Dwarf Iris

It was while wandering through a wild flower nursery many years ago that I broke my vow against instant friendship. The owner had two short rows of miniature Iris – one was limited to enchanting light pastel blue flowers of ineffable beauty. These were not the weak shades so often associated with pale colors. Far from it. The other row contained only snowy white blossoms. "What in the world do you have there?" I asked the dealer. "I simply must have some." "You're looking at *Iris cristata."* he answered. As usual there were only a few coins jingling in my pocket so I was able to buy only one of each. But these were floral bargains without any doubt.

It is an odd thing – and a little sad too – that this wild flower which grows over a large area of the eastern part of the United States is so little known. Ask the next hundred people you see what they think of *Iris cristata.* It isn't likely that a single one will know what you are talking about.

History: In spite of its present obscurity it has been known for a very long time. It was given its still recognized name in 1789 by the Englishman William Aiton, 1731-1793. *Cristata* means *crested.* Friedrich Alefeld, 1820-1872, proposed the name *Neubeckia cristata* in 1863 but this synonymous genus is so outdated that few scientists have ever heard of it. Alton was not the first man on the job. In the British Museum there is a specimen from the herbarium of the American botanist William Bartram, 1739-1823, dated 1764, and described as "a sweet-scented plant, growing five inches high, which spreads much and differs from the Carolina dwarf Iris." This was before our country existed as a nation. Apparently there was time to do a little botanizing while we were trying to win more freedom than the British were willing to give.

Thomas Nuttall, 1786-1859, authored *Iris lacustris* in his *The Genera of North American Plants* dated 1818. *Lacustris* refers to lakes and was a good choice for this Iris is found on the shores of Lakes Huron, Michigan and Superior. There is so little difference in the two plants, mainly in the smaller size of

I. lacustris, that the latter is generally considered only a local form of *I. cristata.*

Description: From the slender, branched, creeping, tuberous, thickened rhizomes rise the bright green deciduous leaves more or less curved, three or four times as long as the greatest width which is below the middle. The leaves are from four to nine inches long, one-quarter to three-quarters of an inch wide, but vary quite a bit. The foliar fans lean outward and bend over at their pointed tips so that the blossoms are not concealed.

The flowering stems, much shorter than the leaves, are only two or three inches long, erect, sturdy and bear one, two or three upward facing blossoms two and a half inches in diameter and come in various light shades of blue, violet and lavender – color tones which are difficult to surpass. The flowers are marked with three raised parallel flutings along the center, the middle one having a white and yellow spot outlined with purple veins. From these fluted falls comes the name *cristata.* I have never seen the sharply triangular, oval capsules.

Rarity: The type, common. The white variety, extremely rare in the wild. From nurseries, scarce. This snowy form appeared in commerce something over 50 years ago. It is unknown whether it was found growing wild or whether it originated in a garden but it is believed that it has been found among collected plants.

Distribution: On hillsides and along streams in open woods. Generally from Maryland south to Georgia and westward to southern Indiana and Missouri. More specifically in Maryland, North and South Carolina, Virginia, Georgia, Kentucky, Missouri, Tennessee, Arkansas, Indiana, Ohio, Wisconsin, Washington, D. C., and doubtless other states as well.

Propagation: Seed is rarely produced from cultivated plants. Even when capsules are obtained from hand pollination the seeds are not numerous, and germination appears to range from very difficult to almost impossible. Over the years I have written to growers in various parts of the country for seed. None have been able to supply me and none mentioned ever having seen any.

From divisions: Cut away the side-growths soon after the

flowering season, or better yet in late summer or early fall. The points of the new roots will be seen then and each of these is capable of becoming a flowering plant the next year. The rhizomes that have flowered die and no new lateral growths will be produced from them. The plants are improved by making annual divisions. The rhizomes are easy to find, often creeping along on the surface of the ground, or very close to it. New divisions should not be allowed to dry out.

Culture: This miniature is easily satisfied. In mild climates full sun or light shade. In the warmer part of the country light shade. I have a plant in full sun in a rockery where the drainage is very sharp, the ground rocky with not much food. Under these conditions it flowers well but makes little increase. In sandy loam containing a preponderance of leaf mold it blossoms profusely. If it isn't given plenty of nourishment the middle of the plant is likely to die out much as does *I. tenax.* It should have plenty of room to spread out, otherwise it needs little or no care.

Nurserymen usually do not stock more than two or three varieties and the white form is scarcer than the colored forms. This is difficult to understand for this white mutation is lovely beyond imagination and is no more trouble to grow than any of the other sorts. In wild stations a great many colors exist. A friend has 25 varieties which he obtained from two collectors in the Blue Ridge area, one working from the Tennessee side, the other from the Carolina. All have not flowered for him yet but he described a clear light blue, a nice orchid-pink, a deep violet as well as the white. I have never seen an *Iris cristata* blossom that was not a pure delight.

Flowering Time: April and May.

Iris douglasiana Douglas' Iris

IRIS DOUGLASIANA Herbert
Douglas' Iris

It was while I was driving along the coastal road of southern Oregon that I first saw Douglas' Iris. Mile after mile they glorified the landscape – huge plants and equally huge flowers splashed the meadows among the rhododendrons and azaleas, among the pines and spruces. I recognized it immediately for there is no other such Iris guarding Oregon's beaches.

About 60 miles north of the California border the obscure Sixes River flows into the Pacific Ocean. I drove 15 miles up a wild logging road along this river – which isn't a river at all but a very lovely trout and salmon stream. I spent four or five days in this botanical paradise – and only the urgencies of home compelled me to leave.

Along the creek, in the logged off lands, the open meadows and under the shade of giant firs, five and six feet in diameter, were literally hundreds of thousands of *Iris douglasiana* plants. It would be conceivably possible to collect a truck load, a car load, or an entire train load and still leave a tremendous number untouched. On some of the hillsides they were growing so closely together that it was not possible to walk without stepping on them. The scattered residents, a few loggers, an optimistic but impoverished prospector or two, and an occasional squatter had no interest whatever in these flowers even though some of them were growing at the doorsteps of their simple homes. They didn't say much but it was obvious that they thought I – from a big city – was, well, perhaps a little odd.

I had never before seen such a sight in all my travels. How many flowers make a million? I don't know, but I am just as sure that there were many times that number on the steep hillsides. Digging a full size plant would be a task that I would not care to undertake. They were three and four feet in diameter – and there was nothing unusual about plants this size. Most of them in this area were this large although closer to the beaches they were noticeably smaller. Why this is so is difficult to say. Perhaps the timbered mountains gave them a little needed protection from the Pacific's winter storms, which can be notoriously violent. Certainly it wasn't the soil for near the sea it is heavily laden with a rich deposit of sand and humus, while inland it is ordinary loam.

No other western Iris offers such great possibilities of color selection and among the myriads of blossoms there was an abundance of choice. I discovered an extremely delicate blue - almost white – with ruffled falls. It is in my gardens today. There were all the light shades, tones and hues of blue, lavender and purples one could imagine. I have never seen a dark colored one. Ordinarily light purples are weak and hardly worthy a second glance. But these were soft, dainty and altogether lovely – reminiscent of much the same effects found in the minute *Iris cristata* which lives two-thirds of the way across the continent.

White forms among purple Iris are usually rare – sometimes virtually impossible to find when a deliberate search is made for them. Such is not the case with *Iris douglasiana.* I made no effort to see how many pure white varieties I could discover. They were too many of them. It would have been no trouble to locate a dozen or so in a half day's search. Among such very faint blues it is a tricky thing to separate the pure albas from the almost whites. I developed a sure method for making this distinction. A calling card held alongside a blossom immediately tells the true story.

It has long been my belief that where alba mutations occur among blue Iris there is a chance – very remote – of discovering a yellow. Among the many thousands of *I. douglasiana* I have examined over the years I have never seen such a blossom. Various other people have made selections from this magnificent species, and some of these have been given horticultural names. None of these that I had heard about were yellow. Never a person to give up – and that is one of the secrets of success with wild flowers as with almost anything else – I wrote to a friend in Gold Beach who lives in this Iris country. Within a few months I received a package from her. Next year the plant she sent me blossomed. And it was a yellow! Not a very good one, perhaps, but yellow nevertheless. It was very light with ordinary or slightly smaller than average blossoms and strongly purple veined. I was simply delighted and mentioned this plant to an Iris fan. To my utmost astonishment she sent me a start from one in her garden. It flowered a year later – and what a golden glory it was – very large blossoms of pure, soft yellow with a delicate trace of lemon veining. It is the most beautiful Iris I have ever seen. The man who made the original discovery had devoted a great deal of time and hard work to obtain the very choicest color forms of *Iris douglasiana.* He has been greatly, almost bitterly disappointed, that no one seems to care much about his efforts. I have never met him but if I do he'll find an ardent supporter.

History: The Englishman, William Herbert, 1778-1847, in 1841, published the still officially accepted name, *Iris douglasiana,* in William Jackson Hooker's, 1785-1865, and George Arnold Walker Arnott's 1799-1868, *Botany of the Beechey Voyage.* Herbert, in the same publication also described three others which are now synonyms. Carl Purdy, of Ukiah, California, gave another, now also synonymous, in 1897. The specific name honors David Douglas, 1799-1834, the famous Scotch botanist who was sent to the west coast of North America during the years 1824-1827 by the Royal Horticulturial Society of London, England. He made another trip in 1830 which ended on July 12, 1834 when he met his death at the age of thirty-five by falling into a bull pit on the Hawaiian Islands.

Dykes, in his great monograph on the genus Iris stated in 1913, "This Iris appears to be confined to the coastal region of California." Mr. Dykes was mistaken for *I. douglasiana* is more abundant in Oregon. The error was natural enough for the earliest discoveries were confined to California: Archibald Menzies, 1754-1842, who was the surgeon and naturalist with the Lord Vancouver Expedition from 1790 to 1795, discovered it in 1792 in Humboldt County; David Douglas in 1833 in a part of California not noted; Behr in 1851 to 1854 in San Mateo County; Henry Nicholas Bolander, 1831-1897, Mendocino County in 1864. Many of our western wild flowers were discovered by land expeditions but Douglas' Iris was first located by ocean voyagers.

Description: From the stout, elongated matted rhizomes come great masses of thick evergreen leaves, rather rigid, ten to 30 inches long, the shorter being near the middle of the plant, three-eights to five-eights of an inch wide, narrowed at the base and gradually tapering to a sharp tip. They are reddish at the base, bright, glossy green above, paler beneath, and finely grooved and ridged the entire length. Those at the middle of the clump are more or less erect while those nearer the outer part of the plant are inclined to curve gracefully outward. This is an effective arrangement for it allows the shorter flowering stems to shower their beauty. These stems are flattened, 12 to 24 inches long, with two or three leaves up to a foot long and a quarter of an inch wide. The leaf-like bracts are separate, about a quarter of an inch wide, up to three inches long, lance-shaped and gradually narrowing to an elongated apex. The flowering stems are erect or somewhat angled outward, and equal to or much shorter than the leaves. The blossoms are often solitary or occasionally two. In some strong growing plants the stem branches once or twice and each lateral stem, three to six inches long, bears from two to five blossoms on pedicels from one to two and a half inches long.

The large blossoms, over three inches in diameter, come in an infinite variety of color forms in the lighter shades. But the shape of the flowers remains fairly constant. 50 to 75 flowers as well as numerous buds on even young plants is not at all unusual.

The capsules, one to two inches long and a half to three-quarters of an inch in diameter, produce a generous number of nearly spherical, or more often somewhat flattened and angled seeds which resemble Brazil nuts.

Rarity: The blue type, very common; the pure whites, scarce; the yellows, extremely rare especially if they are lacking in prominent venation.

Distribution: Woods and open meadows along the coastal areas, mainly in the Humid Transition Life Zone but also in the Upper Sonoran Zone, from sea level to a thousand feet or so. This species is seldom found inland more than a mile or two although in the Sixes River region it was 15 miles from the ocean. In all instances, however, it is always inside the summer fog belt. The northern limit is in Coos County, Oregon, about a hundred miles from the California border. Apparently it is the cooler climate that prevents it from moving farther in this direction where it would not be able to compete with sturdier plants. Its southward limits are to Santa Barbara County, California, about 500–600 miles from the Oregon line. Its occurence is from solitary plants to very extensive colonies. It is easy to see as one drives along the coastal highway during flowering time.

Propagation: Much the same as for *I. bracteata.* Seed is produced in large quantities in my gardens and germination is good. Under favorable conditions it should flower the second and third season – more generally the latter. One large plant can be divided into almost any number of starts. Late summer after the fall rains are established, or more certain survival in early spring.

Culture: No Iris could be easier to grow. I have planted it in the poorest kind of soil, dug out of the basement, where it did reasonably well. Under the great fir trees in the Sixes River drainage basin the soil was ordinary forest loam. Under these conditions individual plants grew to enormous size. Close to the sea they often grow in a sandy humus of high fertility. This is its preference in my gardens. I made a generous sized division and planted it in nearly pure leaf mold with an addition of 25 per cent sand. In three years it developed an extreme spread of 60 inches! This was from leaf tip to leaf tip. The root system, of course, was nowhere near this large. Acid or neutral earths are all right but alkaline ones should be avoided. Good drainage is essential and it is equally happy in full sun or light shade.

Because of its large size and vigorous spreading it should be limited, in rock gardens, to only the very largest unless it is confined to large pots which can be sunk out of sight. A large boulder makes a good back drop and helps conceal bare vertical surfaces.

Like other plants and people it has its limitations. It has withstood near zero temperatures in my gardens but I am sure it will not stand much colder conditions. It is hardy on the southern part of Vancouver Island, British Columbia at about 48 degrees north latitude. It does well in the British Isles except in northern Scotland where our islander cousins have known it for more than half a century.

Americans are not so familiar with its possibilities. This is partially due to its lack of hardiness over much of the country. But I can't help thinking that there is a greater appeal for the unknown – exotic creatures from foreign lands which, in reality, are often less desirable than natives from our own neighborhoods. Nurserymen of the British Islands have done a great deal more with some of our wild flowers than we have. I have obtained some of my best strains of American natives from these foreign growers.

Flowering Time: *I. douglasiana* has blossomed in my gardens from May 21st to June 27th – five weeks of transplanted coastal splendor. Nearer its southern limits it may flower as early as March.

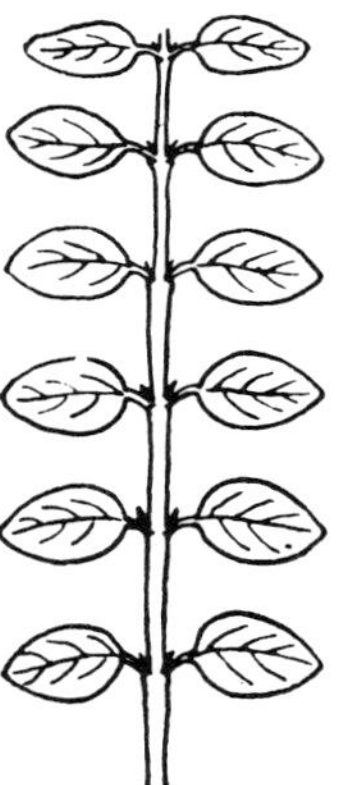

Opposite leaves

Iris gormanii No Established Common Name

IRIS GORMANII Piper
No Established Common Name

This is not only the rarest of Oregon's Iris but one of the most beautiful. It has elicited extravagant statements from lovers of the remarkable genus such as "— —the most dainty and appealing of all native Irises." Such glowing remarks excited my youthful enthusiasm and when I bought one – a low pocketbook prevented purchasing more – I too, was converted.

As the years rolled away and I became deeper and deeper immersed into what has proven to be my life work, I determined to visit the plant in its own home. A letter to a Washington, D.C. botanist who knows where it grows was answered with the vaguest of directions – no help at all. Finally I learned that it was along Scoggins Creek, but who ever heard of such a stream? After a good deal more questioning I found the place. Even today very few people outside of the local settlers are aware of its existence.

A drive 40 miles west from Portland brought me into the heart of its valley home. It isn't much of a place as such things go. Scoggins Creek is about 15 or 20 feet wide and the floor of the valley is from a hundred yards to about half a mile wide rising to low, rolling hills of the Coast Range on both sides. And it isn't a great many miles long. There is a small store at the entrance. Four small lumber mills, a school house and a few homes are scattered here and there. A few are expensive and modern, most very modest, and quite a number are old, tired, and neglected. Grain and cattle are the crops and much of the land is devoted to these enterprises. Like most rural folks the people are friendly. But they know virtually nothing about wild flowers, especially wild Iris. Withal it is as pretty a place as it is obscure – and this just about completes the picture.

I made five trips, totaling 400 miles, before I was able to find this very rare wildling, and the fault was mine. Gorman's Iris closely resembles *I. tenax* and I took it for granted that both would bloom at the same time. When *I. tenax* was in flower I left for Scoggins Creek. I couldn't find a single one and only three of the many people I asked had ever heard of it. Much later I found out that *I. gormanii* flowers from two to five weeks later than *I. tenax.* No wonder I failed! On my fifth expedition I became acquainted with a rancher who had seen one plant, with the very rare yellow blossoms, on his property. He led me and my family to the spot where he pointed out a strip of grazed-over land between a rudimentary road and a fence. It was eight feet wide and 150 feet long. We all started looking but the owner and the three members of my family quickly quit the silly business. There is a forage grass that closely resembles iris foliage. The cattle had cropped everything very short still further complicating the problem. Down I went on my hands and knees and inspected the grass blade by blade. It was slow and tedious work but it paid off when I found the tiny plant. It is in my garden today. That was my only find on this trip.

On later excursions I gave up asking for directions and set out on my own. I took a side road up a tiny creek for a mile or so until I came to some meadows and logged off brush land. Here I hit pay dirt. I spent the entire day in this small area and came home with two dozen selected plants.

The common form of this Iris is light lavender. I have never seen a dark one. The cream colored ones are rare and the yellows extremely rare as are the bronzes. I found one plant that had a yellow and a lavender blossom on one stem. Another rare yellow had miniature blossoms – less than half the size of the others. This treasure is my most highly prized Iris and has a special nook in my gardens. I spent a great deal of time selecting yellow forms for these vary greatly. Most are too pale to be outstanding. But here and there I was able to choose soft medium-deep shades of genuine beauty.

History: It must have been close to half a century ago when Martin Gorman and his friend Earl Marshall visited the valley and discovered the Iris. Mr. Gorman had a passion for accuracy and made no snap judgments. His comment to Mr. Marshall was, "I may have found a new Iris."

Few of his companions realized his greatness for his was a retiring nature. He was born in Ontario, Canada, on November 23, 1853, and died of uremia in Portland, Oregon on October 7, 1926, a lifetime bachelor. A competent botanist, a nationally recognized authority on western wild flowers, his memory is preserved not only in his Iris but in other species of different genera as well as the genus *Gormania* of the Stonecrop Family. Charles Vancouver Piper, who was born in 1867, published the name *Iris gormanii* in 1924 and the world officially acquired another valuable plant. The British were not slow to add it to their gardens.

Description: Structurally this species is identical with *I. tenax.* Taxonomists have been unable to find differences to justify specific standing. The colors of the flowers are the only obvious distinctions. Some authorites consider it only a form of *I. tenax.* Others call it *Iris tenax, variety gormanii.* Gardeners do little worrying about such a matter.

Rarity: The type, with light lavender flowers, scarce due to the limited range; the white rare; the yellows extremely rare.

Distribution: Scoggins Valley in northwestern Oregon. Most of the plants have disappeared due, partially, to indiscriminate collecting. But clearing the land for grain and forage crops has destroyed most of them so that the very few left are mostly in isolated stations. It has been said that the next little valley westward contains a few.

Propagation: Same as for *I. bracteata.* Seedlings will not come true if the parents are near other wild species. A pleasing array of hybrids may result from such proximity.

Culture: Same as for *I. tenax.* The best yellow forms are the most sought and are as valuable as they are rare. All forms of this species have rich golden throats. The lavenders have prominent purple veining radiating delicately from this lovely splash. The albinos and yellows have faint yellow venation which adds much to their special charms. The whites and creams as well as the lavenders hold their colors but even the best yellows, alas, fade into creams with age – the only fault I can find with this distinguished member of a beloved race.

Fully mature plants are a glorious sight with 50 or 100 blossoms showering the garden with floral gold all at the same time – and with more to come. Wild plants do not produce so abundantly. Competition with grasses and other plants for food, moisture, and space does not exist in the garden. This flower – and many others – responds generously to a little human love.

Flowering Time: Spring. Two to five weeks later than *I. tenax*. There is an incredible variation from season to season in flowering time of both *I. tenax* and *I. gormanii.* I have seen *I. tenax,* on very rare occasions, as early as late February and at other times the first buds do not open until early May. I. gormanii's blooming period extends for about two months. During one more or less typical season the first blossom appeared in my gardens on April 24th and the last on June 22nd. As all plants do not flower at the same time it is wise to have a number of them to assure extended blossoming.

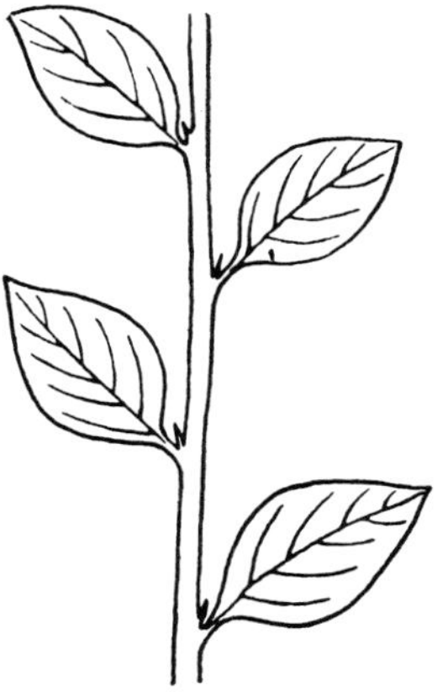

Alternate leaves

Iris innominata No Established Common Name

IRIS INNOMINATA Henderson
No Established Common Name

While an occasional common name such as *Golden Iris* has been suggested I have always heard this species discussed as *Iris innominata.* Perhaps the *Rainbow Iris* would be as good as any for it offers almost as many colors as that ephemeral ribbon arching in the sky.

Although it was discovered much later than almost all the other west coast Iris it has aroused more interest than all the others combined. Thirty or 40 years ago its rugged mountain home was accessible only by boat and a few rough trails. There were a few short roads along the less difficult coastal areas, mainly near the headlands but not into the loftier inland regions. Even today much of this remarkable land can be reached only by foot or nerve shattering one way roads. *I. innominata* lives away from the coastal fog belt in an area of cold winters and hot summers. Its isolation accounts for its late discovery.

History: John and Lilla Leach started down the Rogue River from the community of Galice in extreme southwestern Oregon on one of this remarkable couple's botanical expeditions. Their 125 mile two mule pack journey began on June 1, 1928. A sign read, "Gold Beach 93 miles" but as they did not follow the river all the way the distance was farther. On their fifth day, at Mule Creek, Lilla Leach discovered the first plants of *Iris innominata.* While Lilla may have been the first to see the plant she and John were not far apart and the honor of discovery really belongs to both. They have since found it in many colors over a large part of Curry County in the same corner of the state. It enters into many hybrid strains, usually with *I. douglasiana* where the two species overlap. It was in such an area about 15 miles up the Sixes River that I saw my first *I. innominatas* – half a dozen or so plants surrounded by thousands of *I. douglasiana* in an area where the former was not known to exist. It is probable that I was the first to find *I. innominata* at this station. This was 25 miles or so northwest of where John and Lilla made their first discovery. I think it quite likely that if I had continued further inland away from the diminishing coastal fog belt I would have found fewer and fewer *I. douglasiana* and more and more *I. innominata* and doubled the thrill of my solitary finds.

The history of this plant is as brief as the flowers are beautiful. First discovered on about June 5, 1928 it was named by Louis F. Henderson of the University of Oregon and first published in *Rhodora* in 1930. I do not know of any synonyms and none are needed. An attempt has been made, however, to separate the yellow forms from the purples, the former being referred to as *I. innominata* and the latter, *I. thompsonii.* This hair splitting has been generally discredited and all combined as *innominta.*

Description: From the slender rhizomes large numbers of evergreen leaves grow densely. They are from an eighth to three-sixteenths of an inch wide, up to more than 20 inches long, purplish at the base, deep green above and much paler beneath, with fine parallel grooves and ridges running the entire length, much more prominent above. The leaves very slowly taper to fine points. The older, outer leaves are the longest and they arch gracefully outward to allow the floral stems to display their endlessly varying charms. These stems are six to 12 inches tall, more or less erect or nodding outward, slender and terminate in one, or more often, two blossoms on pedicels from an eighth to a half inch long. The stem leaves are reduced to sheathing bracts two or three inches long and one-sixteenth to three-sixteenths of an inch wide. The floral bracts are broadly lanceolate or oblanceolate, that is three, four, or more times as long as the greatest width which is above or below the middle. They are an inch and a quarter to an inch and a half long and up to three-eighths of an inch wide. The capsules, half an inch in diameter and one and a half long, are full of seed but produced sparingly in my gardens. Dwarf forms are not uncommon and are often considerably less than half as large as ordinary ones except that the flowers of both are much the same size.

While the large numbers of graceful leaves have their appeal these plants are grown for the flowers which are large and come in a great variety of yellows, bronzes, purples and lavenders, some of which are astonishingly lovely.

Rarity: This must be considered a rare plant because of its restricted range. The best and the most sought for colors are more likely to be found in gardens where selections are made generation upon generation. Several *near* whites exist and they are rare but not considered ideal. Two pure whites have recently been discovered but are too new yet to be available for distribution. One was found in the wilds of southern Oregon and the second was produced by careful breeding in the gardens of Dr. Matthew Riddle, a Portland, Oregon Iris fancier whose work with this species is known world wide. These whites, of course, are extremely rare. A double flowering plant with many petals exists. This extremely rare specimen has not been divided. Various other high quality selections both in the wild and garden are very rare and difficult to acquire even from intimate friends. Seed of the *Dr. Riddle Strain* is in much demand.

Distribution: In Josephine County and a large part of Curry County in extreme southwestern Oregon with a lap over into northwestern California, usually in isolated or stations difficult of access, and not near the coast.

Propagation: Much the same as for *I. bracteata,* which see. Pollination is poor in my gardens but there has always been enough seed for my own use and to give to friends and even total strangers. Germination is good. Divisions grow well for me although others have reported just the opposite experience. But parent plants from which starts have been taken are very slow to recover if they do not have an abundance of room on all sides. Apparently they resent dividing under crowded conditions.

Culture: In mild climates full sun or light shade are equally satisfactory. Mine are planted on the north side of the garage in very light shade except during late summer afternoons when the sun strikes them for a few brief hours. Most any ordinary well drained soil will do but the preference is for an admixture of a little sand and humus. Alkaline conditions should be avoided. The leaf spread may be from two to two and a half feet under ideal conditions and allowance should be made to prevent crowding when the youngsters are planted.

My 13 plants were grown from seed I obtained from Dr. Riddle. When they came into flower my first thought was to weed out those with colors less than the best. But after examining all of them closely I changed my mind. I was too soft hearted and too soft headed to destroy any for each was different and all were beautiful. Some of the self sown seedlings from these original 13 were a bit inferior. Occasionally a few flowers will open in the middle of a plant – flowers that are very different from the rest of the clump. This means that a seed has dropped to the ground, germinated and produced an at home loving son or daughter. The contrast can be delightful if both parent and offspring have choice colors.

This species is known for the very prominent divided venation radiating from the bases and covering almost all the area of the falls. The veins have the same but deeper colors of the flowers. Yellow flowers have richer yellow veins, blue flowers more intense blue veins and so on. A more desirable form has either none or very faint veining. Clear, pure blues are very rare in our west coast Iris but *I. innominata* has an occasional specimen which comes closer to this ideal than in any other of our species I have seen. Pure, deep yellows of incredible clarity, amazingly profound bronzes, and the great array of bright colors that characterize this species account for its wide popularity.

Flowering Time: One of the special charms of *I. innominata* is its massive floral display at the height of the season. I have counted no less than 150 blossoms on a single plant at the same time – with a few unopened buds for a little lingering color. In my gardens from the middle of May to mid June. A little later, perhaps, at the higher elevations in its southern Oregon home.

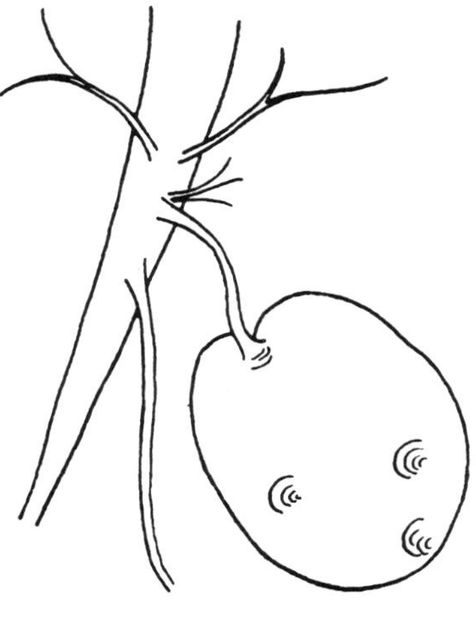

Tuber

Iris missouriensis Western Blue Flag

IRIS MISSOURIENSIS Nuttall
Western Blue Flag

It was on a trip to the western part of Central Oregon that I first saw this desert flag, *Iris missouriensis.* There was a very small clump in the damp soil at the edge of a shallow irrigation stream. To see this Iris – any Iris in that hot and arid land was something of a surprising experience. I do not know of any other species in this far flung genus that will tolerate such a harsh climate. There the winters are severe and the summer sun parches the land. My second encounter occurred some years later when I was returning from a five day study of *Lewisia rediviva* in the Bitter Root Valley of Montana. There were a few of the blue flowers in a wet gully between the great Columbia River and Ellensburg in south central Washington. There they were, blossoming gayly, surrounded on all sides by the unyielding desert. It was dry in late May and all other plants in the vicinity were through for the season.

The third time I met this new friend was on the desert plateau between Goldendale and Toppenish in Central Washington about 30 miles north of the Columbia River. There was a low wet spot – probably spring fed – covering a few acres. In the rich black soil the blue flowers painted a picture of colorful beauty in an otherwise drab landscape. I wandered all over the area, following the cattle trails, looking for that elusively rare specimen, the white *I. missouriensis.* Among the hundreds of plants I found a youngster with a single snowy blossom, and counted myself incredibly lucky. One might think that such a white flower among all the blues would stand out prominently but this is not true. I was only 15 or 20 feet from it before it attracted my eyes. I have had this same experience while hunting other alba mutations, such as *Campanula rotundifolia* and *Sisyrinchium grandiflorum,* where even closer approaches are necessary.

But my last field trip for this Iris was the most gratifying. Boyd Kline, a southern Oregon botanist and nurseryman, and I were heading for a *Talinum spinescens* station east of Ellensburg. He was driving and I was searching the landscape for another white *missouriensis.* Suddenly I let out a yell and Boyd stopped. "I think I see one," I cried, "but I may be wrong. It's over a hundred yards away and I don't think I could see one at that distance." Boyd took a look and he wasn't sure either but we located the rancher who owned the pasture and told him what we were after. He gave us an incredulous look and told us to help ourselves. Indeed he suggested we take them all. Cattle won't eat them but they ate everything else and made the flowers stand out boldly. Sure enough it was the rare alba – a large clump with many flowers. That is why we could spot the whiteness from the distant highway. We found nearly a dozen more of the mutations among the hundreds of blues but took only a few – hoping that the others would become the parents of still more of these albinos.

Undoubtedly others of these lonely sports may be found here and there among untold thousands of the type within its great range.

History: Thomas Nuttall, 1786-1859, named the species in 1834 in the *Journal of the Philadelphia Academy of Sciences,* presumably from specimens collected by Nathaniel Wyeth, the American traveler and trader, "Towards the sources of the Missouri," on his first transcontinental journey in 1832-1833. The two men were friends and Nuttall accompanied Wyeth on his second journey to the west in 1834. The specific name, *missouriensis,* was probably chosen in reference to the place where Wyeth took his specimens. A couple of other names, now synonymns, were offered by William Herbert in 1839, who also established the authoritative name, *Iris longipetala* in 1841. This latter species of the coastal region of central California closely resembles *I. missouriensis.*

Description: The stout, thick and tough rhizomes are covered with old leaf bases from which rise the new leaves four to 24 inches long, one-eighth to three-eighths of an inch wide, and gradually tapering to the tip. They are deciduous, green, and sometimes purplish near the base, turning gray or yellow-brown when dying. They grow pretty much stiffly erect and are shorter than, equalling, or a little longer than the flower stems which are from about eight to 24 inches tall. These floral stems are slender, almost round and naked or with one or two leaves, erect, with the flowers facing upwards or nearly so. Flowers are one to four to each stem but usually two, fairly numerous, large, with light blue falls heavily purple veined radiating from a central spot, often yellow elongated. The standards, lacking venation, are uniformly deeper blue. The albas are golden throated with little or no prominent veining. There is little color variation in a field and this is limited to the more delicate shades of blue. Purple or lavender forms do not seem to taint the clean blues in contrast with *I. tenax* and *I. douglasiana.* The capsules are one to two inches long, one-half to three-quarters of an inch in diameter and produce seed freely.

Rarity: The type, common. The whites, rare. Hundreds or thousands of plants may be examined before one of these lovely mutations is found.

Distribution: No other Iris of my acquaintance covers so large an area. Wet places, from moderately damp to oozy, during the flowering season, but often completely dry during the heat of summer. In hot, arid climates throughout the Great Basin, in the Rockies, North and South Dakota, Arizona, New Mexico, Montana, Idaho, Nevada, Utah, Colorado, Mexico, California, Oregon and Washington east of the Cascade Mountains. On Whidby Island in Washington's Puget Sound. This is a surprising occurrence for no other station is known in the wet climate west of the Cascades. But one of the junipers is also found on some of these islands where they aren't expected to flourish. From low elevations to 10,000 feet in Mexico. The albas will be found with the type. Besides the two stations mentioned above white forms are known in the vicinity of Sprague, Washington, about 35 miles southwest from Spokane.

Propagation: Much the same as for *I. bracteata.* Seed germinates easily.

Culture: This is an easy Iris to grow in the right climate. It requires more than average moisture during the flowering season followed by hot, dry weather so that it can get the rest it needs. As I cannot furnish these conditions in my wet and cool western Oregon gardens it does not do well for me. Foliage is good but the few flowers are of indifferent quality when they appear at all. It does better for me in pure leaf mold half a foot deep where it makes a vigorous growth. Full sun.

It is not generally well regarded although to me it has real charm in its blue garb and great beauty in the pure whites. A tall and stately species it has the real advantage of thriving happily where few others will even survive.

Flowering Time: May into July depending upon climate and altitude. In my gardens from the middle of May into the fore part of June.

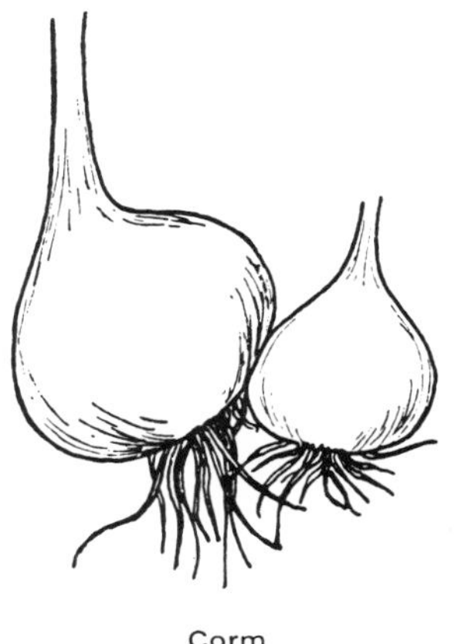

Corm

Iris setosa No Established Common Name

IRIS SETOSA Pallas
No Established Common Name

For many years I have been collecting the wild Iris of northwestern America and *I. setosa* was the last of these to reach my gardens. Its nearest location is in the vicinity of Ketchikan, Alaska, about a thousand miles north of my Portland, Oregon home. And so it was that I had to desert the highways and take to the air mails to acquire this one. I exchanged plants with one of my far northern neighbors and eventually received starts of the rare albino form of this lovely Iris. Seeds also came my way a little later. Now it is anchored firmly among my other native plants.

History: It was first described by Peter Simon Pallas, 1741-1811, from plants he found in Siberia. His account was published in 1820, nine years after his death. From 1822 to 1887 it has had no less than eight synonyms, three of which were generic. *Setosa* means full of bristles, from the bristle-like standards.

Description: From the thick rhizome covered with the fibrous remains of old leaves rise the new ones. They are numerous, sword-shaped, rich green, slightly powdery, usually tinged with purple at the base, from eight inches to two feet long and one-half to one inch wide. As might be expected from a plant which lives in such a cold climate the leaves are deciduous. Doubtless they could not survive otherwise.

The stout flowering stems are closely clustered, from one to two feet tall but regardless of their length they blossom above the foliage. They are deeply forked, bear several heads of flowers of which those on the lowest lateral branch rise as high as those on the main stem. The huge blossoms, up to four inches in diameter, appear pretty much in succession on pedicels from one to one and a half inches long.

The most outstanding characteristic of this Iris, which attracts the eye at once, is the very wide, heart-shaped prominently veined falls. They are quite variable in color, ranging from almost any light or dark shade of blue, lavender, purple, reddish purple or violet. The first one that flowered in my garden was the rare white – unbelievably beautiful and my greatest northland treasure.

Seeds are produced freely and soon become detached and rattle in the thin walled inflated capsules.

Rarity: The type, common within its range. The white, rare. The first recorded account of this white form came from northeastern Asia where it was found in 1909 – almost a hundred years after the species was published. A number of Alaskans have it in their gardens but these people are not dealers and starts are difficult to obtain. It is an oddity that *I. setosa,* which has been known for nearly a century and a half is so little known and so little appreciated.

Distribution: Northeastern Asia: Japan, Sakhalin, Kamchatka, and Siberia. In North America: Coastal Alaska from Nome to Ketchikan. It appears again on the east coast of Canada in Labrador, Newfoundland and south into Maine. It prefers marshlands and other moist places where it often spreads over many acres.

Propagation: Starts are easily obtained from divisions. Those sent me from Alaska arrived in summer after growth was well under way in their frigid homes. They did not seem to suffer from this treatment. Early spring, just as active growth is beginning and after the danger of unseasonal freezes is over, is probably the best time to make the divisions although they can be taken after the fall rains begin.

My first *I. setosa* seed did not germinate. It was obtained from a garden store and may have been several years old. I have since raised them easily from fresh seed planted as soon as it was ripe. The flats contained mostly humus and were shaded. Under ideal conditions they will flower the second season although more will appear the third.

Culture: Writers have told how easy this plant is to grow. That does not entirely agree with my experience or that of some of my Portland friends. In ordinary garden soils it barely holds its own and unless protected from slugs is often badly shredded. In a soil composed almost entirely of leaf mold, with a little sand to prevent compacting and to hold moisture, it has grown vigorously and flowered well. This remarkable Iris, unlike any other North American species, should have a great abundance of moisture during the growing and flowering time, good drainage and aeration, with partial shade to full sun in neutral or acid soils. The albino variety should have the same treatment as the type

Winter, in my mild climate, is not over before the new shoots peep out of the ground among the sad remnants of last season's dead leaves. They show only about a half inch of their tips until warm weather stimulates rapid growth.

This is a highly variable species and accounts for the various forms and varieties that are known among Iris fanciers. A dwarf seems to be quite popular as it blossoms very freely. Some of them are believed to have originated in Alaska and Labrador. Some of the tallest have come from Kamchatka. At least half a dozen forms are grown in gardens and each is obviously distinct but not sufficiently so to justify specific standing.

Opinions differ on the garden value of *I. setosa.* One authority considers it of little account. Another raves over it just as I do. My greatest objection to it is the special soil it needs to thrive in my climate. Certainly it is a gorgeous creature and as it becomes better known it should earn the greater popularity it deserves. Alaskans have suggested adopting it as their floral emblem.

Flowering Time: May in my Portland gardens.

Iris tenax Tough Leaved Iris

IRIS TENAX Douglas
Tough Leaved Iris

The most common Iris on America's west coast and one of the least appreciated is the so-called Oregon Iris, *Iris tenax.* While it may be more abundant in this state it is by no means confined to it. This was the first of the species I became acquainted with when I was a small boy. It grew in the meadows, brush lands and alongside roads on what was then the outskirts of my Portland home. These areas are all gone now, having been replaced with houses and commercial buildings. It isn't necessary to go much out of the city to find them today. As a child we knew them as "flags" – a term so common that it is given in Webster's Dictionary as being used in both Europe and America. Charles the Fifth, sometimes referred to as Charles the Wise, King of France from 1364 to 1380, was so impressed with the Irises that he chose them as the royal emblem of France, the *fleur de-lis.*

When I grew up – physically and, I hope, botanically, this Iris intrigued me and it still does. I have wandered over much of its range, looking for exceptional color forms. Unlike *I. douglasiana* which is likely to display all shades within a colony *I. tenax* generally varies with the locality. Those near Larch Mountain, 20 some odd miles east of Portland, have light colors. At the northern Oregon beaches, often within splashing distance of the ocean, medium pastel lavenders on flowers fully a fourth larger than those inland dominate the open meadows. There is some doubt if these huge blossoms would retain their size and gentle colors if brought away from the sea for in this climate almost all flowers are larger, more vivid and more strikingly beautiful than the same species elsewhere. Towards southern Oregon the deepest and best colors tend to dominate the scene and enrich the picture. Some 80 miles south of Portland I found a plant with such intense violet blossoms in so great profusion which appear over so long a period of time on ideally medium length stems that I named it the "Wiley" variety and have distributed it both in America and the British Isles. About 80 miles north of the California border in the Coquille River Valley between Roseburg and the small town of Coquille all color forms imaginable in the purple-blue-lavender shades occur. This is the only location within my knowledge where all such variations are to be found growing happily together.

I am particularly pleased that this Iris was my introduction to the genus for its endless variations are a constant challenge to find forms better than those I already possess. During its flowering season whenever I am out driving I constantly search the roadsides, hills and meadows for new floral treasures. The only two whites I have ever found I blundered upon merely by chance. One of them was within a 100 yards of my home. I checked the petals carefully and there is no doubt that they were true whites but they acquired a faint purplish cast in my gardens. Other writers have expressed doubt whether wild specimens will retain their colors when moved into cultivation.

History: David Douglas has many plants, including the splendid genus *Douglasia* of the Primrose Family, named for him. But the only one he named, so far as I know, is this Iris. He discovered it in 1825 near Fort Vancouver which is at the confluence of the Willamette River with the Columbia. Indeed, it is difficult to see how he could have missed it for it was very abundant in this area. This was during his first expedition to the west coast between the years 1824-1827. His description of the find was published in 1829 in the Botanical Register under the editorship of John Lindley, 1799-1865. *Ioniris tenax* was offered in 1872 by the German botanist Friedrich Wilhelm Klatt, 1825-1897. This is a particularly appropriate choice for *Ioniris* means *violet Iris* and refers to the typical colors of the flowers. But Douglas' original name remains official. *Tenax* means tenacious or strong. The Indians made ropes from the leaf fibers. These ropes took a great deal of care and work to manufacture with the crude methods they knew and were, consequently, valued highly. David Douglas wrote, "The snare is used in taking elk, and long, and black tailed deer, and in point of strength it will hold the strongest bullock and is not thicker than the little finger."

Description: It is one of the wire-rooted species with slender rhizomes. As the plants become mature they spread out from the center in dense clumps, leaving the middle open. This may be due to the exhaustion of food as the younger plants do not exhibit this tendency and in older ones in my gardens where the soil is rich the centers grow as densely as the outer portions of the root system. The numerous, basal grass-like, semi-perennial leaves are from a foot to twice as long, up to a quarter of an inch wide, and gradually taper to a slender point. They are conspicuously finely parallel veined. The youngest are more or less erect, the older arch gracefully outward to allow the numerous blossoms to show themselves. The slender flowering stems, shorter than the leaves, are up to 20 inches tall with the average a foot to a foot and a half, depending upon individual plants and also shade, where they are taller. They are erect or somewhat turned outward but much less so than the leaves. The stems bear several leaves which sometimes are short and bract-like. They are narrower than the basal ones, varying from one sixteenth to three sixteenths of an inch in width and from two to 16 inches long with an average of perhaps four to six inches. Each stem bears one, or more often two, flowers on pedicels one-half to one inch long. The upper blossom opens first followed soon after by the second. They are three or more inches in diameter and range all the way from the albas through very light, and sometimes weak, lavenders, purples, reddish wines and near blues to intense violets. There are lemon yellows too but few people have ever seen these. The lavender forms have a white spot touched with gold in the middle from which purple veins radiate. The albas have no such white splash, it being replaced with a lemon yellow from which radiate darker yellow outspreading veining – very delicate and very beautiful. The one to one and a half inch long capsules produce an abundance of seed.

Rarity: The lavender type, common; selected forms of the lavenders, scarce to rare depending upon quality; reddish wines, scarce; white, extremely rare; yellows, extremely rare.

Distribution: From southern British Columbia, Canada, through Washington, Oregon to the vicinity of Cape Mendocino, California about 110 miles south of the Oregon border. This covers about ten degrees of latitude, roughly between the 40th and 50th parallels. It is confined to the Humid Transition Life Zone, from sea level up to at least 3,600 feet, from the western slopes of the Cascade Mountains to within ten feet of the high tides of the Pacific Ocean. I have never seen it east of the Cascade Divide for it will not endure that very dry climate. The alba forms are not as likely to be found towards southern Oregon where the colors are much darker than in the northern part of the state or in Washington. Reddish-wine shades may be growing most anywhere in the general range but good ones are difficult to find. An unusually good specimen completely lost its exceptional color when I planted it in my gardens. It became a very good lavender. I have never heard of a true red and doubt if it exists. Albas and yellows are known in the Vernonia-St. Helens area about 30 miles northwest of Portland as well as on Monument Peak, a logged off 4,683 foot mountain about 40 miles southeast of Salem, Oregon's capitol city. It is such a common Iris that it seems futile to mention the various places where it has been reported. Generally it is more abundant in Washington and northern Oregon than anywhere else within its narrow, elongated range.

Propagation: Same as for *Iris bracteata. I. tenax* in its natural habitat or in the garden, if associated with other species, hybridizes readily. Some of the progeny are so strikingly beautiful that they have been given horticultural names. The present search is for that dreamed of phantom, a true red.

Culture: I was fortunate enough to have been given a rich lemon yellow flowering plant. Unlike those of *I. gormanii,* it holds its color with age – a delightful and rare quality.

William R. Dykes in his massive and authoritative monograph, *The Genus Iris* said, "This Iris deserves to be far better known and much more widely cultivated than appears to be the case." The British were quicker than the Americans to recognize the value of Douglas' 1825 discovery. Whenever he could find a ship in the Columbia River he would send his specimens back home. These must have been almost entirely seeds in those days of slow sailing ships. At any rate, it was only a year later, in 1826, when it was introduced into England where it still enjoys a well merited popularity. The horticulturists in this island empire are on the lookout for better color forms and I have had a number of letters from across the seas requesting superior deep violet selections.

Some of the literature on this species emphasizes dry soils. This opinion is somewhat misleading. It will not tolerate wet places. I have never seen it growing with camas which enjoys a great deal of water. There is a plant with foliage amazingly like that of *I. tenax* and it has deceived me many times until I learned that it always grows in very damp spots. Now, whenever I see this plant—whatever it is—in a wet place I do not give it more than a glance for I know it cannot be *I. tenax*. I have often found the lavender flowers along roadside ditches. But they are on the sides or at the top of the ditches, never on the bottoms which are much too oozy most of the year for the Tough Leaved Iris. But this Iris does not have to have dry soils. Any reasonably well drained one, even if damp will do nicely if it is not strongly alkaline.

At the northern beaches it grows in such a rich laden humusy soil that I brought home more than a ton of it for my gardens. I have found some of my very best plants in a clay that was so sticky and impervious that I do not see how anything could live in it. One of my unconverted beds consists of material dug out of the basement. Nothing is more worthless and yet *I. tenax* does very well in it. In a medium of one-quarter sand and three quarters humus beach soil that I brought home especially for my Iris it grows twice as fast as in any other ground I have. This is the ideal medium and it pays startling dividends.

I am convinced that the acidity of the soil has much to do with the intensity of colors of this Iris. The "Wiley" variety, mentioned earlier in this article retained its marvelous deep violet in the original heavy clay in which I found it. But divisions of the same plant, in the humusy material from the beach country, lost a noticeable amount of the very dark shade that accounted for much of its value. In the same leaf mold soil all my reddish tones became lavenders. Soil tests showed the clay had a pH of 6.6 and the humus was 6.1. Neutral soil is pH 7 and higher numbers such as 8 and 9 are alkaline. Lower ones, for instance 4, 5 and 6 are acid. The indications are that Iris tenax in neutral or slightly acid soils will have darker colors than in growth mediums more pronouncedly acid. Crushed egg shells worked in around the roots will slowly disintegrate, help neutralize the soil, and improve the colors without endangering the plants. Horticultural lime will produce faster results but should be used with caution. If too much is added the earth may become fatally alkaline.

In its native habitat it will do equally well in full sun or very light shade. In moderate shade it does not flower so profusely and tends to grow too leggy for maximum appeal. In deep shade it will not spread much and may have few or no flowers. At Ukiah, California, about 25 miles inland and 190 miles below the Oregon border and 80 miles south of its Cape Mendocino limits, a nurseryman has described it as three inches high. The heat and drought of this area accounts for its miniaturization and probably represents its southernmost cultural tolerance.

It is a moderately hardy species, does well throughout the British Islands and in those parts of our country where the extremes of weather are not too severe. Of the wire-rooted species it is one of the easiest to grow.

It is not unusual for a mature plant under agreeable cultural conditions to open a shower of gorgeous blossoms numbering as many as five dozen with many more buds promising continuing garden delights. Mixed with the albinos and yellows of *gormanii.* is a sight for wondering eyes and mute tongues.

I have several dozen carefully chosen specimens of varying colors, tone and hues. They are in ordinary beds; under dwarf fruit and ornamental trees; at the edge of and surrounding a large rock garden; and in pots. It is my earnest hope that these floral treasures of this world will accompany me into the glories of the next.

Flowering Time: Two to five weeks earlier than its first cousin, *I. gormanii.* There is a radical variation of flowering time from season to season, wholly unpredictable within the limits of my knowledge. Once in many years they may begin to unfold their petals in late February. Occasionally the first blossom comes in early May. A more or less typical season, as recorded in my notes: First flower, April 6th, last June 14th, thus covering about two months. A long time for spring flowers and a wholly delightful one.

Rootstock

Iris tenuis Clackamas Iris

IRIS TENUIS Watson
Clackamas Iris

Forty miles west of Portland, Oregon, is the home of Oregon's rarest Iris, *gormanii.* Thirty miles southeast of the same city where I live is our second rarest species, *I. tenuis.* Fortunate indeed am I to live midway between these two very different but very beautiful three-petaled flowers.

It was on a picnic more than a quarter of a century ago that I first saw this shy forest beauty on the banks of the upper Clackamas River at the confluence with its North Fork. I knew it was in that vicinity but finding it was another problem for it was out of flower. Finally I found a tuft of two or three short broad leaves under the deep shade of some native shrubs and I thought my problem was solved. I dug down into the broken rock to be sure to get all the roots but, to my amazement, it had virtually no roots. There was a slender rootstock wandering among the egg size stones which contained only enough humus to barely sustain life. I carefully followed the fish line root for over three feet before it sent down a weak feeder. There was no balling this plant so I coiled the root around my fingers like a piece of grocer's twine and packed the works in damp moss. After a frustrating search that took most of the morning I located three or four more specimens with the same frail structure—and was fully prepared for transplanting failure. I had been warned that this was an exceedingly difficult species to establish in the garden. I tucked it into a bed of leaf mold on the east side of the garage and lo, it quickly sent down a heavy mass of roots as though it had been waiting all its life for such a luxurious home! And in all the intervening years I have never had the slightest difficulty with this rare little Iris.

It was merely by chance that it was growing where I first found it for it does not like such conditions even though it will somehow survive in them. I have more often than not found it under the deep shade of alders, willows and firs where the soil is damp, but well drained during the greater part of the year. I have encountered it along the edges of dirt roads where it was able to withstand running over by campers' cars; on top of rotten fir logs covered with moss, trailing along with roots an inch or so under forest humus. But it is in full sun in rocky ground or in very sandy loam that it is at its best, sending down heavy masses of roots and lifting its arching green leaves and creamy flowers into the mountain skies. In deep somber shade it is understandably a little sullen and does not blossom at all.

Twenty some years ago I gave a small start of this Iris to a nurseryman friend of mine – and promptly forgot all about it for I make many such gifts. I was a bit surprised when I found out, not long ago, that he had nursed this little clump along until he had increased it enough to have a commercial supply. He has shipped it to various parts of the United States and Canada as well as to England, France, Sweden, New Zealand and Australia. This gives some conception of the wide appeal of this dainty little Oregonian.

History: Louis F. Henderson of the University of Oregon first discovered it in 1881 about 30 miles from Portland near the Eagle Creek branch of the Clackamas River, growing in broad mats in the fir forests. The next year, 1882, Sereno Watson, 1826-1892, named and described the plant. *Tenuis* means *slender, thin* and is descriptive of rhizomes, stems, bracts and leaves. Apparently this appropriate name has never been challenged for I have not been able to find any synonyms.

Description: From the long and slender rhizomes with swollen nodes rise the deciduous, soft and thin, light green conspicuously veined leaves. They are from four to 15 inches long, averaging about six, and from one-fourth to three-fourths of an inch wide with the broadest part near the middle, and long and gradually tapered to a sharp apex. These basal leaves vary greatly. I found one plant growing on a rocky bank in full sun with such wide leaves that at first I thought it was a Japanese Iris that had somehow escaped from a distant garden. Some of them arch sideways – a graceful pose I have yet to see in any other wild member of the genus.

The flowering stems are four to 12 inches tall, very slender, bearing two or three thin soft, bract-like leaves two or three inches long. The floral bracts are near or distant and one to two inches long. The one, two, or often three flowers are on slender pedicels equalling or exceeding the bracts. *Iris tenuis* is at once distinguished from all other western American Irises by its deeply forked stems.

The flowers are creamy white with deep, rich, lemon yellow throats from which radiate short yellow, brown or purplish veins. The creamy standards are a faint and delicate purple at their bases. The flowers are small but in delightful proportion to the foliage. I have yet to see another wild Iris in which both blossoms and leaves so completely belong to each other. The flowers are all much alike in size, shape, and color. The nearly spherical capsules, depressed on top, are small, and about half an inch in diameter.

Rarity: Very rare. There is a real chance that a yellow form of this creamy white flower exists and I have looked for it, so far in vain. If it is ever found the lucky person will possess one of the rarest plants in North America.

Distribution: Limited to Oregon at the headwaters of the Molalla and Clackamas Rivers and their tributaries in the foothills of the western slopes of the Cascade Mountains where it shares adjacent watersheds. On the Clackamas River it is found both below and above the small town of Estacada. One may travel miles without seeing any, only to come across a vagrant plant here or there. Or small colonies may be encountered. I have never seen it in abundance at any one place although I have been told that at least one such patch exists.

It is something of a puzzle to me why these flowers have not drifted down both the Molalla and Clackamas Rivers into the Willamette and thence into the Columbia and established colonies all the way. I have found plants on the Clackamas where high water could wash them out and both soil and climate throughout the many miles of these rivers are much the same. And yet this has not happened.

Propagation: Seed germinates easily but pollination is often uncertain and poor. Only a few capsules appear each year in the 16 square foot bed in my gardens devoted entirely to this species. Divisions are readily adapted to new surroundings. I have yet to have a failure from this method.

Culture: Contrary to the conditions in which it is often found in the wild, and some popular accounts, this plant does not thrive in deep shade where few or no flowers are produced. In my mild climate it is at its best in either very light shade or full sun. The rootstocks creep along with good speed so that a tiny clump, in a few years, will make a sizeable bed. It isn't too fussy about soil conditions as long as drainage is good in a neutral or acid medium. But it will make its best and richest growth in a mixture of humus and sand. The only fault it has – if it can be called a fault – is that the rhizomes make such a compact growth that weeding out such pests as Johnson or quack grass is very difficult. I thin out the bed every two or three years for the crowded rhizomes will send out too much foliage at the expense of flowering if ample room is lacking. The surplus plants go into other parts of the garden and to friends and strangers who, once they have seen it in my gardens, are enchanted and simply must have it in their own. It will do well in the rock garden but does not make the close growth as in humus-rich garden soils. In my home I have not seen it send out long, slender, horizontal rootstocks searching for an opportunity to send down feeders in a more agreeable location. It doesn't have to, while in nature, often, there is no other choice. I have only rarely seen a wild plant which was anywhere nearly as floriferous as those in the garden. And those few were living in conditions much like those in their adopted homes.

Flowering Time: Throughout May in my gardens. This is generally a low altitude species but at higher elevations nearer the headwaters of the Molalla, and especially the Clackamas Rivers, blossoming extends into June.

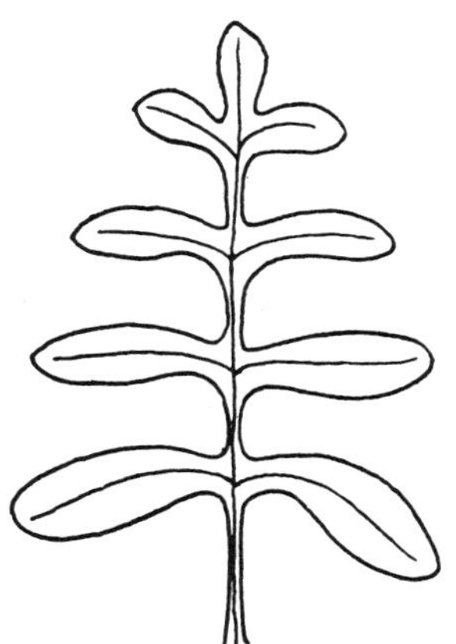

Divided margin

Kalmiopsis leachiana

KALMIOPSIS LEACHIANA (Henderson) Rehder
Kalmiopsis

History: John and Lilla Leach have spent many of their summer vacations in the mountains of southern Oregon where they have traveled over more than 1,000 miles of trails. The Leach's have established an excellent local reputation as druggists. But on the 14th of June, 1930 an event occurred that will make them remembered in the world of botany long after their pharmaceutical activities have been forgotten.

On these expeditions Lilla always traveled in the lead and looked for flowers while her husband kept an eye on the pack animals. On that day they were on a trail in the extreme southwestern part of Oregon when "Lilla suddenly hesitated, gazed at a red patch of flowers ahead and then almost ran to it. She got down on her knees, examining them and exclaimed, 'I have never seen anything like it before! Isn't it beautiful? I believe it is new.' Here she had found a new genus, –. The patch was so small that lest some one might destroy it, we never revealed the location until we had found more and larger patches.

"On May the first the following year (1931), we were going up a long trail of Horse Sign Butte. Here again she saw a rose red patch on the hillside. The trail was steep and the switch backs had to be made, so it was a more deliberate approach, but Lilla experienced the same joy. This time she strongly suspected that it was her best flower "find" in a new location. There were many more plants here; yet within four or five years thoughtless growers have practically dug up and carried away this entire patch of *Kalmiopsis leachiana.*

"We made camp at Miner's Cabin, an old deserted log house where we left our horses feeding in mid-afternoon, and started without wraps or food to botanize the nearby territory. We wandered down the zig-zag trail to Collier's Bar, a distance of nearly five miles, with a loss of 3,000 feet altitude. Here again, growing at about 500 feet elevation, we found Kalmiopsis.

"The next year, June 12, 1932, we found Kalmiopsis in another location, this time on the Big Craggy Mountain at 5,000 feet elevation, a place where very few people have ever been. It is so inaccessible and brushy that six miles in 15 hours is the best we could do, and we came back feeling as though we had been to Hell's Canyon." This account of the discovery of *Kalmiopsis* is taken from an article by John and Lilla Leach, published in the Mazama magazine.

On the nineteenth of June, 1938 the Leach's accompanied by Mr. L. L. Colville, assistant forest supervisor at Grants Pass, and Ed Marshall, ranger at Gold Beach, went to the Big Craggy area to study the country where the flower grows. Although the section they visited is only 35 miles from Grants Pass the party had to make a four day trip by way of Gold Beach to reach their destination. Even today this is no Sunday afternoon excursion.

In an effort to stop vandalism the government quickly closed the area to all human travel under the act "For the preservation of rare and vanishing species."

Forty-five days after their journey the disasterous Chetco fire swept over the entire 200 acre patch and left it in blackened desolation. Some species of plants will spring up from the roots even after such a holocaust.

While it is true that Lilla Leach discovered this plant her husband, John, was only a few seconds behind and both share this unique find.

I very well remember the excitement the Leach's introduction caused. It was reported in the local press. Botanists, expert gardeners, and ordinary sidewalk superintendent citizens were trying to learn more about this astonishing flower. The Leach's were unable to transplant it from the wild but their cuttings rooted. A group of frantic nurserymen got together and underwrote the cost of an expedition to the remote station and engaged Max Ruff to make the journey. Mr. Ruff, who was born on September 9, 1883, was a very expert plant propagator, and was an ideal choice for such a venture.

Kalmiopsis was his favorite flower and he first became interested in it when he saw a plant at the Leach gardens in Portland. Mrs. Leach drew a map for him and he thought there would be little trouble finding them – he had had a lot of alpine experience in his native Switzerland.

He found the place all right – it was on Horse Sign Butte in Curry County. But he couldn't find any of the plants – collectors had cleaned them out completely. He was astonished at such vandalism and couldn't understand how such a thing could happen. His intention was to take cuttings only which wouldn't hurt the plants as deer browse on them without damaging them. Mrs. Leach had told him of another place where they grew so he headed for Collier's Bar.

This called for more walking. He had a horse to carry his equipment; but the nag was more trouble than it was worth. Back he went over the ground he had already covered, following a blazed trail. There was another trail blazed from this one and he had trouble locating it. This last one led down to Collier's Bar. It took him four days to find it. On the fifth day he arrived at the patch after having climbed up to 4,000 feet at Horse Sign Butte and back down again. But the work was well worth the trouble. There were about two acres of *Kalmiopsis* growing in dense clumps with only an occasional evergreen tree here and there.

Having a permit to collect he took 4,000 cuttings, packed them in wet moss and gunny sacks and came home. He had told his wife he would be back in not more than four days and she was worried until he returned after having been gone seven. It was a remarkable trip at that for he covered 140 miles – all on foot. The round trip would have required about 76 miles of walking if he had found them at the first place. Such an ordeal is no longer necessary for trails have been built but the Forest Service no longer permits them to be collected.

Mr. Ruff's most remarkable achievement with wild flowers was undoubtedly his discovery on that trip of a single *Kalmiopsis* plant that was three and a half feet tall and of an equal branch spread. The flowers were a true pink and a little larger than the average. He didn't know it then as it was in August and the blossoms were long since gone. But he recognized the unusual size of the plant as very distinctive. It was growing on a steep hillside against a small pine tree surrounded by a little salal. He took about 200 cuttings and it was fortunate that he did, for when he returned the following year it was gone. A slide had destroyed it. A big boulder had rolled over it, pushed over the small pine tree, skinned off the bark, and came to rest a few feet down hill. Mr. Ruff's starts from this parent shrub were the only ones left in the world.

Contrary to common public opinion Mr. and Mrs. Leach did not discover the *Kalmiopsis.* A mail carrier making his deliveries up the Umpqua River was acquainted with the plant before the Leach's located it in the southwestern part of Oregon. But the postman didn't do anything with his extraordinary information and it was only after the Leach's publicized their find that the stations on the Umpqua, some 50 miles inland from Roseburg, were independently announced. Marcel LePiniec, a Medford, Oregon nurseryman, accompanied by Warren Wilson and Floyd McMullen, 'rediscovered' it there in June, 1955.

Ordinary gardeners, horticulturists and even the botanists were puzzled over the find. No one was quite sure what it was at first, although it was obvious enough that it was a new member of the old and well known Heath Family, *Ericaceae,* comprising about 55 genera and more than 1,100 species distributed over most of the world. This family, as well as a surprising number of others, was authored by Bentham and Hooker.

Dr. Louis F. Henderson of the University of Oregon, born in 1853, was in his late seventies, when he decided it was a *Rhododendron* and named it *R. leachianum* in 1931. The following year, 1932, Alfred Rehder of Harvard University's Arnold Arboretum, established the new genus *Kalmiopsis* and added the wholly appropriate specific designation, *leachiana.* Although one other was suggested in 1943, *Rhodothamnus leachianus,* Rehder's is now accepted as official. It is the only known species, having the genus all to itself. It is closely related to the *Kalmias* named for one of Linnaeus' pupils, Peter Kalm, who traveled in America. *Kalmiopsis* is a Greek name, meaning *Kalmia-like.*

According to Dr. Rehder the *Kalmiopsis* is a throwback from plants which grew during the tertiary period of geologic history.

Description: It grows from six to 12 inches high although it may reach 18 inches where a little shade and moisture are favorable. The three and a half foot specimen discovered by Max Ruff must be considered pretty much as an isolated giant.

The low shrub is freely branched from the base and the twigs are clothed with very fine short hairs. The numerous leaves are thick, dark glossy green, smooth on the upper surface, and densely glandular dotted beneath. This dotting effect requires a lens to be seen easily. The lateral veins are indistinct and the margins are entire. They are alternate, three-eighths to three-quarters of an inch long, and vary from two or three times as long as wide and the sides with a uniform curvature nearly throughout, to egg shaped with the widest part of the leaf above the middle. The leaf stems, petioles, are less than an eighth of an inch long. For its foliage alone it would make a choice addition to our homes. Many a lesser plant, grown only for its green leaves, has genuine horticultural value. But it was the flowers that attracted Lilla Leach when she first saw it and its gorgeous floral display accounts for its very great appeal. The blossoms are on slender stems from three-eighths to three-quarters of an inch long with the former measurement predominating. They grow in terminal, erect clusters of from five to ten flowers with the lowest flowers opening first. They arise from the axils of thin, membrane-like bracts. The buds for the following season are light green and very prominent in autumn.

The wide open, bell shaped blossoms have five spreading lobes, one-half to as much as one inch in diameter. They range from light, delicate pinks to deep rose and the remarkably variable tones and shades have resulted in color selections that have been given horticultural names.

The five celled depressed spherical capsule contains numerous tiny seeds – so small that, like the *Rhododendrons* and other closely related plants, they are difficult to germinate and grow into flowering plants.

Rarity: Extremely rare.

Distribution: From 500 to about 5,000 feet altitude in the mountains of Curry County in extreme southwestern Oregon where it often grows on top of barren boulders, some of which are six or seven feet high, with their roots clinging in the tiny cracks and crevices. They exist in almost no soil and very little moisture. This was the area where the Leach's made their discoveries which were confined to five patches, one of which was burned. All are within the Siskiyou National Forest within a radius of a comparatively few miles. The burned station covered 200 acres, the remaining four are limited to a thousand.

The "new" Umpqua colonies – three are known – are about 50 miles northeast of Roseburg in northeastern Douglas County on the Upper North Umpqua River. This is the much sought for dwarf form, known as the 'Umpqua' or 'LePiniec' variety.

Propagation: Three methods are used, none entirely satisfactory. Along the Umpqua River the plants hang in festoons over the banks. They are simply cut off in sections, making sure that there are roots for each piece, then potted up in a fertile well-drained soil. Sooner or later this system will have to be abandoned, either from depletion of natural stock or by law. However, it is the easiest and most successful.

Hardwood cuttings should be taken in September, with the butt ends dipped in a root growth medium and placed in flats in the greenhouse with bottom heat. The rooting mixture should be three parts glacier sand and one part finely ground peat. They should be rooted by spring. Two years later the first flower buds should appear if all goes well – and there is quite an "if" involved. About 50 percent should root, which isn't bad at all for this particular plant.

The most difficult method is by seed and this is for the expert grower. They should be started in pots with a fertile, well drained soil. If the seeds are covered they will be killed. Simply sprinkle on the surface which should be covered with a very fine layer of coal dust or granite. This is to keep down the moss. Two years may be necessary for germination. When the plants come up the novice may mistake them for some peculiar moss. They are so tiny, virtually microscopic, that they resemble the fuzz on a peach and there may be hundreds in a five inch pot. If moss has a chance to intermingle the youngsters may perish. They should be started indoors, in a greenhouse preferably, and the surface must be kept constantly moist. A cover glass may help but air circulation is necessary to prevent the molds, fungus and other pests from killing the tender crop. If all goes well you may have flowers in four to six years. But only a small fraction of those that sprouted will come to maturity. Much the same methods for growing *Rhododendrons* from seed apply to *Kalmiopsis.*

Culture: Not long after Max Ruff returned from his cutting collecting expedition in the Siskiyous I visited him. He had a great many hundreds of plants in good health and flowering in nursery rows in his lath houses. It was a magnificent sight – one that I never expect to see again. There was an initial wild enthusiasm for these plants and Mr. Ruff was doing his best to supply the demand. But it was only a few years later that the demand dropped sharply. Growing the "Rock Rhododendrons" like the true *Rhododendrons, Kalmias* and *azaleas,* should have been easy. But when ordinary gardeners, and experts too, discovered that their precious plants didn't live long, interest lagged. Today I know of only two growers, and very few retail nurseries bother with them because their losses are too great. Furthermore customers come back and complain that their plants do not live. Being strictly rock plants in the wild one would naturally expect them to live and be happy in home rockeries. It just does not work that way.

I have little doubt if one could start them from seeds in chinks and cracks in rocks they would thrive just as beautifully as they do under the austere conditions in their native homes. But getting such tiny seeds to germinate and produce full size shrubs under these circumstances is nearly impossible. Nature does it by sacrificing thousands upon thousands of seeds to get just one plant. Rooted plants, even if very well rooted, have great difficulty surviving a single season in such an environment. The problem – or one of them at any rate – is to get enough root development to supply the food and moisture the leaves must have to survive in a rock garden which has little of either.

I discussed this mortality problem with John Leach. Besides being one of the co-discoverers he is also an expert gardener. He told me one year he had nine healthy plants. The next season all died but one.

I had a lovely specimen growing in a small planter in a humus soil mixed with a little fine crushed lava. It was on the east side of the house where it had morning sun and light afternoon shade – ideal conditions. It grew and flowered well but the newspaper boy was no Babe Ruth and his faulty aim did so much damage to this distinguished member of my family that I moved it to a semi-shaded spot in one of my rock gardens. Even with tender, watchful care it lasted only a year. I had two others in some extra space between a couple of medium sized *Rhododendrons.* They were in common soil undistinguished from the earth in hundreds of other home grounds. They were in perfect health for a couple of years. But I decided they might be even more contented in the rockery. I moved them and one died the following season. The other survived for two years. I now have one which I planted in a hole two and a half inches in diameter and three feet deep that I drilled in very porous lava rock. I used half humus and half crushed porous lava for the growing medium and it has light shade. The first season half of the top perished and I thought it was a goner. Three years later it had recovered all the loss and was a little larger than when I received it.

I had a long talk with one of the two commercial growers and his advice was "plant it in potato soil." His were in such earth mixed with thoroughly rotted sawdust for moisture retention and drainage. His advice was probably as good as any. Regardless of cultural conditions, however, these extremely beautiful miniatures will thrive for varying lengths of time, then – for reasons that no one understands – they will perish. It may be that they depend upon a bacteria of some kind for their roots and if some of the soil from the wild plants could be added to the growth medium of those in the garden they would live and be happy indefinitely. This bacterial hypothesis is true of some other plants. But in this instance it is only a guess – good or bad, right or wrong, I won't know unless I get some of the original earth.

There is one thing about these frustrating, puzzling, joyful and challenging Rock Rhododendrons that I do know. If it has lustrous, rich green foliage and gloriously beautiful pink blossoms do not tempt the Gods. Leave it alone.

Flowering Time: Sometimes as early as April. Normally in May and June – especially the latter month at the higher altitudes.

THE LEWISIAS Pursh

Lewisia rediviva is widely known as the *Bitter Root.* With this one exception the *Lewisias* do not have established common names. It is true that some botanical writers have offered various terms intended for use by laymen but gardeners and horticulturists have paid little attention to them. This is one of the few genera of plants that ordinary people refer to by their scientific names.

History: Few people, outside of the world of botany, have ever heard of George Bentham, 1800-1884, or Joseph Dalton Hooker, 1817-1911. But it was these two men who named the Purslane Family, *Portulacaceae* – although originally spelled slightly differently. This group of about 20 genera and 220 species contains some of the most beautiful rock garden plants in the world.

Among the best of these are the *Lewisias,* rock dwellers, a genus of American plants found only from the Rockies to within sight of the Pacific Ocean. Every school boy knows of the exploratory expedition led by Meriwether Lewis, 1774-1809, and William Clark, 1770-1838, to the west coast of America during the years 1804, 1805 and 1806. But their lives have been even more indelibly written in the field of botany. Many plants have been named for these explorers including two genera. One of these, Frederick Pursh, in his *Flora Americae Septentrionalis* published in 1814, honored Meriwether Lewis. It was from the rare white form of *L. rediviva* in the expedition's herbarium collection that Pursh named the genus and the first species discovered.

These plants, so similar in basic structure and so widely different, to the wild flower lover, are still in a state of wild confusion among botanists. They have been placed in at least six different genera but the one predominantly accepted today was that originally given by Pursh. More than three dozen species have been described but many of these are synonyms. The first *Lewisia* was described in 1814, the last in 1954 – a span of 140 years. Others are specific names that have been given hybrids by propagators with more zeal than scientific knowledge. Such plants are horticultural clones. About 18 or 20 true species exist.

Description: All are perennials. Several are deciduous. In garden value they range from small, inconspicuous creatures of little interest to the most gorgeously beautiful earth huggers any wild flower lover could imagine. The first blossom of *L. tweedyi* I ever saw, in the Wenatchee Mountains, made me gasp, actually and literally. And I have been gasping ever since.

Distribution: Limited to western North America.

Culture: Those who want to grow *Lewisias* would be wise to serve their apprenticeships on easier rock dwellers. None are easy to grow. None of them like crowding. All are for the expert gardner although in some of the drier climates they present fewer problems than in my wet Portland, Oregon, home.

Evergreen species should be moved in spring or early summer. The deciduous ones which produce fall growth should be transplanted in fall as soon as the rains start but before the ground freezes.

Success can be achieved with all of them by giving the most careful attention to their detailed and somewhat varying requirements. My "know it all" attitude when I first started with them resulted in heavy losses of some of my choicest specimens obtained at the cost of a good deal of travel, expense, and hard work. Now that I know less I am more successful.

Which of the *Lewisias* is the most beautiful? The following list of the better known species, exclusive of hybrids, mutations and varieties, is based upon their garden values, actual and potential, considering both flowers and foliage. It has nothing to do with their rarity or cultural difficulties. None are perfect. All are beautiful:

1. Rediviva *(Best)*
2. Tweedyi
3. Cotyledon
4. Rupicola
5. Leana
6. Brachycalyx
7. Oppositifolia
8. Columbiana
9. Cantelovii
10. Nevadensis *(Least desirable)*

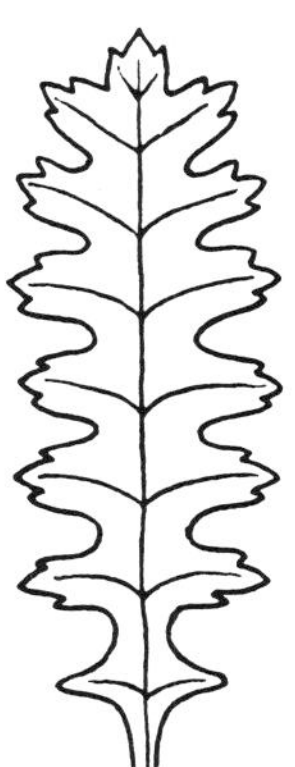

Laciniate margin

Lewisia brachycalyx No Established Common Name

LEWISIA BRACHYCALYX Engelmann
No Established Common Name

The first time I saw the white blossoms of this rare flower was in a southern Oregon garden. Two blossoms were peeping out from under a rock. I wanted some at once and told the owner so. She had only the two plants, and naturally wasn't going to part with them. Anticipating no problems I started circularizing the seed dealers. I wrote every wild flower grower in my long list. I advertised in a rock garden magazine. I tried the British Isles. Those that had been available there rotted out that winter. Finally the southern Oregon lady, who has since become a fast friend, sent me all the seed she had from the two plants. I grew six to flowering size from the original couple of dozen seed. I have since sent Mrs. Byman many other *Lewisias* but am still grateful for her original generosity. Many of my best friends have come to me through wild flowers.

I have found only one person who regards them with indifference and this is hard to understand considering how enchanting these high alpine dwellers really are. One zealot has devoted a large paragraph in his book attempting to tell how they impressed him. He finally settled on "jade-white" and that is probably as good as any for those who are acquainted with this splendid oriental gem.

History: For history of the family and genus see article "The *Lewisias.*"

George Engelmann, 1809-1884, whose name appears frequently in American botany, named and described *L. brachycalyx* in 1868. The specific name he close refers to the short calyx. Two other prominent botanists have since offered other names but Engelmann's is authoritative.

Description: The short, thickened base extends downward into a large branching root. The numerous deciduous light green leaves, moderately fleshy, form a spreading basal rosette which is attractive in its own right. The leaves, from one to four inches long, averaging two, are linear and broadening toward the apex, or lance-like but with the widest part above the middle and narrowing to either end. *L. rediviva's* leaves wither and die before the seed ripens but *L. brachycalyx* keeps its foliage until the seed matures. The flowering stem is not jointed and cannot break off as with *L. rediviva* so that the seed can be collected before it blows away. This is an important harvesting consideration.

In the fall, after the rains start, the leaves come alive again and push up out of the ground but not as vigorously as *L. rediviva.*

There are five to nine petals with the blossoms from an inch to more than an inch and a half in diameter. They are very similar to the rare white *L. rediviva,* although somewhat smaller. Happy, mature plants will send out such a shower of blossoms that they conceal all but the tips of the leaves. The flowering stems are very short so that the blossoms are close to the earth – one of the great charms not shared by all other *Lewisias.* Each capsule may ripen 40 or more typically black, shiny seeds. I would not attempt to identify *Lewisias* from their seeds – they are all much alike in gross appearance.

Rarity: Very rare in the wild. Almost impossible to obtain plants from nurseries and even difficult to buy seed.

Distribution: Gravelly hills and mountain sides, wet meadows at 5,000 to 7,000 feet or higher. In Montana, Utah, Colorado, Arizona, New Mexico, and the Cuyamaca and San Bernardino Mountains of California. Prefers wet places in the spring.

Propagation: At least three methods of propagating *Lewisias* are known with a possibility of a fourth. A fifth has been reported but there is doubt of its actual success. Only one of these, by seeds, works with *L. brachycalyx.* They should be sown as soon as ripe. One of the troubles with growing *Lewisias* from foreign seed is that it is often six months old before it is received. Germination is likely to be poor and if it is a year old, the gamble is much increased. *L. brachycalyx* seed, with me, has produced fairly well – about 30 to 40 percent – but some other species do much better. A good, rich, well drained seed bed – mostly humus mixed with fine rock – is best. If moss appears, before the plants are ready to be lifted, it should be removed carefully. Constant slug baiting is very important. Once these pests devour the foliage the plant is doomed. Under ideal conditions blossoms may appear the second year from seed. An extra season may be required.

Culture: This is a rock plant. It will not survive in ordinary gardens. Plenty of moisture in the spring. Full sun to partial shade, depending upon climate. A cool root run under a rock is a desirable protective device. Leaf mold and crushed rock, with a preponderance of the former will help retain spring moisture. Place a half inch or so of rock chips under the crown to prevent rot. Don't get excited when it dies down in summer. It needs a little dormancy after ripening the seed.

This is one of the best eight or ten members of the genus. I do not rank it quite as highly as *rediviva, tweedyi, cotyledon* or *rupicola* but this is like comparing diamonds with rubies or emeralds. All these, and more too, are in my gardens, and their varying foliage and flowers are a wonderful spring and summer time delight.

Flowering Time: April to June.

Lewisia cantelovii

No Established Common Name

LEWISIA CANTELOVII J. T. Howell
No Established Common Name

One of my botanical friends, Charles Thurman, and his wife, spent a weekend at my home on their return from a field trip to Nevada and California. Among Charlie's specimens was a pot containing four plants of a *Lewisia* entirely new to me. Even the specific name, *cantelovii,* meant nothing. They were obtained from a friend who collected them near the Nevada-California border. The narrow leaves with their bristly margins excited me and I had little success concealing my enthusiasm. Charlie gave me one – perhaps the rarest of all species in this highly variable genus. Neither he nor I had any idea what the flowers were like and I could hardly wait until summer to find out. As his visit was in September of 1963 it was a long wait. It is in this casual manner that many of our native plants have been introduced into horticulture and become garden favorites.

While the one plant was a great delight it only served to whet my appetite. Adequate studies cannot be made from single specimens and I was determined to have more.

History: Long ago I learned that almost any plant from virtually any part of the world can be obtained. Persistence and determination are the keys to success, and patience too. I discovered that John Thomas Howell of the California Academy of Sciences in San Francisco published the first description of the plant. Mr. Howell did not have any of them but referred me to a man in San Rafael who, he said, might be able to help me. After writing back and forth, and exchanging plants I received several of these rarities. They arrived in April of 1964 – very quick work under the circumstances. I potted them in a mixture of half crushed porous lava and half leaf mold and placed them in light shade. They scarcely knew they had been moved into another climate in another state.

I was a little skeptical and puzzled while spring slowly crept around. The flowers surely couldn't be as outstanding as some of the other species or more would have been known about them. Search of the literature revealed only meager information. Still –– ? When the first buds opened the flowers were not as large as I had hoped they would be – about a half inch in diameter. What they lacked in size they more than made up for in numbers and a very long blossoming time. They closely resembled those of the better forms of *L. columbiana.*

Mr. H. C. Cantelow and his wife Ella Dales Cantelow are California outdoors people who have contributed many rare and choice specimens to the herbarium of the California Academy of Sciences located at Golden Gate Park. On May 25, 1941 they were traveling down the Feather River Canyon in Plumas County, California. Three and one fifth miles west of Belden a new *Lewisia* first became known to science. In his diary of that date Mr. Cantelow wrote: "The ride down the canyon was delightful. Well down the gorge, in the granite section on a wet moss-covered wall we discovered a *Lewisia* – new to us. I took one and placed it in a pot. – ." Mr. Howell who was born on November 6, 1903, published the first official description of this plant in *Leaflets of Western Botany,* Volume 3, Number 6, dated April 21, 1942. He named it *Lewisia cantelovii* in honor of the two people who discovered it. Philip A. Munz, in his *A California Flora,* published in 1963 changed the *v* to *w* although Howell says *v* is better Latin.

Description: From the nearly spherical woody base with comparatively shallow roots rise the numerous perennial, fleshy, basal leaves. They are from a quarter to half an inch wide, up to three inches long, slender and widen abruptly near the apex which is rounded, nearly square, or shallowly notched. The margins are very prominently sharp toothed – almost bristly in some specimens. This characteristic is so pronounced that it catches the eye at once and is responsible for a good deal of the charm the plant possesses. The leaves are virtually stemless, and form a pleasing rosette as much as nine inches across although full grown specimens are usually half a foot or less in diameter.

The flowering stems are from six to 12 inches long, averaging nine to ten. A single plant may bear as many as 20. Youngsters may bear only one stem and average fewer than half a dozen. They are inclined outward, freely and openly branched. The slender pedicels are up to half an inch long and bear five petaled star-like flowers. The petals are white or creamy with very narrow, prominent pink stripes.

Rarity: Extremely rare.

Distribution: Only a few colonies are known and these are very small. Some of them are in isolated areas difficult of access. The San Rafael resident who sent me my supply wrote: "Incidently I know why the Cantelowiis are so rare. If the irrigation district hadn't built a flume around the Devil's Slide yesterday's colony would have gone undiscovered for a few more centuries."

From about 1,500 feet to over 3,000, often on wet granite cliffs in yellow pine forests of Plumas and Nevada Counties, California. On the south fork of the Yuba River, Nevada County at about 1,600 feet. Near Belden in the Feather River Canyon, Plumas County. This station is approximately 65 miles west of the California-Nevada border and 135 miles south of the California-Oregon line.

Propagation: Crownal offsets are scarce. They may be cut off, including part of the root to which they are attached, any time in spring or summer and rooted in sand. Some may flower the next year but most will require an extra season. The plants in my wet Portland climate do not set seed but those I gave to a friend who lives in southwestern Oregon's Medford where the summers are drier and warmer, produce a moderate supply. Germination is good and the youngsters may occasionally flower the following season but usually an extra year will be required.

Culture: Study of the conditions in which plants thrive in nature is often a great help in understanding their garden needs. My California friend wrote me: "The colony is growing on a precipitous granite cliff on the south side of the river facing northeast. Some morning sun and afternoon shade. There is a dense covering of moss in which the plants are growing. The roots penetrate crevices where they are present but in many cases the entire root system is in the moss itself which will be obvious to you when you see the specimens. Other plants are growing with the *Lewisias,* principally *Sedum spathulifolium* and *Boykinia elata.*"

They do best in light shade, very sharp drainage, and can stand a considerable amount of drought. I planted some in flower pots in a soil consisting of half leaf mold and half crushed lava rock. Others were placed on their sides in a wall garden and two were tucked into the ordinary rock garden with their roots inserted under a rock. The crowns were protected from excessive moisture by an overhang.

This strictly California native is both exasperating and exciting. The flowers are beautiful but too small and too far apart on stems that are much too leggy for them to appear to best advantage. The leaves are very distinctive and some *Lewisia* fanciers consider them as attractive as the blossoms. It immediately occurred to me and one of my botanical friends that hybridizing might produce some spectacular results. We hope to retain the very desirable leaf characteristics of *L. cantelovii* while creating larger, more colorful flowers in denser clusters. Crosses were made with both *L. cotyledon* and *L. rupicola.* Seed was produced and has germinated at the time of this writing but it will be another couple of years before primary results can be observed. Additional time will be needed for line breeding if the hybrids are fertile. Crosses between species are often sterile and this seems to be especially true among *Lewisias.*

Under ordinary garden and climatic conditions *L. cantelovii* does not seem to be any more subject to crown rot than most other species and less so than *L. tweedyi* and *L. cotyledon.* However, during December of 1964 the temperature in Portland, Oregon where I live, dropped to six above zero F. The freezing spell broke suddenly and was followed by heavy, warm rains. This severe combination was too much. I lost a quarter of my *L. cotyledons* and all but two of the *L. canteloviis.* The survivors were the ones that were protected by rock overhangs. I believe that neither low temperatures nor heavy rains alone would have been particularly damaging. It is unlikely that these extremes exist in its native California home 500 miles southward. This species is too new to horticulture for much to be known of its climatic adaptability. It seems doubtful whether it will thrive in parts of the country where winter weather alternates between sub zero temperatures and warm rains.

The flowers close every night and open again the following day providing the weather is warm or sunny. Otherwise they usually remain closed, especially if it rains. In this respect it is much like *L. rediviva.*

While this comparatively unknown species is by no means the loveliest of the genus it is a worthy addition to the garden. I rank it just below its close relative *L. columbiana,* and above *L. nevadensis.* As a garden subject the most difficult problem is getting it. At the present time not a single nursery stocks it and very few people own even a few plants.

Flowering Time: May and June in its California mountain home. The first blossoms appear in May in my gardens and reach their floral peak in mid July when several dozen will by open at one time on each plant. The display is maintained at a good level all summer and only in the cooler days of early fall do they become less numerous. At the end of November in 1964 a dozen or so buds were still trying to open but were stopped by cold rains. They even survived an inch of snow which did not stick overnight. If the weather had remained dry I believe blossoming would have continued into the middle of December. *L. cotyledon* and *L. rupicola* sometimes have two flowering periods with an in between interval. *L. cantelovii's* is continuous and covers a far longer time than any other *Lewisia* I have ever known. Extending as it does a full half year a single plant may produce as many as 1,000 flowers – or even twice that many. This is hard to believe considering that only a few dozen are open at any one time.

I have never met Mr. and Mrs. Cantelow and it isn't likely that I ever shall. But it is a delight to wander into the garden in late fall when all other species have ripened their seeds and find their *Lewisia's* starry blossoms gazing upwards at their astral relatives millions of miles away.

Lewisia cotyledon No Established Common Name

LEWISIA COTYLEDON (Watson) Robinson
No Established Common Name

Seventy-five feet up the cliff from where I was standing there were two bright pink flashes of color. I put my binoculars on them – and there was no doubt. They were *Lewisia cotyledon.* I was alone in southern Oregon and had no climbing equipment. But I found a low spot a hundred yards away and was able to scale the cliff. Then I worked back until I was directly above the two plants. I couldn't see them because an overburden blocked the view. I worked slowly and carefully down until they were scarcely more than arm's length away. An abrupt drop-off prevented closer approach. Tantalizingly close and I was strongly tempted to chance the few remaining feet. Then I glanced at the sheer cliff face and decided that these two plants were not worth the life of one of the world's mediocre botanists. A year or two later I went back with my wife but they were out of bloom and we couldn't find them.

This was my introduction to this species in the wild. But a friend sent me 500 seeds and a couple of years later I had them flowering profusely in my gardens where the cliffs are no more than five feet high.

History: For history of the family and genus see article "The *Lewisias.*"

The difficulties with *L. cotyledon* aren't confined to cliffs. In 1885, 71 years after Pursh described the first known *Lewisia,* Sereno Watson, 1826-1892, named *Calandrinia cotyledon* and the controversy was on. Benjamin Lincoln Robinson, 1864-1935, in 1897 came up with the name that is now officially established. *Cotyledon* refers to the two characteristic seed leaves. It has also been known generically as *Oreobroma.* Other names are *L. howellii, L. purdyi, L. finchii, L. heckneri;* and varieties *shastaensis, crenulata, ingramii, longifolia, mariana, millardii, minus,* and *elegans.*

No other *Lewisia* has been the subject of so much dispute among scientists and pseudo-scientists. The flowers are all much the same in size, shape and structure though varying in color, but the leaves are radically different. It is true that the floral parts are the most important factors in determining accurate identifications within such large classifications as *orders* and *families*. But within the *genus* the leaves and other vegetative characters assume prominence in separating the species. It was upon the basis of these pronounced leaf variations that so many authors produced so many species and varieties. Scientific researchers are now inclined to group them all together as *Lewisia cotyledon*. My opinion, for what it is worth, follows this line of thought. "Splitting" has been carried to ridiculous extremes.

In wild colonies the different types of each can be found with all sorts of interlocking characteristics. Similarly in the garden, seedlings of one so-called species will produce most or all of the others under identical conditions.

Description: Just below the leaves is the short and thick root one-half to three-quarters of an inch in diameter, which goes down a foot or more in old plants. This underground feeding system is fleshy, a device which permits the plant to store food for the next season's growth as well as to retain water in the dry summers.

The numerous leaves, one to four inches long, form a basal rosette which makes the plants worthy garden residents even when there are no flowers. They are sessile, that is without true leaf stems, very fleshy, brittle when full of water, narrow or wide, broadened at or near the tip, sometimes with a minute point at the apex. The width varies from one-half to one and a half inches with semi-transparent, wavy or strongly wrinkled margins. Or the leaves may be smooth and flat with no trace of marginal transparency. The edges may be smooth or with minute rounded teeth or, on the upper portion with minute sharply pointed teeth. These leaf variations are so pronounced that their accurate portrayal is almost impossible to paint with words.

Young plants may have only a single flowering scape, older ones as many as eight or more, freely branched, two to 12 inches long with the latter length more common, widely spreading. The flowers, an inch or more in diameter, are eight to ten petaled, white, creamy or somewhat yellow with deep pink or orange stripes becoming lighter as the blossoms age. It is this striping which accounts for much of the beauty of the flowers. Occasionally a plant will produce flowers that are all pink with no striping. In their mid season prime the floral display is very showy and a beautiful thing to see. On one typical plant in its second year of flowering I counted 50 blossoms and 416 buds for a total of 566. From eight to 15 seeds at a maximum may be produced in each small capsule. Most, in my garden, produce fewer or often none.

Rarity: Rare, partly due to its limited range and partly because collectors have removed almost all that are of easy access.

Distribution: In stony soils and crevices in rocks from a few hundred feet above sea level to at least 8,000. Limited to the Siskiyous and other mountains in southwestern Oregon and northwestern California.

There are more species of *Lewisias* in Washington, Oregon and California than in all the other states combined. Perhaps their greatest concentration is in the Siskiyous, one of the most distinctive floral regions of America.

Propagation: Cut off the scapes when most of the seeds have ripened but before the capsules have had a chance to scatter the crop. Place them on papers in a cool room. The sap in the branching stems and thick scapes will mature many of the green seeds. When drying has been completed the masses of flowers and stems can be shaken and crumbled to shatter out the seeds. After cleaning I save the debris and plant it too. It is surprising how many plants this chaff will produce from seeds that have refused to come out of hiding. Individual ripened capsules can be harvested one by one but this is a boring and time consuming chore.

Alternate freezing and thawing for a few days each will give better germination. With precious seeds I follow this practice but ordinarily I simply plant them as soon as they are ripe in flats containing equal parts of leaf mold and crushed rock. They deteriorate rapidly. This is why fall sowing is preferable to spring. Germination is excellent and the youngsters will sometimes flower the second season but most take an extra year. An occasional contrary specimen may not blossom until the third, fourth or even fifth year.

Crownal offsets can be removed, cutting closely enough to

get part of the main root if possible. Dip the cut ends in root growth hormone, insert in clean, coarse sand in the shade and they will produce new plants in a few weeks. Cuttings should be taken in spring or early summer. Flowers may come in one year but more often two.

Leaf cuttings including part of the root and axillary bud are said to produce new plants. One of my friends has tried it and so have I. We can get them to callous but not to root or produce new leaves.

Established plants can have most of the leaves removed, retaining only enough at the top of the crown so the plant will not die. New offsets will replace the lost foliage. As soon as they reach fair size they can be cut off and rooted in sand. This defoliation should be done early in the spring.

I have often wondered if multiple crowns could not be produced by cutting off the top of the plants. The theory is sound and I am going to try it on a plant that is not valuable.

Culture: *L. rediviva* is the best known species among *Lewisia* lovers but horticulturists were quick to see the possibilities of the variable *L. cotyledon.* Both English and American propagators have concentrated their attention on it and some remarkable plants have resulted. Hybrids between *L. cotyledon* and *L. columbiana* have been created and are in dealers' stocks. Natural hybrids between *L. cotyledon* and *L. leana* have been discovered in the high Siskiyous. They are intermediate in flowers and foliage between their two parents. A cross between *L. cotyledon* and *L. brachycalyx* has been produced in the British Isles. These are so rare that something more than ordinary friendship is required to obtain them. A friend of mine who has seen my three specimens has declared them the greatest improvement in the history of *Lewisia* culture.

A clear, unstriped yellow of striking clarity, now exists but it will be some time before any quantity is available. Probably not more than a dozen have been grown from the original parent. A pure white of marvelous beauty can be obtained. The nurseryman who has them claims that there are less than a hundred in the world. His ordinary *cotyledons* sell for 50 cents. The snowy white variety is marked at five dollars – and worth the investment.

A dwarf form — no more than four or five inches high with dense masses of deep yellow, orange, or red blossoms has recently come to notice but it will be several years before it can be produced in sufficient numbers to offer to the trade.

Jack Drake, a Scotch horticulturist, has created a strain that contains marvelous pinks, scarlets, deep rose, oranges and cherry reds. Seeds of this improvement are well known in both the British Isles and America. Some of my choicest specimens came from this stock. Even better plants may be expected as the years roll on.

All of these but two — and they have been promised — are in my gardens and a glorious sight they are.

This is one of the more difficult *Lewisias.* Sprinkling with the garden hose in mid summer can be quickly fatal from crown rot. Even in dry climates or near their native alpine homes they can not endure this kindly but mistaken practice.

A mixture of sand and leaf mold is not to their liking. Every year I lose some that are trying to survive in this environment. Half leaf mold and half crushed rock, pea gravel or chips make a good soil. Bits of rock should be placed around the crowns a half inch or so deep to keep excess moisture away. Sharp drainage from crown to tip of root is essential.

I have yet to lose a plant that was placed on its side in cracks between rocks or in holes drilled in boulders. This horizontal treatment keeps moisture away from the crowns. They are wonderfully attractive on the sides of rock walls.

Where root room is limited the plants will take one, two or even three years extra to flower than their more fortunate brothers that have all the depth they need for coolness, moderate permanent moisture and adequate food.

The two cliff-dwelling *Lewisias* I mentioned at the beginning of this article were on a south facing cliff exposed to full sun all day long. But they do not like this excessive sun and heat in the garden. Morning sun and afternoon shade, or very light shade all day long approaches the ideal.

Careful attention to their few needs will assure success, and a beautiful, wonderful floral pageant weeks on end.

Flowering Time: I have had them in bloom from April 16th to June 20th for conventional plants. But there is a special treasure in my gardens that every year gives me an additional treat. After the first crop of flowers has ripened its seeds the second comes on. While this is the only plant of its kind in my gardens it is not particularly unusual for *L. cotyledon* to produce two crops. The scapes are shorter – from one-half an inch to five inches long – and number from six to eight. The flowers are not quite as numerous as the first set and they don't last quite as long. The first buds of the second crop open during the last week of June and last three weeks. In several years this plant has produced only one crownal offset. Apparently the strength goes into the second flowering rather than into vegetative reproduction.

Runcinate margin

Lewisia leana No Established Common Name

LEWISIA LEANA (Porter) Robinson
No Established Common Name

The package from the Siskiyous contained four species of Lewisias, three of which were rare. I obtained them in exchange for a rare botany book. Six of the plants were *L. leana.* This was my introduction to this rare native. I had read about it, of course, but reading is one thing and actually owning it is quite another. This was the only time I ever sacrificed a book out of my library for plants that I could not obtain otherwise. Although I have obtained other *L. leanas* since I have never regretted the deal – something of a horticultural bargain.

History: For history of the family and genus see article "The *Lewisias.*." 1897 must have been a banner year for Benjamin Lincoln Robinson, 1864-1935, for it was then that he established the official names of no less than eight species of *Lewisias* – more than any other author within this genus. One of these was *L. leana.* He kept all the specific names, fortunately, for there is enough confusion among these American natives without that. He simply moved them out of the *Claytonias* and their very close relatives, the *Calandrinias,* where other taxonomists had placed them.

The plant was known prior to that time as *Calandrinia leana.* Thomas Conrad Porter, 1822-1901, described it in 1876. Altogether it has been in three different genera. In going through the histories of the various species I was surprised to discover that Pursh named *L. rediviva* from half to three-quarters of a century before many of the others were announced. Lewis and Clark, who were explorers, not scientists, nevertheless were far ahead of their more erudite fellows.

Description: The branching roots terminate upwards in a thick, fleshy crown from which 40, 50, or even more evergreen, round, or nearly round leaves appear in a basal rosette. They are linear, pointed, one-twelfth to one-fifth of an inch wide, and from one to two and a half inches long. These leaves resemble those of *L. rediviva* more than any other species but they are somewhat larger in diameter. I value these hard to get plants for their evergreen foliage alone. They are a modest powdery green – a delightful quality I have never seen in any other *Lewisia.* Because of this year around display I have planted several dozen more.

One to half a dozen or more stems rise above the ghostly green foliage. They are four to seven inches high and break off from the crown soon after flowering. The freely branched scapes produce a multitude of blossoms which are not crowded, thus adding an extra bonus to a floral bargain. What they lack in size – for the five to seven petaled flowers are only about half an inch in diameter – they make up in numbers. I counted 377 buds and blossoms on one plant, and this is not exceptional. They are a soft pink with deeper rose stripes. Foliage and flowers – an ineffably lovely combination and one I would not be without in my garden of Joseph's floral coat of many colors.

Rarity: Rare, the type plants; the white and bright rosy red, very rare.

Distribution: In rocky places at generally high altitudes – from 6,000 to 9,000 feet. In the Sierra Nevada, Salmon and Siskiyou Mountains. Fresno and Mariposa counties of northwestern California, and Josephine and Jackson counties in southwestern Oregon.

Propagation: By seeds, see under *Lewisia cotyledon.* Crownal offsets are produced sparingly, only one or two appearing yearly on some plants, none on others. For directions see under *L. cotyledon.* According to present knowledge these two methods are the only ones practiced. Rarely more than three seeds are produced in wild capsules. None in my wet gardens.

Culture: In mild climates full sun or light shade suits them well. In warmer areas more shade would be advisable. It is good practice to tuck a layer of small rock under the crowns to prevent rot. This species is a little more tolerant of excessive moisture than *L. cotyledon, L. tweedyi* and *L. rediviva* but occasional losses may be expected if the crowns are not protected. Good drainage, of course, is important. Rocky soil is the answer to this problem. Mass plantings, spaced a few inches apart are spectacular but not more so than individuals tucked into corners or in crevices between boulders.

They will survive a little crowding from other kinds of

plants but if much shaded will refuse to flower. They appear to better advantage with bare rock on all sides or used as a background. At the base of large rocks I like to mix them with *L. cotyledons, L. tweedyis, L. rupicolas* and *L. columbianas,* with no particular order – just as though nature had concentrated them there in her carelessly beautiful way.

The very rare pure white form, mixed with the pinks of the ordinary plants provide a wonderous contrast. If the equally rare cherry reds can be mixed with the snowy mutants the combination will be unequalled and indescribable.

I have only a single plant of this immensely beautiful rich crimson. A friend had promised me a white. When it flowered it wasn't white at all but this amazing bright red specimen.

The ordinary plants – if there is anything ordinary about them – are not expensive but the whites are priced at five dollars. Only one dealer handles *L. leana.* I am sure that wild flower nurserymen are missing a good opportunity in not offering this little known alpine beauty.

Flowering Time: June to August in their high Siskiyou homes. From mid April to early June in my gardens – and a joyous six weeks it is.

Lewisia oppositifolia No Established Common Name

LEWISIA OPPOSITIFOLIA (Watson) Robinson
No Established Common Name

It is virtually impossible to find this white flowering *Lewisia* except when it is in blossom. After spending half a day searching for it on a hillside in southern Oregon where it grows I turned my activities to more profitable pursuits. I have had great success locating out of season plants – a capsule, a dried flowering stem, a dead leaf – all are useful clues. But this time I was a couple of weeks too soon and there was no sign of them among the other spring blossoms. A few weeks later I received half a dozen from a local resident who was able to be at the right place at the right time. They have been in my gardens ever since.

History: For history of the family and genus see article "The *Lewisias.*" Like so many other *Lewisias* bearing his authorship Benjamin Lincoln Robinson, 1864-1935, in 1897 gave this one its still officially recognized name. *Oppositifolia,* appropriately, means opposite-leaved. In 1885 Sereno Watson called it a *Calandrinia,* and in 1893 Thomas Howell decided it was an *Oreobroma.* The confusion was understandable for this is a distinctive plant, quite unlike any of the others.

Description: The thickened, often branching roots, come together just below the crown to form a short heavy base one-half to three-quarters of an inch in diameter. The deciduous basal leaves, few to several, are from one to four inches long, linear, or three or four times as long as the greatest width which is somewhat above the middle and narrowing towards both ends, and are pointed at the tip. The one to three pairs of stem leaves are similar, opposite, and near the base – none on the upper part of the flowering stalk.

The six to eight inch stems are slender, sometimes weak and grow erect or diagonally upward. The one to four stems bear two to half a dozen flowers on slender pedicels from one to three inches long. The excessively long stems with their few, loosely scattered blossoms, are partially compensated for by the flowers themselves. They are surprisingly large, considering the rest of the plant – three-quarters to one inch in diameter.

The eight or ten light pink or Chinese silky white petals, because of their width and arrangement, have a semi-double effect not often seen in wildlings. It is for this appearance, regardless of the rest of the plant, that *Lewisia oppositifolia* has rightfully earned an honored nook in the rockery. The egg-shaped capsules contain from six to 15 seeds.

Rarity: Rare. The variety *Richeyi* is said to be a dwarf and with more flowers. I haven't seen it.

Distribution: On moist slopes from southern Josephine County in southwestern Oregon to Del Norte County in northern California. From low elevations to several thousand feet.

Propagation: By seed only as far as known at the present time. See under *Lewisia cotyledon.* Hand pollination in my climate is necessary.

Culture: This is one of the easier species – if there is such a thing. I made my first mistake by treating it like most other *Lewisias* – sharp drainage in rock soil. The drainage was correct – a must. But they require more than average moisture during the spring flowering season. My plants blossomed and were moderately healthy but not vigorous. Three-fourths leaf mold and one-quarter finely crushed rock gives them adequate drainage and holds moisture well. The question of this combination is not generally well understood. Along with the moisture retention goes aeration. These plants must have air for the roots – the same is true of almost all other plants – even some bog dwellers. The movement of moisture by means of drainage provides this air. A little rock under the crown, like most all other species.

Drying out during the warmth of summer is advisable. Full sun in mild climates to light shade elsewhere is good practice. This small plant should have plenty of elbow room. It will stand a little crowding but the growth will be puny.

Flowering Time: March to May in its wild home. The last two weeks of May in my Portland area.

Cleft margin

Lewisia rediviva 'White' Bitter Root

LEWISIA REDIVIVA Pursh
Bitter Root

At my feet were the bright green deciduous leaves of the Bitter Root, *Lewisia rediviva.* I had crossed two states and entered a third for no other reason than to visit this plant, considerably smaller in diameter than a silver dollar.

I nearly walked on it before I saw the slender leaves. It was a thrilling experience, as fresh in my mind today as it was a quarter of a century ago. I have studied it in three states, collected it for my gardens, and spent hours with the Indians discussing its wonders. It is one of the most beautiful flowers in all America. No other western wildling is richer in legend and tradition. No other *Lewisia* is as well known or distributed so widely in the Far West.

It was on the outskirts of Missoula, Montana, in the Bitter Root Valley, that I found my first plant. I walked a few hundred yards farther until I came to the lonely tent of a full blooded Salish Indian woman who was more than 80 years old. I watched her slip a pointed rod half a foot into the ground and pull back. The Bitter Root plant came out of the loose earth. She tossed it onto the growing pile she was harvesting. Her hands had gathered many thousands of these plants for she had been coming to this same place for the harvest every year since she was a child.

But it was not the harvest she knew as a young girl. Three-quarters of a century before that day many tents dotted the prairie during the late spring when the roots are dug. But when I visited her, there was only the one teepee in the entire valley. It wasn't because the plants had become scarce. In some places they were so abundant it was nearly impossible to walk without stepping on them. But the Indians themselves are nearly all gone.

History: It was one of the most important Indian food plants in the western part of the United States. For history of the family and genus see article "The *Lewisias.*" Twelve miles south of the present city of Missoula, Montana, near the mouth of Lolo Creek, Meriwether Lewis gathered some of the flowers which he pressed and added to a small collection with the notation: "The Indians eat the root of this, near Clarks R. July 1, 1806." This seems to be the first record made of the plant. It was from these flowers that the original botanical study was made.

Dried specimens in Lewis' herbarium showed some signs of life and were planted by Mr. M'Mahon in a Philadelphia garden where they lived for more than a year. And David Douglas' specimens, treated in the same way lived for a short time in the gardens of the London Horticultural Society. Because of its extreme tenacity of life it was entirely logical that it be given the specific name *rediviva,* meaning *restored, brought to life.*

Although it is only a very small plant hugging the prairie it was known to the first white men who came into the country. The French Canadian trappers call it *Racine amere* which means *bitter root.* It is the *Spatlum* of the Indians, the *Rock Rose* and the *Sand Rose* of a few of the whites. As the country became better settled the plant assumed even greater importance. It became the state flower of Montana. A beautiful river, a majestic mountain range and a very fertile valley are named for it. The Bitter Root Mountains are about 200 miles long and are the most imposing offshoots of the Northern Continental Divide, with the highest peaks averaging 8,000 feet. The Bitter Root Valley, named by the early trappers and hunters, averages 20 miles in width and the river, having the same name, flows for 80 miles through the valley with the mountains on both sides.

While the flower is now mostly on the invaders' lands it originally belonged to the Indians. It is hardly possible to discuss one without the other, so important was it in the daily economy of the original Americans. The fleshy root was the part of the plant, which in bygone days, was used so extensively for food. It was at least as important as camas, one of the major causes of the Nez Perce War under Chief Joseph.

The aged Indian woman I watched that day used a steel rod about three-quarters of an inch square and two feet long with a wooden cross bar at the top for a handle. The end was pointed and curved for the first half foot. It was slipped into the ground close to the crown. The T handle was pulled back and the plant came up easily, stripped of most of the soil.

Before the white man and the age of steel the Indians used wooden sticks.

In spite of her advanced age she dug them fully twice as fast as I could with my trowel. Her years of experience and the amazingly efficient tool in her hands made my masculine efforts a little ridiculous. She tossed them in a pile, then sat down and stripped off the bark, clasping the crown with one hand and the roots with the other.

She had an awl-like wooden stick about eight inches long, half an inch in diameter at one end and pointed at the other, hanging from her waist. I couldn't imagine what it was for until I saw her use it to remove bits of the bark which adhered in the crotches of the fleshy roots.

The crop is harvested while the plants are in bud. The root isn't collected after flowering as by that time it is exhausted and the bark is difficult to remove. At about the same time the blossoms open, the leaves disappear and do not renew growth until the fall rains. For this reason the plant is almost impossible to find in the middle of summer.

The outer layer of skin is dark reddish-brown and is only slightly bitter. Beneath this layer is a carroty-orange colored inner bark not much thicker than a piece of newspaper. It is very bitter. The raw inner root is pure white and somewhat starchy, a little tough and stringy, definitely bitter but not unpleasantly so. If the roots are eaten without removing the orange inner bark the bitterness is much more pronounced and definitely distasteful. They are often eaten fresh during the harvest. Boiled for ten minutes they become jelly-like and make a good soup. The dried roots have to be boiled twice as long. Drying is simple. The roots are cleaned and spread out in the sun for half a day or so. Then they are stored in sacks and can be kept for one or two years.

One person – meaning a skilled Indian – can gather two gunny sacksful in a week and such a quantity is quite valuable. I was told that such an amount in the old days would purchase a horse or a wife.

I boiled some of the fresh roots and in a few minutes the toughness and stringiness was completely eliminated. Nearly all the bitterness disappeared too. The Indians used the liquid from the boiled roots as a cough medicine. I drank some of it and it was extremely bitter. There is some question of its value in treating coughs as the bitter principle is one of the glucosides – closely related to the carbohydrates. They are not recognized in modern medical practice as having therapeutical properties. But the root itself is very nourishing as it is rich in hemicelluloses.

It is sometimes prepared alone or cooked into soup with meat or bones. In the old days the Salish Indians baked it in the ground. This was the only method they knew of baking for they were entirely without pottery or even basketry. A pit was dug and a very hot fire kindled in it. When the bed was reduced to glowing coals, red willow sticks, with the sap still in them, were criss crossed over the fire bed in the form of a gridiron. This was blanketed with green grass, ordinarily bunch grass, two or three inches thick. The grass was covered with moist earth then another coating of green grass was added. The bitter roots were then placed into the pit and covered with more grass and a thick layer of earth. Another fire was kindled on top of the heap and the roots were allowed to bake for ten minutes. The same method was used for camas, except the fire on top was kept burning for 12 to 18 hours. They were more often dried and stored for winter use, however.

The Bitter Root is more desirable as a food than camas, because it is easier to dig and prepare. The camas bulbs grow six inches or more deep. They have to be skinned, baked and dried before storing for winter. Bitter Root preparation is much simpler. Both skinning and drying are easy and fast. When cooked they are starchy and really a very good food if you don't mind the mild bitter flavor. The roots do not boil to pieces as potatoes do, and a half a dozen good sized roots are enough for a meal.

The annual ceremonies associated with the harvest are nearly a thing of the past. The chief sets a date and calls the tribe together. He chooses a few of the older women who know best how to collect the roots, and the same women are usually chosen every year. Most of the older women now have rheumatism so younger ones have taken their places. One man is selected as the leader of the women. This leader prays for the success of the harvest. Then he and the chosen women go out into the prairies and dig enough roots for the dinner that day. The roots are cleaned and only certain Indians are allowed to cook them. Then they have their feast, which consists of meats and other foods. No general digging is allowed before the feast. Afterwards any Indian is free to harvest it any time and in any quantity. This was the general ritual of the Indians at Camas Prairie, and Mission Valley, Montana. It is doubtful if this ceremony will be practiced many more years.

The Bitter Root is dug first then comes the camas and wild sweet onion harvest. Although few white people care about the Bitter Root as a food, complaining of the flavor, the red men valued it highly. It must be remembered that sugar was completely unknown to the Indians, and there was no honey until bees were introduced from Europe. Bitter Root soup was sweetened with camas. Service berries were also used for the same purpose. I found this fruit more abundant in the Bitter Root Valley than I have seen it any other place.

Although the Bitter Root has been collected in great quantities for centuries, it is still common today. The Indians collected only the larger plants. Many of the smaller ones were old enough to flower and scatter their seed, assuring a sustained yield year after year.

I was puzzled why the Indians go to the extra work of harvesting the Bitter Root when potatoes are much easier to grow. The answer is simple. They are not an agricultural people and their habits, customs and traditions have been fixed for unknown centuries, consequently their adaptation to changing conditions is exceedingly slow. Some of the older Indians have not learned to speak English. Routines which they have known since legendary times, they do skilfully and easily, but anything new is often beyond their abilities. The elderly Indian lady, who could dig the roots so much faster than I, handed me her 'dollar' watch to set. She didn't know how to pull out the stem to move the hands.

The best Bitter Root fields in the valley are within the city limits of Missoula itself and southwards. It is only a matter of time until these fields will disappear. Construction of homes and plowing of fields is eradicating them. The Indians will not suffer from this loss, however, as they too, are little more than a memory. In 1923 only 20 per cent of the Indians on the nearby

Flathead Reservation, were full blooded. 25 years later, in 1948, there were only 12 per cent – less than 400 pure bloods out of a total reservation population of 3,700. It won't be many years before death and intermarriage will see the last of these simple and friendly people who do not fit into the white man's way of life.

On an early Sunday morning I stood on a hilltop high above Missoula, with the Bitter Roots and other wild flowers all about me. I looked upon the homes and cultivated fields below with the river in the middle, and the sentinel Bitter Root Mountains on both sides guarding the fertile valley. Suddenly floating through the clear spring air came the music of church chimes playing "Oh Come All Ye Faithful." It was the voice of the white God calling his children to prayer. I thought then of the prairie before civilization came to plough its fields and build its homes. And I thought of the ancient Indian woman in her solitary camp and of the Great Spirit who, in ages past, called her ancestors to harvest the Bitter Root growing so abundantly in the peaceful valley. I was witnessing the final harvest of a vanishing plant. I was gazing upon the last of a great people who, with their legends and traditions, were scarcely more than a memory.

Description: The Indians' primary interest in their Spatlum was in the fleshy roots. They are much branched – six or more main roots with side feeders – and from four to eight inches long, descending from a short base a half or three-quarters of an inch in diameter. Where there is a crack in a rock or a crevice the roots go down almost vertically. Above solid rock, where opportunities to seek the depths do not exist the roots tend to sprawl parallel with the surface of the soil, which may not be more than a couple of inches deep.

In the fall, after the rains start, the new leaves begin their growth. This may be as early as September in my Portland gardens and as late as December east of the Cascades where the climate is more arid and the rainfall more limited and often later. They do not make their complete growth until the warmth of spring. The leaves, which resemble thickened fir needles are from three-quarters of an inch to more than two inches long, linear, grass-like, tapering uniformly to a dull point. They are slightly flattened and prominently concave beneath on the upper half of their length. Numbering three dozen or more in mature plants they make an altogether pleasing rosette.

In the spring the fat, grayish brown buds, a dozen or more, appear in the middle of the rosette. As the flowers spread their 12 to 18 petals the leaves wither and by the time they are in full bloom scarcely a trace of the needles can be found. This is the most astonishing sight I have ever seen on the prairies – miniature water lilies floating on the desert sands. For the size of the plants the flowers, dainty, silky chalices, are huge, two to three inches in diameter each on its own short stem. Earth-hugging in compact clusters of creamy white or the richest profound rosy pinks imaginable, there is nothing in all the world of *Lewisias* to compare with them. They are my favorites in this spectacular genus – even surpassing the very lovely *L. tweedyi.*

They open on warm days, close at night or when the weather is rainy, too cool or cloudy. The three or four dozen stamens provide ample pollen for those who care to try hybridizing. Up to two dozen black, shining seeds are produced – the product of pollenizing the six to eight styles.

Rarity: The type with pink blossoms, common. The white form, rare. There is always the possibility that a yellow blossom might occur where there are white ones. I am still seeking such an extreme rarity among the Bitter Roots.

Distribution: It is fortunate that the most beautiful of all *Lewisias* is the most abundant and widely distributed. They are found in the Arid Transition Zone, often at low elevations but up to several thousand feet. I have never found them except on top of solid rock or in gravelly soils and they are never seen in wet climates. They range from British Columbia to southern California and eastward to the Rockies in Colorado and Arizona with probably their greatest concentration in Montana's Bitter Root Valley. One may travel miles on end in country which is ideally suited to them without finding a single plant. Then, when least expected, you may come upon a small patch with only a few specimens or walk through an arid meadow containing untold thousands. Why this is so I do not know – probably chance plays a heavy role in this unordered scheme of things. Whites occur in pure or almost pure stands or in patches where they dominate the pink. I have never seen a white alone in a field of pink.

The first white was reported by Meriwether Lewis on July 1, 1806, near the mouth of Lolo Creek in the vicinity of Clarks River, Montana. A patch has been reported on the old Blewett Pass Highway in the State of Washington where they are mixed with but are more abundant than the pink. Two small colonies have been located in the nearly treeless Steens Mountains of extreme southeastern Oregon. Another station is near Antelope, Oregon, 50 or 60 miles south and a little east of The Dalles. Years ago I was told they were found on the Oregon shore of the Columbia Gorge approximately opposite the mouth of the Klickitat River. I tried several times to find them there out of season but failed. Finally, in desperation, I looked when they were in flower. True enough there were a few scattered white blossoms. Indiscriminate collecting has virtually wiped out this station. On the Washington side, not far from the Klickitat, a large meadow contains many thousand of these snowy flowers with only an occasional pink. This is private land but I have been fortunate enough to obtain permission to collect specimens. They are associated with such other arid prairie delights as the Grass Widows, *Sisyrinchium grandiflorum;* Yellow Bells, *Fritillaria pudica;* the distinctive shooting star, *Dodecatheon poeticum;* the early sunflower, Gold Star, *Crocidium multicaule* and a host of other wildlings. This is one of my spring time pleasure grounds. Undoubtedly other stations of the white *Lewisia rediviva* exist but they can hardly be numerous.

The intensity of colors in the common pink forms vary radically. Fifteen miles east of Ellensburg, Washington on the highway leading to the Columbia River there is a small colony. Some of the flowers are a very pale, weak pink mixed with a few better ones. On a trip to this station a companion, who had never seen *L. rediviva* before, exclaimed at their beauty. And he was right for any Bitter Root flower is lovely.

Those near Missoula are very good soft pinks and worth the five days I spent with them. Here they are found mostly on the open prairies but on hillsides too, among lupines, delphiniums, phlox, pentstemons and native grasses. The soil was mostly sand and small gravel rich in the leaf mold of centuries. This is the only place where I have ever seen them in close proximity with other plants, where they were often half hidden. There were quite a few young plants which resembled the mature ones except that they had fewer leaves. But the best I have ever seen, incredibly pure, live pinks of the richest shades imaginable, live in a small colony about 13 miles east of Goldendale, Washington on the road to the small community of Roosevelt. This virtually desert land, stony and with very poor fertility is the home of these gorgeous blossoms – in violent contrast to their sterile habitat. The owner has allowed me to collect some of them and they are in my gardens today.

Propagation: By seeds only. The flower stems are jointed and as soon as the seeds are ripe they break off. By this time they are pretty well dried and are so light that the wind easily blows them away, often scattering the seeds as they go. Harvesting the crop is a tedious chore. If the stems are broken off too soon the seeds will not be sufficiently ripe to germinate. A day or two later the capsules may have scattered their fruit upon the ground where it is virtually impossible to see it or the entire structure may, literally, have gone with the wind. As the capsules on the same and different plants do not all ripen at the same time a close watch for a couple of weeks may be necessary to collect all of it. These black seeds are in a closely huddled group at the base of the capsule and it is necessary to tear it completely apart to see if it contains any. The first season I was too casual in examining for seed and lost it all, on the assumption that if it wasn't obviously in sight none had been set. Unlike some of the other members of the genus in my gardens, *L. rediviva* produces moderate but consistent crops.

Planted in full sun as soon as they are ripe in flats containing half crushed lava rock and half leaf mold they come up in the spring as thick as wheat. I have often thought one seed must surely produce several plants although I know this is ridiculous. The following winter, however, most of these yearlings rot out unless they are kept dry. Far more than 90 percent are lost under these conditions. In the Goldendale-Roosevelt station mentioned above I have dug the mature plants in ground so muddy in winter that I had to wear boots. But this was just after a heavy rain and in a few days the soil returned to its meager winter moisture. They simply will not stand this extreme wetness for any length of time.

Sometimes plants will be found with two, three or four crowns and intergrowing roots. These can be cut apart and grown as single plants. Apparently this is a case of natural root grafting. There is no useful purpose in making these separations as they are more beautiful in compact clusters. I have tried splitting them from top to bottom, through crowns and roots, cutting them into both halves and quarters. Most of these divisions died and I ended with fewer plants than I started with. The few survivors were slow to re-establish themselves. To the best of my knowledge they can be grown only from seeds. There are no crownal offsets as with some of the other species.

Culture: In the drier climates where constant freezing can be expected all winter this isn't much of a problem. Frozen earth is dry earth. But where winters go back and forth from freezing to thawing or in places where freezing does not normally occur but where there is a good deal of rain the Bitter Root has a difficult time surviving. But there are ways of adapting them to these unfavorable conditions.

Sharp drainage is absolutely essential. I obtain this with a mixture of half crushed lava and half leaf mold – both drainage and food are provided with this mixture. But that alone is not enough. At least a half an inch – and preferably more – of crushed rock, pea size and larger, tucked around the crown will prevent rotting. It is not possible to over emphasize this detail. Inattention to it cost me numerous valuable plants until I learned not to fight nature.

This is the only *Lewisia* of my acquaintance that demands full sun to flower. I tried them in a planter box with morning sun only. They did not live. Neither low winter temperatures, high summer ones in full sun, nor mid year drought will hurt them. Excessive water is their deadliest enemy. Planting in holes drilled in very porous rock with a mix of leaf mold and crushed rock will suit them nicely if the holes are large enough and deep enough to give the roots ample room. If they are cramped in these holes they will live but flower only sparsely. They like chinks and crevices in rocks too. But in all cases plenty of rock chips under the crowns is essential, very essential. Mass plantings or in clumps shows them off to good advantage. An even better effect is obtained if a white is included with the pinks. Or a circle of whites with a few pinks in the middle will give an astonishingly beautiful contrast. They can also be placed on their sides in rock walls, blending the whites with the pinks but with a preponderance of the latter. While the rare white forms are lovely the best of the rich, glowing pinks are even more magnificent and I prefer to use the whites to accentuate these richer colors.

The biggest problem in using these white *L. redivivas* is to acquire them. I know of only three American and one British nurserymen who handle them and they all obtained their starts from me. I believe our native plants can best be preserved, in most cases, by seeing to it that they are propagated and distributed into our gardens.

Slugs are a minor problem. They sometimes eat the upper ends of the leaves and seem to prefer the tender growth. The problem is not serious and presents little or no threat of survival. Adequate control is obtained by baiting during the fall, winter and spring when the leaves are present. *L. brachycalyx* and *L. rupicola* are the only other *Lewisias* in my gardens that are attacked by these pests.

This species, like a number of others, flowers better in the garden than in the wild where sufficient food and adequate moisture are not necessarily available. The rich leaf mold and humus I mix with rock is responsible for the superior blossoming I get in my gardens. Give them plenty of food and you can expect plenty of flowers.

Cultural summation: Full sunshine, sharp drainage, a collar of rock around the crown, and moisture control.

Flowering Time: In the southern part of its range where spring is in a hurry, as early as March. Farther north and at higher altitudes varying from April, May, June and into July. During my visit to the Bitter Root Valley they were just coming into flower in late May, but exact dates are not necessarily reliable as seasons vary considerably. Meriwether Lewis made his find on July 1st – fully a month later than mine although he was only about 12 miles south of where I first saw them 142 years after he did. The white and the pink blossom about the same time and both are equally hardy.

In my Portland, Oregon gardens they have flowered as early

as May seventh and as late as June 17th – a goodly span for a glorious flower.

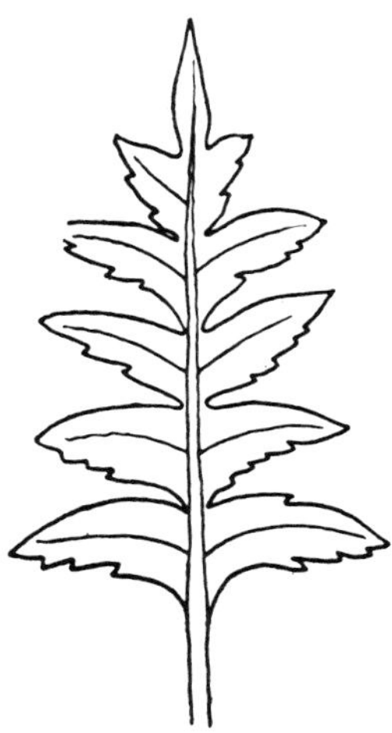

Parted margin

Lewisia rupicola No Established Common Name

LEWISIA RUPICOLA English
No Established Common Name

Saddle Mountain is in extreme northwestern Oregon. The Pacific Ocean, ten or 15 miles westward can be seen from its three thousand foot top. It isn't much of a mountain as far as height is concerned in this part of a rugged country. But botanically it has a good deal of significance for upon its sides some species of plants are found that grow nowhere else in Oregon and, in some instance, in only very few other places in the northwest.

From the campground at its base it looks like an enormous boulder, and that's what it is. A pleasant trail leads to the top some three miles away. For the first half of the distance the path leads through a forested area. Then it abruptly changes into the open with a little steeper grade. A little more than two hours, at a leisurely pace, brings the hiker to its double top, largely barren of trees in the sparse soil. At the first of these peaks I left the trail and climbed to a small, grassy meadow. It was there that I saw my first wild *L. rupicola.* They were scattered here and there – never abundant – in the humusy, thin soil. I found a few others in a little broken rock and skimpy earth on both sides of the trail. I climbed to the top of an immense solid rock plateau and found a few more, often in soil that was no more than an inch or two deep. In these instances the roots had found small cracks that allowed them to penetrate to permanent moisture.

All of them were on a south exposure where they received full sun all day long. I more or less expected this, for its close relative, *L. columbiana,* I found under similar conditions on Hamilton Mountain. This is another small peak just west of the Cascade Divide in the Columbia Gorge, 30 some odd miles east of Portland on the Washington side of the river.

Saddle Mountain is an Oregon State Park and the removal of plants and seeds is forbidden. I knew this, of course, and recognized the plant at once for I had already obtained some of them from a nurseryman in Bothell, Washington, nearly 200 miles north of my Portland home. I also grew quite a number from seed that I obtained from a dealer in Scotland.

While I was studying these plants on the mountain I had to laugh a little. There I was, smack in the midst of them in their native home, scarcely two hours drive from where I live. And yet I had to send two or three times that far to get the plants and across a continent and an ocean for the seed. This is a common experience. It is often easier to get our own natives in the British Isles and continental Europe than it is right here in the west where they have been growing for a good many thousands of years. Applied to plants there is a good deal of truth in the biblical saying, 'A prophet is not without honour, save in his own country.'

Lewisias are generally from dry climates and it is really surprising that this species thrives close to the ocean where the rainfall is heavy.

History: For history of the family and genus see article "The *Lewisias.*" For a long time *L. rupicola* – which means growing on cliffs or ledges – was considered a form of *L. columbiana.* This latter species was considered a *Calandrinia* when it was first described by Oregon's first resident botanist, Thomas Howell, in 1887. In 1893 he changed his mind and placed it among the *Oreobromas.* Robinson, in 1897, made it the present *L. columbiana.* It wasn't until 1934 that Carl S. English Jr., of Seattle, Washington established *L. rupicola* as a seperate species. The distinction was justified for these two species, though closely allied, are so different in gross appearance and in detail that each deserves its own individuality in the world of flowers.

Description: The thick base of the root just below the crown branches into fleshy roots four inches or more long. The perennial leaves are deep, rich green above and paler below with a distinct longitudinal ridge running the entire length. They are thick, narrow, and widened at the tip, up to two inches long, a quarter of an inch wide at the broadest part, abruptly pointed at the apex, and with entire margins. They form a close, basal crown with those in the middle as little as an eighth of an inch long. They become progressively longer towards the outside of the cluster with those at the base of the rosette the longest and lying flat upon the ground. An ordinary mature plant will be about three and a half inches in diameter with 60 or more leaves.

One of the great charms of this rarity is the crownal offsets. I have seen as many as eight in the wild and one in my garden has 14. These side crowns snuggle closely to the parent plant and create a compactness unknown in any other *Lewisia* – a graceful growth that makes this species outstanding for its foliage alone. These crownal offspring, two to two and a half inches in diameter, are usually somewhat smaller than those with only a single crown. With so many rosettes one would expect the plants to be quite large but the short stems create a density that belies this thought. One of mine with eight rosettes is only four inches across. Another veteran with 14 is five inches in diameter. Under favorable conditions these side crowns will start to appear in three years although this varies markedly with different individuals. When planted in holes an inch and a half in diameter drilled in porous rock the restricted root room does not induce crownal offsets and the plants may be only an inch to an inch and a half across. Flowering is also more restricted and an extra year or two may be needed for them to appear.

The slender stems, from one to several to each plant, arise diagonally to a height of four to eight inches and terminate in open clusters of flowers about an inch in diameter. The seven to ten petals are rose-pink with narrow stripes which are a much deeper and richer red. The ovate capsules are very small and contain only a few or no seeds.

Rarity: Very rare due to its limited range and collecting restrictions in some areas. It is not difficult to obtain, however, as a few nurseries handle it. It is sometimes offered as *L. rupicola,* or as *L. columbiana variety rosea.* This latter name can be misleading. Sometimes it is actually *L. rupicola,* or it may be one of the more colorful forms of the variable *L. columbiana.* I have never seen a white form but one may appear some time, somewhere.

Distribution: Washington in Grays Harbor County, formerly known as Chehalis County, in the extreme western part of the state. Saddle Mountain was for many years believed the only place in Oregon where it grows. There are a number of other mountains in this rugged section of the Coast Range that have been but little explored by botanists. Most of them have no trails leading to or up them and are, consequently, difficult of access in this brush choked land. Loggers have roamed over a good deal of this terrain but their interests are in trees. So it was only in 1964 that another station was located on Onion Peak, about 15 miles southwest from Saddle Mountain. Both are about the same elevation. An effort is being made to have this peak declared a special state park to preserve this species from wholesale collecting. It is quite likely that other patches will be found on the bare, rocky tops of some of the other nearby mountains.

Propagation: Crownal offsets can be cut off in spring or summer and rooted in sand in the shade. But multi-crowned plants are so much more attractive than those with single rosettes that it seems a pity to destroy this charm for such a purpose. The only other method is by seeds. When most of the flowers have faded and the capsules matured I cut off the stems, place them on papers in a dry cool room and let them complete the ripening process from the stored sap. Then I crumble the material in my fingers and a surprisingly large number of seeds are often found when the examination of individual capsules reveals only a few. They should be planted as soon as ripe in flats containing at least three-quarters humus that is decayed until it is soil, and one-quarter fine crushed rock. Germination is good with fresh seed but that I have obtained from overseas is usually half a year old. These do not produce many plants.

By mid-summer the youngsters should be large enough for removing to their permanent positions. On Saddle Mountain I found extremely few plants that had been produced that year. Nature's chance germination with this species, as with most all others, is very poor.

Culture: Transplanting evergreen *Lewisias* should be done in spring and early summer. Mortality as high as 25 to 50 per cent may be experienced with autumn and winter moving. In spite of the fact that I found them in full sun on Saddle Mountain, in the garden they do a little better with morning sun only and light shade in the afternoon.

In a rich soil composed mostly of humus with a little crushed rock to promote drainage they do ever so much better than in their native homes. Growth is better, faster and they are more floriferous.

One of my plants with seven crowns had two dozen blossoms out at one time and over 100 buds. Another with five crowns, a little later in the season, displayed 76 flowers at one time with 375 more either having already flowered or yet to come. At the height of the season I counted 129 blossoms on a different plant with additional buds.

The only fault with this *Lewisia* is the over-long stems. The effect would be greatly enhanced if they were much shortened. There is a chance that a dwarf form will appear some day.

Slugs are not consistent in their attacks upon the foliage. Weeks may go by with no sign of them. Then, overnight, half the leaves may be eaten down to stubs. If baiting is not done at once the rest of the leaves may disappear the following night, leaving only a green nubbin of a crown. Strangely enough the plants soon recover and send out new foliage so that within less than a year no sign of damage can be seen.

Most plants will flower the second season from seed. Occasionally a third season will be required. Rarely a plant will blossom the first year but only sparsely and late. Three or four years should yield fully mature specimens except for those with numerous crowns. This multi-rosette growth may not appear at all in poor soils. Under rich, but moist and well drained conditions some of the extra crowns appear the third season. Those with eight, ten, 12 or more are veterans and highly prized. They may be anywhere from five to ten years old. More than ordinary friendship is needed to induce an owner to part with one.

L. rupicola is remarkably tolerant of excessive wet. I have not placed the usual layer of small rock under the crowns of any of mine and have yet to lose a single one from this or any other cause. The same applies to *L. columbiana.* Rot induced losses have occurred among all my other species – the bane of the *Lewisias.*

My list of favorites in "The *Lewisias*" article places *rupicola* fourth, just below *cotyledon.* This is because the latter is the most variable of them all, both in flower and foliage, and therefore has a far greater potential for hybridizing between species, and improvements within the species than any of the others. *L. rupicola* specimens are much the same in all respects. Otherwise I would place it ahead of *L. cotyledon.*

Flowering Time: In my gardens the first buds have opened as early as May 12th and the last on June 26th – 45 days. A second crop is quite common, but not on all plants. They appear in late July and often go through August, September and October. During this last month a few buds may still remain but fail to open due to the increasingly cold weather. Five months of floral delight.

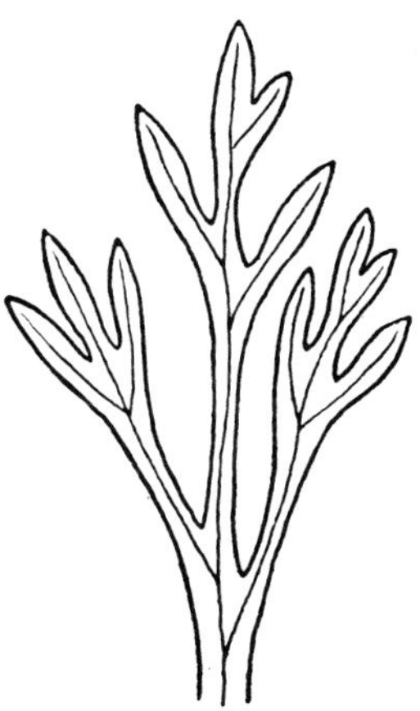

Dissected margin

Lewisia tweedyi
No Established Common Name

LEWISIA TWEEDYI (A. Gray) Robinson
No Established Common Name

A granite boulder as big as a house was resting on the steep hillside in the Wenatchee Mountains. As I slowly climbed up to it I wondered why such an enormous ball of solid rock hadn't roared down the slope, smashing everything in its way. I struggled around its east face until I reached its upper surface, then slowly worked down the other side. Just below it there was another boulder, weighing a ton or so. As I rounded this comparative midget a single blossom of *Lewisia tweedyi* greeted my widening eyes.

I stood there gasping with astonishment at this remarkable flower – the first I had ever seen. I recognized it at once from the descriptions I had carefully read about it, for there is no other plant like it in the Wenatchees or anywhere else.

I had traveled through the Cascades and over two mountain passes on a three day trip for no other purpose than to collect and study this very rare beauty in its native habitat. My collecting permit allowed me to take 12 plants but this was the only one I was able to find. I went back to the forest ranger's office where one of the staff offered his help. We went a couple of miles to just outside of the forbidden Tumwater Botanical Area where we found a few more. I collected ten, sufficient for my purpose, and spent the rest of my time observing the conditions under which they lived.

Leavenworth, in the geographical middle of Washington, is a little town of about 1,500 and much like many other communities of its size. It nestles in a tiny valley surrounded by several mountain ridges rising almost vertically for 5,000 feet or more. These peaks, and the streams at their feet, come together at Leavenworth where the Wenatchee River flows through the hamlet. This setting gives the residents an awe-inspiring view such as few other communities in all America can claim. The clear, rushing waters, the snow streaked mountains and the tiny plant I had traveled so far to see all combined to make that 20th of May a day I shall long remember.

These plants were at about 1,200 feet although they are found on the mountain ridges at 5,000 feet or more. All that I saw were on a south slope in very light shade with a little sun filtering in here and there. They were among scattered trees consisting of the Ponderosa Pine, Western Red Cedar, Douglas Fir, Alaskan Yellow Cedar, Engelmann Spruce, Little Sugar Pine, Lowland White Fir and Lodgepole Pine. This mixed stand of forest trees indicated an overlapping of those from the wet west side of the Cascade Mountains with the ones of the drier eastern slopes where the Wenatchees are located. This growth told me a great deal about the climate which further research confirmed. The summer temperatures rise to 100 degrees or more and in the winter the thermometer drops as low as 30 below – *L. tweedyi,* therefore is hardy. The pines indicated sparse precipitation – 17 or 18 inches of rain plus another five or six inches in the form of snow to a depth of four feet or more. This snow and freezing is important. It means that the ground is frozen solid and under these conditions is dry, protecting the *Lewisia* roots from their deadliest enemy, rot.

The warm sun on the south slopes melts the snow and the plants can start their season's growth in these locations by about the first of April. Later, of course, on north slopes and at high altitudes.

The soil for several inches deep was a combination of decomposed granite in the form of coarse grit mixed with the leaf mold of ages – exactly what this *Lewisia* likes. Beneath was solid granite with cracks here and there for the ever-seeking roots. I brought back 100 pounds or so of this marvelous soil, although I would have preferred a truck load.

All the plants I found were on steep slopes – about 30 degrees or more. Some were upright, others were on their sides, peeping out from under boulders. I found one under a flat rock, where the crown was at the opening of a miniature cave. There was just enough room for me to get my arm, with a trowel in my hand, inside where I carefully loosened the root. I had to reach in to shoulder depth to get all the root system. In my one-tracked stupidity it never occurred to me that this was an ideal den for a rattlesnake or two. At any rate the owners, if any, weren't home and I removed the specimen safely. The root at the base of the crown was much thicker than my thumb and it was over two feet long – much like an old piece of rope. There were a few ticks in this country too but I gave little attention to these pests. I was looking for *Lewisias,* not trouble.

History: For history of the family and genus see article "The *Lewisias*." There is such a great variation in both flowers and foliage in this genus that it is understandable that the botanists themselves were uncertain what some of them were when they were first discovered.

Asa Gray, 1810-1888, first named this one *Calandrinia tweedyi* in 1887. Thomas Howell, 1842-1912, changed it to *Oreobroma tweedyi* in 1893. Then Benjamin Lincoln Robinson, whose name appears so often in the study of this genus, in 1897 gave it the now officially adopted *Lewisia tweedyi.* All of these authors have honored Frank Tweedy who was associated with the North Transcontinental Survey which was organized in connection with the Northern Pacific Railway. Tweedy, and T.S. Brandegee, also a member of the Survey party, collected it. Tweedy found it on the Wenatchee's Mount Stuart about 15 miles southwest of Leavenworth. Except for his association with this unusual member of the Purslane Family, Mr. Tweedy seems to have disappeared into the mists of history.

Description: The root of Tweedy's *Lewisia* is extremely thick, branched or not and sometimes two or three feet long although usually much shorter. The basal portion just below the very heavy crown is much larger than many other *Lewisias* due presumably to the numerous offsets. These crowns, half a dozen or more, grow so densely that they detract from the appearance of the plant.

The numerous, evergreen, smooth, light green leaves with entire margins are up to half a foot long, including the stems, those nearer the middle of the basal rosette being the shorter. The blades, sometimes shallowly notched at the apex, are up to two inches wide, egg-shaped with the widest part above the middle. The petioles, three-eighths of an inch wide, are as long as the blades, somewhat flattened with the edges turned upward forming a shallow groove, and widened to three-quarters of an inch at the base. The underside of the stem is strongly ridged at the base and less so upwards until the ridge becomes obscure near the tip of the blade. The leaves are leathery, inconspicuously veined, and lighter green on the underside. These leaves, are very different in appearance from all other *Lewisias* and at once identify the species. A mature plant will be eight inches in diameter.

The several flowering stems protrude just beyond the leaves – a delightful arrangement unfortunately not found in all the other species. They are numerous in mature plants – a dozen or more – slender, leafless, but with thin small bracts. There are several buds scattered at intervals along the stems, the terminal one flowering first. The eight to 12 broad petals open widely creating a saucer rather than cup-shaped blossom of truly royal beauty. They are up to three inches or slightly more in diameter, cream colored or often tinged with apricot or pink near the tips of the petals. The petals are by no means individualists. They close and cling together as age overtakes them, being replaced with those lower on their scapes. The egg-shaped capsules are small and contain up to 12 to 20 seeds, usually fewer, and in my gardens more often none.

Rarity: Very rare due to scarcity within the limited range. An extremely rare pink form exists, both in its alpine home and in cultivation.

Distribution: From about a thousand feet or less to more than five thousand in the Arid Transition Life Zone. Limited to the Wenatchee Mountains of Central Washington. Stations at Mount Stuart, both sides of Tumwater Creek, Chumstick Creek, as well as other places, sometimes at the top of high ridges.

Propagation: Seed is produced only meagerly in my gardens – some seasons none. Sow as soon as ripe in flats containing equal parts of leaf mold and small or crushed rock. Some of my friends report poor success but germination with me has been excellent over a period of years. The seedlings make a good growth the first year if the soil is fertile, flowering the second or third season. Seedlings up to one year old are unusually resistant to rot – very much unlike their mature relatives.

Crownal offsets may be cut, as close to the main root as possible, treated with root growth hormone and placed in the sand filled cutting box. These root faster and easier than any other *Lewisia* I have ever tried, with never a failure. They should be taken in the spring, summer, or very early fall. Cuttings taken during the first of November stay alive but do not root at this time of the year. They flower the second or third season. As these crowns are produced in abundance, more than any other *Lewisia,* this is a quick way of multiplying stock.

Culture: This majestic queen of the kingdom of flowers has been praised for its beauty and criticised for its uncertain and often short reign.

Because of their somewhat flattened blossoms they appear bigger than they are and have been described as the largest of the family. But a ruler quickly dispels this erroneous concept. *L. rediviva* flowers present themselves as chalices and appear smaller, but in diameter both are equal. I have even found an occasional Bitter Root blossom exceeding *L. tweedyi* in size. This inhabitant of the Wenatchee Mountains has petals of a satiny texture and is startlingly beautiful. But its flowers are nowhere near as colorful as *L. rediviva's* which takes top honors in sheer loveliness in my opinion. Neither American or British writers share this opinion nor do most of my friends. But place the blossoms side by side and decide for yourself.

One of my plants had 17 flowers and 34 buds for a total of 51, which was not at all unusual. Other plants may have twice as many. Youngsters going into their second year may have half a dozen or less. The rosettes, more upstanding than *L. cotyledon's* for instance, make a more compact growth and, with the profusion of flowers are a wonderful sight to behold – another reason for eagerly awaiting the warmth and color of spring.

I had heard so many stories of the difficulties – and impossibilities – of growing this plant that I was hesitant to make the attempt. But these problems are exaggerated and arise largely from ignorance of the few conditions required for its survival and health. True, it is the most difficult of all the *Lewisias.* True, it is for the expert gardener. It is *not* true that it cannot be conquered. Failures and successes revolve around a single factor as a rule – crown rot. Once this is overcome the other necessities usually fall into place and are easily handled. No competent rock gardener need hesitate to try *L. tweedyi.*

In the Wenatchees where I first studied them I found evidence that even in this dry climate some of the crowns had rotted off. But they were replaced with offsets and the plants survived. In my wetter climate the death of a single crown almost always means the end of the entire plant. Placed vertically in the garden or in pots they rarely survived more than one season no matter how carefully I had fulfilled all their other needs. The answer is simple – turn them on their sides or place them under the protection of an overhang where moisture cannot get at the crowns. I have a planter box on the front porch, with an east exposure where very little rain can get to the plants. Under these conditions *L. tweedyi,* facing straight up, does very nicely.

Other considerations must be understood and handled correctly and in detail. Many plants are lost in winter which is what can be expected when they are not given their needed protection. But with the warmth and drier days of spring when the flowers are at their best the beginner is lulled into a sense of security – the hazards, apparently, are over and the challenge has been met. It is quite a shock then to discover that some of them wither and die overnight. I had heard of this peculiarity but did not believe it until it was brought to my attention abruptly and bluntly. The crown rots and the whole plant is only a memory. Besides turning the plants on their sides the other cultural requirements to prevent this catastrophe are:

Perfect drainage. Broken or crushed rock mixed with an equal amount of humus is a good combination.

An inch of small rock under the heavy crowns. This is the vulnerable part of the plant and moisture must not be allowed there at any time. If there is any question it is far better to err on the dry side. I have never heard of any *L. tweedyi* dying of thirst. The leathery leaves and massive root system will store a great deal of water.

Old leaves are dying nearly all year round but late in the season when the new growth has replaced those of the previous year the process is more rapid. These should all be removed, both for appearance and to help provide aeration. Stagnant air retains moisture.

All side crowns should be removed likewise for even better aeration – this cannot be overdone. These offsets are often so dense that removing them safely is difficult. I use a long narrow bladed knife made for this purpose. The leaves are so crowded that some guesswork is involved. I once cut off an entire plant. The root stub died – they will not grow from roots – but I cut off all the crowns and used them for propagating stock. Leaving only the central crown improves the looks of the rosette as soon as a few new leaves fill out the emptiness. I usually perform this surgical operation just after flowering time to get the maximum floral display and still early enough to root the cut away offsets. Some I use in my own gardens and others are given or traded to friends – half the fun of growing wild flowers is in the giving and receiving.

If the above directions are followed meticulously there is no reason why an expert gardener cannot grow them. I have had mine for a number of years and know another fan who has had them for more than a quarter of a century. Very few nurseries handle them but the prices are not much higher than for the other better *Lewisias.*

They can take quite a bit of heat. Temperatures of 100 degrees, while not common, are known in their native Wenatchees and they can easily take 30 below zero.

Each plant should have enough room to display its charms. Mass plantings are not as effective as individual ones because of the large number of flowers arising from each. They do not like crowding any more than any other *Lewisia.* A place in a rock wall suits them ideally, either in sun or light shade. It does well in the alpine house too, where moisture can be controlled.

If all this seems too much trouble, remember that success will give you one of the rarest and most beautiful wild flowers that North America has ever known.

Flowering Time: May, June and July, depending upon elevation, in the Wenatchee Mountains. In my gardens the first flower appeared one season on April sixth and the last on May 24th. Two established plants sent out a second crop. The first bud opened on June 17th and the last faded away on August first. The second flowering was not as abundant as the first – nine to each plant. This is about what can be expected most years.

Lilium bolanderi Bolander's Lily

LILIUM BOLANDERI Watson
Bolander's Lily

My first experience with this unusual lily was a delightful surprise. All my later relationships with it were also surprises, but mostly exasperating, frustrating and disappointing. I had received an unexpected package from a friend in southwestern Oregon. It contained a plant about six inches high with a single trumpet-like flower quite unlike any other I had ever seen in size, shape or color. There was no label or notation of any kind. At first I thought it must be some strangely beautiful *Fritillaria.* I examined the bulb and did not find any of the rice-like scales so typical of that genus. The scales were those of the true lilies. From then on it didn't take me long to discover that I had the rare and distinguished Bolander's Lily. I planted it immediately. It was in such excellent condition, as though it had been collected only a few minutes before, that I photographed it at once. It was fortunate that I did for the next year it struggled feebly above ground and died before the end of the season.

My southern Oregon friend, Rosamond Hess, knew I was as enchanted with it as she was so she sent me two more plants. They failed to survive the winter. But we weren't quitting. She sent me another. It came up about two inches in the spring and looked very promising – then it slowly withered away. Next year Rosamond sent me some seeds. They germinated the following spring and now, in their second year they are healthy and show promise of beauty to come. But my experience with this difficult plant as well as that of others who are more skillful than I, adulterates my hopes with skepticism. But under the right circumstances this plant can be grown and flowered. Under the section on *culture* I'll tell you how it is done.

History: This lily was named and described officially in 1885 by Sereno Watson (1826-1892) of Harvard University in honor of Henry Nicholas Bolander, (1831-1897). Tastes in lilies vary greatly. To me Bolander's is one of the very best of the approximately 20 species of American and Canadian lilies, about half of which are natives of the Pacific States.

The Lily Family, *Liliaceae* is a very large one of wide

distribution comprising about 120 genera and around 1,250 species. A few of the genera are of little interest but many are among our most beautiful plants and occupy important positions in our gardens. Some are trees but most are perennial herbs arising from corms, bulbs or rarely, rootstocks.

The true lilies are among the most spectacular members of the family. There is a wide difference of opinion as to the number of species. Estimates run from 50 to 300 or 400. Probably those that are entitled to specific rank number around 100. There are, of course, a great many hybrids that have been developed over the years and new ones are being constantly added to horticultural lists. They are very closely related to the *Fritillarias* which usually have smaller corollas and are more uniformly campanulate. The lilies generally have funnel shaped flowers. The *Fritillarias* either have coated bulbs or rice-like scales while the true lily bulbs always have scales which are never rice-like. This is one certain way to differentiate the two genera.

The lilies are native only to the northern hemisphere and extend around the world. They are found in India, China, Japan and other parts of Asia as well as in Europe. They are not found in South America, Africa or Australia. Their southern limits are Florida and the Neilgherry Mountains of India. Northward they are limited to Siberia and Southern Canada.

Description: Bolander's Lily grows from an ovate bulb, an inch to an inch and a half long and approximately as broad. It consists of numerous lanceolate, not jointed, scales an inch to an inch and a half long. The stems range from six to 40 inches high. These taller dimensions are very unusual, however. In my gardens they were six inches high and under good cultural conditions may often average a foot and a half. The stems are stout and the leaves are mostly in whorls with one to three solitary ones below each whorl. The leaves are from an inch to two and a half inches long, and from a quarter to over an inch wide, powdery, paler beneath, thick, somewhat sharp pointed to more blunted. They are egg shaped in outline with the wider part of the leaf above the middle to lance shaped but with the wider part of the leaf above the middle.

The flowers borne near the top of the stem are horizontal or somewhat nodding and may number from one to an unusual eight with an average of two or three on pedicels an inch or an inch and a half long. As lilies go the blossoms are small, an inch to an inch and a half long or slightly more and funnel form in outline. The six petals of equal length are about half an inch wide, as long as the blossoms, considerably longer than wide and with the sides nearly parallel for most of their length but tapering somewhat from the middle or below the middle.

The upper third of the blossoms are somewhat spreading with the tips of the petals slightly or not at all recurved. They may be dull red, brownish red, reddish purple, and liberally dark purple spotted. These color descriptions may sound rather dull and drab but they do not do justice to the flower – a diminutive lily of exquisite beauty and a joy to possess.

Rarity: Very rare. This plant has never been abundant in any one place and its range is limited. One dealer lists the seed at three dollars a packet. Nurserymen generally do not propagate lilies for which there is only a limited demand, finding it more profitable to depend upon collectors of wild stock. This is particularly true of *L. bolanderi* which is far more difficult to grow than most of our other native species. Many of these plants bought from nurserymen die due either to ignorance of how to handle them in the garden or to planting in climates to which they are not adapted. These are the reasons Bolander's Lily is becoming ever scarcer to the extent that it is threatened with eventual extinction.

Distribution: From southern Josephine County in the Siskiyou and Coast Range Mountains of southern Oregon into the Redwood belt of Siskiyou, Del Norte and Humboldt Counties, California. It is found on rocky talus slopes, open stony ground, dry chaparral hillsides, and dry rocky ridges. One text book describes it as inhabiting wet places about springs and meadows. This is a very questionable statement. I do not believe it could withstand such conditions although some of our other native lilies thrive under such circumstances.

Propagation: I do not know of any other genus of plants which can be grown in so many different ways. Five different methods can be used although, of course, not all of them can be utilized with any single species. At least two methods can be used on all species and many of them will respond to three.

Commercial growers use methods which will produce the greatest number of flowering plants in the shortest period of time. There is one exception to this generalization. Hybrid lilies will not come true to type from seeds. This is the only sexual approach. The other four are vegetative and produce progeny like the parents.

Seeds: Plant one-half inch deep in flats in early or late spring. Most seeds will produce flowering plants the third year. Slower growing sorts may take four, five, or even six years. The number of seeds a mature plant will produce varies radically. Some species will ripen as few as a half dozen; others hundreds or even thousands. This is a mass production way of increasing stock if the parents are pure blooded and have not been cross pollinated with other species.

Division of offsets: With many species, and hybrids too, this is one of the best and easiest ways of increasing stock. A maximum of about six offsets may be obtained in a single season from a mature bulb. They form at the base of the parent bulb, on the underground stem above the bulb or on the end of the stem. The divisions are taken in the fall from two to four weeks after flowering or immediately after the seeds ripen. This is the only time the bulbs become really dormant and many species do not thrive well if they are disturbed when the roots are growing actively. The clumps should be dug carefully and the large flowering bulbs replanted immediately where they are intended to remain permanently. The smaller ones may be planted in beds about four inches deep until they are large enough to flower. This is usually in two or three years.

Scales: These are often broken off when handling the bulbs. Or they may be removed deliberately. The best time is during the dormant season in the fall. If propagated indoors under heat they should be planted just below the surface. If outdoors an inch or two deep – no more than the latter. They may be placed upright or, preferably, horizontally turned on their sides. One or more tiny bulbs usually will grow from the base of each scale. They will be large enough to flower in three years generally although a few may require only two. These youngsters, however, will not be full sized bulbs in so short a time with this method, or any of the others.

Bulbils: Some species produce small dark green or deep purple bulbils or bulblets in the upper leaf axils. None of the native Americans do this, however. A single plant may produce as many as 50 of these peculiar growths. They should be removed as soon as they are ripe but before they drop to the ground. Planted one inch deep a few will flower in two years but most will require three.

Stem rooting: A few species are stem rooting or semi-stem rooting. Pull up the stems in late summer after flowering and heel in trenches. Up to 24 bulbs per stem may be grown with this technique and they may be expected to flower in a minimum of two years but three are usually required. Commercial propagators rarely use this system any more but the home gardener may find this a fascinating process and well worth the little effort required.

Propagation Methods for L. bolanderi: Seeds and scales. Offsets are produced too but is not very practical with this species. Several years are required for them to appear, and then only a very few will be produced.

Culture: Some species grow in bogs with the tops of the bulbs barely under the surface of the wet soil. The roots may go deeply into the muck but the bulbs themselves are always above the mud and well drained. These moisture lovers do well as a rule in ordinary well drained garden loam. So do most other lilies. A light sandy soil is generally preferable but I have seen untold thousands of healthy, vigorous lilies of many species growing in full sun in good friable soils such as might be used for raising potatoes. Good drainage is a must. If water collects around the roots in winter the bulbs will rot. Many species like a little shade. Mixed with rhododendrons or in front of fences or walls with lower growing shrubs in the foreground makes pleasing arrangements both for the plants and the gardener.

Bolander's Lily has very different requirements, however. It is the only American species that is sufficiently short to be pleasing in the rock garden where a little partial shade will add to its contentment. It is one of the most difficult of all lilies to grow and as exasperating as a badly spoiled child. Give it the sharpest drainage imaginable – like the stony soil in which it thrives in its native habitat. Don't let a soft heart make you soft headed with the garden hose. Too much water is deadly after flowering. It simply will not succeed in my Portland, Oregon home where the annual precipitation is about 44 inches. For untold centuries it has lived where the rainfall amounts to about 16 or 18 inches a year and in an atmosphere with a lower humidity. From these hereditary conditions it will not budge. Even in drier climates than mine plants will go on flowering year after year until, suddenly and for no understandable reason, they will die. This is so discouraging that I know a nurseryman who has given up on them. But by keeping them coming along from seed or scales their beauty can be enjoyed every year. Once you have seen them in flower I am sure you will agree with me that the effort is well rewarded. They resent moving. When possible it is desirable to plant the seeds where you want the mature plants to have their permanent homes. Mature bulbs should be planted five or six inches deep.

This is a plant for the expert gardener – one of the reasons it lacks popularity. The other principal fault lily hobbyists find with it is its stature. Most gardeners like to boast of how tall theirs are. Height, however, is no criterion of beauty. Balance between stem, foliage and flowers is more important and there is a slow trend to recognize this relationship as more desirable then mere length of stem.

Flowering Time: Lilies bloom from late spring until early fall. But July is the month for *Lilium bolanderi* to display its shy beauty.

Lobed margin

Lilium kelloggii No Established Common Name

LILIUM KELLOGGII Purdy
No Established Common Name

While I have not seen all the species of lilies in the world I am acquainted with all the American and Canadian ones. If I had to choose one among them as my favorite it would be *L. kelloggii,* so obscure that it doesn't even seem to have a common name. I had it in my gardens for a number of years where it was as happy as I was to possess it. Lily bulbs, while too bitter for most human appetites, are edible. Field mice are not so particular and when they finally discovered my few plants they quickly disappeared. So did the field mice. I saw to that.

I have never seen it in the wild and it may well be that I never shall. It is too rare to find except by blundering upon it. The occasional collectors who supply the commercial growers are reluctant to reveal their sources of supply. This is probably a good thing. Indiscriminate collecting might soon place it among the increasing number of our extinct natives.

History: It was discovered by Henry Nicholas Bolander, (1831-1897). But Watson, who named *L. bolanderi,* confused Bolander's specimens with those of another species and *L. kelloggii* remained undescribed until Carl Purdy of Ukiah, California dedicated it to the memory of Dr. Albert B. Kellogg,(1813-1887) in May of 1901. Purdy introduced it into cultivation when he listed it in his *Price List of California Bulbs,* edition of 1905. *Index Kewensis* gives Purdy's 1905 catalogue as the work in which the plant was first published. This seems to be erroneous by four years. But there is so little information on this plant in western botanies, either old or new, that it is difficult to know just what happened. Purdy was a well known wild plant collector and grower during the first part of this century. My extensive library gives a brief description of it in a volume published in 1925, devoted to California flora. Only one later work even mentions it although it is a well known species among commercial lily growers of the Far West. I have never seen it in any gardens except my own although it is easy to grow, given the right conditions, and a pure delight to gaze upon.

Description: The smooth slender stems grow from two to

four feet high. Those in my garden were nearer the former figure. The leaves are mostly in whorls but with a few single ones scattered along the stem. The bulbs are small, from an inch and a half to two inches in diameter. The flowers are from one to 15 with an average of three or four. The six petals are strongly curved back to the stem, very much in shape like the well known tiger lily. The flowers are rather on the small side, around one and a half to two inches in diameter and two inches long. What they lack in size they more than make up in delicate fragrance. A vase of the cut flowers will quickly perfume an entire room. The ones I had in my garden were white with bright pink spots. This combination was strikingly beautiful and the entire effect was one of graceful daintiness. There are also pinks that are just as lovely when they first open and turn to a deeper rosy purple. Some of them have a central yellow line and flowers that are all yellow have been reported but these are so rare that few nurserymen have ever seen them.

Rarity: Very rare. Few nurserymen have them and those that do have only small supplies.

Distribution: Somewhat obscure. The literature on this wonderful wildling's range is fragmentary and not at all complete. In California it follows the inner margin of the Redwood belt in northern Mendocino County to Del Norte County. It is also known in Josephine and Jackson Counties of southern Oregon. I have made a number of field trips to some of these counties at various times of the year but have never seen it there. I suspect it is limited to more or less isolated areas.

Propagation: Mostly by seed and scales. Also by offsets which takes several years and produces very few. For details see instructions under *Lilium bolanderi.*

Culture: Good drainage in full sun or light shade. This is a comparatively easy lily to grow if allowed to dry out after flowering. Otherwise it will rot. Any good friable soil that does not allow water to collect around the bulbs will do nicely. Plant six inches deep. Moles and mice are their worst enemies. Metal mesh screen fine enough to keep out the latter will solve this problem nicely. There is no reason why this wholly desirable flower cannot be kept healthy and happy in the home garden indefinitely.

If you like our native lilies this one should be, by all means, included in your plantings.

Flowering Time: Late June and July.

Lilium parryi Lemon Lily

LILIUM PARRYI Watson
LILIUM PARRYI variety KESSLERI A. Davidson
Lemon Lily

The very fragrant Lemon Lily is not one of my neighbors. Its alpine home is 1,000 miles south of mine in the valley. But that does not mean that I cannot see it in local nurseries or have it in my gardens. It was in one of these commercial fields containing thousands of plants of a great many species and varieties that I first met this gorgeous species of a splendid genus. There were only a dozen or so of them in the vast field of many colors. The demand for species lilies is much more limited than that for the numerous hybrids that may be more popular but certainly not necessarily more beautiful. Furthermore, Parry's Lily is not easily obtained by nurserymen or anyone else. Its collection on public lands in California is now prohibited by law as it should be.

History: It was named by the well known botanist of Harvard University, Sereno Watson (1826-1892) in 1878 in honor of Charles Christopher Parry (1823-1890) who is also prominent in American botanical circles. The variety *kessleri* was named by Dr. Anstruther Davidson, a Los Angeles physician, 1860-1932, It seems strange that more than 40 years elapsed from the time the first western American lily was discovered until the last was introduced into cultivation at the very beginning of this century when the country was well settled and explored. And only three of these were named before the 1870's.

Description: The smooth, slender stem, from two to five feet high, averaging about half way between, comes from a small, scaly rhizome-like bulb often irregular in shape, usually about an inch in diameter and two, three or even four inches long. It is thickly covered with small scales one-half to three-quarters of an inch long, jointed, white or light yellow in color and rarely tinged with pink or purple. The horizontal leaves are from four to six inches long and one-third to one half an inch wide, tapering both ways from the widest part which is above the middle. The lower ones are usually in whorls, the upper scattered.

The flowers are borne on short, stout pedicels. They are

horizontal, funnel-shaped, two to four inches long and with the same width, the upper third widely spreading or recurved. The petals are about three-eighths of an inch wide with the apex gradually tapering. Each plant generally bears one or two flowers but under cultivation they may have as many as a rare ten. The chocolate brown anthers are prominently displayed and are very attractive. Technical descriptions of plants must be a little dull and boring to all but ardent botanists and they reveal little of the true beauty of flowers. Yellows are often weak, pale or muddy with a tendency to fade. Not so with Parry's Lily. The flowers are a pure lemon yellow, minutely and sparsely purplish brown dotted on the inside. Of the dozen or so yellow species of varying tones and hues this would be my first choice for the garden.

Lilium parryi variety kessleri: This is a wild form and not a horticultural adaptation. The flowers are larger. It grows a little taller than the type, makes a more vigorous growth, has more abundant foliage, and is better adapted to gardens. It comes true from seed. It is also more expensive. The wholesale price is fifty per cent higher than that of the type.

Rarity: The type, very rare. The variety, extremely rare. Collectors have decimated the supplies which were never abundant.

Distribution: The type: Moist places about mountain springs and meadows in the San Gabriel, San Bernardino, San Antonio and San Jacinto Mountains of southern California and eastward to Arizona, at elevations from 4,000 to 9,000 feet. The variety *kessleri:* Same habitat as the type but rarer and with a more limited range.

Propagation: From seeds and scales. Also by rare offsets which require several years and is not practical if rapid increase is wanted. For detailed instructions see under *Lilium bolanderi.*

Culture: This is a difficult plant to grow although it need not be. In spite of the fact that it grows in moist places in its native home it will thrive in ordinary well drained garden soils in either full sun or partial shade. Like most lily bulbs of the same size it should be planted about five or six inches deep. After flowering the plant goes dormant and should be allowed to dry out. The greatest cause of failure with this species is the too ardent use of the garden hose after the blossoms have disappeared.

It rots the bulbs – sure death. It is generally considered semi-hardy and will do well in climates that are not too severe.

Flowering Time: Late June and July and August depending on altitude.

Loiseleuria procumbens Alpine Azalea

LOISELEURIA PROCUMBENS Desvaux
Alpine Azalea

When I opened the package I received another Alaskan surprise. Though full grown, the *Loiseleuria* was only an inch high. Some *Rhododendrons* grow taller than a one story house and it seemed incredible that this tiny miniature could be a close relative of such floral giants.

Few people have ever heard of it and fewer still have it in their gardens, mostly because of its largely far northern home. It is a very difficult plant to acquire unless you have a sympathetic friend who lives near its chilly habitat. It is only the rare nurseryman who handles it.

History: It belongs to the great Heath Family, *Ericaceae*, of Bentham and Hooker. For the history of this family see under *Kalmiopsis leachiana*. The genus *Loiseleuria* was named in 1814 by Nicaise Auguste Desvaux, 1784-1856, in honor of J. C. A. Loiseleur-Deslongchamps, 1774-1849, a Parisian physician and botanist. So it is that a little known genus consisting of but a single species in a very large family was named for a man who, though well known in his native city, is now all but forgotten. The specific name, *procumbens*, which means trailing on the ground, was given at the same time. It accurately describes the outstanding habit of the miniature. It has had at least three other generic names one of which was *Azalea*.

A horticulturist, who is pretty well informed, told me that it is the ancestor of all our azaleas. I have been unable to discover further information on this fascinating hypothesis.

Description: It is a low, smooth, subshrub, repeatedly branched with the branches long and widely spreading. The evergreen leaves are leathery, margins entire, blunt tipped, with short leaf stems. They are considerably longer than wide and the lateral margins are parallel for most of their length. They are paler green beneath with a prominent ridge. A hand lens is quite a help in noting these details for the crowded leaves are only an eighth to five-sixteenths of an inch long. The bell shaped, five lobed flowers are usually pink but white forms are not at all uncommon. Even when not in blossom these white variations can usually be told by their lighter green leaves. These whites can be found in the vicinity of Juneau, Alaska. The tiny bells, about one-fifth of an inch in diameter are born on short pedicels in terminal clusters of from one to five. The floral and vegetative parts are in delightful miniature proportions although a hands and knees position is necessary to enjoy their dwarfed beauty.

One authority says they are usually under four inches tall. Maxcine Williams, an Alaskan botanist who has furnished me much of my field information says: "I have never seen them of any such height so would say two inches at most." Mine are less than one inch.

Many alpine plants have to hug the earth to survive in their icy homes so they make their growth by spreading. Such is the way of life this Alpine Azalea has adopted. Maxcine Williams: "I've seen a few up to eighteen inches across. In a garden, no longer kept up, one was at least two feet across. Anderson, (a well known Alaskan botanist) says 'sometimes forming mats up to eight to 12 inches in diameter but usually much smaller.' I have seen patches much larger but they were probably composed of several plants. However, as a rule, individual plants are well under 12 inches." The comparatively large plants are many years old as the growth is slow.

Rarity: Extremely rare in nurseries or gardens. Within its wild range it is from scarce to fairly common. One Alaskan says it is never abundant. Maxcine Williams: "I'd say that it was abundant in all places I have ever seen it. On top of South Newton Peak at Nome there was a stretch of maybe 50 feet that was a pink carpet. That is the most I've ever seen in one spot before but there were many other beds on both Newton and Anvil Mountains of several feet in extent. I've never seen that much on Juneau's mountains although I have seen good sized beds here and there above timberline."

Distribution: It seems to be a contradiction that a plant could be so little known but so widely distributed. Mostly confined to the subarctic regions and high mountains above timberline of the northern hemisphere. From the easternmost sector of Asia eastwards over Arctic America to east Greenland. South to New Hampshire and the 49th parallel, and in Alberta, Montana and California. Also in the northeastern European-northwestern Asia area. In the northern Urals, northernmost Scandinavia, Scottish Highlands and numerous other stations. Its obscurity must be ascribed to its lofty home where it is difficult to visit.

Propagation: Three methods. For seedling propagation seen under *Kalmiopsis leachiana.* Softwood cuttings: Take in June or July from season's growth of non-flowering wood. Treat with rooting compound and place in shaded flats containing three parts glacier sand and one part finely ground peat. Half-hardwood cuttings taken a little later and treated the same way. Layering is easy but limited in the number of plants that can be produced. Place sand under the branch, pin it down, cover it with peat and keep moist. This process should be done in April and the layers cut off the following year and potted up.

Culture: In collecting wild plants the beginner is tempted to take the largest ones he can find. This is a mistake. They are much harder to keep alive than small ones until they can become adapted to their new homes. I have made this tempting blunder in the earlier stages of my outdoor career but learned better the hard way.

It doesn't like pots and will not flower well in them. But if such containers must be used they should be large.

This is a rock garden subject and it is not easy to handle until it becomes acclimated. A study of the conditions it prefers in nature will aid in determining its domesticated requirements.

As they are usually found above timberline they get all the sun available. But in its northern home this will often mean only partial sun. In these lands temperatures are seldom very high so partial sun or light shade and a cool place in the garden is recommended. But these conditions must be altered to suit the grower's climate. More shade in hot regions.

One wild observer: "Favors more or less dry and often exposed, peaty or gravelly habitats, frequently forming rather close and tough mats in open spots in the heath." This dry condition can be misleading. After flowering it needn't have much moisture but requires well-watering in the spring. In gravel moraines below glaciers it grows thickly until the alders encroach. Then it dies out. It does not thrive under trees and resents crowding by other plants. That is why it has climbed the alpine slopes where competition is no great problem. In the rockery, therefore, it should not have to fight for its life with sturdier growers. Half leaf mold and half crushed rock is an excellent medium.

Very sharp drainage is absolutely essential. Neglect of this requirement can be fatal. Red spider may attack. Two sprays with a suitable contact insecticide eight to ten days apart will destroy both adults and the newly hatched young.

Flowering Time: Late spring and summer, depending upon altitude and climate.

Incised margin

Moneses uniflora One Flowered Pyrola

MONESES UNIFLORA (Linnaeus) Gray
One Flowered Pyrola

History: The generic name of this perennial comprising only a single species was exceedingly well chosen in 1821 by the English botanist Richard Anthony Salisbury, 1761-1829. It comes from two Greek words, *monos,* single, and *esis,* delight.

Description: As might be imagined it has a solitary flower, at the summit of a slender scape two to six inches high. The nodding blossoms with five waxy white or sometimes rosy petals are from a half to three quarters of an inch in diameter. They are as lovely and dainty as they are inconspicuous among the larger surrounding plants found in the woodlands where it grows.

Although each stem boasts of but one lonely very fragrant flower the plant itself has no hermitic tendencies. It is frequently found in little colonies like the *Pyrolas* which develop from the creeping subterranean shoots. The rich, damp forest duff in the coniferous woods it enjoys encourages this spreading habit and is an important consideration when growing it in the home garden.

The glossy, deep green leaves with short flat stems, are attractive in themselves. They are rounded, or nearly so, obscurely veined with fine, indistinct obtuse teeth, opposite or whorled and clustered at the ascending ends of the underground shoots, which root and make new plants in a friendly colony.

It is very closely related to the *Pyrolas,* the Wintergreens and, as might be expected, have been confused with that genus. Quite logically, under these circumstances, there has been a confusion of names, both botanically and common ones. One Flowered Pyrola is one of them. Others are *Moneses brevicaulis, M. grandiflora, M. reticulata* and *M. verticillata.* Also *Pyrola uniflora.* In general appearance and nature of the leaves it more closely resembles the small *Pyrola secunda* than any of the others.

The top of the flowering stem is bent over as though the weight of the blossom is too heavy for the slender scape. But after the flower has pollinized and the ovary begins to develop the stem begins to straighten until the five celled subglobose capsule with many minute seeds is looking straight up at the sky. *Moneses* has this distinctive trait in common with another of its relatives the saprophytic Indian Pipe. *Monotropa uniflora,* of the Heath Family.

A slightly different variety *M. uniflora reticulata* has been described but resembles the type so closely that it is pretty much a matter of botanical hair splitting and needs no particular elaboration in this work. Its leaves are ovate, acute or acutish, rather sharply serrate instead of crenate and with more prominent veins than the type.

While the *Pyrolas* and *Moneses* are similar their differential identification is easy enough. If the capsule splits open from the summit downwards it is a *Moneses.* If the capsule opens from the base upwards it is a *Pyrola.* A less scientific method that will delight that wonderful person, the wild flower lover, is simply this: If it has only one flower to the stem it is *Moneses.* If there is more than one blossom it has to be a *Pyrola.*

This is one of the most delightful of all forest fairies and richly deserves an honored place in the wild garden. But few of us are wise enough and fortunate enough to make it happy there.

Rarity: *Moneses uniflora variety reticulata* is rare, partly due to its limited range. *M. uniflora,* the type, is from scarce to rare depending upon the part of the world in which it grows.

Distribution: The variety, *reticulata,* is found from southern Alaska along the coast to Vancouver Island in British Columbia, through Washington and Oregon west of the Cascade Mountains to Humboldt County and the neighborhood of Mount Shasta in California. Also in the Cascade and Blue Mountains of Oregon.

The type, *M. uniflora,* has a much greater range and is primarily a mountain plant growing from moderate elevations to comparatively high altitudes in moist woodlands. It is limited to the cooler parts of the northern hemisphere. It is found in Switzerland, other parts of Europe and northeastern Asia. In America it grows from Alaska across Canada to Labrador. On the west coast southward through British Columbia, Washington, Oregon and into California. Going eastward in Utah, Colorado,

New Mexico, The Rocky Mountains, Indiana, Minnesota, Pennsylvania, Maine, Rhode Island, New York, and doubtless many other localities.

Propagation: By no means easy but it can be done by the careful gardener experienced in handling difficult plants. Divisions can be made in October or April, springtime probably being the preferred season. Potting mixture should be composed of humus mixed with coarse sand and never allowed to dry out. Spring divisions should be kept shaded and the same conditions are preferred for those made in the fall although the cooler weather at that time of the year makes this less important.

Where growth is vigorous the decumbent stems can be pinned firmly to the rich earth. This layering should be done in the spring and the plants the following spring should be ready for potting up. Cuttings can be successful although slow to root. Take them in June or July, treat with root growth hormones, and they should be ready for fall transplanting or can wait until spring. One of the greatest difficulties in propagating this plant is the slow rate of growth. A considerable amount of time is required to obtain a sizeable stock.

Seeds are scarce and they are extremely small. Sow in fall or spring on sterilized moss or peat over a very rich humus soil. A glass covering will be a real help in preventing drying out which could be fatal. Leave alone until two true leaves appear then pot in late fall or spring in rich, well drained soil. Two years are required to make sizeable plants from seed. Sometimes heavy germination may be obtained but if even a few grow there is cause for rejoicing.

Culture: If entire plants are taken from the woods late fall or spring are the best times. Large clumps of soil, disturbed as little as possible, should be dug and planted in shady places in rich, permanently moist soil, and otherwise left alone. The same rules apply to nursery or home grown stock. Wild flower dealers sometimes offer seeds and plants of the *Pyrolas* and other related genera of the heath family. If these plants are from cultivated stock they should be much better rooted than wild collected specimens and ever so much easier to adapt to garden conditions.

Flowering Time: May, June, July and August, depending upon altitude and climate.

Crenate margin

Monotropa uniflora Indian Pipe

MONOTROPA UNIFLORA Linnaeus
Indian Pipe

A deliberate search for the Indian Pipe is likely to end in failure for it is by no means common, and yet many people have seen it at one time or another. Perhaps the best way to find it is to come upon it unexpectedly in the woods. Under these circumstances the snowy plant will make one gasp with its waxy, translucent beauty. Each time it is encountered represents an exciting discovery for its rarity is matched only by its white loveliness, doubly accentuated by the shady forests it seems to prefer.

The entire plant has a fascinating whiteness which is peculiar to the Indian Pipe alone. While there are other white plants in nature none has the pure shiny white transparency that covers the entire plant from petals, sepals and stem right down to the ground and even below the surface of the soil.

History: While it is scarce enough to be a memorable event whenever it is encountered it is by no means a recent discovery. It has been known from early times for Carl Von Linneaus, the father of modern botany, described it in the first edition of his *Species Plantarum* published in 1753.

Description: It is remarkable that a plant which has been known to both science and nature lovers for so many years has so few common names. One of them, the Corpse Plant, is wholly unfair to this forest beauty. Another, the Indian Pipe, is well chosen from the North American point of view, for each stem, when the flower is at its best, terminates in a nodding blossom resembling, in a glorified way, a smoking pipe much like those used by the original Americans. Other names are Ghost Flower and Ice Plant. It is the best known and one of the most appreciated of that rare group of plants, the saprophytes, which grow around the globe. The flowers are oblong and bell-shaped. *Monotropa* is from the Greek. It refers to the terminal flower being once turned, that is nodding when young then slowly becoming more and more erect with advancing age until the entire flower and stem stand perfectly erect upon full maturity. This is a curious fact which I have not observed in very many other plants. When growth has been completed the seed ripens in the ovoid capsule in this completely vertical position. *Uniflora* refers to the single flower on each stem, unlike in this respect, its rare forest companion, the Phantom Orchid.

It is a Tertiary relic but, unlike a great number of other plants of this by-gone age, it has not disappeared. Although the mushrooms and fungi are deprived of green coloring material they are primitive forms of plant life and are not related to the Indian Pipe. It is a true flower, of the Heath family, closely related to the *Pyrolas, Rhododendrons,* blue-berries and manzanitas.

The first time I saw this ghostly flower was on the Fourth of July – an easy date to remember. It starts to blossom in late June at the lower levels and goes into August at the higher elevations of around 2,000 or 3,000 feet. If you know where to look in March you can dig down into the rich soil and find what resembles, to a marked degree, lead bee-bee shots. These are the sleeping stems which, in three or four months, will come into full blossom and later in the season remain as blackened stems.

Monotropa is a perennial and the new shoots often push their snowy heads through decayed tree leaves and the partly decomposed stems of last year's flowers. It is strange that a plant which produced an abundance of flowers last year may produce fewer this season or may die altogether. Occasionally, of course, more flowers will appear from the same plant than grew the former season. Many plants have more blossoms and become larger as they grow older. Definitely this is not true of the Indian Pipe. They grow from six to eight inches tall, and each plant will consist of half a dozen or so flowering stems, crowded so closely together that they lose much of their distinctive charm and individual beauty. The entire clump would have a much greater appeal if the stalks were more widely spaced. This is the only floral fault I can find with this plant. Generally the larger the clump the more dense the growth. I counted one plant which had more than 150 flowering stems. Occasionally there will be a plant with only a single blossom.

The Indian Pipe may be easily distinguished from the Phantom Orchid. The latter turns brown when it is dying and the former almost jet black. The Phantom Orchid is slightly cream colored and usually has several flowers on each stem while the Indian Pipe will only rarely produce two and usually only one.

The Phantom Orchid sometimes flowers in clumps of two or three but it is nearly always alone. The Indian Pipe rarely produces only two or three stems, and it flowers a full two weeks later than the Phantom Orchid, although the two are in flower at the same time. But the Phantom Orchid is well beyond its prime when the Indian Pipe is at its best.

Because the forests are being destroyed the Indian Pipes, which depend upon its shade, are, like the Indians themselves, slowly vanishing from the face of the earth.

Saprophytic plants contain no chlorophyll which is the green coloring matter in normal plants. Through the action of the sun this material manufactures starch and sugars from water and carbon dioxide. Plants which do not have it cannot manufacture their own food. The Indian Pipe is one of them. There is no question but at one time in its remote ancestry it too manufactured its own food, but throughout the ages it has come to depend more and more upon the predigested material it found in the soil until today the trend has been completed and its life depends absolutely upon decayed vegetation. Its green leaves, having lost their function of producing food, have been reduced to the white scaly bracts that characterize the entire plant.

Some of the botanies I have used in preparing this article disparage *Monotropa's* necessity of living upon the products of other plants. But in one way or another this is true of all plants and animal life. Animals either live upon each other or upon plants. And plants themselves derive some of their sustenance from the decayed remains of other plants. This is one of the immutable laws of nature and should not carry with it any trace of opprobrium.

While it seems to prefer the extreme depths of the coniferous woods where only saprophytes can grow it is sometimes found in more open spaces which it shares with some of its lower growing chlorophyll-bearing companions.

This ghostly flower of the forest appears incredibly fragile and it is. Whenever it is thoughtlessly touched by a human finger a black spot appears. Any twig dropping upon it does the same thing. Finally the entire plant turns black as if resenting intrusion upon its privacy. This peculiarity might be considered strange indeed until it is remembered that neither you nor I care to be handled by total strangers. This blackening is caused by a soluble ferment having the property of an oxidizing agent, and a tannic principle playing the part of coloring matter. In some Materia Medicas it is recommended for nervous diseases and those of the eyes. It is applied externally, fresh or preserved.

What began so inconspicuously beneath the soil early in the spring and grew into such remarkable charm and ineffable beauty in the full maturity of mid summer finally fades into dull grays and blacks as the season comes to an end. But the dying flowers continue to lift their heads to the heavens, proudly offering a new crop of seed for a new generation of plants for the coming new year.

The Indian Pipe has neither enemies nor friends. No disease and no insects attack its frail foliage. No bee is drawn to its delicate fragrance. No butterfly is drawn to its home beneath the trees and humming birds never visit it at all. It is a solitary dweller of the deep forests where it creates its magic beauty completely unattended.

Rarity: Rare.

Distribution: Japan, Korea, the Himalayas, Switzerland. In North America from Alaska to California and from Labrador to Florida, and even in South America. It flourishes from sea level and in the timbered areas of the mountains.

Propagation: Unknown. While I am sure it can be done, I have not succeeded in growing this plant from seed. Nature is continually experimenting in an attempt to adapt each plant to its particular environment, and by means of reproduction to secure the preservation of the species. In the seed of the Indian Pipe, this experimentation has culminated in the production of large quantities of seed so minute that there is very little food stored in each to permit germination. Nature in her zeal has largely defeated her own purpose. This is one of the reasons the Indian Pipe is one of our rarer flowers. Nearly every blossom produces seed abundantly in contrast to the Phantom Orchid which produces very little, often, in fact, none at all. Seed scattered on the surface of the ground consisting of rich leaf mold, in a shady place should offer the best chances of success. But many thousands of seeds might well be required to produce a single plant. Divisions taken from wild plants would be almost certain to fail.

Culture: Unknown. I have brought entire plants with large clumps of soil from the woods and planted them carefully in my gardens. All have failed in spite of all my skill and all my knowledge. Saprophytic plants seem to completely reject moving. It may be that the total lack of chlorophyll prevents the growth of new feeding roots so the plant can adapt itself to a friendly but unfamiliar habitat. Once successfully established in the garden it should be left completely undisturbed.

Flowering Time: Late June, July and into August, depending upon climate and elevation.

Pentstemon barrettae Barrett's Pentstemon

PENTSTEMON BARRETTAE Gray
Barrett's Pentstemon

Before starting out on an expedition to find a plant I have never seen I first search the literature for clues to its exact location. This is often a big help – a time and work saver, and certainly a practical approach to uncertain field work. This was my introduction to *P. barrettae.*

I spent the better part of a hot day scrambling over talus slopes and skirting the foot of sheer cliffs. The directions given in a publication devoted solely to *Pentstemons* gave its location five miles east of The Dalles, Oregon. I worked several miles on each side of the designated place and found no trace of it. All the other botanical texts gave other locations. None of them were correct or even nearly enough so that success was possible within reasonable time limits.

Finally a new friend gave me instructions that were so exact I walked right up to the colony with no hesitation whatever. The days spent in the search were well worthwhile for this is one of the most unusual of all *Pentstemons* and one of the most valuable for the garden.

History: The *Pentstemons* belong to the Figwort Family *Scrophulariaceae.* This large family, comprising about 200 genera and some 3,000 species, was named by that prominent botanical team, Bentham and Hooker. As might be expected of so large a group it is of wide geographical distribution.

The genus was named by John Mitchell, 1676-1768, in 1748. This is definite. Beyond this point the confusion begins. It has been given at least seven different generic names between that date and 1862. But the original name holds today. In a vague sort of a way there are some 230 species but no one knows for sure. They are by far the most plentiful in the western part of the United States. At least one species comes from Kamchatka and northern Japan. They extend from Alaska in North America to Guatemala and grow in every one of the 49 continental states. *Pentstemon* is from the Greek and refers to *five stamens,* four of which are fertile. The fifth is sterile and usually bearded. Closely related genera have only four. Among these the genus *Mimulus* resembles the *Pentstemons* so nearly that a stamen count may be necessary to make positive differentiation. The *Mimuli* are water lovers and are most often close to streams or oozing banks while the Beard Tongues, one of the few common names for *Pentstemons,* prefer drier places.

They are deciduous or evergreen perennials, and grow from a few inches to several feet high. Blossoms are from tiny to comparatively huge, usually of purple in various shades but include pinks, reds, whites and a very few yellows.

The genus is so large and many of the plants resemble each other so closely that some taxonomists have almost despaired of bringing order to chaos. They have been divided into subgenera and these into sections and subsections. Further confusion arises from free natural hybridizing. Sometimes one plant will have two different specific names and varieties are plentiful.

P. barrettae, however, stands alone in some respects. It was first described by Asa Gray in 1886 in his *Synoptical Flora of North America,* presumably from specimens collected by Mrs. Barrett from the Oregon side of the Columbia River. Specimens were supplied from Klickitat County, Washington by Wilhelm N. Suksdorf.

Description: The most outstanding characterisitc of this species is the evergreen leaves. They vary considerably in size and shape. They are very thick, leathery and have a succulent texture somewhat like that of Sedums but not otherwise. They run from an inch to five inches long, averaging two; from half an inch to one and a half wide. From egg shaped with the broader part toward the stem and much longer than broad, to two or three times as long as wide and the sides with a uniform curvature nearly throughout and to those considerably longer than wide and with the margins parallel for most of their length. The edges are sparingly broken by more or less irregular projecting fine points or evenly and sharply indented with the small projecting points acute. In the warmer part of the year they are an olive green with a powdery silver coat that is as distinctive as it is charming. In the winter this silvery effect fades and is replaced with a purple bronze that is much different than the summer garb but no less delightful. I do not know of any other of the numerous *Pentstemons* that have such large and showy leaves with so strong an appeal.

The flowers are tubular and terminate in expanded five lobed tips, two of which are upper and the remaining three lower. The lilac or rose-purple blossoms are an inch and a quarter to an inch and a half long, and three eighths to half an inch wide. They are a slightly darker and richer color when just opened but otherwise remarkably uniform in their light hues. The plants are very floriferous, the blossoms often appearing so densely as to half conceal the beautiful foliage.

Plants growing in crevices in the sheer basaltic cliffs will average half a foot to one foot in diameter. On talus slopes that are almost all rock the roots will penetrate so deeply that they will find food and permanent though very little moisture. This seems to be exactly what they want. I have found such plants the usual foot to foot and a half tall but fully four feet in diameter by actual measurement. I pried a large slab of rock off the cliff face to lift out one of the plants that was about eight inches high and half a foot in diameter. The root system was fan shaped, a foot wide and over two feet long! This gives an indication to what extent rock plants will go to assure a permanent supply of food and moisture.

Rarity: Extremely rare. Rare plants are often difficult to obtain. But this one is so distinctive and so desirable that it is well recognized in both British and American wild flower gardens. Some of the nurseries dealing in native flora stock it. Because of its semi-domesticity and its cliff-side inaccessability it isn't likely to become exterminated.

Distribution: On sheer basaltic cliff faces, talus slopes, and flat but very stony ground. Near Mosier, Oregon adjacent to and paralleling the Columbia River Highway for a distance of about a mile. Within easy view of passing motorists. Between Bingen and Lyle, Washington, approximately opposite Mosier. Nowhere else in the world as far as known. These three small towns are on the eastward slope of the Cascade Mountains where the precipitation is considerably less than on the westward side.

Propagation: Most *Pentstemons* are easy to propagate and Barrett's is no exception. I have had excellent germination from seeds sown in the fall. If the source of supply is from isolated plants they should come true to type. But if any of the *fruticosus* group are nearby hybrid seedlings may be expected. Natural crosses are very prevalent among some members of this genus. Near the Mosier station where I collected my seeds the only other *Pentstemon* I saw was *richardsonii,* one of the deciduous sorts.

Cuttings from the season's growth root easily in damp sand kept in the shade. I have yet to have a single cutting fail to root. Mid to late summer when the new growth has had a chance to partially ripen is probably the best time but I wouldn't hesitate to take them at any other season.

Culture: Some of the directions for growing this plant in the garden are erroneous. Allegedly, some writers consider it difficult, requiring definite shade or sun treatment. In the wild I found them on the north side of cliffs where they received little sunshine except possibly very late in the day. I have found them exposed to full afternoon sun. I climbed to the top of the cliffs. There, in a shallow basin, in full sun all day long, they seemed just as healthy as elsewhere. At the Washington station they are exposed to full afternoon sunshine. They flower a little more luxuriously with an abundance of sunshine. Sharp drainage is a must but this need is no different than what many other members of the genus require. It is strictly a rock plant. I have never seen it growing under any other conditions. This is one of our best garden Beard Tongues. I can't help feeling, however, that it would be much better if the flowers were a little richer and deeper in color.

If large plants are wanted in the rockery give it a place where the roots can wander freely in the stony soil. It can be kept within more confined limits if the roots are given less room to roam. But it will not do well if it is planted in holes drilled in rock although the *Pentstemons richardsonii* and *menziesii* will tolerate a considerable amount of these drastic restrictions. Perhaps the best place for a small *P. barrettae* is in a tiny crevice with plenty of sun.

Flowering Time: April to June, depending upon the season. One of the nice qualities of this plant is its comparatively early blossoming time.

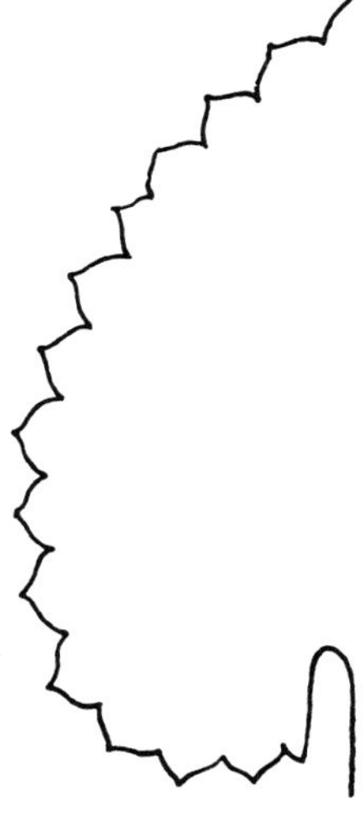

Dentate margin

Pentstemon cardwellii 'White' Cardwell's Pentstemon

PENTSTEMON CARDWELLII Howell
Cardwell's Pentstemon

The summer sun reflected on the barren rock such a fierce and deadly heat that I drank over a gallon of water that afternoon – and it wasn't enough. I was on the lava beds of Oregon's upper Hood River Valley not far from the base of Mt. Hood, searching that desolate area for wild flowers. The porous rock was comparatively new for there were only small amounts of humus in the faulted surface. Plant life of any kind was sparse. And it was no wonder for this was the hottest place I had ever been. I did not understand how anything could live, let alone thrive, in that incredibly dry and terrific heat. Nevertheless it was in a narrow crack in that once molten rock that I saw my first *Pentstemon cardwellii.* There were only a few of them, close together as though seeking companionship in that hostile environment. It was with some effort that I was able to free the roots of one plant from its tenacious hold deep in the crevice where it had been compelled to go to reach a little moisture to combat a great deal of heat. There was no trouble transplanting it successfully into my gardens, partly due to my great care to keep the roots moist, and partly that this is a tough, hardy individual, inured to taking punishment.

I knew it was a *Pentstemon,* of course, but in the tangled maze of this frustrating genus I couldn't be sure which it was. My friend, Nettie Gale, one of Portland's outstanding authorities on our native flora, identified it as *P. fruticosus cardwellii,* a synonym.

Only one plant rewarded my searches in that forbidding lava flow but I was as happy with my treasure as I was to get out of the place. Certainly there are much hotter regions where life can endure but I shall gladly leave them to sturdier spirits than mine.

History: This valuable addition to the rock garden has a unique history. It was first named and described in 1901 by Thomas Howell in his *A Flora of Northwest America.* Mr. Howell, 1842-1912, was Portland's first resident botanist who produced a flora of his part of the country. He had a brother who was a successful grocer. Thomas Howell, himself, was a poor man but thoroughly dedicated to his profession. He was so impoverished, in fact, that he could not afford to hire printers to publish his book. Nothing daunted, he learned to set type and did the work himself. It wasn't much of a success at first but today it is a rarity and sells for $15 to $50 a volume and it is very difficult to acquire at any price. I have a copy of it in front of me to help in preparing this account. Mr. Howell predicted he would be remembered long after his brother was forgotten. The passing years have proved the accuracy of his conviction.

Dr. J. R. Cardwell for whom the plant was named and Howell must have been good friends though I have no records to verify this belief. Dr. Cardwell came to Oregon in 1852 and became one of the prominent horticulturists in the early history of the state. He was the first president of the Oregon State Horticultural Society which was organized somewhere about 1885 (the exact date seems obscure) and retained his position for nearly 20 years.

Both Howell and Cardwell have gone to their horticultural Valhalla but the botany of the one and the *Pentstemon* of the other are still with us and will be for an untold number of years.

Undoubtedly years will pass before all differences are resolved and order will come to this chaotic genus. A few efforts have been made by determined individuals to provide exact specific determinations and end the confusion. Some have given up in sight. Some authorities have placed *P. cardwellii* as a subspecies of *P. fruticosus* which in itself has had 13 different names including three that were generic. The most recent publications have given *P. cardwellii* specific standing, separate from its close relative, *P. fruticosus.*
tive, *P. fruticosus.*

Description: It is a shrubby plant with loosely clustered stems from often elongated woody rootstocks. They are spreading or sometimes with their lower parts resting upon the ground for support, from four to 16 inches high outside of the flowering shoots. The size depends partially upon the amount and richness of the soil and the available moisture. The leaves are glossy evergreen, leathery, firm, from three-quarters to an inch and a half long and one-third as wide. They are either narrow with the margins nearly parallel for most of their length, narrowly egg-shaped, or nearly egg-shaped with the curvature nearly the same throughout and two or three times as long as wide. The margins are remotely and evenly sharply indented with small or finely acute projecting points. The leaf stems are short, flattened and prominently grooved.

The flowers have short stems of nearly uniform length and are borne on one side of the main stem with the lowest opening first. The bright purple trumpets an inch and a half long appear above the foliage. The clusters are few flowered.

It is distinguished from *P. fruticosus* by its larger, wider, more abundant compact leaves and is so much more floriferous that it half obscures the foliage.

Rarity: Scarce, the type. The white form is extremely rare. I have personal knowledge of only three people who have found it although undoubtedly numbers of others, too, have had this delightful experience. It is not particularly difficult to acquire. *Pentstemon* lovers often have it in their gardens and are willing to distribute cuttings. It can also be purchased from an occasional wild flower nursery. A horticultural variety, *roseus,* which I have not seen, has rose colored flowers.

Distribution: Drier locations at moderate to high altitudes in the Cascade Mountains of Washington and southward to Josephine and Curry Counties in southern Oregon. My first discovery of this plant was at about 3,500 feet. *P. fruticosus* has a much wider distribution.

Propagation: True to type seedlings may be difficult to acquire if the seeds are taken from plants that grow near other species, either in the garden or in their native habitat. They hybridize freely. But, like most *pentstemons,* they may be expected to germinate freely. Plant in fall. Cuttings of the season's growth root readily. Take in mid or late summer after the wood has had a chance to harden a little.

Culture: This isn't much of a problem if its simple requirements are attended to. *Pentstemons,* with few exceptions, require sharp drainage. This, with plenty of sun will provide healthy plants. Compactness in rock plants makes them ever so much more attractive than those with sprawling growth. This may be achieved by limiting the food and confining the roots to a very small area.

Flowering Time: Spring to early fall. The first blossoms, in May or June, simply blanket the plants with their rich purple trumpets. Following this early display occasional spikes keep coming on until early autumn, usually in September, when especially if not allowed to seed in the spring, the show is repeated with a somewhat less glorious performance. The rich green leaves in pleasing proportion to the size of the blossoms, the compactness of the foliage and the extended flowering season make this a delightful possession for the discriminating rock gardener.

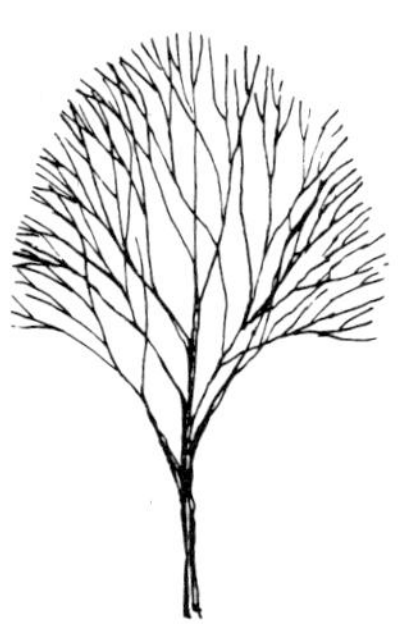

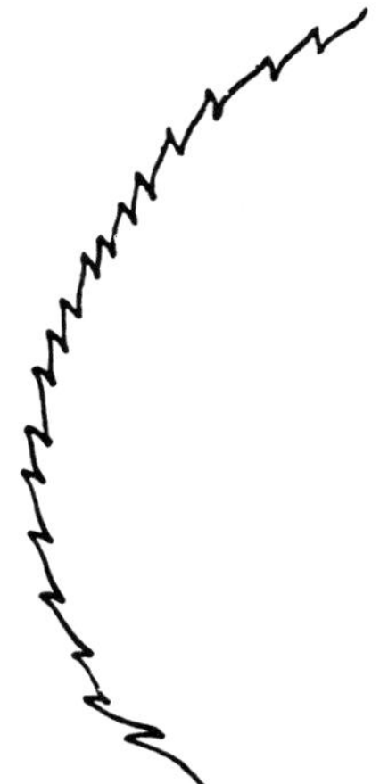

Serrate margin

Pentstemon menziesii 'White' Creeping Pentstemon

PENTSTEMON MENZIESII Hooker
Creeping Pentstemon

Menzies Beard Tongue is one of the three most important *Pentstemons* I like to have in my gardens. It is a long time and cherished friend. Our acquaintance began many years ago. I was driving from my Portland, Oregon home to Mount Hood when, from out of a corner of my eye, I saw a flash of brilliant purple at the edge of the highway. I pulled over, stopped, and walked over to this new discovery. There, growing in the miscellaneous humus, sand, and general debris usual to such places, was a dwarf form of *P. menziesii.* It was a bare three inches high, flowers and all, growing in a layer of duff less than two inches thick on top of the asphalt pavement – hardly the sort of situation where you would expect to see a *Pentstemon* or any other desirable flower. But there it was in the driest kind of soil, in full hot summer sun, a solid mass of blossoms, as though saying, "friends, this is the way I like to live."

It was inevitable that I should find it early in my career for it is found on most of the mountains of the Cascade Range near my home.

History: It was first described and named in 1838 by the famous English botanist Sir William Jackson Hooker, 1785-1865, in honor of Dr. Archibald Menzies, 1754-1842. Menzies was the surgeon and naturalist with the Lord Vancouver expedition to the Northwest Coast from 1790 to 1795. Prior to that time Menzies had visited the northwest coast in a trading ship and made some plant collections. He first collected specimens of the *Pentstemon* named for him, at Nootka Sound on the west coast of Vancouver Island, British Columbia. One might think that this would be the end of a simple story but such is not the case. Today, one and a quarter centuries later, the taxonomists are still squabbling about the right name for this variable species. One of the forms has entire leaves while *menziesii* is more or less toothed. The former is now generally considered the subspecies *davidsonii,* although there are still differences of opinion upon this. Other forms of *menziesii* have been given subspecific names based upon minor variations of flower or foliage. There is a good deal of this hair splitting among scientists. Many people, including myself, suspect that some of this is done for the purpose of increasing personal prestige. At best it does little or no good and at the worst adds to the confusion of a science that is still struggling for stability.

Description: The stems of Menzies' Beard Tongue are shrubby near the base. They are freely branched, spreading or creeping on the surface of the ground where there is enough soil for this accomplishment, and matted. From two to eight inches long they turn upwards near the tips. The leaves are numerous, round or two or three times as long as wide and with the sides uniformly curved nearly throughout. They are from a quarter to one and a half inches long with margins broken by more or less irregular projecting points. The leaves gradually taper into stems from an eighth to half an inch long depending upon the size of the leaf and the individual plant.

In the gay days of summer the thick evergreen leaves are shiny green. With the arrival of winter the foliage compensates for the gloomy atmosphere by taking on the richness of reds, wines and bronzes.

The flowering branches are from three-quarters to less than four inches high generally although the amount of moisture available and the richness of the soil allow greater variations. The flower clusters have few blossoms but, as the stems are numerous, a plant may be a mass of color. The tubular flowers are one to one and a half inches long terminating in a five lipped corolla, two upper and three lower.

The blossoms vary radically in tones and hues of purple and lavender. Those on Larch Mountain, a 4,000 foot peak a few miles east of Portland, have weak, washed out lavenders that aren't worth a first look, let alone a second. On an old rock quarry at the base of Mount Hood on the southwest side at about 3,500 feet the inflorescence is a brighter and richer purple, well worth collecting. The ones I first discovered on the edge of the road 1,000 feet lower were even better. The color forms are so markedly different in garden value that starts of some offered to friends would be excellent gifts. Others, entire plants, might well be disposed of to an obnoxious person.

A plant in a very rocky place may have tiny leaves and be

no more than an inch or so high and scarcely wider. Others, in more generous surroundings can grow as tall as six or eight inches or even more and spread over a square yard or so, losing, under these conditions, much of their appeal.

Rarity: Ordinary plants, common. More dwarf and better color forms, unusual. True blue and clear pink forms are said to exist. If this is true, I have never seen any of them. They would be extremely rare. White, extremely rare.

There is a fraternity of gardeners, loosely organized at the best, but ordinarily not united at all. These folk are scattered from the Atlantic to the Pacific; from South America to Alaska. Indeed there is no continent that does not claim at least a few. Some contacts are made through the three rock garden societies, one in America and the other two in the British Isles. More commonly one person discovers a kindred spirit who contacts a third and in the course of a few years correspondents are in touch throughout the land. They freely exchange plants or make one sided gifts. It was by this method I located a man who gave me my start of the white *Pentstemon menziesii.* I am as happy with it as he is with the *Lewisias* I sent him.

Distribution: From near sea level to at least 7,000 feet. Alaska has a few *Pentstemons* but *menziesii* does not go quite that far north. It starts in British Columbia where it was first discovered on Vancouver Island near Nootka Sound. It travels the Cascade and Coast Ranges through Washington. It is found on Saddle Mountain in the northwestern part of Oregon and on the slopes of Mount Hood and adjacent lesser peaks in the Oregon Cascades. Most of the literature limits it to British Columbia and Washington. But I suspect it goes much farther south in Oregon than Mount Hood, as does its subspecies *davidsonii* which was discovered by George Davidson on Mount Shasta, California at an altitude of 12,300 feet.

Propagation: I suppose this species would come easily from seed although I have never tried it and don't intend to. Cuttings root freely from season's or last year's growth and produce results much faster than seeds. The branches lying on the surface root readily and tenaciously along much of their length. They do not do this, of course, if they are lying on solid, impervious rock. But if there is any soil at all roots will appear and take hold. The branches of one of my plants have crept over the bare, soiless surface of a porous lava rock. This was enough for many roots to work their way into the tiny pores. I simply cut them free from the parent. Now they are going it alone with virtually no food and have assumed that delightful dwarfness so much desired.

Culture: Good drainage and full sun are its requirements. It is important to start with plants of good color and form either from nurseries or wild stock. I drilled a hole six inches deep and an inch in diameter on top of a semi porous rock and planted one of the miniatures in it. The soil is half humus and half crushed lava. It makes virtually no growth from year to year but sends out its delightful stone hugging blooms each season. In another spot I have provided ample root room but very little food. This treatment has kept the plants close to the surface, compact in foliage but allows spreading almost without limit. It is a mass of wonderful color when in blossom where it has crept over the top of a boulder and cascaded down the side. Perhaps the most important consideration in obtaining massive flowering is to provide a minimum of food but sufficient room for the roots to have a little permanent moisture.

The variety *davidsonii* usually lives at high to very high altitudes which normally are above where *P. Menziesii* grows. Apparently it has a strong determination not to survive in my close to sea level garden. Several attempts have all ended in failure. It will appear fairly healthy for a few weeks or even months then wither and die. I had one plant that flowered nicely but briefly before it passed away. I have never been able to keep one for an entire season. The type, *P. menziesii,* is easy.

Flowering Time: June to August, depending upon altitude.

Entire margin

Pentstemon rupicola 'White'

Rock Pentstemon

PENTSTEMON RUPICOLA (Piper) Howell
Rock Pentstemon

If I could have only a single species of *Pentstemon* from all that wonderful and varied genus of plants *rupicola* would be my choice made immediately and with certainty that there would be no mistake and no regret. It has all the earth hugging floral and foliar qualities in balance and proportion; in the softly pleasing tones and shades of color associated with those precious stones, the emeralds and rubies. Truly it is the gem of rock flowers in the world of plants.

The Gorge of the Columbia River with its jagged peaks, rushing streams and verdant canyons has been my favorite hiking and wild flower hunting grounds for nearly half a century. I took my first lonely trip into that rugged country when I was a boy of sixteen. No year has passed since that has not seen me climbing its cliffs, traveling its deer trails, and searching its meadows. During those unnumbered journeys the Crimson Beard Tongue, *Pentstemon rupicola,* has been a favorite companion. I have seen it in flower and in seed; in snow and in sun every month of the year.

There is a ridge I like to climb. It is a hands and knees ordeal to reach the knife edge top a thousand feet above the great river. Here I can see for endless miles up and down the vasty gorge. It was merely by chance that one April day I arrived there at just the right time. Glancing through the vine maple trees a hundred yards away a flash of bright pink struck my eyes. I worked my way down the sharp slope until I came to a boulder as big as a house. There in a narrow crack were three of my favorite beard tongues covered with flaming blossom. They didn't seem to mind the deep shade although I had never seen them in so dark a place before. They usually prefer a north facing cliff where the light shade, the coolness and the little extra moisture provides the conditions that gives them the most luxurious foliage, the gayest and most abundant flowers. It is a true cliff dweller – *rupicola* refers to its habit of growing in the broken rock and general debris that has fallen off towering rock walls. Rarely it is on flat surfaces but always with a rock underlay an inch or so below.

One day I crawled out on a promontory jutting a hundred feet or so into the Columbia River. At the extreme tip the barren basaltic rock was a reticulated mass of tiny weathered cracks. There must have been a little soil in these tiny veins although I couldn't see any at all. Only two plants were growing in that stern and desolate tip. Both were my Rock Pentstemon, rounded, compact, three inches high and glorious with clear glowing bright pink trumpets. All day long, from the early eastern dawn to the lengthening shadows of afternoon, these hardy creatures endured the torrid sun burning down from the Columbian skies, doubly intensified as it reflected from the bare rock. They suffered the hot drying winds that sweep, sand laden, down the gorge from east of the Cascades, just as they suffered the bitter winter gales that rage through this mighty canyon. It must have taken years for the roots to struggle down the minute cracks to reach a meager but permanent supply of life giving moisture. Few other plants have been able to survive this impossibly harsh environment.

Winter rains freezing in the cliff face seams exerts an enormous pressure. When the ice melts the pressure is relaxed and the loosened rock often crashes to the bottom of the stony walls, taking plants with them. This rubble is an easy source of wild flowers, including our *P. rupicola.* All one needs do is pick them up and pack them in damp moss. This is a delightful way of collecting compared to the hard work of cutting away the rock with cold chisel and single jack hammer.

History: Thomas Howell, Portland's famous early botanist, was the first scientist to describe and give this species its present name from specimens found on the dry cliffs of Mount Rainier in the state of Washington. The account appears in his *A Flora of Northwest America* published in 1901. It was also called *P. newberryi* variety *rupicola* by Charles Piper in 1900 but this synonym no longer has official recognition.

Description: The stems are shrubby, freely branched and spreading mat-like close to the ground with woody bases. From two to ten inches long, the ascending ones usually are about three inches tall but sometimes twice that high. The leaves are numerous and make a compact growth which accounts for half its vegetative charm; the other half comes from the light green prominently powdery texture, a very delightful effect. This combination is not confined to this species nor to the *Pentstemons* but wherever found it is a universal improvement. The leaves are thick very short stemmed, round or somewhat lengthened, from half an inch to occasionally twice that long, wavy margined or with the edges broken by more or less irregular finely projecting points.

The flowering stems are from an inch and a half to three inches high but the blossoms always rise just above the leaves. The few flowers on each stem, clear, glowing, deep shell pink are condensed near the tip, the lower ones opening first. But there are so many stems that the massive effect of neat compactness is one of very great beauty. The person who is not moved by the sight of a pink springtime fire glowing on a cliffside must have a heart as cold and gray as the rock to which the plant clings for life.

All the *P. rupicolas* I have seen in the Columbia Gorge and adjacent mountains have had much the same tones of lively pink, deeper in bud than in full blossom. Plants average about six inches in diameter but I have one of exceptional rich color in my garden that is twice that size.

In Oregon's Crater Lake National Park and adjacent territory they are fully as floriferous and even more so than in the Gorge of the Columbia. But in this southern part of the state the blossoms have a gentle shade of lavender mixed with the pink that is of a soft richness I have never seen in any other plant. Flowers with tinges of lavender can range from very bad to excellent. This one is unexcelled. Driving around the Rim Road of the Lake at an elevation of between 7,000 and 8,000 feet we discovered a *P. rupicola* I shall never forget. It was only 20 or 30 feet from the edge of the road and so close to the base of the south facing cliff that it would have been no great feat to climb right up to it. It was perfectly symmetrical in circular outline, over two feet in diameter and so densely covered with remarkably dainty lavender pink blossoms that the powdery green leaves could not be seen at all. I wanted it more than I have ever wanted any *Pentstemon* in my life. What a sight it would have made in my rockery!

There were only two reasons I did not take it. It took me fully half a day of hard work and eloquent talking to obtain a collecting permit which did not allow me to remove plants so near the road. And my conscience would not let me take it. I have never regretted leaving it. Thousands of visitors can enjoy it compared to the few who visit my gardens.

Rarity: The type, scarce. Usually a few plants are scattered here and there with comparatively long distances in between. Occasionally a colony will be found that has several dozen plants. The white form, extremely rare. I have never seen it in the wild. My plant was purchased from a wild flower nursery which obtained it from a grower in northern Washington. Presumably it was discovered as an isolated plant growing among the ordinary, but no less beautiful pinks.

Distribution: From central Washington to northern California on both the east and west slopes of the Cascade Mountains. A few feet above sea level in parts of the Columbia Gorge to 8,000 feet in the mountains.

Propagation: Seeds germinate easily enough and the plants raised by this method will come true to species providing the seed was taken from isolated plants. Natural hybridizing is the bane of seedling grown *Pentstemons.* One of my large plants has root layered itself from every stem that touched the soil. These can be cut off close to the base and transplanted to new locations all ready for flowering during the coming season. This can be done in the autumn or early spring or, where frozen soil does not interfere, during winter. Cuttings of the season's growth strike very easily. I usually take them in late spring or summer but they are so eager to root that success can be expected in the fall too.

Culture: Good drainage is the principal requirement. I use a mixture of half leaf mold and half crushed lava rock. This takes care of the drainage nicely and provides both food and moisture for the entire season without watering. In mild climates they can be planted in shade or sun. In my Portland garden I give them morning sunshine and afternoon light shade. The results are excellent. In warmer parts of the country mild shade all day might be preferable. If they are given too much food and ample room for the roots to wander the plants tend to sprawl loosely and much of their charm is lost. I have drilled holes an inch and a half in diameter and eight or ten inches deep in porous lava boulders. Planted in these holes in a mixture of crushed rock and leaf mold the growth is vigorous but compact and the flowering is good. In two or three seasons a small plant in one of these holes will cover an area six or eight inches across and completely conceal its artificial home. All attempts to plant them in the tiny crevices where they are found in nature fail. That must be done by germinating the seeds themselves in such cracks and babying them along until they can take care of themselves – an extremely difficult challenge.

Wild plants removed from cracks in cliffs usually do not have good or extensive root systems. Old plants with very woody bases adapt to new homes with reluctance and are better left alone. Young plants are by far the best especially if you can find them on a rock slide or talus slope where there is a good deal of soil mixed with the broken rock. These often have quite a few feeding roots which can be removed with little damage. Some specimens have leaves twice the size of others nearby. These choicer plants may not retain their distinctive foliage if they do not like their new homes. Occasionally part of a plant will die back for no obvious reason. It will be unsightly for a time but when the damaged parts are pruned out the remainder soon recovers and fills in the open spaces. This may be a fungus. At any rate it is not a particularly serious problem. It also occurs on *P. cardwellii.*

An occasional white mixed in here and there with the pinks offers a contrast that is pure joy.

Flowering Time: April to August. The blossoming time varies from year to year to some extent but depends mostly on altitude. Near the river in the Columbia Gorge they splash the cliffs with bright fire in the spring. At high elevations they have to wait until their white winter blanket has melted away and the warming sun arouses them to a brief new season of alpine beauty.

Pterospora andromedea Pine Drops

PTEROSPORA ANDROMEDEA Nuttall
Pine Drops

History: Unlike its close relative, *Hypopitys*, the Pine Drops is largely free from the confusion of generic and specific synonymous names for it stands alone. It is the only member of its genus and has refrained from the world traveling *Hypopitys* has enjoyed. Occasionally it is called Giant Bird's Nest and Albany Beech Drops. The only other scientific name it has had is *Monotropa procera*, no longer recognized. It was first described by Thomas Nuttall in 1818 in volume one of his *The Genera of North American Plants.* The generic Greek name, *Pterospora*, refers to wing-seeded.

Description: This is a strange plant and an astonishing one. Mr. Nuttall described it as an evanescent annual – a statement I found difficult to believe, thinking that perhaps this great botanist had made a mistake. But there was no mistake. The slender pedicels soon recurve and the entire plant dies early. It lives for only a single season. How it has managed to survive throughout the untold centuries is beyond my understanding. Its minute seeds are extremely numerous but, like most of its saprophytic brethren, there is so little food stored in them that the chances of any of them germinating and producing plants seems remote indeed. Nevertheless they can be found scattered across the land in the shade of our pine forests.

The stout but slender erect stems, usually solitary but sometimes in clusters of several are from eight inches to five feet tall with a foot and a half about average. Much of what could be a beautiful plant is lost by this great height. These stems are yellowish, brownish or reddish brown, fleshy in texture and covered with a viscid pubescence sufficiently adhesive to trap insects which are often found dead on the stems. The entire plant arises from a thick ball-like matted mass of fibrous and very astringent roots about two inches in diameter. The flowers are numerous, ivory white, nodding on recurved pink pedicels, urn shaped and narrowed at the throat. They are dainty and definitely attractive but far too small to give good balance to a plant with such extraordinary stems. They are borne in an elongated, narrow open raceme.

The leaves are scale-like, crowded below, linear-lanceolate, one half to one inch long, while the upper ones are smaller and scattered.

In the winter the dry, dark reddish stalks are ornamented with depressed globose capsules a third to a half an inch in diameter – offering a woodland charm at a time of the year when there is little else to attract attention.

All plants belong to one of four great classifications known as *phyla*. The lowest in the scale of evolution are the *thallophytes*. These include such plants as the fungi, mushrooms and other *saprophytic* and parasitic plants. The next higher *phylum* is the *bryophytes* which comprises the true mosses and the liverworts. The distinction between these two plants is a technical one and most people call both mosses. All of them are chlorophyll-bearing plants which is likewise true of the third *phylum*, the *pteridophytes*. This group includes the club mosses, creeping plants which in gross appearance resemble the true mosses; the horsetails, *Equisetales*, and the ferns. The highest *phylum* is the *spermatophytes*, the flowering plants.

It is one of the remarkable quirks of nature that the lowest *phylum* of plants contains members which are totally without green coloring matter while the plants in the next two higher *phyla* all have chlorophyll to manufacture their own food. But the highest *phylum* of all does contain members that have no chlorophyll whatever and many of these, which are natives of North America, are in the heath family, *Ericaceae*. Thus there is a great leap from the lowest to the highest *phylum* to find nonchlorophyll bearing plants with none whatever in the two *phyla* in between. It would be entirely reasonable to expect to find saprophytic plants among both the bryophytes and pteridophytes but such is not the case. It will take a much better informed person than I to explain this apparent botanical puzzle.

Rarity: Rare.

Distribution: Under oaks, pines and other conifers and it has a wide range but is limited to temperate North America. On the West Coast from British Columbia through Washington and

Oregon and into California. In the middle states in Colorado, New Mexico, Arizona, South Dakota, Michigan. In the northeast in Quebec, Nova Scotia, New Hampshire, Pennsylvania and as far south as northern Mexico. It is generally considered a mountain flower and is found as high as 9,000 feet although usually much lower.

Propagation: This plant must be considered difficult to grow from seed along with the other saprophytes described in this book. But it has one advantage over its near relatives. It is an annual and such plants often germinate their seeds much more readily than those from perennials. If plants which live for only one year were not able to produce new seedlings the entire species would not survive beyond a single season. I have never tried to grow this flower but I believe there would be a fair chance of success by scattering the seed on top of soil rich in decayed vegetation in a shady place.

Culture: Unknown. If this plant can be established it should not be allowed to be crowded by competing flora. Saprophytes usually are not found in close proximity to other plants. Careful scattering of seeds yearly would be vital to a continued succession of flowers.

Flowering Time: June, July, and August, depending upon climate and altitude.

Pyrola aphylla Leafless Wintergreen

PYROLA APHYLLA Smith
The Leafless Wintergreen

History: This lovely forest dweller is a distinctive plant for it is the only member of the genus of ten or 15 species that is totally without green foliage. It is, therefore, a true saprophyte, completely dependent upon decayed vegetable matter for its nourishment. It is one of the very few genera of plants whose members comprise both chlorophyll bearing plants and those completely devoid of it, and every gradation in between. The genus was given its recognized name by Linnaeus in his *Species Plantarum* published in 1753. *P. aphylla* was named in 1814 by J. E. Smith, 1759-1828.

P. aphylla, like all its widely distributed brothers and sisters, has beautiful, dainty nodding blossoms as though they are more interested in the soil at their feet than in any wonders of air and sky above their heads.

The common name, Wintergreen, means, simply, that the leaves remain green all winter, a characterisitc shared with many other plants, which with one exception, do not bear this name. *Gaultheria procumbens,* is the other. It is native to the middle western states and is a source of wintergreen oil, none of which is found in the *Pyrolas.* The generic name too, is somewhat misleading. It is a diminutive of the word *Pyrus,* the pear tree, from a fancied resemblance to the foliage of that tree. Inasmuch as the *Pyrolas* have leaves of quite varying shape, Carl Von Linnaeus, the great Swedish botanist, must have had a much better imagination than I possess.

Description: The flowers of *P. aphylla* are variable, pink or reddish but lighter colored than the truly beautiful *P. bracteata.* The four to 14 inch scapes are closely clustered where there are many from the same plant although it is common to see others with only one flower stalk. This clustered arrangement, the many nodding flowers, and the five concave petals to each blossom give the plant much of its charm. The leaves are reduced to a few reddish lanceolate bracts. The entire plant is light red or pink. Another form has cream colored flowers. Occasionally a plant will be found that has traces of green in the flowers, stem and reduced leaves, indicating the saprophytic process hasn't been quite completed.

It is an eye catching, startling sight to find it in the deep forest where it is usually alone or sometimes associated with others of its saprophytic kind, the Indian Pipes, Phantom Orchids and Coral Roots. If one is fortunate enough to find all these together in one place, as I did, he will never forget it.

Rarity: Rare.

Distribution: In the Coast Range, Cascade and Siskiyou Mountains from British Columbia, Washington, Oregon, California and eastward to Idaho, western Nevada, and western Montana but never common anywhere within its range. The genus is circumpolar, being found from Alaska to Labrador and south to Georgia, Michigan, South Dakota, other middle states, and into Mexico. Also in the British Isles, and northern Asia. *P. aphylla* prefers low elevations. Other members of the genus grow as high as 9,000 feet. Most grow in rather dry soils but at least one species is a bog plant.

Propagation: This genus is as exasperating as it is beautiful. Seed is scarce and almost as fine as dust – a characteristic shared by most of our saprophytes. It should be scattered on top of the soil consisting mostly of leaf mold or on a surface of sterilized moss in a shady place. The seedlings, when you are fortunate enough to get any, should be left alone until two leaves appear. Then they may be potted up in a rich mixture. Sizable plants should be produced in about two years. Thick germination is very rare as, indeed, is any germination at all. Both April and October are recommended times for making divisions but this is a hazardous venture, more likely to fail than succeed.

Culture: It is rare indeed to find any of these *Pyrolas* in the home garden for they are extremely difficult to transplant successfully. If you can get some of the underground offshoots which Mother Nature intends to use to produce plants for the next season you will have a fair – and only a fair – chance of success. As for taking the mature plants that is a thoroughly discouraging business. They don't wither much if at all. They stay surprisingly fresh and attractive. But that is all they will do. They will not send out any new roots. Weeks, even three or four months later they will still be green. Then, before you know it they will perish. I dug a nice plant of *Pyrola aphylla* once. I never did find how deeply the roots went. At 12 inches they disappeared under fir tree roots and were still going down at that depth. At another time I dug several clumps of *P. picta,* the roots of which were only two or three inches deep. They remained alive for an entire year and even sent out a few new green leaves. Then the plants perished. The secret is to stimulate growth of new roots. If that can be done they can be established safely. Treating with root growth hormones may be helpful. I once rooted a leaf of *P. bracteata* in water. The roots struck near the base of the leaf but no new leaves appeared. I am sure more work with this method might well be crowned with success. How a plant can be so difficult in the garden and so abundant and healthy in forested areas in the mountains defies the imagination and develops the vocabulary.

Divisions or transplants of wild plants made in October or March or April in early spring offer the best opportunities of success. Large clumps of soil, carefully planted in shady gardens and never allowed to become dry offer the best opportunities for success.

It is a minor tragedy that these plants with their varying foliage, some entirely green, others with creamy margins and veins, and flowers ranging from whites to pinks and lovely reds make such beautiful ground covers in the forests and are so utterly lacking in our gardens. If through knowledge, great skill and loving care you are able to make them contented at home, leave them alone. Then they will be happy and so will you.

Flowering Time: June and July.

PYROLA APHYLLA PAUCIFOLIA Howell

This plant differs from the type *aphylla* in that it has a few reddish green leaves near the base of the scape one or two of which may be small orbicular in size and shape. Apparently it hasn't quite decided whether to go the whole way and live entirely upon decayed vegetation or to continue to manufacture a little of its food through the action of the sun on the small amount of chlorophyll remaining in the vestigial leaves. It was named by Thomas Howell in 1901 in his *Flora Of Northwest America.*

Rarity: Very rare. Much more difficult to find than the type *P. aphylla.*

Distribution: Same as the type.

Propagation: Same as the type.

Culture: Same as the type.

Flowering Time: June and July.

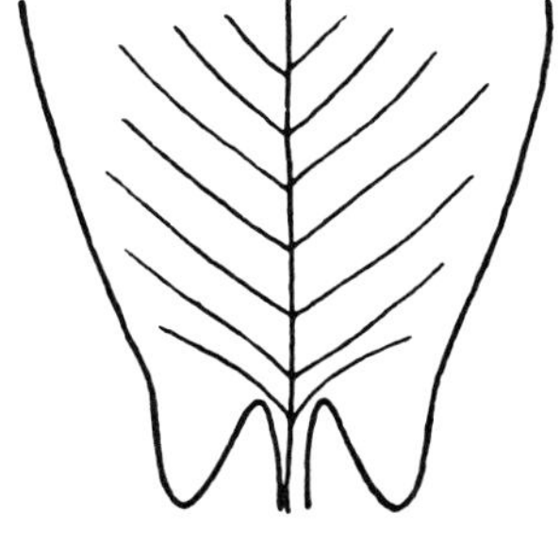

Auriculate base

Ribes sanguineum 'White'

Jack Hausotter Photo

Red Flowering Currant, White Form

RIBES SANGUINEUM Pursh
Red Flowering Currant

My introduction to the Red Flowering Currant was explosive. When the neighbors heard the news that World War One was over on November 11, 1918 they got out their guns and shot off all the ammunition they had. My father was one of them. The only weapon we had was a shotgun. Dad blazed away in the general direction of the front lawn, neither knowing nor caring much what he hit. It was too dark, that night, to tell anyway. The end of the war in Europe marked the beginning of a war in the Wiley family when mother discovered that the head of the family had blown her young Red Flowering Currant out of the ground. She had gone to quite a bit of work and trouble to transplant it out of the woods. In a day or so, however, the Wileys, like the rest of the world, were at peace. We never did get another currant. I suppose mother was a little discouraged with father's warlike proclivities and while he enjoyed his home, shrubs were not a matter of life and death in his scheme of things.

It was a small plant, unbranched and only about three feet high but it had flowered that spring and I'll always remember its bright crimson blossoms. Since then I have seen it often during my spring time out door travels. A number of varieties have been introduced to horticulture but my greatest enjoyment of this species has been finding it in the open woods, brush lands and meadows where it is common enough and very spectacular in early and mid spring. At this time of the year it is the most colorful shrub in its far western home. Its only competitor at this time is the brilliant spathes of the skunk cabbage which shower the swamps with great yellow flowers. It is quite a sight to see the red currant blossoms surrounding a marsh splashed with huge nuggets of floral gold. The Rufous Hummingbirds complete the spectacle as they dart gracefully and colorfully from shrub to shrub in their never ending search for nectar.

History: The currants have been kicked around in a confused sort of way for many years. Linnaeus put them in what is now the Saxifrage Family, *Saxifragaceae,* in the first edition of his *Genera Plantarum* published in 1737. Subsequent taxonomists have placed them in no less than ten other families. Some of our recent authorities have left them where Linnaeus believed they belonged. The latest decision, however, is that they should be in the Gooseberry Family, either *Ribesaceae* with two genera, *Grossularia* and *Ribes;* or *Grossulariaceae* with two distinct genera, *Ribes,* the currants, and *Grossularia,* the gooseberries.

The two genera are easy to distinguish. Among other characteristics the gooseberries are armed – thorny, while the currants have no such weapons. The number of species of *Ribes* in the world varies with the opinions of the writers. About five dozen appears to be fairly correct. They are distributed mostly in the subarctic and north temperate regions of both the old and new worlds and in America extend southward to the Andes.

The origin of *Ribes* is obscure. It may have been derived from *ribas,* the Arabic name for *Rheum Ribes,* a species of rhubarb but not the one grown for its edible stems. I cannot see any logical relationship between a rhubarb and a currant. But the frightful mess that characterizes botany may be one reason why those who spend their lives in this field do not necessarily live as long as their fellows who are engaged in more orderly work such as mathematics where two and two always make four – and no arguments.

The species *sanguineum,* which means *bloody* or *blood-red* in reference to the color of the flowers, was named and described by the Polish botanist Frederick T. Pursh, 1774-1820, in his two volume work *Flora Americae Septentrionalis* published in 1814. He left Dresden, where he was educated, in 1799 for Baltimore. After spending nearly 12 years in America he returned to Europe in 1811. Pursh did not travel to the western part of the continent. It was probably from the specimens that were collected by Lewis and Clark on their transcontinental expedition that Pursh made his identification for his account reads in part: "–. On the Columbia River. M. Lewis. March. –" While three other names have been offered since, Pursh's is still accepted as authoritative.

Description: *R. sanguineum* is an erect, deciduous shrub from four to 12 feet high, well branched and somewhat spreading. The young twigs are clothed with very fine short hairs, but the older ones are smooth. The palmately veined leaves are round kidney shaped in outline, mostly three lobed but sometimes five. The lobes are rounded, prominently veined, edged with small teeth, dark green and covered with very fine short hairs above and grayish beneath with fine densely matted hairiness.

The blossoms are borne in closely flowered drooping clusters (racemes) from two to five or six inches long. They are tubular, terminating in five wide spreading star like lobes that are simply enchanting when observed closely. They range from soft pink to brilliant crimson and have a spicy aroma which accounts for the name, Incense Shrub, which is occasionally used.

The round blue-black berries are from three-eighths to one-half an inch in diameter and are covered with a heavy white bloom. Both in flower and in fruit this is a very beautiful shrub and deserves better recognition for its garden value. The berries are edible – sweet but flat flavored and on the dry side. The flavor improves somewhat when they become dead ripe, but they have more eye than stomach appeal.

There are a number of horticultural varieties. *Splendens* has dark, blood red flowers. *Flore-pleno* is a double form. But the most exciting of all is the White Form. A few years ago I attended a lecture given by Dean Collins, a well known horticultural editor and writer. During the course of his talk Mr. Collins mentioned a white flowering mutation he had in his garden. I went out to look at it and found it growing between two of the red flowering ones. The racemes were much larger than those of its adjacent neighbors and I was greatly impressed with its value. During the late 1930's Mr. Henry Henneman, an ardent native plant lover, was roaming the woods somewhere in western Oregon – the exact location is obscure – and found the original parent plant. He realized he had found a rarity, took some cuttings, propagated them and gave Mr. Collins the one growing in his yard. Mr. Henneman has gone and no one seems to know what happened to his wild discovery. Mr. Collins gave me some cutting material and I have distributed the resulting plants to various growers so that its survival is assured.

Rarity: The type, common; the horticultural varieties, rare in the wild and equally difficult to find in nurseries; the white variety, extremely rare.

Distribution: At low elevations, mainly in the Humid Transition Zone in British Columbia, Washington, Oregon and northwestern California where it grows in the Coast Ranges and into the foothills of the western slopes of the Cascades. It might be found sparingly east of the Cascades but the drier climate would not meet its requirements and I have not seen it there. The variety *glutinosum* grows from Lincoln County, Oregon to northwestern California. It differs but little from the type.

Propagation: Seeds germinate easily but this method is not often used as the resulting plants will not come true to type. Mound layering in summer is occasionally practiced. Budding or grafting is utilized when quick increase of rare varieties is wanted. In Europe currants are sometimes grafted high on the species *odoratum.* These are trained to single stems forming little standard trees. The effect can be quite beautiful. American commercial horticulturists might be overlooking an opportunity. Parking strips too narrow for ordinary trees would be well suited to these miniatures. Tree roses for this purpose are frowned upon by many women because of the thorns which tear clothes.

The common method of propagation is from cuttings. Mr. Collins gave me material from his shrub on two occasions. Some of those I obtained in the autumn I placed in a sand cutting box outdoors in the shade. I cut them into short sections, leaving one or two buds below ground level and two above. I had nearly 100 per cent success. Those I gave to two expert propagators all died. They used bottom heat indoors. Evidently this promoted the growth of fungus which was fatal. The basal and middle parts of the greenwood shoots I took in late spring rooted easily, while cuttings of the terminal growth rooted with difficulty and some of them not at all.

Culture: This is a delightfully easy plant to grow. It prefers a little shade although I have seen scores of wild specimens exposed to full sun. These were usually in somewhat dry places and the combination inhibited their growth. Any ordinary good garden loam with a reasonable amount of moisture suits them nicely. But it adapts easily to adverse conditions. Annual thinning of new basal growth gives a neater appearance. Only occasionally will the upper parts need pruning. A spacing of ten or 12 feet will permit them to retain their individuality and display their distinctive beauty.

Currants are hosts to the spores which are responsible for the fungus disease, White Pine Blister Rust – a serious affliction of our forest trees. Consult your state department of agriculture before shipping to various parts of your own state or to other states.

Flowering Time: Late March, April and May, depending upon altitudes and seasonal variations.

Sarcodes sanguinea Jack Hausotter Photo Snow Plant

SARCODES SANGUINEA Torrey
Snow Plant

It is a rare plant that has a genus entirely to itself. The Snow Plant is one of these, and rightly so, for this bright red saprophyte is quite unlike any other plant in North America and perhaps in the entire world. A member of the heath family, *Ericaceae,* which includes a number of other plants devoid of green foliage among which is the Indian Pipe, *Monotropa uniflora.* These two plants, closely related, share a magnificent beauty, one pure crimson and the other just as pure white. Both are greatly admired by those who are fond of that limited group of plants, the saprophytes. These two are among the very few at the top of the pinnacle of floral beauty.

The common name, Snow Plant, is to some extent misleading. It does come up through the snow and flower while there is still whiteness all around. But more often it pushes its way through the cool wet earth immediately after the snow has melted. As the snow line goes higher and higher with the advancing spring *Sarcodes* follows close behind so that there is a succession of bright red blossoms reaching to loftier alpine elevations. Occasionally a late snow storm will reblanket the exposed earth and the scarlet Snow Plants will stand magnificently above the white expanse.

It is generally quite useless to search the alpine slopes for this elusive beauty, its color the bright red of pure arterial blood, standing alone in vasty fields of snowy white, is much too rare for any such good fortune. But if you should chance upon it you will never forget its lonely and ineffable beauty, its glorious scarlet splendor.

At the base of the plant, late in the season, one or more well formed shoots may develop for next season's growth. Time is precious in the high mountains and nature takes every advantage of the brief spring and summer. The flowers must awaken, push rapidly through the earth, blossom, ripen their seed, and prepare for the winter's long sleep while their lowland cousins are pursuing a more leisurely life. Near the end of summer, which may mean as early as August or September, the red color has faded and brilliance has been replaced with the dull and drab tones of fall.

The plant is edible. When boiled it is said to be quite tasty. I don't know and never expect to. It is no part of my nature to care to eat this or any other of nature's marvels that is so extremely rare and so utterly lovely. All this aside from the stringent law that forbids removing the plant. It is so showy and so spectacular that tourists have endangered its very existence. Others whose consciences are less sensitive than mine claim it will remain fresh for several days when picked.

History: It is not at all a new discovery. The pioneers had not been out west for many years until John Torrey, the New York botanist, wrote the first official description of it in 1854. Dr. J. M. Bigelow collected specimens in full flower in the Sierra Nevadas. He was with the government expedition in 1853 and 1854 to survey a route for a railroad from the Mississippi to the Pacific Ocean.

Description: The fleshy stems are from an unusual low of three inches to 15 with an average of about a foot. The leaves, untold eons ago, must have been green like all other normal plants. Now they are reduced to red scales. The five lobed bell-shaped flowers in a dense raceme are on the upper half of the stem, and are mingled with long, graceful curling bracts. The foliage on the lower part of the stem consists of narrowly ovate red leaves up to two inches long while the upper ones are narrower and more scattered. The tissue is translucent and when a shaft of sunlight strikes the plant it glows with a marvelous brilliance as though lighted with an inner fire.

The plants may grow in clusters, as many as 15 coming up together. But those with only a single stem have a distinctive glamour that is peculiar to solitary individuals.

The generic name, *Sarcodes,* is from the Greek and means *flesh-like. Sanguinea* refers to the *blood-red* color of the entire plant.

Some of the plants have a tendency towards the decumbent – that is with the base of the stem resting on the ground for some distance until it turns upward. This detracts from its charm and is one of the few faults that can be lodged against a largely blameless flower.

Virtually every botany that covers the range in which *Sarcodes* lives describes it. But enough of botanical descriptions. The exacting, formal and cold language of science can never hope to present this plant as it lives in the forest. It is here that the layman comes into his own. He knows little about technical terms and cares less. He knows only that a Great Power gave us this flower; that no artist's brush, however skilled, can equal the magic that nature required thousands of years to create. The untutored layman knows too, that when he finds one of these plants words are as inadequate as the painter's palette, and he is as silent as the great mountains towering over his head. He either feels this plant in the ultimate depths of his soul or he feels nothing at all.

Rarity: Very Rare.

Distribution: At altitudes from 4,000 to 9,000 feet in coniferous forests, especially among the redwoods and true firs. In the Siskiyou Mountains of southern Oregon, in western Nevada. In California in the Siskiyou, Trinity, Sierra Nevada, San Gabriel, San Bernardino, San Jacinto and Santa Rosa Mountains.

Propagation: Unknown in cultivation. While the plant produces many seeds it is unlikely that attempts to germinate them in the garden would be any more successful than with any of the other saprophytes. Scattering them on top of soil rich in humus and in light shade would offer as good an opportunity for success as any. In climates where cold weather does not occur it would be advisable to freeze the seeds for a few days, then thaw followed by more freezing. This procedure sometimes stimulates germination and may produce good results. No other method of propagation would be likely to succeed.

Culture: Unknown. It should be planted in a soil consisting of rich decayed vegetable matter for this is the kind of material the plant needs for nourishment. It should not be crowded by other plants and should be left undisturbed by cultivation or any other horticultural practices. In his book *With The Flowers And Trees In California* written about 50 years ago Charles Francis Saunders reports having seen it "–planted in lard kettles and set for decoration on the porches of mountain cabins; for it appears to be a favorite posy with mountaineers, the most careless of whom could hardly fail to notice it flaming up at his feet." In spite of the stem arising from a thick fleshy mat of roots it isn't likely that these plants were actually growing in the lard pails. No doubt they could survive for the one season but, like almost all other saprophytes, it is almost certain that they failed to live through the following year.

Flowering Time: May at the lower elevations into July at the higher, following at or immediately below the snow line.

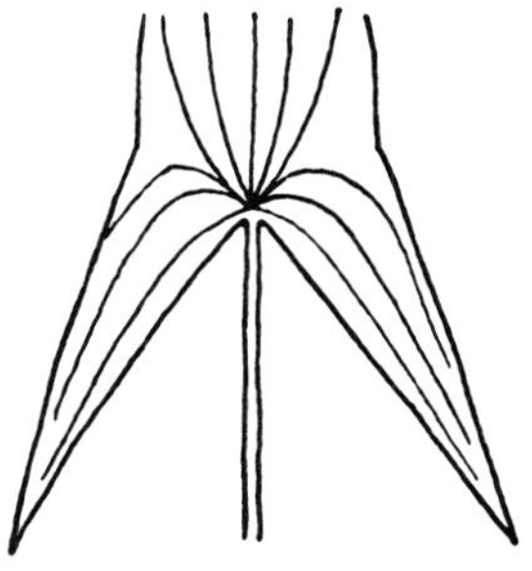

Sagittate base

Saxifraga tolmiei Jack Hausotter Photo Tolmie's Saxifrage

SAXIFRAGA TOLMIEI Torrey and Gray
Tolmie's Saxifrage

It was at the foot of a talus slope above timber line on the north side of Oregon's Mount Hood that I found an earth hugging plant about half a foot in diameter. The leaves were bright green little blobs, much like those of some of the *Sedums.* But *Sedums* like dry places, in some instances with so little soil and moisture that most other flowering plants cannot survive. This plant was obviously thoroughly contented with the volcanic sand in which it was growing thoroughly soaked with icy cold water from a glacier a thousand feet or so above. *Sedum?* No. Then what was it? I was in too big a hurry to make a field study for I had a long walk ahead of me to get back to base camp. I removed part of the plant and balled it with my bare hands. Water ran out of the ball – almost pure sand with an incredibly minute amount of humus.

After a dinner cooked over an open fire that evening I examined my find more carefully. Sepals five, petals five, stamens ten. The same count as the *Sedums* but it couldn't be a stonecrop under these drowning conditions. It was *Saxifraga tolmiei.* I have found this plant a few other times but always under the same conditions: around 6,000 feet, in full sun, with roots in a loose sandy or pumice soil and thoroughly soaked with free running ice cold water. What radical conditions! Freezing wet below and alpine sunshine hot above.

This is not only a curious little alpine but a fascinating one and altogether quite lovely with its white or light yellow star shaped blossoms above the quaint foliage.

History: It belongs to the rather large and diverse Saxifrage Family *Saxifragaceae,* named by Bentham and Hooker, comprising about 35 genera and 450 species of wide geographical distribution. (Another authority claims about 75 genera.)

The genus *Saxifragia* was originally named in 1735 by Joseph Pitton de Tournefort. The spelling was changed slightly to *Saxifraga* by Carl Von Linneaus and was published in 1737 in the first edition of his *Genera Plantarum.* About three dozen different names have been suggested between then and 1837. The name comes from two Latin words, *saxum, a rock,* and *frango, to break* in reference to the fact that many species grow in clefts in rocks. Another explanation is that some people believe that certain species will cure bladder stones.

About 250 species have been recognized, nearly all of the north temperate zone, and about 67 of these are native to North America, 27 of which occur in the Pacific States where *S. tolmiei* lives.

This species was first named and described by John Torrey and Asa Gray in 1840 in volume one of the *Flora of North America* from a specimen supplied by Sir William J. Hooker, the great English botanist. Dr. W. F. Tolmie had been a student of Sir W. J. Hooker. He went to Fort Vancouver, in what is now the state of Washington in 1832 as a medical officer to the Hudson Bay Company. He died in 1886.

Description: The prostrate stems are woody below, from four to 16 inches long, and freely branched. The evergreen leaves, from a quarter to three-eights of an inch long, are smooth or with a few long bristles at the base, thick, rigid and bright green. They very much resemble some of the *Sedums* that have more or less globose leaves. One of the charms of the plant is that the leaves are densely crowded – a character that would spoil many plants. The flowering stems are an inch and a half to three inches high and appear above the foliage. They are loosely few flowered but, as the stems are produced in abundance the entire plant is often covered with starry blossoms about half an inch in diameter or slightly less. The entire effect is so enchanting that I would be glad to have it in my garden.

Rarity: Rare, mostly because of its inaccessibility and lack of abundance in any one place.

Distribution: Usually above timberline, from 5,000 to 10,000 feet, in sandy soils near perpetual snow. From southern Alaska southward through British Columbia, Washington, Oregon, and in the Sierra Nevadas to Tulare County in California. The *typical* form with *shorter leaves* and the *flowers few and sometimes solitary,* does not occur south of Washington.

Propagation: Unknown. Books are full of descriptions of

Saxifrages and instructions on their propagation and culture; how easily this is accomplished and how readily they take to the rock garden. True enough about most of the widely varying and often very beautiful species. But none of these authors mention *S. tolmiei.* I have yet to find an authority who can tell me how to propagate this unusual plant. Theoretically it should come readily from cuttings. I have never tried it but would expect total failure. Seed should be sowed on the surface of a pot filled with fine soil and covered with paper and glass to keep them close and dark. This direction applies to Saxifrages in general and it might be worth attempting with this one. It is sometimes true that mature alpines will not survive at lower levels but that the same plants raised from seed will be able to adapt to a foreign environment. The rare success with this method is worth the attempt.

Culture: Unknown. This is a delightfully healthy plant in its alpine home where it enjoys the companionship of other high born flowers. *Erythronium parviflorum* taken from the same lofty meadows does very well in my gardens. But not *S. tolmiei.* I have made several attempts and so have some of my friends. All have failed. I have tried a rich, loose garden loam; a pure leaf mold and sand mixture; its very own mountain soil. I have tried with ordinary moisture. My last experiment was in its native soil in a pot sitting in a deep dish full of water so that the roots would always be abundantly wet and always nicely drained. The plants looked all right for a week or so. Then they slowly and steadily declined until, in a month or so, they completely disappeared. It may be that it is one of those intractable plants that can never be permanent guests in our gardens. Or it may have some simple little secret that, once known, will answer the problem. There are very few gardeners who can supply flowing icy water all summer long. It may require chilly nights. Long winter rests. Anyone of these, a combination, or some unthought of requirement could be the solution.

Flowering Time: July and August, varying with the altitude and season.

Sedum spathulifolium pruinosa Cape Blanco Sedum

SEDUM SPATHULIFOLIUM subspecies **PRUINOSA** (Britton) Clausen
Cape Blanco Sedum

Sedums, as a group, arouse very little of my gardener's enthusiasm. 15 or 20 years ago I wasn't thinking of them or any other particular plant when I was walking on top of a bank just above the ocean near Bandon on the southwestern coast of Oregon. I was on one of my periodic field trips searching for new plants.

Suddenly, at my feet, I came upon a small colony of stone crops that were distinctly different from any I had ever seen before. The green leaves were as white as though they had been dipped in flour. This was a good Sedum for its ghostly leaves alone no matter what the flowers might be like.

They were growing at the extreme edge of the bank well within salt spray splashing distance of the ocean during winter storms. Like most of the species of my acquaintance they were in full sun. That, of course did not mean much as the weather at the Oregon coast is mild – rarely very warm in summer or cold any other part of the year. The soil was a loose sand and humus mixture so that it was easy to lift a few specimens with my bare hands to remove them to a new home. In spite of having lived in three different places since that time I still have them in my gardens.

History: The Stonecrop Family, *Crassulaceae,* to which the *Sedums* belong, comprises about 20 genera of 500 species. Among the more interesting members are the *Dudleyas* and *Gormanias.* The family was named by Bentham and Hooker whose names appear frequently in the world of botany.

Carl Von Linneaus gave the genus its officially recognized name and described it in 1735. *Sedum* comes from the Latin *sedeo, to sit,* on account of its lowly habit – they like to cling to rocks. They occupy an important position in the family, comprising about 200 of the 500 species and are found mainly in the temperature regions of the northern hemisphere but a few grow in the Andes of South America. As might be excepted in so large a genus a good deal of confusion has existed in the group and some of it continues to the present time. At least 11 other generic names have appeared but the one Linneaus gave it still survives.

Sir William Jackson Hooker, 1785-1865, the great English botanist, gave the *specific* name and described it in 1832 in his *North American Flora.* It has been afflicted with at least four others since that time, all of which are now in synonomy.

But here is the astonishing thing, the almost incredible circumstance. I searched all the literature I could locate – and there was a great deal of it – and could find no reference whatever to the specimens I had found near the beaches of Bandon. It had the general characteristics of *S. spathulifolium* but the flour-like color of *Dudleya farinosa.* At one time I thought it might be a strange form of *Dudleya* but that was too far fetched to be likely. I puzzled over it for years and never came to any definite conclusions that were satisfactory. It was not a new plant to wild flower growers. It was commonly known as the Cape Blanco Sedum and had been collected and grown as such for I don't know how many years. It was only in the second edition of Dr. Morton Eaton Peck's *A Manual of the Higher Plants of Oregon,* published in 1961, that a scientific description and a name for this *sub-species* finally appeared – 129 years after Hooker named the *species!* Robert T. Clausen gave it the subspecific name *pruinosa,* which refers to a frosted appearance due to fine hairs or scales. Undoubtedly Mr. Clausen's work with *pruinosa* appeared in some scientific journal or similar work prior to Peck's publication. That is the way new plants are customarily brought to public attention.

S. spathulifolium has two or three named varieties including *purpureum* and *rubrum.* It is a common plant and has a much wider distribution than *pruinosa.*

Description: The most outstanding characteristic of *pruinosa* is the dense flour-like encrustation on the leaves. One might think the entire plant was covered with a very beautiful frost except that frost does not ordinarily appear where it lives. In the winter the frosty appearance becomes less prominent and is largely replaced with a truly pleasing reddish bronze if the plants are exposed to the sunlight. Those in the shade retain much of their summer garb. But the whitish material falls away in flakes as it is replaced with a new coat.

The stems are stout, creeping or with the stems resting on the ground for most of their length before they turn upward. They may be up to eight to 12 inches long – two or three times that of the type – and often leafy throughout.

The leaves are in rosettes, wider and rounded near the tip than at the basal end. They are broader and much thicker than the type and often deeply notched at the apex. Those of the flowering stem are larger than the basal ones. The blossoming stems are few and small with dense clusters in which the terminal or central flower blooms first. The stemless, or nearly so, flowers are on spreading branches. The entire stems are from two to six inches high – well above the earth-hugging leaves. The four or five clear light yellow petals are egg shaped, four to six times as long as broad and tapering gradually to the apex. The flower cluster is from one to two inches wide and the blossoms about half an inch in diameter.

Rarity: Rare.

Distribution: Steep slopes, cliffs and banks on rocky islets and the mainland coastal area from Vancouver Island, British Columbia through Washington and Oregon into California. I have never found this plant abundant anywhere although I have not covered its entire range.

Propagation: *Sedums* can be grown from seeds but I have never tried it and don't intend to. I do not know of any plant easier to propagate from divisions or cuttings. One method is to simply grab a plant and pull part of it up, roots and all and replant. Or break off a stem with rosettes attached and plant. Any time, spring, summer or fall will do nicely. Rooting is extremely easy. In fact the problem isn't so much how to increase stock but how to prevent too much spreading and encroaching on other plants.

Culture: Most *Sedums* prefer sunny locations and *pruinosa* does well in such positions where the climate is extremely mild. In my Portland garden sunny treatment does not prevent good growth but the foliage tends to a yellowish tinge due to too much heat. Light shade is much preferred. They do best in a loose sandy or leaf mold soil which should be well drained. Rock crevices make good homes for them as long as they can get a little soil and moisture. The thick stems and leaves hold moisture well and they can stand a considerable amount of drought. They do well as potted plants indoors – a trait not common to wildlings.

Many *Sedums* grow so rapidly or spread to various unwanted places in the garden from cuttings broken off by wind or animals that they become pests. *Pruinosa* has a minimum of this disagreeable habit. It is my choice as best of the native American *Sedums* and fully equal to any I have seen from Asia or Europe.

Flowering Time: May and June.

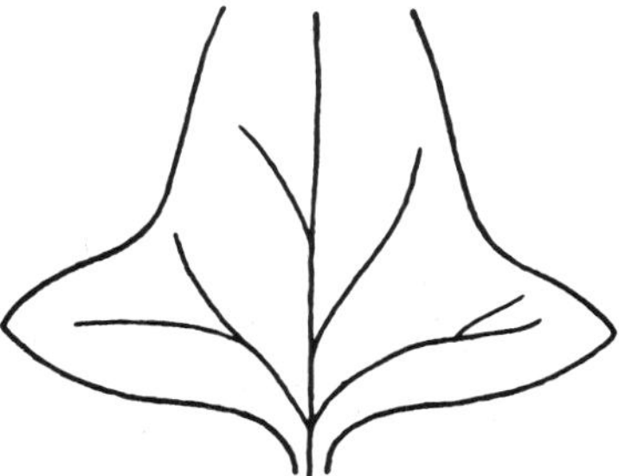

Hastate base

Sedum spathulifolium 'Rubrum' Broad Leaved Stonecrop

SEDUM SPATHULIFOLUM Hooker 'Rubrum'
Broad Leaved Stonecrop

As a race I don't care much about the Sedums. They like to wander around and take up squatter's rights – often where they are not wanted. I kicked the worst of these horticultural hoboes out of my garden and kept the good ones. This red-leaved variety of the common *S. spathulifolium* does a little of this traveling but, on the whole, is a thoroughly desirable resident.

A chance acquaintance, whom I had only seen once before, came over to my house one day. I gave him a few rare little ferns and he gave me a nice start of this Sedum. I never saw him again and I have no idea where he obtained it. But it has thrived with me in light shade, and in full sun too, and I have distributed bits of it to various friends.

History: For the history of the family, genus and species see the article on *S. spathulifolium pruinosa.*

Description: The flowers are yellow like the type species, the leaves are much the same size and shape. In summer both leaves and stems turn a rich, deep red and are very powdery. These two characteristics make it particularly appealing and I am very happy to have it. In the winter much of the red disappears from the surface of the leaves which are then neither green nor red but a somewhat uninteresting shade in between. And the glaucous quality is also subdued on the upper side. Beneath, however, some of the red color shows through the still heavy glaucous coating, combining into a soft ruby pink that is pure delight.

Rarity: Extremely rare in the wild. Obtainable from a few nurseries at moderate prices. *S. spathulifolium* is a variable species and I have seen a great many thousands of these plants during the years of my extensive wanderings but have never found this red leaved form.

Distribution: With the type species. From British Columbia through Washington, Oregon and into California in both the Coast and Cascade Ranges. Also in California's Sierra Nevadas. A defeatist attitude accomplishes little. Nevertheless a realistic outlook suggests that the likelihood of finding this variety in the wild is remote in the extreme.

Propagation: Same as *S. spathulifolium pruinosa,* which see.

Culture: Same as type species. Both *pruinosa* and *rubrum* in adjacent colonies make a pleasing contrast and accentuate the values of both.

Flowering Time: May and June.

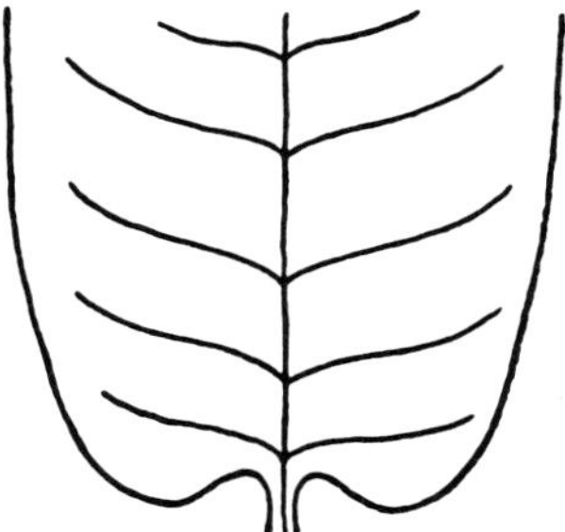

Subcordate base

Shortia galacifolia Oconee Bells

SHORTIA GALACIFOLIA Torrey and Gray
Oconee Bells

In a shaded place in my gardens in Portland, Oregon, Oconee Bells, the plant with the melodious name, is living as happily as though it were in its native soil 2,400 miles away. My home is not far from the shores of the Pacific Ocean while this *Shortia* lives in the high mountains of North Carolina near the Atlantic. But spanning the continent was no more difficult, indeed less so, for this flower than it was for the early pioneers who settled the west.

Few people can rightfully claim to be without a fault and the same is true for plants. But if Oconee Bells has any shortcomings they must be minor and obscure. Any reasonable effort to establish it in the garden is very much worthwhile. Reports have been made that this is a difficult accomplishment but with me it has been wholly tractable and a pure delight.

Beauty and rarity do not necessarily go hand in hand but in this instance they are a perfect unity. This unique little creeper surpasses by far all the native American ground covers. And it may well be that there is no other ground cover in the rest of the world that can equal its all around loveliness.

History: Its history has been accompanied by minor differences in dates, geographical placements, and taxonomic confusion, all of which is understandable. Various genera have species in both the old world and new. When European botanists visited our continent it was often easy for them to determine that a new species belonged to the same genus as one from Europe. The similarity of flower and foliage made the determination simple. Examples are the *Erythroniums* and *Gaultherias.* But the *Shortias* were completely unknown to science when the distinguished French botanist Andre Michaux discovered the one American species in the high mountains of Carolina in 1788. (Some give the dates as 1780 and 1789.) But his collected specimen was in fruit rather than in flower and the Frenchman Louis Claude Marie Richard, 1754-1821, did not describe it when he wrote Michaux's *Flora Boreali-Americana.* Asa Gray, the American botanist, examined Michaux's specimen in Paris in 1839 and with John Torrey founded the genus *Shortia* in 1842 in honor of Dr. Charles W. Short, a Kentucky botanist.

A great search was made for the plant in the mountains of the Carolinas but it eluded rediscovery until 1877 when it was finally brought to public notice by George M. Hyams who found it near Marion, in McDowell County, North Carolina. (Some give the date as 1878 and my map shows Marion to be in South Carolina. Another reference says C. S. Sargent made the rediscovery in the Great Smoky Mountains of North Carolina in 1886, and that it is restricted to Sapphire County. All these differences are important only to the extent that they reveal what this little flower has endured since Michaux's days.) For a hundred years all trace of the living plants was lost and it was believed to be extinct. The difficulty seems to have stemmed from its very limited range.

It belongs to the *Diapensiaceae* Family of Bentham and Hooker which consists of six genera of nine species – a very compact group.

Shortia galacifolia's leaves resemble those of *Galax* with which it grows and this accounts for the specific name. There are only two species in the genus, the other, *S. uniflora,* is native to Japan and was named in 1871 by the illustrious Russian systematic botanist Karl Johann Maximowicz, 1827-1891, a writer on Asian plants. Maximowicz placed it in the genus *Schizocodon.* It was decided, however, that the Japanese plant was a true *Shortia* and it is now in that genus.

Description: The leaves are all basal, and are among the few American natives that are desirable for their foliage alone. They are evergreen and in the spring and summer are a bright shiny green with the venation a prominent lighter and more delicate green giving a marbled effect which has a charm all of its own. During the colder part of the year they turn a lively vermillion and remain that way until the warm days of spring transform this horticultural chameleon back to its conventionally attractive color.

I have a leaf on my desk while I am writing this account. The texture is slightly leathery, round or egg shaped with slightly wavy margins. The one I am looking at is two inches long, half an inch wider, slightly heart shaped and faintly notched at the tip. Others are blunt tipped and may be half again as large. Young plants have much smaller leaves. The stems are slender, three or four inches long, and closely clustered. The long petioles give the leaves a chance to spread out and eliminate what would otherwise be an overly compact effect which would rob the plant of the daintiness it possesses. The slender flowering stems arise from the base of the plant from three to eight inches and each terminates in a single flower slightly nodding above the reticulated green leaves.

These blossoms cannot be casually dismissed, but must have a paragraph to themselves. The clear white bells are a full inch across changing to rose with age. The five lobes are delicately frilled at the tips – a floral offering of feminine daintiness unsurpassed in American woodlands. Mother Nature must have been proud of her creation for she produced these blossoms in abundance. I counted more than four dozen on a single plant. I feel like a blundering, inarticulate fool in attempting to paint a grammatical picture of this extraordinary plant. Once you have seen it you will know what I mean and how I feel.

Rarity: Very rare, due mostly to its drastically limited range. Abundant in a few stations but becoming ever scarcer due to collecting. There is an even much rarer variety with flowers that are a delicate pink from the first and plants with semi-double blossoms also occur. Considering the very great rarity of the plant one would expect it to be virtually impossible to obtain, that it would be prohibitively expensive, or both. Astonishingly enough quite the opposite is true. Not many nurseries offer it but those that do ask anywhere from a dollar and a half to as little as ten cents and in quantities from one to a thousand.

Distribution: Limited to a few small stations in the mountains of North Carolina and South Carolina.

Propagation: May be grown from seed which germinates easily if fresh. But this is a leisurely method as the youngsters grow very slowly. Also they are a trifle fussy until they get a little age behind them. Seed, however, is difficult to obtain as the flowering stem usually withers away before maturity. Early summer cuttings root readily in a mixture of moist peat and sand with a preponderance of the former material. The cutting box should be in the shade, of course. Increase is generally made from divisions of established clumps and from runners. A little care is required for success with this method but the expert gardener shouldn't have much difficulty. Most evergreens do better if transplanted or divided in early spring just as new root growth is well under way.

Culture: Few people live near enough to its native habitat in the Carolinas to collect wild stock and this is just as well, both to help conserve the wildlings and for the gardener. Nursery grown specimens have much better root systems and are easier to establish. Ground covers often have underground stems,basal branches, or both, which can be used for propagating. Such plants, if grown in pots have much better root systems than sections cut out of peaty soil. If a dealer offers both, the former will be the better buy even though it may cost a trifle more.

Most of mine are planted on the north side of the house in a bed 18 inches deep composed of 50 percent leaf mold, 25 percent coarse sand and 25 percent rich top soil. They are very much at home there now but were a little slow to establish themselves. Others are in the rock garden where they get just a little afternoon sun. In this spot they are scattered among the boulders in a mixture of crushed rock and leaf mold. Another location gets sun all morning and up to around one in the afternoon. I had more trouble adapting them to this place due to the extra heat. Most of the older leaves died back but new ones soon took their place. The soil medium is the same as that in my main planting. The extra light reddens and bronzes the foliage much sooner than it does where direct sunshine never gets to them.

Oconee Bells does well in partial sunshine where the weather does not get too warm. Its requirements are simple but absolute: Good drainage and an ample supply of humus, leaf mold – loose and fertile. A few gardens are fortunate enough to possess these natural conditions. Most of us, however, have to create them. Under ordinary garden treatment such as might be given most domesticated plants the *Shortias* will struggle along for a season or two before giving up in despair. They should be given enough room to expand by means of their searching underground root system. Furthermore any plant as distinguished as Oconee Bells shouldn't have to fight for space, food and light with other lesser dwellers in our gardens.

They can also enjoy life as pot flowers. This system is often used in England where our *Shortia* is more fully appreciated than in its native land.

There are two questions *S. galacifolia* presents that do not seem to have convincing answers. Why does not this plant, which does so well in its native Carolinas, appear in other parts of the country? Its ordinary needs have existed for centuries in many other places. This question is more pronounced with Oconee Bells but is found in other genera as well. I have puzzled over this problem for a great many years. While a number of solutions have occurred to me none of them are entirely satisfactory. The other question: Why is it that this plant, which is lovely the year around and so spectacularly beautiful when it flowers in the spring, is so seldom found in gardens? It is true that it hasn't had much publicity; that it is more or less obscure. It is also true that it has been available for over three quarters of a century; that it can be readily obtained at a trivial cost.

Flowering Time: Early spring. March and April in McDowell County, North Carolina.

Silene hookeri var. *ingramii* Jack Hausotter Photo Ingram's Indian Pink

SILENE HOOKERI variety **INGRAMII** Tidestrom and Dayton
Ingram's Indian Pink

My experiences hunting *Silenes* have been a little frustrating. The first I ever saw was a nondescript plant that had floated down from the mountains and seeded on the banks of an irrigation ditch in Central Oregon. I decided if it was typical of the *Silenes,* of which I had heard so much, I couldn't get interested. Many of them are little more than weeds. But, at their best, they well deserve all their far flung popularity.

The first good one I found was *S. hookeri.* Although I was looking for it I didn't expect to find it so soon for it was considerably north of its described range. The little clump of three or four plants was surrounded with those horticultural shotgun guards, poison oak. Undoubtedly they are still there. The following day 20 miles or so north of Grants Pass in southern Oregon I found them in scattered abundance on top of a bank in the light shade of evergreen trees. Although it was spring the soil was getting quite dry.

I got out my narrow bladed shovel and went to work. And what a job it was! The crowns were only two or three inches below ground and I was certain I could get the few specimens I needed in a few minutes. I was never more mistaken in my life! From the crown a deep rootstalk headed for the middle of the earth. I went down two feet in the impoverished, unyeilding soil. Then I quit. How deeply those determined roots go I have no idea and I have little intention of finding out. I abandoned this futile job and looked for very young plants – those that had not yet had time to go deeply. But it was difficult to tell a new plant from an old one without digging. I finally collected several and, in spite of great care, only one survived. The obvious lesson, learned at the cost of a good deal of sweat, was don't dig them in the spring.

The common name *pink* is misleading. It has nothing to do with the color of the flower but rather with its deeply lobed and scalloped petals. Pinking shears are still used to make ornamental edges on cloth, leather and other materials. And it is from this practice that the common name arises. Others are *Catchfly* and *Campion.*

History: Among gardeners the *Silenes* are the best known of the approximately 55 genera and 1,300 species of the *Chickweed,* of *Pink Family* as it is sometimes called, *Caryophyllaceae.* This name, originally spelled *Caryophylleae,* was designated by Bentham and Hooker, and is still authoritative. The family is pretty well distributed but is most abundant in the temperate regions.

Like the family itself, the *Silenes* are widely scattered. There are anywhere from 250 to 400 species, depending upon whose opinion you care to accept, about four dozen of which are native to the United States. It is a variable genus too in its life habits, comprising annuals, biennials and perennials. *Silene* is a Greek name of one of Bacchus' companions who was described as covered with foam. It is also connected with the Greek *sialon,* saliva, alluding to the stickiness of the herbage of some species. This is so pronounced that one variety is known as *viscida.*

The genus has been known for a very long time. Linnaeus named it in 1735 and it is also listed in the first edition of his *Genera Plantarum,* dated 1737.

S. hookeri was described by Torrey and Gray in their *A Flora of North America*, published in 1838-1840. Their notation was quoted from Thomas Nuttall's manuscript: "Woods of the Wahlamet, Oregon. The only specimen I have seen was collected by Dr. Gardiner." The variety *ingramii* came along much later. Tidestrom and Dayton named it in 1929 in honor fo Douglas Ingram of the United States Forest Service who was an excellent botanical collector. It was merely by chance that I was able to add part of Mr. Ingram's botanical library to mine and I would not part with these volumes for any price.

Description: Hooker's Pink, like its variety, *ingramii,* grows from a very deep seated perennial rootstalk although the parts above ground are deciduous. The plant is more or less grayish due to a growth of fine, whitish curled hairs, not glandular. There are several to many stems from the base, erect or more regularly with the lower part resting on the ground for some distance before turning upward, two to ten inches long, unbranched or sparingly so. The leaves, including the petioles, are either from one to three inches long, three or four times as long as the greatest width which is some distance above the middle and with a narrowing toward both ends, or gradually widening from the base to the pointed tip. The blades taper at the base to a winged leaf stem.

The flowers are either solitary or in clusters of two or three at the tips of the stems or in the upper leaf axils, on slender pedicels one-half to one inch long. The calyx, one-half to three-fourths of an inch long, is cylindric-funnelform and becomes greatly distended with the development of the seed. Its hairiness is so delicate that it is difficult to see with the naked eye.

The petals are cleft into four linear lobes, the middle pair the largest. The flowers are about an inch in diameter and vary from white to deep rose or bright red. The broadly egg-shaped capsules contain numerous seeds.

Rarity: *S. hookeri* is rare due to its more or less limited range. The variety *ingramii* is extremely rare because of the drastically limited territory in which it grows.

Distribution: *S. hookeri:* Dry ground in sun or light shade west of the Cascades in the Transition Life Zone generally at low altitudes from Yamhill County in the Willamette Valley of northwestern Oregon not far south of Portland, southward to the Siskiyou Mountains of northern California. I have never seen it as far north as Yamhill County. Much more abundant in southern Oregon.

Variety *ingramii:* Limited to an area of about 20 miles in diameter with Roseburg in southwestern Oregon as the center.

Propagation: It is possible to transplant wild plants in full bloom if they are planted immediately in coarse sand and leaf mold before withering. But at least a foot of the main tap root should be collected with each plant. *S. ingramii* transplants from wild stock easier than *S. hookeri.*

Increase can also be made from small rooted side shoots taken above the crown in the fall, but this is a difficult and uncertain process and is likely to result in a good percentage of failures.

For quick results nursery stocks raised from seed and grown in pots are easy to establish in the garden. They are well rooted and hardly know they have been moved.

Silenes are best grown from seed unless unusually good specimens are wanted for propagation. They will not come true from seed. The flats should contain coarse sand, rock chips, or other gritty material mixed with an abundance of leaf mold. Seed should be planted in late October or early November. In the greenhouse they will usually start sprouting within 20 days and keep coming on for weeks. If sown outside the seeds should produce their youngsters by spring. Greenhouse grown stock will produce flowering size plants by July.

Culture: The *Silenes* have an undeserved reputation for being difficult to grow. Getting them established is the biggest problem and this isn't really hard to do if their needs are understood. I have seen them growing on dry hillsides, even when in flower. This means good drainage in a very deep soil. The same growth medium should be used in the garden as in the seed beds but there must be ample room for their incredibly long tap roots. Most of the wild ones I have seen were in light shade but they do equally well in full sun in most climates.

Too little watering of some kinds of plants can be fatal. It is very certain that some flowers can be just as severely damaged by over enthusiastic use of the garden hose and these two particular *Silenes* are among them. They come from a country that is dry in the summer. Once well established, summer irrigation should not be practiced to enable the rootstalks to ripen. The wetter the climate the more important it is to provide perfect drainage.

Nursery grown stock can be planted any time but late summer or early fall is best. As soon as the autumn rains begin the young shoots push through the soil and only await the warm days of spring to make an active growth. Except from well-rooted potted stock spring planting is unwise.

Silenes have been grown in Europe for a great many years and are better known across the waters than in our own land. Many species, some of which are very popular, are annuals. The discriminating buyer will be wise to learn the life habits before buying. I do not care for annuals. Besides the chore of yearly replanting, self sown seedlings will pop up in places that I have reserved for other treasures. Another disadvantage is that good color forms cannot be assured with annuals. Vegetative propagation of selected perennials will ultimately result in a more colorful garden with a minimum of upkeep.

The crowns should be two or three inches below the surface of the soil. It is from these subterranean crowns that the fine, fleshy shoots appear and as the plants advance in age, year after year, these increasingly heavy tap roots send out more and more spreading stems. In my earlier attempts to collect them from the wild I did not understand this peculiarity. I would come across what looked like a nice clump of a dozen or more youngsters and immediately conclude that I could get all I needed in one big scoop of the shovel. It wasn't long before I learned to avoid these enticing veterans and concentrate on those juveniles that had only two or three stems and a less involved underground feeding system.

Soil fertility doesn't seem to be nearly as important as drainage. I have found them in earth so impoverished that it appeared to be utterly worthless. But there they were growing, not vigorously but very beautifully nevertheless.

S. hookeri and its variety *ingramii* are the American jewels among the *Silenes,* few of which are grown in our gardens. It seems strange that these very lovely plants are so little known. Not many nurserymen handle them and I have rarely seen them in gardens other than my own.

They are ideally suited to the rockeries where their roots can be tucked deeply into the narrow crevices between boulders. Once their roots are firmly and deeply established all they ask is to be left alone.

For the large rockery *S. hookeri* may have greater appeal than its variety *ingramii.* In the course of time a single plant of the former will cover several square feet and present an incredible display. *S. ingramii* seldom gets more than a foot in diameter and will be in better proportion in more limited areas. *S. hookeri* has more interesting blossom forms with its deeper cut petals and varying shades and hues of the lighter pastels. But, besides being much rarer, *ingramii* often has somewhat larger flowers of deeper pinks, rose, cherry reds, and some apricots. It is my favorite of all the *Silenes.*

I have one plant with bright red blossoms tucked into a small hole I drilled in a rock. It gives me three or four blossoms each year but where there is more root room a four year old plant will have as many as 50 flowers.

S. ingramii has recently been crossed with *S. californica* which has less desirable vegetative characteristics but more vividly brilliant scarlet blossoms. These hybrids are simply out of this world.

Flowering Time: Both *S. hookeri* and *S. ingramii* flower at the same time, as early as mid April and into July. Nursery stock will blossom on and off until frost. Indian Pinks sometimes show their gay colors on Thanksgiving Day.

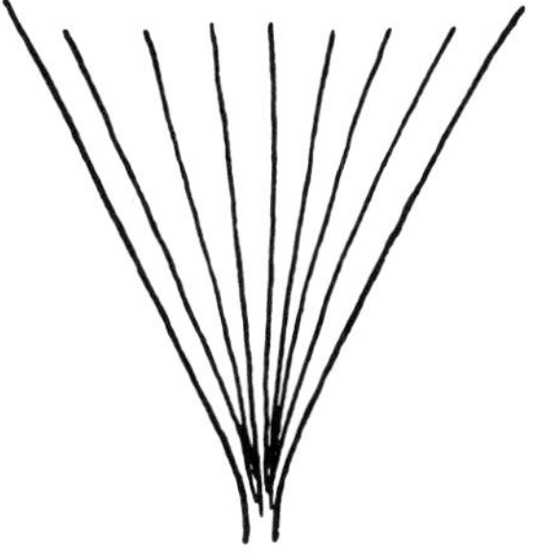

Cuneate base

Sisyrinchium grandiflorum 'White' Grass Widows

SISYRINCHIUM GRANDIFLORUM Douglas
Grass Widows

If there is royalty among flowers, and what plant lover can doubt it, the Grass Widow is the queen of the *Sisyrinchiums.* The clear purple bells, opening to a full inch and a half in diameter, with the golden anthers, is a beautiful sight when viewed alone. But a single blossom is no less striking than an entire field containing tens upon tens of thousands of plants all bowing and dancing in the spring breezes.

I have known these plants since I was a high school boy when I used to travel from Portland up the Gorge of the Columbia to Hood River with one of my teachers on weekends to work in his apple orchard. But my most memorable visit with these spring blossoms was ten or 15 years ago.

It was on Memaloose Island in the Columbia River where the Indians have buried their dead since legendary times. The lofty hills of the Cascades rose high from either shore while at my feet among the native grasses were a hundred or so Grass Widows, their purple blossoms a royal tribute to the ancient people deep in their long and lonely sleep beside them. The great silence was unbroken even by the whisper of a breeze. A loneliness I have never before known swept over me. Here was the ineffable beauty of the living flowers. Here were the souls of a forgotten race awaiting their Resurrection.

Among these few blossoms there was one with the whiteness of milk, the purity of snow – a flower I knew existed but had never seen before. Among the others were a few with cream colored stripes and two that were clear glowing pink, the only ones with this particular bright color I have ever seen. In a little while I left the sandy island but I am sure the *Sisyrinchiums* are still flowering there every spring just as I am certain that the Indians are still sleeping their eternal sleep undisturbed except by the occasional wandering vandal.

With the passing years my interest continued to grow in this rather common but uncommonly beautiful flower. I was determined to find some of the white ones and bring them to my

Portland gardens. My wife and I set out upon a field trip for this sole purpose. We visited hillsides where the purple flowers were growing in great profusion and with great vigor in the tiny water courses they need at this time of the year to be at their best. We searched vast open meadows, walking slowly and examining plant after plant and never spotting that elusive white. We traveled over 250 miles. We strolled among how many? 50,000, a 100,000, twice that many? Who knows? It was a slow process and a painstaking one. You might think a snow white flower among the rich purples could easily be seen from considerable distances but usually this is not so. The plants grow so densely in places that it is necessary to be within no more than 50 feet to see one and half that distance is much better. It was getting near the end of a long day and about time to go home. But I decided to try one more meadow. Within a hundred feet from where I entered it I found one white flower, not an outstanding plant by any means as the blossom was small but it had the clarity I was looking for and it was better than none at all.

This, and a subsequent trip for the same plant, were the only two occasions in my long career that a deliberate search for a rare flower was crowned with success. The other time I had a young man with me. We kept about a hundred feet apart as we walked slowly up a long and gentle slope. Within less than an hour he came over to me. There was a happy grin on his face and in his hand was a clump of large, clear white blossoms – exactly the splendid specimen I had been dreaming of. I took it home, and planted it in its own sandy loam in a three inch deep hole I carved out of a very porous lava boulder, – exactly the conditions I felt sure would make it happy in its transplanted home. How wrong I was! It never came up the following spring and I have never found another like it. I had overlooked one vital fact. Its native habitat was semi-desert with much less rainfall than we get in Portland. I should have added a goodly mixture of sand with the native soil. The purple type does well in my gardens but whites are often weak and need greater attention.

History: The *Sisyrinchiums* belong to the Iris family, *Iridaceae,* comprising about 57 genera and 1,000 species of both temperate and tropical regions in both hemispheres. Other close relatives are the orchids and lilies. There are about 150 species of *Sisyrinchiums,* all native to North America and the West

Indies. The name was first applied by Theophrastus, the Greek philosopher and naturalist who lived somewhere around 287 B. C. He used it in reference to a bulbous plant related to the *Iris.* At this period in ancient history, of course, neither the new world nor this genus had been discovered. It was Carl Von Linneaus who gave them their present name in the first edition of his classic *Genera Plantarum* published in 1737. They have been placed in at least nine other genera since then, one of which is still recognized as the correct designation by some authorities for the species with which we are concerned in this article.

David Douglas discovered it near Celilo Falls on the Columbia River in 1826. Although other earlier explorers must have seen it prior to that time it was he who gave it the first official description which was published in 1830. The latest scientific name is *Sisyrinchium douglasii.* Another prominent one is *Olsynium grandiflorum.*

The purpose of the taxonomists – those botanists who are concerned with the naming of plants – is to place each one in its correct place in relationship with others. It is intended to clarify a still badly confused science. But repeated changing of scientific names often compounds the confusion among laymen. Botanists do not have an exclusive right to these names. They belong to the public too. It is usage which provides the ultimate stability and it seems that the most popular designation for this most beautiful of all *Sisyrinchiums* is still *S. grandiflorum.*

Description: The stiff, erect stems are powdery silver green with narrow deeper green stripes. In this respect they are unlike any other plants within their range. They grow from three inches to a foot high and come either singly or in tight clumps of more than a dozen. The flowers are so large, up to an inch and a half across, that they appear to make the plants top heavy. They grow on short slender pedicels from near the top of the stems. The blossoms have six equal divisions and three stamens tipped with rich golden anthers in delightful contrast to the purple. The spreading, somewhat fleshy roots are an inch or two below ground.

I don't know where the name Grass Widows comes from. They are also called Blue Bells although they are never blue even if some of the other species are.

Rarity: Common, the purple type. Scarce, striped ones. Most of these do not have clear, sharp striping. Unless they do they are not particularly attractive. Really good ones are harder to find. Rare, the white form as it is usually found. Very rare, the white with large clear flowers. Very rare, clear pinks.

Distribution: Dry areas. British Columbia, Washington, Oregon, northern California and eastward to Idaho, Utah and Nevada. Rare west of the Cascades in Washington and northern Oregon due to too much rain.

Propagation: Can be raised from seed although this isn't done very often as they are easy to divide. This should be done in early spring after the shoots appear above ground.

Culture: Not at all difficult once their simple requirements are understood. In their native habitat they are usually in full sun although they do well in the light shade of pines and oaks. In every place where I have found them they were in a rich sandy loam with rock just a few inches below. Sometimes this layer of soil is so thin one wonders how they can survive. They will endure dry hillsides and the tops of rocks but do much better in springtime streams where the ground is so wet during flowering that boots have to be worn to keep from getting soaked feet. After the blossoms have disappeared the ground begins to dry. Then the tops disappear and the roots endure a long summer drought.

In the garden excessive spring moisture isn't necessary but allowing them to remain dried out all summer is essential. This last and sharp drainage are the keys to success. In wet climates they should be treated as rock garden plants.

Flowering Time: This varies remarkably. In my gardens I have had them blossom sparingly at Christmas. Other years they wait until March. East of the Cascades where they grow so abundantly the shoots are rarely visible just out of their winter sleep before January and even then are difficult to find. In eastern Oregon and Washington I have seen them in early March although they are generally at their best during mid April when they mingle with the dainty Yellow Bells, *Fritillaria pudica.* This is a sight worth traveling far to see and groups from western Oregon and Washington make annual trips to the other side of the mountains for no other purpose. In other regions and higher altitudes they will appear as late as May and June. While individual blossoms have only a very brief existence others on the same plant take their places and different plants flower earlier and later. Over a month elapses from the time the first appears until the last is gone.

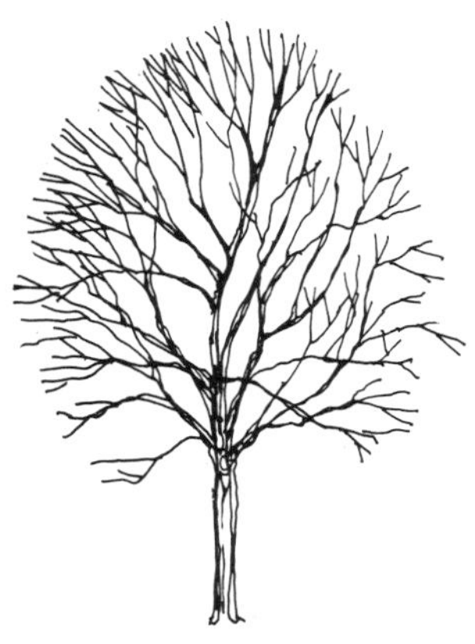

Synthyris lanuginosa Woolly Synthyris

Insert: Harold M. Johnson Photo

SYNTHYRIS LANUGINOSA (Piper) Pennell and Thompson
Wooly Synthyris

The enthusiasm I had for these distinctive members of a small genus was considerably greater than my initial success. I received five plants from a dealer who lives in the mild, wet climate of the Puget Sound region of northwestern Washington. One went into a rich leaf mold soil in light shade where I had other *Synthyris* growing nicely. Two others went into pots so they could be moved to more congenial places if circumstances seemed to warrant it. The remaining two I tucked into holes in porous lava rock where they were protected by an overhang. My *S. rotundifolia* and *S. stellata* continued to thrive but the first three *S. lanuginosa* slowly weakened and finally disappeared. Only those two in the rock holes survived.

History: The Figwort Family, *Scrophulariaceae*, comprises about 200 genera and some 3,000 species of wide geographical distribution. It includes the well known *Pentstemons*, the similar Monkey Flowers, *Mimulus*, and the European Foxglove, *Digitalis*.

The genus, comprising 14 or 15 perennial species grows from the Rockies to the Pacific and from California to Alaska. The generic name was given it in 1846 by George Bentham when he was 46 years old, from a Greek word meaning *closed doors*, in reference to the capsule valves. Charles Vancouver Piper, in 1906, called this species *S. pinnatifida* subspecies *lanuginosa* because of its close resemblance to *S. pinnatifida* – a native of the high mountains in Utah and Idaho. In 1933 Pennell and Thompson reduced it from its subspecific standing and gave it the now authoritative *S. lanuginosa*, which means *woolly* or *downy*. This word has been very useful to me. Whenever I see it in a wild flower catalogue describing a plant outside my experience I know it may be something exceptionally good and I do not hesitate to place an order. Generally the money is well spent.

Description: If it were not in flower anyone who should see it for the first time would hardly think of it as a *Synthyris* so strikingly different and greatly more beautiful is it than any of the other species with the single exception of its closest relative

S. pinnatifida. Most of the others have leaves that are more or less circular in form. The botanists say it is grayish downy throughout except for the almost smooth sepals. This is true but it seems to me that a frosty, light green, in keeping with its lofty, frigid home would be more appropriate and more accurate. This lovely silvery green is very pronounced on the young tender leaves, much less so on those a year old, and almost indistinguishable on the dead ones. The perennial leaf blades are finely divided. The primary segments are in about four pairs, each of which has one or two pairs of segments which are again toothed or sometimes more irregularly developed. If this is confusing think of a small delicately divided fern leaf. It is for this lacy texture and frosty green color that the plant is greatly admired and worthy of a place in any expert's garden.

In outline the leaf blades are about one and a half inches long, approximately half as wide and with petioles as long as or slightly exceeding the blades. The scapes, usually leafless, or sometimes with a few small bracts below the flowers, are higher than the foliage. The spike-like flower clusters are from one-half to two inches long. The tubular flowers have four wide spreading lobes that make them almost wheel-shaped. While the deep blue blossoms are only about a quarter of an inch wide their numbers make them conspicuously beautiful above their gorgeous foliage.

Rarity: Extremely rare.

Distribution: At very high altitudes – the Arctic-Alpine Life Zone – in stony locations in the Olympic Mountains of northwestern Washington and nowhere else in the world. It has been found in Marmot Pass and on Mount Angeles, one of the prominent peaks of the Olympics. This region is part of the Olympic National Park. Getting a collecting permit in our National Parks is extremely difficult. I had to make several contacts and negotiations covering about a month before I was allowed to take a few specimens. And even then a guard – a perfectly charming person – was sent along to see that I kept within the limits of my written permit.

Propagation: The heart shaped seeds with the point of attachment at the tip, give an upside down appearance. One of the big difficulties of growing them from seed is to get it. However abundant they may be in their alpine home, in its lowland, artificial haunts it is rarely produced. It flowers nicely in Scotland where it is well known, but in that island it never sets seed. Most members of the genus come readily from seeds but this one, due to its icy home, should be planted in the spring in wet climates to eliminate chances of rot. In its native haunts the seeds are frozen and covered with deep snow all winter. Freezing means that they are dry and can not rot. The flats should be shaded and the soil mixture should be rich in humus with stony material for good drainage. The youngsters should be ready for transplanting the following spring and another season or two, with the best of luck, should produce the first flowers.

Divisions are easier and faster. They should preferably be taken in early spring and placed in their permanent places or in a flat for another season. Late summer or early fall divisions can also be made, or immediately after flowering. In this latter event they need ample water and protection from summer heat. At least one season will come and go before blossoms can be expected and several years may elapse before the glow of success will sparkle in your eyes for this is a contrary plant. Those who have had no difficulty reproducing *S. rotundifolia* or *S. stellata* should not look for any such ease with *S. lanuginosa.*

Culture: Skilled knowledge and climate are the determining factors in not only making this most beautiful of all *Synthyris* live but thrive. The nurseryman in the Puget Sound area who sent me my original stock wrote: "This *Synthyris* is really not satisfactory material for the open garden. For seven years I've grown several collected plants on a scree. My experience with them has been much the same as the experience of other plant collectors in this coastal area. It will grow strongly and flower moderately for a year or two after being brought from the mountains. But rather soon it weakens in the garden and merely goes on in a half life, making little increase and flowering not at all. Flower buds will form in the autumn. Then the alternate frosts and thaws of our coastal area will cause them to rot. The plant needs less water and more dormancy than it can receive in the open. In a cold frame *S. lanuginosa* might handle very much better."

My Scottish correspondent who lives in a colder and drier climate says: "The plant grows well here if looked after, but never sets seed. The plants I have date back to a collecting trip in the Olympics in 1933! This says something for the longevity of this plant, having survived six years of complete neglect during the war." This man had kept them alive for 28 years at the time he wrote the above quote.

My experiences have been in between the two but more like those of my Puget Sound friend. Mine too is a wet climate. Planting on its side, sharp drainage, a little morning sun, and protection from too much moisture, especially in the wet seasons, are the secrets of keeping both plant and owner happy.

Flowering Time: June or later in the high mountains, depending partly when the snow is gone. Earlier in the lowland valleys.

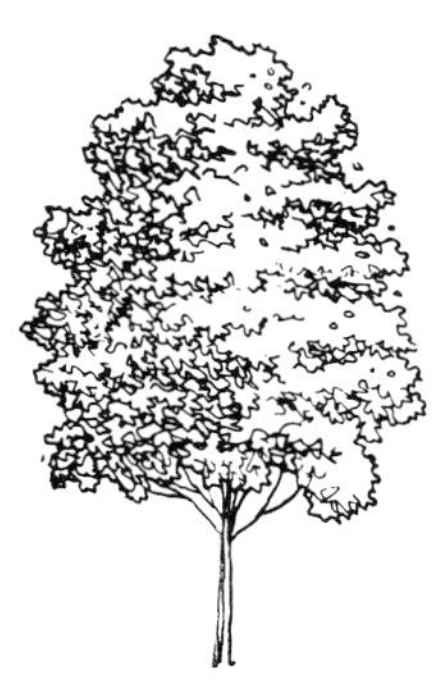

Acuminate apex

Columbia Synthyris

Synthyris stellata

SYNTHYRIS STELLATA Pennell
Columbia Synthyris

Oneonta's Gorge, a spectacular side canyon in the even more spectacular Columbia Gorge, is scarcely more than 30 miles east of Portland – not much more than half an hours drive. It was there, my favorite floral retreat, that I have spent many happy hours, enjoying the great vistas that stretch to the horizons, while at my feet many a wild plant greeted my eager eyes. This area, so close to home and yet so remote from the distractions of civilized life, has been my outdoor playground since I was a boy, long years ago. And it was there, in the shade of Oneonta's towering cliffs that I first saw and admired this Starry Grouse Flower.

I didn't know its name, except that it was a *Synthyris.* Indeed when I made my first solitary trip to this place at the age of 16 it didn't have one and it was 13 years more before the botanists decided what to call it. I didn't discover the plant, of course. Many others had seen it too, and some nurserymen were selling it under the erroneous name of *S. reniformis.*

The vandals have not been as active as usual at this particular station throughout the passing years. The plants seem to be as abundant now as when I first admired them not many years short of a half a century ago.

History: For the history of the family and genus see article on *S. lanuginosa.*

In his *Western American Alpines,* Dr. Ira N. Gabrielson mentioned it as "An as yet unnamed form (soon to be described) from the Columbia Gorge." The following year, 1933, Francis Whittier Pennell, 1886 - 1952, gave it the official name, *S. stellata,* which means *starry* and refers to the shape of the blue or purplish blue flowers. Mr. Pennell's choice was accurate, descriptive and has never been challenged.

Description: Like all of its sisters it is an evergreen perennial. When the old basal leaves wither away new ones take their places. They are from one to more than three inches wide, those on young plants or new foliage being the smaller. The growing leaves are medium green on top and lighter below, somewhat shiny at first but losing their gloss with age. The largest leaves are thickened and feel like soft, high quality leather. The blades are round kidney-shaped to round heart-shaped, with margins shallowly to deeply and prominently lobed, except near the basal portion where the lobes are less noticeable. Each lobe is generally from two to five toothed with some of the teeth having one or two smaller teeth on the sides of the larger. To anyone who has used a cross cut saw these teeth give the impression that the saw filer didn't know his business. But on the leaves the marginal irregularity offers a delightful aspect to a plant that is already well endowed with charm. Unlike *S. lanuginosa* it is neither powdery, hairy nor finely cut and divided. The slender petioles are from one and a half to two times as long as the width of the blades. Nature has been wise to provide these long leaf stems to prevent over crowding and the consequent loss of appeal.

The flowering stems, from six to 12 inches high, averaging about eight, are erect or declined in the middle of the plant and the rest are outward spreading. The leaves on the lower part of the flowering stems are much smaller than those from the crown, fan-shaped, narrowed at the base with sharply toothed margins. Farther up the stem the leaves become reduced to conspicuous nearly stemless leafy bracts. The flower clusters are from three to six inches long, growing closely together with the lower opening first. The floral display, rising well above the foliage, continues over a period of weeks and often more than half conceals the broad green leaves. The tubular blossoms with four wide spreading lobes somewhat resemble stars but I can't help feeling that if the lobes numbered five the effect would even more closely approximate the popular conception of our heavenly bodies. The crop of flat seeds is uncertain.

Rarity: Very rare, the type. The white extremely rare.

Distribution: In the Humid Transition Zone of the Gorge of the Columbia where it cuts through the Cascade Mountains. Only a few feet above sea level near the river and on the adjacent hills in shady moist places. One authority says it does not grow on the sunnier Washington side of the river. Another cites both sides. I have not seen it on the north shore but it is likely that it does live there in the cooler side canyons. About 30 miles east of Portland is as far west as I have yet to find it and it isn't likely that it travels eastward beyond the rainy areas, where it is replaced with another species. A rough estimate would limit it to between the 30 and 60 mile posts from Portland. I have never found more than a few dozen plants in any one place and often there is quite a distance between stations. I have nearly always found it either between mossy rocks or on top of rock.

Propagation: Comes very easily from seed which is difficult to acquire. None of those in my gardens have ever set any. This seems to be the experience of others, including English gardeners who are well acquainted with the genus. Sow in the fall or spring. In my climate, autumn is preferred. Divisions are easy from the crownal offsets, which however, are produced slowly. In my mild climate they may be taken either in the fall after the rains have started or in early spring so that the roots may become well established before the arrival of warm weather. Both methods may be used on the extremely rare white form.

I have never seen this white variety in the wild. A friend obtained ten seeds from England. All germinated and all produced white flowers!! The progeny from white mutations of plants usually either revert to type or produce only an occasional white youngster. Evidently this is a fixed white blossoming form. A white variety – whether or not it is this particular one I have not been able to determine – has been known in the British Isles for more than half a century.

Culture: Wild plants can be collected easily. Where they are rooted between rocks they can often be removed with the fingers and packed at once in the moss which surrounds them. In more exposed locations only a trowel is needed. My limited collections have always been made in the spring and all have quickly adapted to my gardens without even withering. In mild climates they do well in either light shade or partial sun. In the hotter parts of the nation sun should be excluded. In nature they are often in moderately deep shade but do not flower as well as in the open. A rich, humusy soil is better than an impoverished one but either will do. Moderate supplies of water and good drainage are more important. Given these they will outstrip their wild bretheren.

I have yet to see one in the woods that is as large, as

healthy, or nearly as floriferous as those in my gardens. They delight in a shaded spot in the rockery. Good places are in crevices between boulders or at the base of a rock large enough to make a suitable background. They will tolerate crowding by other species of plants but, like people, do much better if given room to expand and display their beauty.

A certain amount of confusion has existed in the past, even among nurserymen, about accurate identification and buyers have occasionally discovered what they paid for was not what they received. *S. stellata,* due, I suppose, to its rarity, is not often listed in catalogues. Once it is acquired problems are ended. It seems to be disease and insect free, requires little care, and blossoms beautifully most of the spring.

Flowering Time: March, April and May.

Acute apex

Talinum okanoganense Okanogan Talinum

TALINUM OKANOGANENSE English
Okanogan Talinum

It would be not only possible but almost a certainty that a person could stand on top of a colony of these plants without knowing it. This would be true, not only in the winter when the plants have lost all their leaves but in the summer too. They are so small and hug the ground so inconspicuously that they are difficult to see except when they are in their glorious blossom.

The plants in my garden always surprise me in winter. They are so barren and the branches, lying prostrate on the ground, appear to have gone to another world. A close examination reveals a trace of life. But still I wonder if they will come up in the spring. They always do unless a sudden cold snap comes on after the sap has begun to flow. In that case, as with many other plants, good-by.

When not in flower they might easily be mistaken for *Sedums.* But such an assumption would be far from true. They are not even in closely related families.

I obtained my first plants from a nursery. When they arrived I looked at them closely. They were so small I wondered if I hadn't been a victim of a horticultural swindle. But I knew the man who sold them to me was not that kind of a person. When they flowered a few months later my doubts were resolved. It was the greatest botanical bargain I have ever known and I was mighty lucky to get these splendid dwarfs.

History: They are honored members of the fascinating Purslane Family, *Portulacaceae* which consists of about 20 genera and 220 species. Among them are such distinguished plants as the *Spragueas, Portulacas,* the beautiful but difficult *Lewisias,* the *Montias, Claytonias* and *Calandrinias.* The family is widely distributed but most abundant in temperate regions. It was named by that famous English botanical team, George Bentham, 1800-1884 and Joseph Dalton Hooker, 1817-1911, the son of an even more illustrious father, Sir William Jackson Hooker.

Michael Adanson, 1727-1806, of France described and

named the genus *Talinum* in 1763 from an aboriginal name of a Senegal species. Two other generic names have since been offered, one in 1789 and the other in 1808 but neither are now recognized as official. They are found in Africa, Asia, Peruvia, Venezuela, Chili, Mexico and in various parts of the United States, numbering about 50 species. A number of them have been classed with the *Calandrinias* to which they are closely allied. Some genera have suffered the wildest kind of confusion. It is refreshing to work with one that has not endured such a fate. They are herbaceous plants, sometimes shrubby at the base and often grow from a tuberous root. The larger ones may grow two feet high or more. I haven't become acquainted with all of them, of course, but of those within my limited experience *I. okanoganense* is the smallest and by far my favorite.

It isn't at all surprising that a plant which is so inconspicuous nearly all the time and not at all prominent even when in flower was not discovered until nearly all the native plants of the Pacific Northwest were well known. What is astonishing, however, is that two different people, working entirely independently of each other, found it almost exactly simultaneously.

Mrs. Way discovered it on Mount Baldy near the Thompson River in British Columbia. She submitted her findings to Miss Alice Eastwood through C. W. Armstrong of Vancouver, British Columbia. Miss Eastwood described it and named it *T. wayae* in *Leaflets of Western Botany* in November, 1934. Carl S. English Jr. of Seattle, Washington located it in Okanogan County, Washington. He named and described it in the *Proceedings of the Biological Society* of Washington, D. C. in October of 1934. *T. wayae* is now considered a synonym, English having established priority by only one month. Botanical priority is based upon publication dates. There can be a considerable lapse between actual discovery and publication. Which of these people really first found the plant? No matter. It is a very choice addition to our knowledge of northwestern flora and to our rock gardens.

Description: If there ever was an earth hugger this is it. The entire plant, flowers and foliage, is scarcely an inch high. The spreading and numerous closely clustered stems from short basal offsets are from three-quarters to two inches long. The thickened root is perennial. The grayish green leaves are from three-sixteenths to half an inch long and usually nearer the former. They are round, cylindric and elongated and closely resemble some of our *Sedums.* The most obvious difference is that *T. okanoganense* has a more spreading habit. The flat topped flower cluster is from one to one and three-eighths inches high consisting of from one to nine blossoms. The creamy white five petaled flowers are half an inch or slightly more in diameter. The centers are a delicate yellow or sometimes pinkish. The blossoms are tiny wide open stars gazing upward at their astronomical namesakes millions of miles away.

A large plant may be two to four inches in diameter with the flowers a delightful proportion to the small branches and tiny leaves. A true miniature with charm and loveliness equal to that of any other plant of similar size.

Rarity: Very rare. Flowers that are all pearly white with no trace of yellow are found and are extremely rare.

Distribution: Range very limited. Mountains of southern British Columbia and south into Okanogan County, Washington.

Propagation: In drier climates this is not too difficult. Seed is produced freely but is tricky to collect. A day or so too early and it is green. Shortly after it is fully ripened it shatters out and is lost. The ovoid capsules need to be picked when the seed has just completed ripening but before it has had a chance to escape. The winter climate is too wet in my Portland home for good success with these seeds. They usually winter rot. Drier places will produce better results. Cuttings root fairly well but my trouble is to keep them moist enough to root and sufficiently dry so they will not decay.

Culture: Give them the very best drainage and plenty of sun in the cooler parts of the country. A little less if yours is a hot climate. They will take a lot of drought, having lived with it all their lives. I drilled one inch holes in porous lava boulders and planted some of them there in soil consisting of half leaf mold and half crushed rock. Others were put in open spaces in the ordinary part of my rockery. It is important to see that competing plants do not crowd these dwarfs. They have a right to the very little room they need. See to it that they get it and you will be greatly rewarded.

Flowering Time: From May at lower altitudes to August

in the higher mountains. That so tiny a plant will have a blossoming time of several weeks is as astonishing as it is pleasing.

Obtuse apex

Spiny Talinum

Talinum spinescens

TALINUM SPINESCENS Torrey
Spiny Talinum

It seemed quite useless to look for wild plants on the desert country I was driving through in south central Washington. I was returning from a five day trip to the Bitter Root Valley to study Montana's lovely state flower, *Lewisia rediviva.* About halfway between the tiny hamlet of Vantage on the Columbia River and Ellensburg, Washington, I caught a flash of bright rosy pink on top of a ten foot bank. I stepped across a few strands of barbed wire – the remains of a long abandoned fence and the end of an optimist's dream of security in a frustrating and desolate land.

The flowers were large and their rosy red petals partially obscured the spiny ball-shaped cactus growing out of the thin stony soil. Beautiful to be sure but such plants drown in my winter wet Portland gardens so I left them alone. But I looked around a little further. There was a fine cut-leaf violet, equally impossible and a scattering of a few dozen Bitter Root plants in flower. Among these interesting desert plants and a few odds and ends of weeds there were some peculiar creatures quite unlike anything I had seen before.

They resembled, in a vague sort of a way, Tolmie's Saxifrage but I knew that water lover wouldn't have lasted a single day under those despairing conditions. It also looked a little like a *Sedum.* But I had never heard of a desert stone crop. More out of curiosity than any real enthusiasm I dug a couple of the smaller ones. The roots were shallow and I had them out of the ground, packed and moistened down in a couple of minutes.

At home I planted them in stony soil, like their desert home, and gave them a place in full sun. Although it was late in May when I found them and the desert was already quite dry there was no sign of flowers. It wasn't long, however, before some very slender stems began growing upwards. Not much later some pure magenta flowers with golden anthers appeared. The blossoms were so startlingly beautiful that I gasped in wonder. How could such a joyous plant live in such an environment?

The bitter winter winds rage over those barren rolling hills. And in the summer the intense heat blazes down on the dry soil and hot basaltic rocks. No wonder the discouraged rancher moved to a gentler climate.

It was the Rock Pink, *Talinum spinescens,* of course. I felt like kicking myself for not gathering a few extra specimens for my friends.

History: Mr. W. D. Brackenridge and Dr. Charles Pickering were the botanists with the exploring expedition of Captain Wilkes. It was during the spring and summer of 1841 that these two scientists, attached to Lieutenant Johnson's party, set out to explore the interior of what is now the State of Washington. John Torrey, 1796-1873, the very competent New York botanist named and described this plant in 1874 in the story of the Wilkes Expedition. It was no doubt from the herbarium specimens collected by the two scientists that Torrey was able to make his determination. So it happened that a lovely desert flower was given to America in 1874, a year after John Torrey passed away. His name appears freely in the annals of North American botany and is well known to plant scientists. This lonely plant still bears his name and is a fitting tribute to the end of a great career of an even greater man.

The nomenclature of this plant has suffered little confusion. In 1891 Otto Kuntze, a German botanist, offered *Claytonia spinescens.* This is now considered a synonym and Torrey's original designation is still official.

Description: *T. spinescens* is said to grow from five to 11 inches tall but I have never seen any greater than the lesser height. It may be that in more salubrious circumstances the greater stature may be found. It is freely branched from a short stout woody base. The short branches are quite thickened. In the winter they are covered with a mass of short sharp spines which are the persistent midribs of the former leaves for this is a deciduous perennial. The naked branches during the dormant season are nothing worth looking at except for their curious appearance. At this time they seem more dead than merely sleeping. In the spring a mass of pimple-like pink protuberances appear. These soon expand into linear succulent leaves half an inch to an inch long and somewhat resemble thickened fir needles.

These fleshy green leaves effectively conceal the heavy stems. At this time, even before the flowers appear the plant is a worthy garden dweller. Large ones, in the wild, are six inches in diameter with the average about half that size. I have visited the site of my original discovery many times and have yet to find a tiny seedling. Apparently, wind blows the seeds away and the sparse, stony soil is a difficult environment for seeds to germinate and send down tiny roots deeply enough to survive the severely hot and dry summers.

The slender but stiff and wiry flowering stems are from four to ten inches high with the average much closer to the former figure. They terminate in a cluster of half a dozen to a dozen or more buds. The upper ones open first into upward facing five-petaled blossoms which do not last long but are quickly replaced with others. This habit assures a flowering period covering a number of weeks.

These long, thin stems remind me of a skinny girls legs and really do nothing whatever for the plant. If they were as shortened as those of *T. okanoganense* this wonderful plant's only fault would not exist.

Rarity: Rare. I have been unable to run down rumors of double flowering forms and those with white blossoms. If they exist, and it is likely that they do, they must be extremely rare.

Distribution: From Okanogan County in north central Washington south to the Wenatchee Mountains of Chelan County and continuing southward to the Oregon border. The literature on this plant confines it to the State of Washington. However a small colony has been located in Central Oregon since the current literature was published. It is possible that other stations will be discovered.

Propagation: *T. spinescens* does not consistently set seed in my Portland gardens. Some years there will be none at all. Other seasons only a little can be harvested. In such a wet climate as mine germination is not satisfactory. Drier locations should offer good success, especially if the seed is alternately frozen and thawed for a few weeks in the refrigerator. Cuttings can be rooted in sand in the spring and summer but a delicate balance between enough moisture to enable rooting and not enough to cause rotting is good practice. Self sown seedlings will often flower late the same season in suitable climates. Rooted cuttings, like the mature plants themselves, grow slowly.

Culture: All the wild *T. spinescens* I have ever seen were in sharply drained, rocky soil. They don't like competition. None were growing close to other *Talinums* or any other species of plants. These same conditions should be provided in the garden. They like full sunshine. Their succulent leaves and thickened stems hold enough moisture so that they can withstand a considerable amount of drought. For this reason I give them little or no moisture in the summer. A moderately loose rocky soil with a little humus will allow the roots to penetrate deeply enough to reach permanent moisture and sufficient food for good health. Many desert and alpine plants will rot out in wet climates. This is one that doesn't. If a few warm days in late winter start the sap to flowing and a cold spell follows the change can be fatal. This lack of hardiness is not confined to *Talinums.* It applies to many plants, domesticated and wild.

Flowering Time: June to August depending upon altitude and climate. *T. spinescens* blossoms a little later than *T. okanoganense.* The first flowers to appear are not numerous but become more abundant until a heart warming peak is reached. Then they become less and less frequent until the final lonely blossom ends the season.

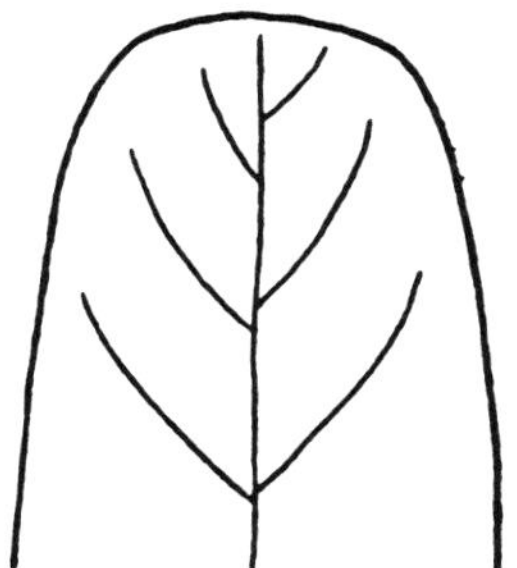

Truncate apex

Trillium grandiflorum Large Flowered Wake Robin, Rare Double Form

TRILLIUM GRANDIFLORUM (Michaux) Salisbury
Large Flowered Wake Robin

My home not far from the shores of the Pacific is more than a thousand miles from the nearest wild *Trillium grandiflorum* and yet it does well in my gardens. Going in the other direction it has been shipped across the Atlantic where it is well known in the British Isles. One English writer has gone into ecstasies over it: "– a plant unsurpassable anywhere for heartiness of habit, charm of manner and purity of bloom. – and should be planted everywhere by the thousands; its only fault being that its excessive beauty and goodness attract as much love from slugs and mice as from gardeners." It is just as popular in America where it is collected avidly, grown commercially, and distributed freely from ocean to ocean except for a few states where conditions are too harsh for even its great adaptability. It is the largest of the white flowered species and is exceeded in size only by one of the sessiles with huge red blossoms that lives in the western part of our country.

It is the most variable of all the *Trilliums* and some specimens that have comparatively narrow petals are not particularly outstanding. But those with wide and long petals – and they are not abundant – are extremely beautiful. Anyone who has seen these large blossoms will recognize at once that the extraordinary width of the petals is responsible for the great appeal these flowers have wherever *Trilliums* are grown.

One of my midwestern friends makes a yearly excursion to Michigan's upper peninsula where mutations are found. He has sent me some of them. One had small petals that were entirely green and I had to look closely to distinguish between petals and leaves. Others had one or two more than the typical three petals. A few had four, five or six petals, some of which were snowy white. Most of the mutations he sent me were streaked and striped with narrow or broad bands of green or had green margins with the middle parts of the petals pure white. There were both petioled and sessile leaves. They ranged from all white to all green flowers with almost every imaginable combination. Most of these mutations are oddities, interesting for their peculiarities rather than because of much floral appeal. Occasionally one will be found, however, that has a good deal of charm and is well worthy of the little care and limited room it occupies. There is also a tendency for some of these to revert to the original flowers both in color and number of petals. Some of these have needle-like capsules that appear to be sterile. It is difficult, however, to believe that, due to their wide distribution, they reproduce solely from divisions of the rhizomes. Most of these have stamens and pistils. But there is another form which will not revert to type, the stamens and pistils having become petals.

These double forms may have up to 30 or more petals and some of them are astonishingly beautiful. They are of two general types: 1. Trumpet, with the petals in the same position as the typical blossoms, flaring outward. This is also sometimes referred to as Camellia flowered. 2. Gardenia, with the outer petals turning outward and the inner ones in a tight curling cluster around the center. My midwestern friend has found them only in rocky soil. This may or may not be coincidental. These mutations of *T. grandiflorum* are not limited to Michigan, however. They have been found in Ontario, Canada, New York, Ohio, Minnesota, and doubtless numerous other places. Nor are they confined to *T. grandiflorum,* many other species having been found with this strange growth.

The California plant wizard, Luther Burbank, claims to have crossed the western Leopard Lily, *Lilium pardalinum* with the western *Trillium ovatum.* This is a remarkable circumstance. While both are members of the Lily Family they are in different genera. Crosses between species within a genus are often difficult or impossible but between two different genera are quite far fetched. These hybrids were dwarfs with broad, lily-like foliage. The blossoms resembled *Trilliums* with three very broad, flat, greenish-white or yellow petals. These interesting hybrids lacked vitality and all died but not before Mr. Burbank photographed them.

History: Carl Von Linnaeus named the genus *Trillium* and described three American species, *T. cemuum, T. erectum* and *T. sessile,* in the first edition of his *Species Plantarum,* published in 1753. In this same edition he also included the closely related genus *Medeola,* and at the earlier date of 1735 he introduced the other of the two allied genera, *Paris.*

Some modern authorities have placed these plants in the Lily of the Valley Family, *Convallariaceae* or in John Lindley's Wake Robin Family, *Trilliaceae,* which he proposed in 1836. Most, however, have left them in the *Liliaceae* of Bentham and Hooker.

Mediola is an American genus of only one species found from Nova Scotia to Ontario, Minnesota, New York and southward to Florida and Tennessee. The name comes from *Medea, a sorceress,* in reference to the supposed healing powers it possessed. It has two whorls of leaves, the lower numbering from five to nine and the upper three to five. The shape of the leaves suggests the *Trilliums* but the flowers do not.

The genus *Paris* has nothing to do with the famous French city on the Seine river. The name comes from a Latin word for *equal* in reference to the regularity of the parts in units of four – eight stamens, four petals, four sepals and four leaves. The last, apart from the one extra leaf, are much like those of the *Trilliums* but the flowers are quite dissimilar. There are about 40 species native to the British Isles, Europe, and Asia.

Trillium comes from the Latin in reference to the parts coming in units or multiples of three – three sepals, three petals, six stamens, a three or six angled or lobed ovary. Certainly this is an appropriate name and the three others that have been offered since Linnaeus' time are generally known only to botanists and are now in obsolete synonomy.

There is a good deal of dispute among taxonomists as to exactly how many species exist. Six different sources give as many opinions: 20, 24, 25, 30, 31, and 50 including some varieties in this last figure. Most are North American's and 43 of our adjacent 48 states claim at least one species. Southern Canada has about seven. Four are native to Japan and two are from the Himalayas.

Trillium rhomboideum variety *grandiflorum* was given by the French botanist Andre Michaux in 1803. In 1805 Richard Anthony Salisbury, 1761-1829, established the now authoritative *T. grandiflorum.* The specific name, very appropriately means *large-flowered.*

It may or may not be the most beautiful – gardeners like to argue over that – but it is certainly the best known and anyone who grows *Trilliums* should have a choice spot for this renowned species.

Description: The usually stout stems of *T. grandiflorum* are from eight to 18 inches high – usually nearer the latter height – and grow from a scarred rhizome. The age of the plants can be determined by the number of scars on the rhizome sheaths. The three large, broad leaves are sharp pointed and an inch and a half to three inches below the single flower supported by the more slender, erect or somewhat inclined peduncle. The three large, broad snow white petals are strongly veined and sometimes turn soft pink with age. The blossoms are generally from two to three inches wide but one English writer, in his wild enthusiasm, describes a variety with flowers from four to six inches across. I have a plant four and seven-eighths inches in diameter in its natural position and, spread out six and one-fourth inches.

The fruit is a spherical, greenish-white, slightly six-lobed berry-like capsule from one-half to one inch in diameter.

Rarity: The white type, common. The variety *roseum* is rare. It is pink in bud and blush pink in blossom. Whether it will come true from seeds is very doubtful. Nurseries hardly ever list this variety and very few have it. Those that do can dispose of their stocks to regular customers without including it in their catalogues. In spite of its scarcity it generally sells for the same price as the white.

The mutations with all green flowers or with striped and streaked white and green blossoms are likewise rare. I do not know of any dealer who sells them. They are too difficult to obtain. My dozen and a half plants were obtained through two Michigan friends. And it takes loyal friendship to get them at all.

The double flowering varieties with the stamens and pistils reduced to petals do not revert to type. The best of them are extremely beautiful and just as rare. My friend who makes annual pilgrimages to Michigan's upper peninsula has promised to send me one if he finds any. This is virtually unheard of. Of course I don't expect to receive such a gift. For all practical purposes they are virtually nonexistent. There is a man in New

York State who is said to have two or three hundred of these doubles. Many people, including myself, have written to him. He keeps these letters but does not answer until some whim or other strikes him. Then he will sell a few, allegedly for 20 dollars each. But years may go by without a reply. But Mr. X doesn't worry in the least. He has a monopoly upon the supply and can easily sell all he possesses. One of my correspondents tells of a person who had a few to sell. One that he was offering for five dollars wasn't particularly impressive. Another he sold – and this was a single plant – brought him 100 dollars. This is probably the highest price any *Trillium* fan has ever paid and it has started quite a discussion among those who collect these flowers. I wouldn't pay that much because I simply do not have the money and probably wouldn't spend it if I did. On the other hand if I were offered 1,000 dollars to find such a plant in the wild I would be forced to reject the opportunity. A person would be almost certain to spend far more than that in actual cash to say nothing of the time involved in what would likely be a futile effort. It is quite possible to spend a lifetime in the outdoors without discovering a single one of these extremely rare flowers. I know several people who possess a few but neither money nor the obligations of friendship will avail to induce them to part with any. And I know better than to strain a cordial relationship by even making such a suggestion. Probably no other American wild flower mutation is so sought after – and so futilely.

Distribution: The mutations are presumed to cover the same regions as the type. From Canada's Ontario and Quebec provinces southward into Minnesota, Michigan, Indiana, Ohio, Kentucky, New York, Pennsylvania, West Virginia, Virginia, The Carolinas, Georgia, to Florida. Also Missouri and Tennessee. In rich woods, ravines, wooded upland slopes and in the mountains to 5,000 feet or more. Its wide range indicates a high degree of adaptability to gardens in various parts of America and in foreign lands.

Propagation: Seed should be harvested as soon as the capsules are ripe – preferably as they split open but before the seed drops. Many species have the seeds in a mucilaginous, sticky mess before they are removed from the capsule. This material is so slippery and insoluble that it is virtually impossible to clean them by ordinary washing. It is much more practical to break open the ripened ovaries and spread them out on papers in a warm dry room. After the masses have dried it is quite simple to crumble them apart and either plant at once or place in cool storage with a relatively moist atmosphere. Seeds can be damaged by becoming too dried out.

Rapid increase is by seeds. They should be planted as soon as ripe or in the fall before the first heavy frosts. As the seeds ripen in summer they may be planted and left dry until the fall rains. But once they become wet they should not be allowed to become dry on the under side next to the soil. They may be scattered on the surface of the earth or shallowly covered – the latter method being the preferred one due to better moisture control. But I have had hundreds volunteer near the parent plants where nature has deposited the seeds. Old leaves and general debris had covered them sufficiently to retain the necessary dampness. Germination is better if the seeds are frosted. That is why spring sowing is not recommended.

It is during the early months of the year when the soil is warming and the humidity is beginning to drop that most failures occur. It is very difficult to keep the bottom sides of the seeds constantly moist. This is the most important requirement for growing *Trilliums* and ignorance of or lack of sufficient attention to this detail is the common reason for the remark, "I can't grow *Trilliums.* The seed doesn't germinate." Once this problem is conquered the rest is easy.

From seed to first flowering requires a minimum of four years and it is unusual for many to blossom that soon. The fifth and sixth years will usually see most in flower although under some circumstances it may take seven. At least one species requires up to 11 years. An unseasonal frost may cause delay. Also different batches of seed vary widely. Some may not send up their first single leaves until the second year. Poor soil, crowding by unrelated plants, lack of adequate moisture, are causes of retarded growth, not only with *Trilliums* but with many other kinds of plants. The seed beds should consist of rich, well drained, moisture retaining soils. And they should be well shaded, partly to conserve surface moisture and partly to provide protection from excessive heat.

Two years after first flowering are necessary for the plants to achieve full maturity in the ordinary sense of the word. At this time only one stem can be expected from each rhizome. After more years have elapsed – and the exact number is variable – a single rhizome may send up two or three stems, each with a solitary flower. This generally represents the ultimate attainment and such plants may be considered floral patriarchs although an occasional plant may be found in the wild with a dozen or more stems.

A much easier and much slower method may be used to propagate – simply leave the plants alone. The rhizomes, as they advance in years, will sometimes develop offsets and these can be separated after the seeds have ripened and the tops have died. This is in late summer. I prefer to leave these clumps undisturbed and use other means of acquiring more plants for the clusters make compact, natural bouquets which display *Trilliums* in their greatest glory. Offsets are produced less than one per year per parent plant over an extended period of time. This, of course, is not a satisfactory procedure in a world rushing madly to its own destruction.

Other systems have been tried. Rhizomes have been cut lengthwise, making right and left halves with generous roots on each. They have also been sliced horizontally, leaving most of the roots on the under half and the stem bearing part on the upper half with some attached roots. Both of these experiments have terminated in all parts simply rotting away.

But Walter E. Thwing developed a system of vegetative propagation which is sometimes successful. Mr. Thwing started his triumphal experiments in 1946.

In mid July he took an established potted plant that had produced two stems and two blossoms in April and removed the soil with a hose until the crown of the rhizome was exposed. The feeding roots were left undisturbed. He cut a notch about one-sixteenth of an inch wide and the same depth two-thirds of the way around the crown just below the growing bud. The plant was then covered with soil again and the pot was plunged into the ground in the shade. Three months later, in October, he uncovered the plant and found three strong new shoots coming from just below the notch with more showing, and the original growing bud was unharmed. The plant was covered again for the winter.

In April of the following year, 1947 – nine months after the operation – seven plants appeared, four of which were strong enough to flower. In July, a year after the operation, several well developed little rhizomes and a rash of new buds were disclosed when the soil was removed again for an examination. Three months later, in October, the entire plant was removed from the pot and the roots washed clean of soil. Five of the new rhizomes were strong enough and had sufficient roots of their own to be separated from the parent plant. They were cut off and potted separately and the parent was repotted.

In the spring of 1948, 14 plants came up, six from the parent and eight from the new rhizomes.

In 1949, less than three years after the notching surgery, there were 25 plants with 16 flowers. The original rhizome produced 16 plants and six blossoms, representing a total plant increase from two to 25.

In another test Mr. Thwing partially notched a rhizome just below the bud just as he did with the successful experiment. But this rhizome was freshly dug including the roots. After the surgery it was replanted. It died, the double shock of surgery and transplanting apparently was more than the plant could survive.

The two basic principles of the Thwing method are notching rather than complete dissection of the crown and bud, and operating only on established plants without disturbing the roots. It is possible to perform the necessary surgery on plants growing in the ground but it is much easier to handle those that have been potted. They can be operated on at bench height. The ones I have notched were growing under a plum tree and I found removing the soil, reaching down into the hole with a razor blade and doing the delicate excision while on my hands and knees was both hard work and difficult.

This system of propagating the rare double *Trilliums* fails much more often than it succeeds. It should not be attempted on these very valuable mutations until sufficient experimenting has been done on ordinary specimens to acquire the skill necessary without killing the plants.

Culture: *Trilliums* are not difficult to handle under garden conditions. They will tolerate almost any well drained soil unless it is alkaline. But they prefer a moist rich medium with an abundance of leaf mold in partial sunshine to moderate shade. Although the rhizomes may be quite deep in their wild homes four inches measured from the top of the rhizome, for the species is ample in the garden. The best time to plant is when they are completely dormant – after the tops have died down but before the buds begin to grow in the fall. Selected plants must be dug, however, when they are in flower. Or, better still, staked at that time and transplanted when dormant. I have gone into the woods during dormancy where I knew the plants were abundant and failed to find a single one. Even the dried foliage almost always vanishes. Most people dig the wild plants as I have, when they are in flower and with reasonable care they survive nicely. The bloom is made mostly from the food stored in the fleshy root the previous season. When transplanted in full blossom, however, the shock is usually great enough to require at least two years, and more often three, before they recover their full vigor.

Mass plantings give a striking effect, especially if mixed with some of the lacy low growing ferns that do not hide *Trilliums'* snowy blossoms. I like to plant them in tight clumps of half a dozen or a dozen, and leave a foot or two of space between each group. If this is done after a good deal of study has gone into the effort the result can be one of the most strikingly beautiful in all the world of wild flowers.

T. grandiflorum will fit nicely into the shadier parts of medium to large rock gardens where moisture and soil fertility are right. Between *Rhododendrons, Camellias* and other similar evergreen shrubs where the spacing is much more than is needed a few tight groups of *Trilliums* are spectacular spring time delights. They can also be mixed with dwarf *Iris* and *Erythroniums.* The combinations are limited only by human imagination and visions of floral beauty.

Flowering Time: April, May and June depending upon climate and altitude.

Trillium hibbersonii Rock Trillium

TRILLIUM HIBBERSONII Wiley
Rock Trillium

A mile or two westward and more than 2,000 feet below him the endless Pacific Ocean thundered against the shores of Vancouver Island. Eastward, nearly a third of the way around the world was the place of his birth, Lancashire, England. But nestling in a small rock crevice at his feet was a dwarf *Trillium* that John Arthur Hibberson had never seen before.

A hundred and fifty miles from his family in Victoria and 8,000 from his native England, with the virgin forest, the massive cliff and the distant ocean as his only companions he was as solitary and lonely as ever a man can be. Little did he know that the miniature plant he was looking at would bring his name renown wherever *Trilliums* are known; wherever wild flower lovers grow them.

At that moment magnificent vistas, great forests and towering cliffs were not his interest. He had found a *new* plant and he was well aware of it. He had never heard of this *Trillium* before and, indeed, there is no reason to believe that anyone else knew it existed. With his miner's pick Mr. Hibberson dug it out of the hard rock and collected six or seven others he found growing nearby. There can be little doubt that he was the first to collect it.

Considering that the plant was not in flower at the time and the vast number of plants of many species that were all around him Mr. Hibberson deserves considerable credit for his astuteness for he was not a botanist. He was a surveyor and timber cruiser working for a private company. But he was an excellent observer and had a considerable knowledge of the trees, shrubs, flowers, grasses and even the mosses of Vancouver Island and other parts of British Columbia. Without his insight and rich experience it is entirely possible that it would be still undiscovered. Certainly its appearance in our gardens would have been delayed for a long time.

History: John Arthur Hibberson, July 10, 1881 - August 21, 1955, was born in Lancashire, England, and emigrated to

Canada in 1907 where he became a naturalized citizen. He was 57 years old when he found the first specimen of the plant that now honors him. This event occurred on Monday, April 25, 1938. From his diary of that date: " – Another hard day climbing around rock cliffs. Some good hemlock and balsam. Saw small species of *Trillium* on rocks at 2,000 feet." That is all. It is not often that the exact date and circumstances for the discovery of a new plant are known.

This, one of the four miniatures in the genus, was the last of the *Trillium* species to be discovered. It isn't likely that there are any more. It is certainly one of the most beautiful. I rank it among the four best and for the life of me can not decide which deserves the highest rating. The others are the deep maroon form of *T. chloropetalum* which has the largest flowers of them all if length of petal is considered the determining factor; *T. grandiflorum* which on a rare occasion will produce a blossom six inches in diameter; and *T. rivale,* a west coast dwarf which very much resembles *T. hibbersonii.* Robert J. Hibberson, the son of John Arthur Hibberson, naturally enough considers their *Trillium* the loveliest of them all. I am not the kind of a person to dispute the judgment and good taste of a friend I respect and admire.

A year or two after he made his find his wife, Mabel, asked him why he did not go back and collect more before vandals destroyed them all. He said there was no need to worry about that as the plants were so difficult of access and so isolated that they were safe. Dr. Adam F. Szczawinski, Curator of Botany, Provincial Museum, Victoria, B.C., expressed a similar opinion. Neither of these convictions, sincere as they unquestionably are, can be taken very seriously. Collectors go everywhere plants exist anywhere in the world. No unusual plant is safe and many are threatened with extinction.

Mr. Hibberson never made another trip to the place of his discovery. This was at Boat Basin on the inward top of Hesquiat Harbour at an altitude of 2,000 feet and inland about one and a half miles. The first specimen he saw was growing on a cliff fully exposed to terrific storms, sun and the severity of winter. He planted his collection in his Victoria gardens. But the story does not end there.

According to Dr. Szczawinski, he, Dr. Taylor of the University of British Columbia, and others re-collected it in 1956 on the west coast of Vancouver Island at an unspecified location. Probably another collecting trip was made in 1957. On July 7, 1958 Drs. Szczawinski and Taylor found more on the banks of the Clennyuck River, Kyuquot Sound at an altitude of about 400 feet. Presumably other unsuccessful attempts to find the *Trillium* were made but the dates are obscure. Probably these futile expeditions were undertaken in the early 1950's.

An occasional brief account of this unusual *Trillium* has appeared in newspapers and once in a magazine. A few were grown from seed along with their parents in the botanical gardens of the University of British Columbia. Interest faded into indifference. Twenty-eight years came and went after Mr. Hibberson made his discovery before any scientific work was done on the plant. It was merely by chance that I first heard of it in 1963 and it was not until July 17, 1966 that I started the active research which culminated in this presentation of a new species of *Trillium* to the world.

Description: As might be expected from a plant which is dwarfed above ground the rhizome is small, measuring about three-eighths of an inch in both lengeh and width in young flowering specimens.

In height from ground to the three leaves they vary from about half an inch to four with an average of approximately two. The blossoms add half an inch so that a tall plant will be no more than a generous four. Considering that some of the other species attain two and a half feet this is a tiny member of a generally robust genus.

The leaves are acute or acuminate, an inch to two and a half long and about half that wide. They are normally sessile but occasionally a short petioled one will be found. Peduncles are short, stout and abruptly turned just below the flowers. The sepals are shorter than the petals which are three quarters of an inch long and half as wide. The flowers open a clear pink and slowly fade with age to a near white. I do not know of any other *Trillium* which is consistently all pink although *T. rivale* does rarely produce marvelous pink blossoms and so does *T. grandiflorum* although in lighter shades. *T. undulatum*, *T. stylosum* and one or two others, either usually or occasionally have more or less pinkish petals. It is the enchanting color and the comparatively great width of the petals that makes *T. hibbersonii* one of the most beautiful in a genus noted for its loveliness. The capsules are almost perfectly spherical, being often a little wider than tall and they contain anywhere from 15 to 144 seeds by actual count, averaging 60 to 70.

Rarity: This is by far the rarest of all *Trilliums.* It was Dr. Szczawinski's estimate that there are no more than 120 to 150 plants existing in the wild. This, of course, is a figure based upon incomplete exploration. Nevertheless there is no question of the extreme limitations of the natural populations. According to Dr. Taylor the largest colonies do not contain more than two dozen or so plants. In cultivation I know of only nine gardens which contain any and of these not more than three are blessed with as many as half a dozen old enough to flower. The rarest single specimen of any *Trillium* is probably the one in the botanical gardens at the University of British Columbia. It is a tetramerous plant, that is with the parts in fours or multiples of four – four leaves, four petals and so on – instead of the usual threes. Teratological forms are well known in other *Trillium* species but this seems to be the only plant of its kind in *T. hibbersonii.* As propagation in gardens continues on an expanding scale it is likely that others will appear.

Distribution: Probably more limited than almost any other member of the genus. Due to the extremely rugged, isolated area where it grows on the west coast of Vancouver Island, and the small amount of exploration that has been done, the extremes of its range are unknown. Three stations have been discovered: the northernmost is at Kyuquot Sound; the middle one is Nootka Sound and the last is Hesquiat Harbour at the southernmost known limits. This covers a latitudinal range of from 50 degrees 11 minutes to 49 degrees 28 minutes north. Unconfirmed reports also have it at Clayoquot Sound which is 11 or 12 miles southeast of Hesquiat Harbour. It is quite likely that other locations, both within and outside its known range, will be found. Present evidence indicates that no great numbers grow at any one place. I have asked some of the few scattered residents in the areas to look for them. All have failed. The altitudinal range established by exploration is from about 400 feet to more than 2,000. It is likely that it is indigenous to both lower and higher elevations.

Propagation: In some instances by offsets from the parent rhizomes but usually by seed. *T. hibbersonii* produces more offsets than most any other member of the genus. Not all of its rhizomes, however, possess this hoped for characteristic. I have two that do. One of them had five small youngsters attached to the parent when I received it. I did not remove any of them until the following year when the plant had recovered from transplanting shock. One was still too small to risk separating but the other four were teased loose from the tangled feeding roots and planted individually. In the course of time, after maturing, all of these as well as the original parent, should continue to yield further progeny. But it is doubtful if any can be depended upon to average one a year.

Seed production seems to be reliable both in the wild and under cultivation, in varying climatic conditions. Plants set seed at Portland, Oregon; Victoria, Vancouver, Kelowna and Savona, British Columbia at elevations from sea level to 3,000 feet and with temperatures lower than 20 degrees below zero F. Some species of *Trilliums* do not set seed without artificial pollination when moved away from their native habitats. Fortunately *T. hibbersonii* is not one of these.

As with other *Trillium* species seed germination is not entirely reliable. Robert J. Hibberson in Victoria, B.C., has had virtually 100 per cent success over a period of several years. Another Victorian, who is a competent nurseryman, planted seed in four pots under seemingly identical conditions. One pot produced new plants profusely. The other three not at all. Bob Hibberson plants his seed immediately after ripening, three-eighths to one half an inch deep in a soil mix composed of equal parts of coarse sand, light loam, and peat moss. Equally satisfactory results may be expected if planting is delayed for as much as a year. Cover and keep damp until the fall rains if you use the Hibberson method. If the seed is allowed to dry out after having been kept moist all summer germination may be reduced. The seed flats should be shaded. Little or no germination can be expected if they are in the sun.

Culture: The closely related species, *T. rivale,* is found as deep as ten inches in its native soil. If *T. hibbersonii* is planted at this depth death is almost certain. It should be not more than one inch from the surface of the soil, measured from the top of the rhizome.

As with all other *Trilliums,* this one should be shaded. But unlike nearly every other species it prefers rocky conditions. I use a mix composed of one-fourth crushed lava rock and three-fourths leaf mold. Bob Hibberson uses lots of tuffa, coarse sand, rotten wood and light garden loam topped with a quarter of an inch of vermiculite. Mr. Hibberson's plants couldn't be healthier.

This species was originally found growing in a crack in a cliff face. Others have since been located in a dry creek bed between vertical rocks. All the evidence I have indicates that it always thrives in rocky places. In cultivation it should have the same consideration.

This is a delightful flower for tiny nooks and crannies in the rockery or in other isolated spots where it can be seen and enjoyed. It should have an abundance of room so that it is not obscured, overshadowed or crowded out by larger and more robust plantings. It appears to best advantage in clumps of half a dozen or more. It is too tiny and too dainty for solitary blossoms to make much of a floral display. With a background of some of the very dwarf native ferns such as the Maidenhair Spleenwort, *Asplenium trichomanes,* or the equally distinctive Lace Fern, *Cheilanthes gracillima, T. hibbersonii* makes a wonderful sight in a small rock garden. Plantings adjacent to other larger *Trilliums* are distractive and in poor taste.

Hardiness: In its native habitat it has endured an all time known low of seven degrees below zero F., and in the interior near Savona, B.C., it has survived maximums of 103 degrees F. and minimums of 37 below zero F. In these latter stations, however, it should be remembered that the nights during hot summer weather are always cool and in the winter deep snow cover gives important protection. There is some doubt if it could live in climates where there are alternate periods of severe freezing and thawing.

Flowering Time: About two weeks before *T. ovatum.* In Victoria, B.C. gardens it begins to flower in late March and goes into the latter part of April. In its original habitat, probably about the same time. varying, perhaps, a week or two one way or the other due to differences in altitude and oceanside weather.

Trillium ovatum Western Wake Robin

TRILLIUM OVATUM Pursh
Western Wake Robin

When I was a small boy I used to accompany my parents on their woodland expeditions in the spring to collect bouquets of *Trilliums.* Many other Portlanders did the same thing. And when I was old enough to go alone I continued this bad practice – wholly ignorant that I, and my other forest colleagues, were helping to destroy this white flowered creature. Of course, digging them, logging, clearing land for the plow and building new homes are even more devastating. I no longer pick the flowers although I occasionally dig specimens for my gardens and for study. Since I became a student of botany many people over the years have asked me the same question: "Does picking *Trilliums* kill the plants?" I have always believed that the answer was 'no' but this was guess work and I had no specific knowledge. So I decided to find out.

On April 17, 1962 I dug six plants from the woods and planted them under the shade of an apple tree in my gardens. The plants were in full late blossom but had not turned wine colored as they do when the flowers age. They came from ordinary woodland soil and were planted in similar earth.

Four of the plants had two stems each with one blossom on each stem, making eight blossoms. Two of the plants had one stem each with one blossom on each stem, making two blossoms. The six plants, therefore, had a total of ten stems and ten blossoms. The stems were removed at the time of planting and the rhizomes were watered. Except for weeding they received no other care or attention until April 8, 1963.

On that date nine stems had appeared. Two of these consisted of one small leaf each. Five of the stems had the usual one blossom each. The two remaining stems had the customary three leaves each but no flowers. Three of the plants had two stems coming from each rhizome. Three of the stems had leaves with very little green, most of the leaf surface being notably yellowed.

The plants that in 1962 had ten stems and ten blossoms in

1963, within nine days of being a full year from planting, had nine stems and five blossoms, all exhibiting an inhibited growth of varying minor degree. Only one blossom set seed. The capsule was very small and contained only a few seeds.

On April 14, 1964 all the six rhizomes planted in April 17, 1962 were still alive. Four of the plants had two stems each just as they did when I first planted them but only three of these had flowers on both stems each. The fourth rhizome had two stems but no flowers. The remaining two plants had one stem each with one flower each. Three plants had some slight yellowing of the foliage but not as much as in 1963. In 1964 all the plants had three leaves each against the two in 1963 that had only one leaf each.

On July 6, 1964 six flowers had set seed capsules. Four of these were small but with seeds. Two were normal size and shattered out the seeds.

Statistical summation:

Original plants in 1962: 6 rhizomes, 10 stems, 10 flowers, 4 with 2 stems.
1963: 6 rhizomes, 9 stems, 5 flowers, 3 with 2 stems.
1964: 6 rhizomes, 10 stems, 8 flowers, 4 with 2 stems.

Two years after the inception of the experiment the six plants had the same number of stems but had two flowers less than in 1962, and lacked four capsules of the ten that normally would have developed in 1962, if the parts above ground had not been destroyed.

It must be remembered that these plants suffered a double shock. They were brought in bare rooted and that is an ample reason for them to have had to struggle to re-establish themselves as vigorously as they were in their original home in the woods. Then to have their chlorophyll-bearing organs removed at the same time was somewhat analagous to having an appendix excised at the same time as an operation for the amputation of a leg. At least one more year, and more likely two, will be required for these plants to recover their full original vigour. This experimental procedure cannot be compared to the lesser damage plants suffer when they are picked in the woods. I therefore instituted a further experiment to simulate these conditions.

On April 10, 1963, I removed the stems from two plants that had been established for one year. One rhizome had two stems and two flowers. The other had one stem and one flower. Total: three stems, three flowers.

On April 14, 1964, the plant that originally had two stems and two flowers had one stem and one flower. The other rhizome that originally had one stem and one flower had one stem and no flower. At least one more year, and more likely two, will be required for these plants to make full recovery. There was no yellowing of foliage.

As might be expected established *Trilliums* can be picked with less damage than those that are picked at the same time they are transplanted. Nevertheless there can be little doubt that picking wild *Trilliums* every year that they flower will ultimately result in the destruction of the plants, and must account in part for their gradual disappearance from the vicinity of large cities. These experiments were performed with *T. ovatum.*

While wandering through the forests searching for native plants I have noticed how delightfully *T. ovatum* mingles with its woodland companions. The delicate pink bleeding hearts, blue violets shyly hiding their heads and the bolder yellow species, the earthly *Oxalis,* several ferns, and in the moister places the sessile species *T. chloropetalum* all live their peaceful lives in the shade of the alders, the maples, cedars and firs. Luther Burbank noted that the flowers and leaves are larger and the rhizomes shallower in the shade than they are in warmer and sunnier spots.

History: For the history of the family and genus see the article on *T. grandiflorum.*

Frederick Pursh described and gave the still authoritative name of *T. ovatum* in his *Flora Americae Septentrionalis* in 1814. Pursh established his identification from plants collected "On the rapids of Columbia River," (at the foot of the Cascades) on April 10, 1806 by Meriwether Lewis of the Lewis and Clark Expedition. These men, and the renowned Scotchman, David Douglas, who came west about a score of years later, must have been very busy collecting their herbarium specimens in the Pacific Northwest for their names appear frequently in the annals of botany of this part of the continent. This explains why so many of our western plants became known to botany at a time when very little exploring had been done so far from the well settled east coast. Salisbury established *T. grandiflorum* only a year before Lewis discovered *T. ovatum* more than a thousand miles away. At least four other names have been given since, but all are now synonyms.

Description: *T. ovatum* has been called "The Pacific Coast Representative of *T. grandiflorum.*" Although this isn't quite accurate there are some similarities. The best flowers of the Western Wake Robin compare favorably in size and beauty with those of the better ones of *T. grandiflorum. T. ovatum* is also a muchly varied plant in petals, colors, and double flowered mutations but to a lesser degree than its eastern relative.

The stout stems grow from six to 20 inches high, with an average of about a foot, from a horizontal or sub-erect fleshy rhizome that is from five to seven inches below ground. The leaves, in whorls of three, are wide and sharp pointed. The peduncles are from an inch to three inches long terminating in single, slightly nodding snowy blossoms, turning from light rose to darker shades of purple with age.

The fleshy, berry-like winged capsules are from half an inch to one inch in diameter. They open on maturity and slowly discharge the seeds. When the ripe but green colored capsules first open the seeds are a glutinous mass, difficult to separate.

Rarity: The ordinary, run of the field plants, are common. There is a radical variation in the length and width of the petals, and consequently in the size and beauty of the flowers. Many, most in fact, have short and narrow, short and wide, or long and narrow petals. Only occasionally will a flower with very wide and very long petals be found. This is a lovely form and I have spent many hours in the *Trillium* fields searching for these elusive plants. Strangely enough an entire patch may contain only the less desirable forms while another station of many acres close by will yield several dozen of the better ones. Over the years I have found and established in my gardens over a hundred of them. They can hardly be considered rare but certainly they are scarce.

Once when I was on top of a cliff several thousand feet above the river in the middle of the Columbia Gorge I discovered two plants with young clear pink blossoms. These are extremely rare and I have never seen any others like them. They were not the vinous shades that come as the flowers age. Occasionally a flower will be found that is a deep, rich maroon when the blossom is fairly young. The first time I encountered this form was at a wild flower society meeting where it was displayed as a colored slide. None of the members at the time knew what it was. This scarce to rare form I have seen only a few times in my many years of woods wandering.

Nearly every year our Portland papers report *T. ovatum* mutations that have been found in the area. Most of these have one, two or three extra petals and those who plant them joyously in their gardens find that they often revert to type in subsequent seasons.

Like the double flowering *T. grandiflorum*, that has replaced its stamens and pistils with leaves, *T. ovatum* too has its extremely rare multi-petaled mutations. I have searched for a great many years and examined thousands upon thousands of plants and have yet to find a single one. They are so rare as to be almost nonexistent. But I have three of these treasures well hidden in my gardens. They are descendents of a parent that was found by chance in the mid 1920's, 20 or so miles east of Portland. The original owner had let it increase until there were at least 30 progeny. This man has passed away and no one knows what happened to most of his plants. However, a start of them was given to another fancier. A few years ago when I met him this person had increased his stock to nine. Before that time he had 12 but he gave three to a nurseryman who unwisely planted them where visitors could enjoy their delights. They disappeared one night. In return for $35.00 worth of work and money I obtained the three. Another three went to the trusting horticulturist. This particular flower has more than two dozen petals with the stamens and pistil absent and is one of the choicest *Trilliums* I ever expect to own.

A chance acquaintance showed me a colored slide of a *Trillium ovatum* that had the three normal green leaves but arising above them on two separate peduncles were two normal, three petaled flowers, one to the stem. The only information I was able to get was that it was found somewhere in the general Portland area and its fate is likewise unknown.

There is a clump of about a dozen plants of the Trumpet type of double flowering *T. ovatum* in the University of Washington Arboretum at Seattle. This very beautiful specimen was transplanted from the wild and, so far, has eluded those few people with questionable ethics.

Plants are continually, endlessly, trying to become better adapted to their environment. This is in order that they may be successful in the battle for survival with other competing species. Ordinarily this adaptation is a slow process and covers thousands upon thousands of years. But occasionally Mother Nature produces a change in a hurry – a mutation. Most of these experiments are failures in that they are less able to survive the bitter struggle than their normal parents.

Such are the multi-petaled *Trilliums* that have lost their powers of sexual reproduction through the transformation of stamens and pistils into petals. This leaves them only the slow and uncertain vegetative reproduction by offsets. In the higher forms of plant life this means lingering but certain extinction. But bring them into the protection of your garden and they will return your love, as long as you give it, with their unique and very rare beauty.

Distribution: British Columbia, Washington, Oregon, to central California, Idaho, Montana, Wyoming, Nevada, Utah and Colorado. From sea level to several thousand feet in the mountains. It prefers moist, open woods. Contrary to common belief shade is not a necessity in itself. It needs the coolness that the shade provides. In Hood River's upper valley at 3500 feet altitude I found a *T. ovatum* growing in full sun, protected only by stunted native grasses. This plant was in good health and was able to live under these unusual conditions because of the comparatively mild daytime temperatures and the cool nights.

Propagation: Same as for *T. grandiflorum.* The Thwing Method may or may not work with *T. ovatum.* This surgery, performed on five plants, failed to produce offsets.

Culture: *T. ovatum's* flowers do not all peep out of the ground at the same time. This variation may extend over a period of about a month during the active growing season. In the wild the plants die back and disappear when the hot weather dries the soil. In the garden some of mine have kept their leaves alive until early November although they were far beyond their prime. At the same time some of the other plants of the same species had lost their leaves and had sent up tight new green shoots about half an inch above ground where they remained until the warmth of the next season stimulated further growth. So it is that *T. ovatum's* foliage can be seen year around in my climate. The flowering buds will often start to open before they are much more than out of the ground. Stem height will continue to increase until it reaches full length even though some of the blossoms may be wide open before then.

T. ovatums from the western part of its range is lacking in hardiness in the middle western states and other parts of the country where winters are severe.

The *Trillium ovatum* from Montana and that general area is a variation of the species of the Coast Ranges. Of 500 rhizomes from the Montana stations that were planted in Oregon's Willamette Valley, only a couple of dozen came up and flowered like ordinary *T. ovatums* three years later. A few others sent up weak flowering stems. The other rhizomes remained alive and seemingly healthy under ground. The foliage of plants from the two areas differs too.

Those who insist upon picking these *Trilliums* will find that they make excellent vase flowers. If withering should occur before they can be brought home their stems should be put into water and left outdoors overnight. After reviving they will keep fresh in the house until natural aging and fading destroys them. If they are brought into the house when withered they will not be able to recover in the warm, dry atmosphere.

Other cultural needs are the same as for *T. grandiflorum.*

Flowering Time: March, April, May, June and into July, varying with the season, climate and altitude.

Trillium rivale Brook Trillium

TRILLIUM RIVALE Watson
Brook Trillium

My trip to southern Oregon for the express purpose of finding *T. rivale* started badly. Before undertaking such expeditions I search the literature to learn as much as possible about where the plants I want grow. While this is often a big help it is rarely that exact locations are given. That is what happened in this instance. I stopped to see some friends a few miles east of Grants Pass on the Rogue River. They knew of the plant but had no idea where it grew. I decided I might be too far north so dropped about 40 miles southwestward to the tiny community of O'Brien, a few miles above the California border. Then I drove westward for two or three miles over a one way dirt track, got out of my car and walked up the banks of a recently dried stream bed.

There in the loose sandy soil mixed with rocks and boulders I found my first plants. Quite a thrill it was, and surprising too for these diminutive beauties had gone deep for permanent moisture. A few were only half a foot down but most were ten inches and sometimes even more! I could hardly believe it for the much larger *T. ovatum* of my childhood around Portland is usually only six inches deep and never ten. But then Portland has a much wetter climate than *T. rivale's.* There was very little humus or other nourishment in the sandy material they seemed to enjoy and I was able to reach their deep rhizomes with trowel and bare hands. But they were far from easy to get. Roots from the shrubs and trees that provided them light shade were a handicap and the stems had, from the collectors viewpoint, the bad habit of going under a rock that was usually too big to move.

This was a little discouraging so my companion and I started back until we came to a steep south facing slope partly shaded by pines. More from curiosity than from any real hope of finding *Trilliums* under those very dry conditions, my companion and I decided to take a quick look. Astonishingly enough we found a small colony, partly exposed to full sun, growing in fist size and smaller broken rock that had tumbled down the hillside in ages past. This was stout trowel work and quite futile. The rhizomes were just as deep as the first ones we located and the stems twisted and writhed among the shattered stones where there was very little soil. Getting any of these called for a better vocabulary and more patience than either my companion or I possessed. So we tossed our tools into the car and headed for Takilma, ten or 11 miles eastward. This little village consists of a forlorn general store and a few scattered houses. The grocer didn't know what we were talking about when I mentioned *Trilliums* so we were on our own again. A one way dirt road leads southward towards the California border two or three miles away. One of the forks of the florally renowned Illinois River flows close to the road. In the moderately deep shade of trees and shrubs on the sandy banks of this lovely stream we blundered into another patch. These too were in much the same sandy soil with virtually no loam. There were just as many boulders and roots and the rhizomes were just as deep, and the digging just as frustrating. But we finally acquired what I needed for my studies. Then we spent quite a number of hours in further searching to see how abundant they were. We found that they grew in relatively small to very small patches with intervals of often quite a number of miles where there were none at all. We packed our few plants carefully to keep them cool and moist and headed for Portland at the northern border of the state, something like 300 miles distant. The bad part of such a journey is arriving home for by then continual driving and working in the field from daylight to dark takes its toll. So it was on this trip but nevertheless I planted them at once. When this task was completed I sighed contentedly and was happy.

History: For the history of the family and genus see *T. grandiflorum.* The well known American botanist Sereno Watson, 1826-1892, made an excellent choice when he described this shy treasure in 1885 and named it *T. rivale* which means *brook loving.* One might wonder why this species was introduced to the scientific world 71 years later than *T. ovatum* when both are found about the same distance westward. The answer is simple enough. The great Columbia River was one of the major liquid highways the pioneers traveled when crossing the continent or going inward when they journeyed by ship around Cape Horn. Both David Douglas and the Lewis and Clark Expedition did much of their far western exploring along this river. Neither traveled southward as far as the Siskiyous. Their collections, examined by systematic botanists, resulted in the early classification and publication of new species when others, just as important but farther from trade routes, remained unknown for much longer periods of time.

Description: The stems rise from a deep seated rootstock. They are often no more than two or three inches high but three or four is the average in my gardens. Some botanists describe them as tall as ten inches. I have never seen any this high and it is just as well. Dwarfness accounts for much of their peculiar charm. Occasionally a specimen will be found with sessile (stemless) leaves but usually the petioles are from one-fourth to one half as long as the one to three inch leaves which are narrowly egg shaped, rounded or heart-like at the base from which they widen rapidly to their maximum somewhat below the middle. Then they taper to the apex which may be from a dull to a small sharp point. The leaves are either unmarked deep green or the veins may be prominently cream colored. This variation is strikingly beautiful. They are never mottled as are some of the other species including the white flowering *T. sessile californicum* which I have found growing along stream banks in the area where *T. rivale* makes its home. Both types of leaf variations are found growing side by side. The slender peduncles are from one to over four inches long, erect or more usually curved downward. These declined flower stems compel the blossoms to nod, greatly adding charm upon charm. Nor is the end yet. The petals are either clear white or gorgeously painted by Nature's magic touch with innumerable fine purple dots leaving only the tips pure snow. Plants with both white or purple dotted petals are found in the same patches and each may have plain or cream veined leaves. Some of the buds are pink when they open and turn white with age – quite the opposite of both *T. ovatum* and *T. grandiflorum.* An extremely rare form is pink from bud to blossom without ever becoming white. The flowers are comparatively large and they are still more appealing for their prominent deep lemon yellow anthers. None of the variations I have described are sufficiently important to justify new botanical names and, to the best of my knowledge, none have been offered. Watson's original one still stands alone.

The literature on *Trilliums* is replete with accounts of double forms of many species but I have found no such references to *T. rivale;* know of only one person who has ever seen or heard of them and I have but three in my gardens. They do exist, however, and it is a red letter – no, a crimson –day when one is discovered.

Rarity: The type species, very rare. The pink, extremely rare. This determination was based upon the scattered stations within its very limited range.

Distribution: Usually along stream banks in light to medium shade in southern Josephine and Curry Counties of Oregon to Siskiyou and Del Norte Counties in northern California. Near the mouth of the Rogue River in the vicinity of Gold Beach and in the neighborhood of O'Brien. Also on the banks of a tributary of the Illinois River a few miles south of Takilma in Oregon, and at Big Flat, 30 miles east of Crescent City, California. Prefers low altitudes in the Humid Transition Zone, but friends have located them at elevations as great as 3,000 feet.

Propagation: Same as for *T. grandiflorum.*

Culture: Much the same as for *T. grandiflorum* except that it needs a gritty soil. Also see culture for *T. hibbersonii.* Plant two to three inches deep. Those I have in my rockery in light shade are scarcely more than an inch high while others, collected from the same station, are three or four inches tall in damp leaf mold and top soil. The rhizomes should be adjacent to or under a rock. In the wild there are large leaved and miniature forms which have nothing to do with soil or moisture. Either small or large plants can be found in barren stations or in rich, moist earth. In the Illinois River Valley the big leaved form is not reported above 1,500 feet while in the Coast Range Mountains the small leaved one is at home at about 3,000 feet. Surveys are not complete enough to know whether altitude is necessarily the determining factor in the size of the plants. Those who are seeking the smaller form, however, will do well to hunt at the higher elevations.

Friends of mine, who try to spend their vacations in the Siskiyous, discovered a patch ten feet wide that was so dense they could not walk through it without stepping on the tiny blossoms. A planting of similar size in the shaded garden if isolated from all other flowers, would be a joyous sight. It would be an expensive one too. For the space occupied they cost more than most other American *Trilliums* and plant for plant are the third highest priced.

Few dealers stock them, partly because collected plants are nearly impossible to get. Sales are more limited than other species too, due to the necessarily higher selling prices. Collectors will not dig ten inches for the same fee that they get for other *Trilliums* at half that depth. They are not nearly as well known as some of their larger relatives and for this reason are not found in many gardens.

T. rivale, like many other members of the genus, seems to be disease free and slugs are only a minor threat. The rhizomes are small and can dry out if moles, gophers or field mice tunnel under them. Any one fortunate enough to possess the extremely rare pink form would be wise to plant it in pots or heavy mesh wire (not galvanized) baskets for protection from these subterranean pests. With constant slug baiting the rare ones should be safe. Most of mine receive ordinary garden care. In hardiness it is about the same as its western relative, *T. ovatum.* It is not recommended for frigid climates.

The genus *Trillium* can boast of only four earth hugging treasures. One is the miniature *T. hibbersonii* from Vancouver Island, discussed in this book. The second is *T. nivale,* native of the middle western and eastern states. It is too bad that these names are so much alike in spelling and pronunciation and it is perfectly understandable that this has been a source of confusion. But *rivale* refers to *brook loving,* and *nivale* means *snowy* or *white.* The fourth is *T. govanianum,* a strange creature from 12,000 feet in the Himalayas.

If I had to choose from among these four, *T. rivale,* the Gem of the Siskiyous, would occupy a dual place with *T. hibbersonii* in my floral loves. It isn't the largest, the showiest, or the best known but it is one of my favorites of all the *Trilliums.*

Flowering Time: Late March, April and May. At least one systematic botanist has suggested that *T. rivale* may have been derived from *T. ovatum* through a dwarf mutation and other changes. At any rate, like its larger cousin, *T. rivale's* blossoms do not all appear at once and, consequently, the flowers may be seen over a period of weeks, enchanting spring time weeks.

Zauschneria latifolia California Fuchsia

ZAUSCHNERIA LATIFOLIA (Hooker) Greene
ZAUSCHNERIA LATIFOLIA variety ETTERI
California Fuchsia

There was a flash of bright crimson along the side of the mountain road. I pulled off to the side and stopped. It was the California Fuchsia, *Zauschneria latifolia,* the first I had ever seen. It was growing in a tiny crevice at the foot of a cliff where there was very little soil and even less moisture. In spite of these harsh conditions and exposure to the full heat of the summer sun it was a thriving, mass of brilliant red tubular flowers. I took a cutting or two and this wonderful plant has been in my gardens ever since. Like so many of the better things of life it was merely by chance that I found it for, while I was on a plant hunting expedition, I was looking for other treasures and had not expected to find this one.

It is difficult to understand why this colorful native is not more popular. I have seen it in less than half a dozen gardens. Like most all plants, and people too for that matter, it is not entirely perfect. The worst fault it possesses is that it dies down in the late fall and winter, leaving a mass of dead leaves and stems which are unsightly.

History: The genus was named in 1831 by Karel Boriweg Presl of Bohemia, who lived from 1794 to 1852, in honor of Dr. M. Zauschner, a professor of natural history at the University of Prague. It belongs to the Evening Primorse Family, *Onagraceae,* which comprises about 20 genera and 600 species. Some of these genera do not resemble others at all in general appearance and yet they are closely related.

There are five species of *Zauschnerias,* all native to western North America. Because there is a considerable variation in the plants there has been a good deal of confusion among various authorities as to which plants belong in which species. Three of these, which are now recognized as distinct species, at one time all had the same name. Also at least seven sub-species and varieties have been named, making this one of the most confused and misunderstood genera, considering its small size, that I have ever encountered. *Z. latifolia* has been called *Z. californica* variety *latifolia, Z. tomentella, Z. glandulosa, Z. pulchella, Z. canescens* and *Z. velutina. Z. latifolia* was given this name in 1887 by Edward Lee Greene, 1843-1915, although W. J. Hooker gave it another name in 1850.

Description: In *Z. latifolia* the slender stems are from six to 20 inches tall. It is about a foot high in my gardens and makes a compact plant of numerous softly hairy stems, branched above with the basal parts on the ground before turning upwards. This decumbent character destroys the charm of some plants but in the *Zauschneria latifolia* it has quite the opposite effect, giving a spreading, more rounded appearance with a massive show of flowers which conceal the basal parts. The leaves three-quarters to an inch and a quarter long are numerous, mostly opposite, stemless, lance shaped to ovate, pointed, with the margins broken by more or less irregular finely projecting points, or nearly smooth, with long soft, not woolly hairs, or sometimes hairless. With the variations in the size, shape, margins and hairiness of the leaves alone it is no wonder that so many differences of opinion have been expressed by botanists. I have one plant in my garden which has leaves so radically different from those of all my other *Zauschnerias* I wondered for a long time if it could be another species entirely.

While the foliage and general manner of growth is somewhat pleasing it is the flowers themselves which make this western native so outstanding. The blossoms three-quarters to an inch and a quarter long, are bright scarlet, tubular or funnelform with the base of the tube expanded then narrowed into a long tube terminating in four sepals and petals with the opening widely expanded and the entire floral structure the same brilliant red. The flowers are produced in such large numbers at the height of the season, in my gardens at least, that they partially obscure the foliage. Such a plant, in full blossom, is a wonderful sight indeed and is even more delightful because it is at its best when most other natives are either completely through or have only a few straggling blossoms left.

Some of the other species grow as much as two or three feet tall and may be desirable in parts of the garden where they can be used as background material or mixed in with larger sized plants. *Z. latifolia* is well suited to the rockery. It, and all the others, like full sunshine, sharp drainage, and can tolerate an amazing amount of drought.

The *Zauschnerias* are among a limited group of natives which Oregon law prohibits removing from public lands.

The variety *etteri* grows only three or four inches high, has beautiful silvery white foliage, and is a wonderful garden plant when used to its best advantage. As a ground cover on steep slopes or planted at the top of a vertical wall and allowed to cascade over the side its scarlet flowers, a few inches above the frosty leaves, make a spectacular sight.

While the foliage and manner of growth vary greatly the blossoms are much the same in size and vivid coloration in this species.

I have been unsuccessful in discovering the source of the white form of *Z. latifolia.* A nursery in southern Oregon has one plant. Presumably it was discovered as a mutant somewhere in that general area growing wild among its scarlet companions. Starts have been obtained and it is now available from dealers. Interplanted here and there among the conventionally colored type it provides a contrast that accentuates both.

While one of the common names is California Fuchsia it is misleading. It is neither confined to that state nor is it a *Fuchsia.* Other common names are Humming Bird's Trumpet, and Balsamea.

Rarity: *Zauschneria latifolia.* Scarce.
Zauschneria latifolia etteri. Rare.
Zauschneria latifolia 'White'. Extremely rare.

Distribution: The type plant and its varieties from southern Oregon in the Coast Mountains in Curry County and along the lower Rogue River to southern California and western Nevada. From a few hundred feet to 9,300. Other members of the genus extend farther eastward to Utah, Arizona and the Rocky Mountains. All prefer dry slopes and ridges.

Propagation: Increase is by seeds, cuttings and divisions. Seeds should be sown in fall or as late as March. This method of propagation is no guarantee that seedlings will come true to variety.

The decumbent stems have a tendency to root when they have an opportunity to send feeders down into soil that is not too rocky. In light, dry soils it likes to spread underground too. These characteristics make divisions easy. I like to take them in the fall of the year when the new shoots are just appearing. By the time spring has come they are well established. But spring divisions are successful too.

Cuttings from basal shoots can be taken in spring or summer. They should be rooted in sand in a shady place and be ready to flower the next season. The *Zauschnerias* are among the easiest of plants to propagate. I have never had a failure from divisions and the few cuttings that did not succeed were taken from the tops of the stems instead of the heavier basal parts.

Culture: Full sunshine. A loose, rocky soil with sharp drainage although this last is not necessarily very important unless too much moisture is present. At the end of the season when the foliage has died down it should be cut an inch or so above the ground to remove the unsightly, colorless stems and leaves. Some people consider the plant undesirable due to the unkempt appearance of the woolly seeds but pruning back as suggested removes this objection. It is remarkably tolerant of drought. If only an evergreen form could be developed we would have a plant as nearly perfect as anyone could hope for.

In some of the colder parts of the country it needs either heavy coverings of loose, aerated mulch or taking into the cool greenhouse until the threat of severe weather is over. In wet climates it has a tendency to lush leafage at the expense of flowering. Holding back the moisture where it is possible is the answer to this problem.

Flowering Time: In my Portland, Oregon gardens the first blossoms usually appear in late June. July or August sees them a mass of glorious color. Then the blossoms become a little more sparse until the frosts of October or November put an end to the season. In its natural habitat flowering covers about the same period of time, late June in the warmer areas at low altitudes to as late as November in the higher mountains in the southern part of its range.

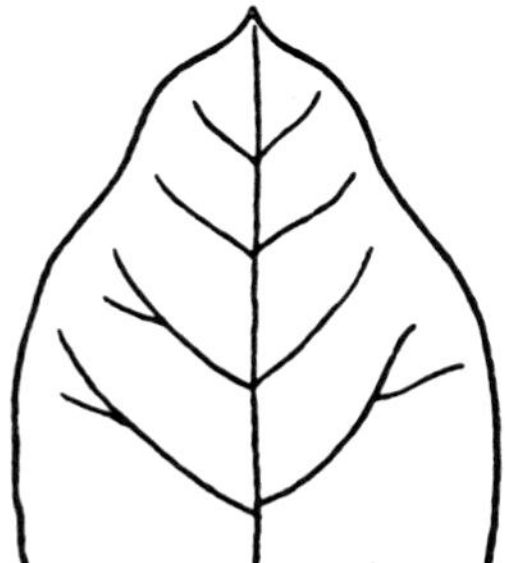

Mucronate apex

Author collecting *Douglasia laevigata* near top of 100 foot cliff

ROCK GARDENS

This type of gardening presents infinite variations but before undertaking construction it is essential to understand two basic precepts: 1. What does such a garden represent? 2. What are the needs of the plants that are to be grown in it? Many a beginner neglects these principles and, after years and experience have added to his wisdom, becomes annoyed with his efforts in the first and frustrated with the second.

The first consideration is the position of the rockery in relationship with the rest of the landscaping plan. A pile of boulders in the middle of a lawn, surrounded with formal plantings, falls far short of the ideal. It should be placed where it will blend so smoothly and naturally with the terrain that it automatically becomes a part of it.

It should not be shaded by shrubs or trees. It is true that some plants need protection from the sun but this can be provided by the rocks themselves, on their north sides. A well placed rockery will be part of but independent of the adjacent plantings. It represents, in miniature, a concentration and a variety of plants that cannot be found wild in any one place.

The second problem to consider is the choice of the stone – where there is one. This is where the novice is likely to err badly. In many parts of the country the best material is difficult or impossible to obtain. Volcanic lavas which are full of expanded gases during the solidification process have a porous cellular structure that will absorb great quantities of water during heavy rains and will retain some of this moisture for considerable lengths of time. This rock tends both to prevent the accumulation of stagnant water and provide the thirst needs of roots in hot weather. My rockeries are composed of this type of stone. More impervious basalts and granites may have to be substituted and these will do nicely if the drainage is better. The color of the rock is very important. Mine is red because gray was not to be had. The tendency for the beginner is to choose the most vividly hued boulders as violently contrasting as possible – achieving a terrestrial rainbow. This may create a geological spectacle but it distracts the attention from some of the

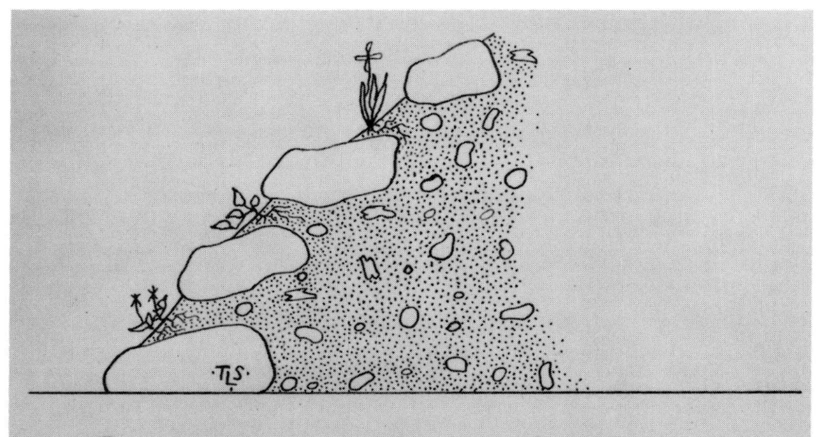

Wayne Olsson Illustrations

most beautiful flowers. The basic purpose of the garden is violated – to provide homes and to glorify plants. The somber grays are subdued and act as background for the flowers. When boulders and blossoms are in the right relationship with each other the picture may well exceed belief.

Once the kind of rock has been chosen the next decisions are the shapes and the placing. A series of rounded boulders may be perfectly natural but also perfectly monotonous. A wide selection of different sizes and shapes are needed: spherical, oblong, somewhat flattened for overhangs, indented, and curved. Sharp corners do not give the illusion of age in most cases and nature does not go for straight lines. These rocks should be placed to give the impression that they have always been there – exactly where they belonged. Often a large boulder can be used as a center of attraction with lesser ones working up to it, becoming larger and larger the closer they get and, in the other direction being reduced until they terminate in a rubble strewn talus slope. If such a scheme is carefully planned the effect can be astonishingly effective.

When planning a rock garden provisions should be made for its enlargement, even though you may be positive that it will never be done. It is surprising how rapidly all the space will be filled with plants and you suddenly discover that you have still others and no room for them. If allowances have not been made for this event you may find yourself compelled to put on an addition that will be as unlovely as a lean-to on the back of a house.

It is rare indeed that sharp loose rocks are found in nature standing on end. But many a 'first time' rockery features this incongruous setting and is nothing less than a ridiculous monstrosity. With rare exceptions they should be placed flat in the ground. On the other hand a good design is not that of a symmetrical dome. It has a central peak with lesser ones here and there at a distance. There are ridges, valleys, slopes, hollows, tiny meadows, and a talus slope or two. Each of these features should be constructed with the exact species of plants for which it is intended, with thought for color, size, spread, shade, sun, and moisture needs.

A common belief is that the rock garden should include a pool or stream. This can provide a pleasing variety if it is

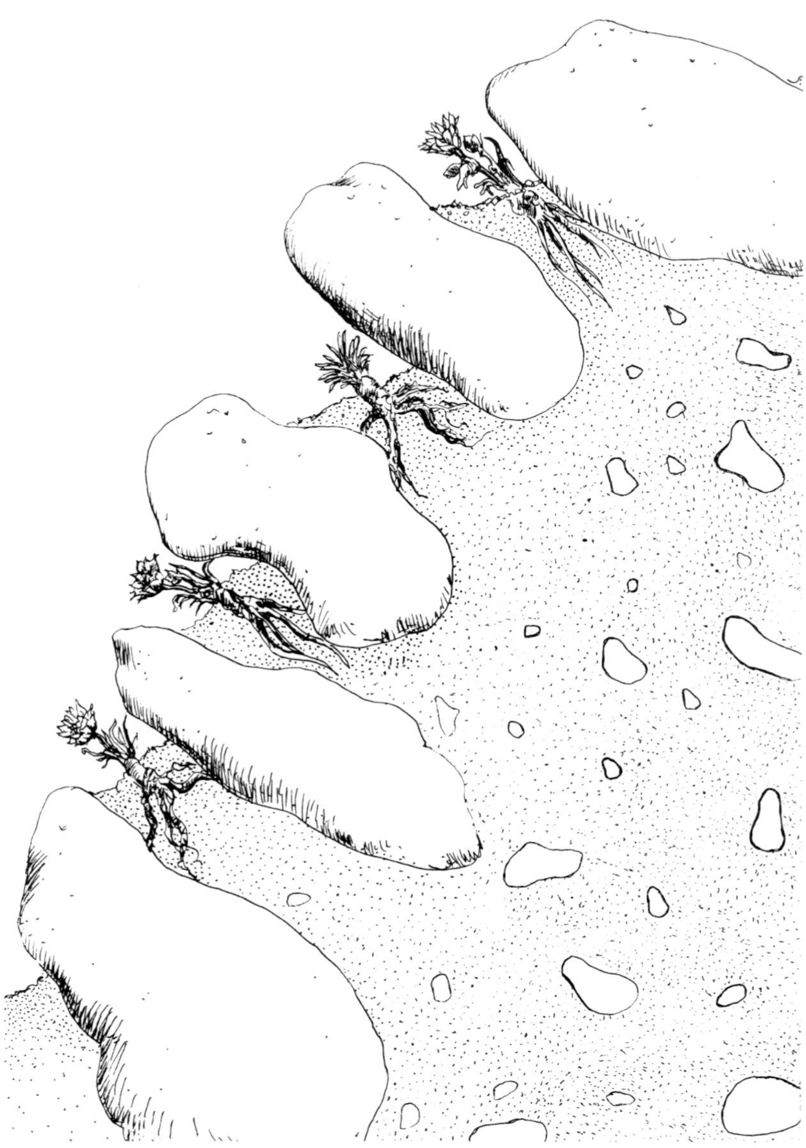

Rocks placed for drainage into the interior which is composed of coarse sand, humus, loam, chips and small rocks for moisture retention and drainage.

relegated to a minor aspect of the overall picture. There are many stream bank rockeries in the mountains, and while they are beautiful at first glance, they are monotonous. Usually only a few different species are strewn along their borders. For every such scene there are from hundreds to thousands of natural rockeries that do not have water.

Some huge boulders may be placed with the larger part of their bulk above ground to give height. But for every cubic foot of rock above the surface at least two should be buried. The larger rocks, the smaller ones and other material must provide the three essentials of successful rock gardening: sharp drainage, adequate and limited permanent moisture, and a cool root run. The roots should be able to grow for considerable distances into crevices and pockets between rocks and under them to sufficient depths where temperatures and moisture are stabilized, cool in summer, warm in winter, and moderately moist all year. Alternate freezing and thawing as well as stagnant water can destroy plants, and often do. One way to help prevent this calamity is to provide overhangs under which the plants can be tucked away from excessive moisture.

The larger, surface rocks should be sloped so that rainfall will drain into the interior. Rocks with the outer ends sloped downwards drain away moisture and allow roots to dry out. If underground rocks are placed so that water collects stagnation will drown the roots. The base and supporting material should be composed of very coarse sand, humus, loam, chips and small rock. I use one-half leaf mold and one-half crushed volcanic rock ranging from rough sand up to fist size stones. Heavy clays can be modified with generous additions of humus, sand, rock chips, pea gravel and peat. Animal manures and commercial fertilizers should be used sparingly to prevent ungainly growth and the loss of compactness which is one of the important charms of alpines.

Too much emphasis has been put upon acid or lime conditions. Most rock plants will thrive under neutral conditions or those that vary within reasonable limits one way or the other.

Shade lovers from warm climates need only light shade or full sun in milder areas while those that grow in the shade in cool regions need even more shade in the hot ones. Plants that thrive in full sun in their own moderate territory need protection from the heat of the day where temperatures are higher. Far western valleys and coastal regions have cool nights which allow plants to recover from the drying they endure during the heat of the day. Similarly, high altitude plants in full sun recover during their chilly nights and when brought to lower elevations need some sun protection. Many of these alpines have their roots frozen – and therefore dry – all winter and it is very important to protect them from the alternate freezing and thawing that destroys them in their adopted lowland homes. Desert plants have their own special necessities. Sharp drainage and dryness are essential. They are more likely to perish from too much rather than too little water. Some of them can go for months without rain.

Once the construction is completed it only remains to put in the plants. When there are more of them than room the temptation is to crowd them in anyway. This is one of the surest ways of destroying the entire effect you have worked so hard to achieve. Each should be separate and distinct from all others with an exposure of rock face or talus in between.

With all the various factors to be considered in creating a high quality rockery it is obvious that much hard work and disappointment can be eliminated by doing all the preparatory designing on paper before a single rock is moved into position.

SPECIALIZED ROCKERIES AND PROCEDURES

Flowers On Bare-Faced Rocks

Wild plants are often found growing in cracks in otherwise solid rock and thriving there even though these cracks are incredibly small. In removing some of these plants with a cold chisel and single jack I have often noted that the root systems would be living off less than a teaspoonful of soil and with moisture content that was scarcely detectable. In some cases there would be less than one-fourth that much, and yet these plants often bloom abundantly and are healthy, compact and robust – qualities we admire.

Attempts to transplant mature wildlings into such crevices in rocks in our gardens almost always fail. Those in nature started from seeds and as they slowly pushed their roots into the tiny cracks and sent their leaves out into the light and air, they were able to adapt to these astonishing conditions.

There is no way to determine how many seeds must drop from parents higher up into these incredible places before a single plant is produced. The chances are fantastically against any seeds lodging in the right place and the odds that any will germinate and live to maturity are almost as great. Thousands, tens of thousands, and more, are wasted before one is able to perform its alloted task.

Repeating this phenomenon with mature plants fails because the roots are not able to penetrate deeply enough fast enough to provide both food and moisture for the development of healthy foliage. Drought and starvation, but more particularly the former, account for the deaths.

In rockeries, where there are large boulders often there is too much bare surface. This dull sameness can be both relieved and beautified by simulating the natural crevices that will accommodate mature plants. The method is simple, practical and if done carefully there will be no obvious evidence of man's mimicking natural processes.

I drill holes in the rock half a foot or so apart, the spacing depending upon the anticipated spread of the plants. The degree of success and the amount of hard work, depend upon the kind of rock. Basalts, granites and other similar materials are too poorly drained and too hard for practical drilling. A soft, porous rock is best. That is why I chose volcanic lava. I use carbide tipped drills with extensions welded on to increase the length. They are graduated from ½ inch through ¾, 1, 1¼, and 1½. I drill a number of one-half inch holes first, change bits and enlarge, until they are full size. This system is much more practical than starting with the largest because doing all the work with the one and a half is very slow. I use a one-half inch capacity electric drill. A firm grip must be maintained at all times as hard spots in the rock occur and a sudden violent twist could sprain or break a wrist.

Flowers growing in holes on bare faced rocks

The cost of the drills would not justify the results unless quite a number of holes are needed. Ordinary, less expensive, steel drills dull too rapidly.

The holes should be angled downwards at anything from 30 to 45 degrees for a triple purpose: 1. To permit drainage inward to the roots and for additional absorption into the adjacent rock for storage. 2. To prevent rains washing away the soil if the holes were horizontal. 3. To make planting and firming the soil around the roots easier and still allow the crowns of the plants to be placed horizontally.

I like to drill the finished holes at least a foot deep and as much more as circumstances will permit. Sometimes the rock is too small for the hole to be any deeper without coming out the other side. Again, hard spots may be encountered that are almost impossible to drill through with the largest bit. In this event I use the smallest one to go deeper to facilitate drainage. I drill interconnecting holes in large rocks, going straight down the middle from the top of the rock until it goes through the bottom. Then I sight along a shaft to make the side holes intersect with the main one. This takes a little care so that they will meet. This means that both food and moisture can be interchanged throughout the entire interlinking system.

In the largest rocks an interconnecting system may be more difficult if not impossible. In this event individual holes are usually adequate. The porous nature of the rock takes care of the drainage in these blind holes. If the rock is nonporous, or comparatively so, it will be necessary to continue on with the half inch drill to the bottom or far side to allow for the drainage. Most of the holes should be drilled so that the crowns of the plants will be on their sides. With some species this is absolutely essential to prevent rot.

Many plants need holes fully one and a half inches in diameter to give enough root room. A one and a half inch drill in soft lava usually results in a two inch hole which is an excellent size. I try to space the holes in such a way that the plantings will be completely informal. There is no such thing in nature as holes in straight lines. I can imagine little that would be more artificial or ugly. I try to choose indentations for holes that will make the finished effect appear as though the plants simply had to grow there. I take advantage of every overhang, placing a hole immediately below to protect the plant from rain. With some species, such as *Lewisia tweedyi* and *Synthyris lanuginosa,* this represents the difference between success and failure.

The exceedingly porous nature of the lava I use holds large quantities of water without flooding so that moisture is no particular problem. For filling the holes I use one-half crushed lava with the largest pieces less than half an inch in diameter, and one-half leaf mold, varying the proportions to meet the needs of individual plants. The combination of moisture retention, drainage, and sufficient food for good growth, but not too much room results in a healthy, compact foliage with good flowering if the right species are chosen.

Medium or small plants are preferable to large ones. They have more limited root systems which are easier to tuck deeply into their new homes.

Planting Tools For Rock Holes

I use three planting tools: a three-sixteenth and a three-eighths inch in diameter metal rod and a half round square ended trowel one inch in diameter and five inches long made from stainless steel tubing.

Planting The Holes

First I dampen the soil as it is very difficult to moisten adequately after it is in the hole. I put a thin layer on the lower side of the hole then, using one of the rods, usually the larger, to lift the roots I insert them as deeply as they will go until the crown of the plant is barely outside the entrance. The half round trowel is used to slide the soil as closely to the bottom as possible. The larger rod pushes it clear in and firms it around the roots. Tiny air pockets are closed by tamping lightly with the smaller rod. When the hole is three-quarters filled I add a little water, complete the planting, and water lightly again. I always leave a small amount of space at the entrance for watering during hot days until the newcomers are well established. From one to three extra seasons may be needed for flowering in these holes than under conventional plantings. The growth is generally slower and more limited. And weeding, thank heavens, is eliminated.

Species For Rock Holes

Pentstemon richardsonii makes an immense growth. The best *Pentstemon rupicolas* I have ever seen in a garden were in such holes. *P. menziesii* is delightfully dwarfed under these conditions and so is *P. barrettae*. *Campanula rotundifolia* is nicely dwarfed in foliage but retains full floral size in vertical holes. The *Sedums* seem to prefer vertical treatment too as they tend to break off or become stragglers when horizontal. *Lewisia rediviva* has never suffered the common and fatal crown rot in my wet climate with this treatment although it is slow to respond with blossoms. Some of the other *Lewisias,* including *tweedyi, cotyledon, rupicola* and *columbiana* are a little slow to flower but do not drown when placed horizontally. This is especially important with the fussy *tweedyi.* The *Talinums okanoganense* and *spinescens* also adapt nicely in both vertical and horizontal positions. Such dwarf ferns as *Cheilanthes gracillima* and *Asplenium trichomanes* take readily to this horticultural captivity. So do the exasperatingly difficult *Kalmiopsis leachiana* and the water sensitive *Claytonia nivalis.* *Silene hookeri* and its even lovelier cousin *S. ingramii* flower well but with fewer blossoms. *Townsendia exscapa,* the midwestern dwarf with the astonishingly large pink daisies, drowns everywhere in my rockery except in one of these holes.

I do not know if this 'hole in the rock' culture is my own invention even though I never heard of it before I created it. At any rate much more experimenting is needed to find out what plants will endure it, which will thrive, and, more important, the species that will survive in these holes that would otherwise perish in wet climates. Undoubtedly many, many others besides the ones I have mentioned will grow and beautify otherwise bare rocks. The possibilities seem almost as limitless as the rewards.

Special Small Rockeries

Rock gardens need not be large to be beautiful. A modest one can be just as lovely if it is correctly designed. Such a plan can be built around a single boulder of almost any size depending upon how extensive the garden is to be. The important consideration is that the center of attraction should be on the boulder itself and all other lesser rocks should be in proportion.

Once the boulder is selected the site should be prepared. Dig out the dirt about two feet deep or more and replace it with rock of fist size and smaller down to what amounts to coarse sand mixed with equal amounts of leaf mold. This excavation should extend at least a foot beyond the extreme edge of the finished work so that plants can be set in around the perimeter. Then drill an interlinking network of holes in the boulder as discussed under "Flowers On Bare-Faced Rocks." After this is done move the rock into its permanent location. If it is too big to manhandle put it on planks with pipes beneath for rollers. It will move easily up to the final positioning with blocks and tackle. Pipes can be used as levers to make whatever final adjustments are needed. Thought should be given to which side should face the sun. If most of the plants are to be sun lovers the maximum surface should be in that direction – or vice versa.

At the foot of the drilled boulder smaller ones of varying size should be placed, creating pockets, crevices and tiny moraines. Below these, if the drop off is abrupt, smaller rock rubble can be used to create miniature rock slides and talus slopes.

The plants, like the rocks should be in proportion to their surroundings. Large specimens will ruin the illusion of balance and great care should be used in their selection.

In the back yard I have such a rockery built around a boulder 32 inches high, 30 wide, and 40 long. The overall size, which includes the subsidiary rocks and talus slopes, is 58 inches wide and 62 long. This rather small creation contains over five dozen plants of more than a dozen different species with room for more and is the outstanding feature of my gardens. As I planned to use more shade lovers than sun worshippers I placed it so that the gentler slopes were on the north side. The main rock was chosen for its irregular but natural shape.

This 12 by 18 inch planter box contains eight plants of three different species of *Lewisias*

I have a rockery in a brick planter box on the front porch. This entire garden measures 12 by 18 inches and features a rock set several inches into the soil. The above ground portion has a hole drilled through it from top to bottom. This miniature stone is irregular in shape, six inches wide, eight long and five high. A *Lewisia* is growing in the hole and seven others of three different species complete the display.

Another small rockery which has caused a good deal of comment is built on top of a concrete patio. There is no reason why a garden must have an earth base as long as drainage is good.

The framework was made of redwood two by fours. Cedar, cypress, or any other rot resisting lumber would do just as well. I placed them on top of each other edgewise, two high, drilled the nail holes to avoid splitting and nailed the ends together. To hold them rigidly in place I drilled vertical holes near the ends on all four sides and drove in three-eighths inch pipes. These holes were made to fit the pipe snugly and the top of the holes with the pipe ends showing, were filled with putty. These walls were, thus, about eight inches high. Planks of that width would be suitable but the two 2 by 4's are less inclined to warp. The frame was painted forest green.

On top of the concrete where the large boulder was to be placed I prepared a bed of six inch rocks and filled the space in between with my regular mix of half crushed rock and half leaf mold.

The choice of the boulder was very important and I was fortunate to be able to find one that was somewhat irregular in shape, flat topped and partially hollowed by nature. I enlarged the opening with my carbide tipped drills, making the holes as close together as possible and over a foot deep. It wasn't necessary to drill through the bottom as the porous material gave free drainage. A cold chisel cut away the thin walls left by the drill and I cut the outside walls until they were from two to four inches thick – as thin as I dared make them without danger of breakage. There was no attempt to smooth the inside as the rough interior was better suited to seeking rootlets. Then I drilled holes downward at 30 to 45 degrees from the outside to

Small rockery built on top of concrete patio

the interior so that the entire system was interconnected. With some help, the boulder was lifted into place and smaller stones, with more than half their bulk buried below the surface, were put into supporting positions. One of these, facing a corner of the framework, has a hole drilled completely through from top to bottom. All the remaining space was filled with the usual soil mix up to nearly the top of the frame. The drilled holes and the open top of the boulder were filled with plants and others had their roots tucked under its base. A wild honeysuckle was planted in one of the holes I drilled at the back of the main rock. I trained it up a pipe which has side arms for hanging baskets. While the entire garden is only 42 by 48 inches it could be made almost any size as long as the principal boulder is in the right proportion.

If a rock of good contour is not available one can be shaped easily. It should be soft and porous for good drainage and ease of cutting. Lava and pumice are good. Professional landscapers working with rock walls use hatchets and hand axes to carve these stones. It is simply amazing how quickly they can shape a soft stone any way they want it. If a flat topped one isn't to be had, turn a rounded one on its side and chip it down to a smooth surface. Sides that do not have a desired conformity can be reworked the same way. After the rough chopping is done lighter strokes should cut away all ax marks. A few depressions and overhangs are easy to make and add something to the natural effect. Then the top can be cut out as described above. Drilling the side holes finishes the stone, and you are ready for the planting and flowers without end. In two or three years mosses will blanket any trace of harshness.

The Building Block Rockery

This semi-formal structure has some unusual advantages. It can be made almost any height, length and width. Construction is simple, comparatively easy, and economical. Best of all, in regions where suitable rock is not to be had these blocks can be purchased.

They come in two kinds of materials: concrete, which is

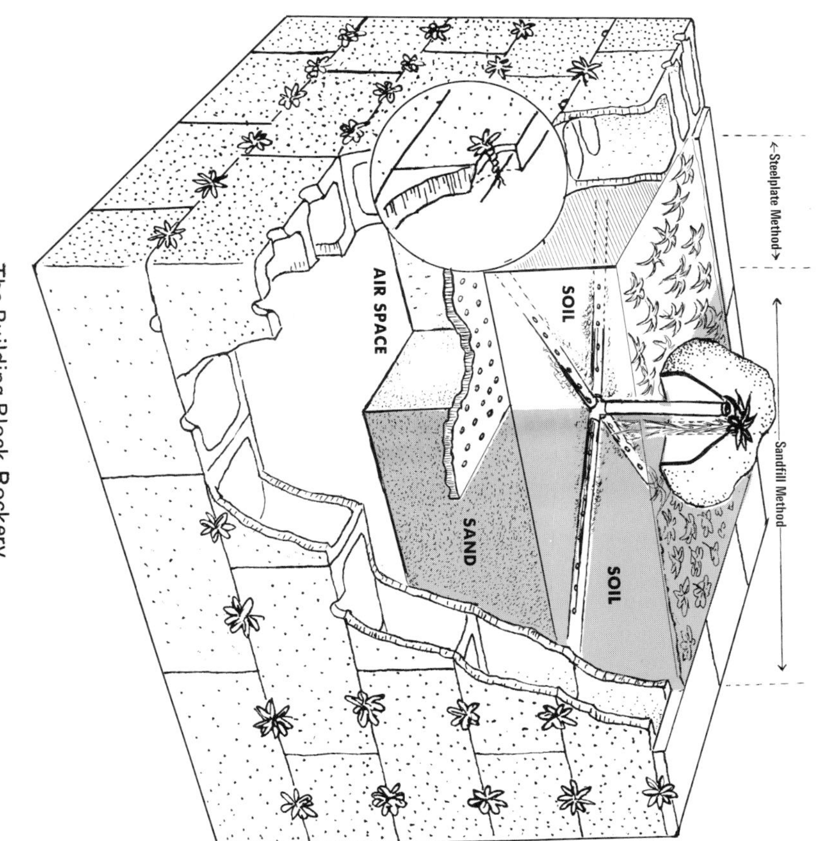

The Building Block Rockery

lower in cost, but heavier to handle, and more difficult to grind and drill; and so-called 'pumice' which is also referred to as 'light weight' and various other trade names. It is manufactured from raw shale which is placed in a rotary kiln and heated to nearly 2,000 degrees F. At this temperature it becomes rubbery and almost molten. Carbon dioxide gases are given off which expand the material and leave it porous. Then it is cooled, crushed and pressed into the finished blocks.

This is the type of block I use. It is so porous drainage and irrigation through them approach perfection. It can be drilled, ground, shaped with a wood rasp and chiseled. The best size is eight inches wide and high by 16 long. Each block contains two holes from top to bottom, measuring about five by six inches. The outside walls are one and a half to two inches thick.

The first step, after deciding upon the site, is to prepare a flat surface and check it with a carpenter's level. Next add a layer of sand about half an inch thick for adjusting any soil irregularities. Then under where the blocks are to go lay down a quarter inch mesh wire screen: galvanized iron, stainless steel, aluminum, copper, brass or some other corrosion resistant metal. This will prevent rodents from tunneling upward and feasting on your horticultural treasures.

The next step is very important: laying the first course. Mortar the ends and place them firmly together. Check carefully with a straight edge, carpenter's square, and level for accuracy. If this first course is level, straight, and the corners square the rest will be easy. But adjusting each block to a near perfect position is tedious and frustrating. Light tapping with a mallet will take care of minor corrections; greater ones will call for adding or removing some of the sand.

All courses, especially the first one, should be set before adding the next. The mortared joints can be broken loose if they are not thoroughly cured. Allow three or four days between courses. Each course should be staggered so that the middle of one block will be immediately above and below the joints of the upper and lower adjacent courses. The best way to make a good job of this locking system is to start at the corners.

Two kinds of mortar are available. The conventional material allows for adjustments in length and height. This will yield a perfect job if skillfully done. The blocks should be wet for better adhesion.

A new substance resembles very fine grey sand and is mixed with a milky liquid to form a thin paste. It is applied in 25 cent piece size dabs, four on each end – one to every corner – , and eight on top. It makes an extremely strong bond and allows the blocks to be set flush with each other. As it does not allow adjustments in either direction it is not favored by professionals. Building blocks cannot be made absolutely the same size because of lack of uniform shrinkage. But for short walls this is usually not an important consideration. The amateur mason, using this bonding agent, can lay blocks several times as fast as with ordinary mortar. That the joints are not absolutely tight is inconsequential. This system should not be built when the temperatures are below 40 degrees F., and the blocks must be dry.

Drill inch and a half holes through the top of the outside wall of each block, one for each cavity. (Corner blocks take three holes.) They should slope downward at 45 degree angles so that soil can be placed over the roots of the plants to the outer wall face. The drilling can be done after the blocks are in place but it will be faster and easier to use a drill press. Smooth the holes with a heavy, half round wood rasp.

The cavities should be filled as each course is completed and cured. Pack it firmly and water thoroughly, then add more soil to take care of the settling. It will be easier to do the planting at this time too although it can be done later without much difficulty.

Capping stones, one and one-half inches thick, should be placed in position without mortaring so they can be removed for servicing the top layer of plants.

The middle may be left open but a much prettier garden with room for more plants can be created by utilizing this space. Fill it with coarse sand up to about the depth of two blocks (16 inches) from the top. The sand will hold water and act as a reservoir to feed moisture through the block walls to the roots. Earth will not provide good drainage. Peat moss and sawdust will keep settling for a long period and will require adding soil to the top of the garden. Gravel will not hold enough moisture. Complete the filling to the top of the capping stones with rock garden soil. Wet it down, and add more to take care of settling. Then place an irregular rock of an eye-pleasing size in the middle, and plant the entire area.

Irrigating through the porous inner walls can be important, especially in hot, dry climates. One way is to drill a hole through the top of the middle rock and extend a half inch pipe down about six inches. Then take a four way fitting known as a 'cross', drill a hole through the top and weld on a sleeve. Attach capped pipe extensions to each of the four openings and screw the device on to the half inch pipe. These extensions should point to the four corners of the rockery and terminate within six inches of the walls. Place an inch of pea gravel above and below the pipe extensions to prevent clogging. These extensions should have one-eighth inch holes drilled half a foot apart on each side of the pipe and on the capped ends. The top of the vertical pipe should extend just enough above the top of the rock to attach a hose connection. Another, larger, hole should be drilled through this middle rock as closely as possible to the one for the pipe. This is for a leafy plant to help conceal the adjacent pipe.

The same device can be brought up from the bottom and fitted with an elbow so that the pipe can be run under the wall to the outside with a hose connection at the end. It might be necessary for the end of the pipe to be slightly below ground level outside the wall for drainage to prevent freezing. In this event scoop out a hole big enough to attach the hose easily.

Either approach to the problem will be satisfactory. But the water should be turned on just enough for a gentle flow. A strong stream will cause interior washing away of material and possibly settling of the plants. This irrigating should be continued for five or ten minutes – just long enough to wet the sand and soil completely without flooding. If water is seen running from under the walls the flow has been either too fast or too prolonged. The outside of the walls can be irrigated by playing a garden hose or a sprinkler upon them for a short period. The capping stones can be removed from the top course for attention or watered by filtering through them. The top of the middle of the rockery can be irrigated with a light spray.

In cold climates a very important advantage of filling the open middle of this rockery is the prevention of freezing from both sides of the blocks as is the case if the middle is left open. If this protection is not provided in regions where winter weather conditions are severe plants should be chosen that can tolerate low temperatures. *Lewisia tweedyi* and *L. rediviva,* for instance, are the only members of the genus that can be expected to survive minus 30 degrees F. It would be a waste of time, money and space to use other *Lewisias* under these circumstances. The same principle applies to the Block Wall Garden.

There is another way of converting the open middle area into a garden without sand fill. With a power grinder cut a ledge an inch wide and a quarter of an inch deep all around the inside edge of the top of the third course down. This will be 16 inches from the top, exclusive of the capping stone. The grinding can be done after the course is in position but the work will be easier if each block is ground before it is placed into position. Then fit a one-fourth inch steel plate on the ledge after first drilling holes half a foot apart over the entire area for drainage. Coat with roofing tar, asphalt or some other rust resistant paint. Spread a one or two inch layer of small rock on top of the plate to keep the holes from clogging. Finally fill with the planting mix and finish as with the sand fill method. The thickness of the plate will vary with the area of the opening. Irrigating through the inner walls with pipes below the two top courses is not practical with this system as it is with the sand fill although it can be used on the two upper courses. Or sprinkling the top surface with a garden hose will be satisfactory.

The Building Block Wall Garden

Rock wall gardens have been built for a great many years and some of them, especially in Europe where they are better known, are very beautiful. The *Building Block Wall Garden* is no different than the *Building Block Rockery* except that it is built in a straight line. Each course can feature plants or only the top course. If all the blocks contain plants the effect can be much more striking than a bare concrete wall, a wooden fence, hedge, or any other property line device. What little watering is needed can be furnished by playing a garden hose or sprinkler on the face of the wall. The porous rock absorbs a great deal of water. The uppermost course is irrigated with a soil soaker strung along the top of the capping stones. Adequate water will reach the plants through the caps within ten or 15 minutes. The only other maintenance is the occasional replacing of a plant or two. Weeding is eliminated. I do not know of any other wall or fence that will repay such high floral dividends with so little upkeep.

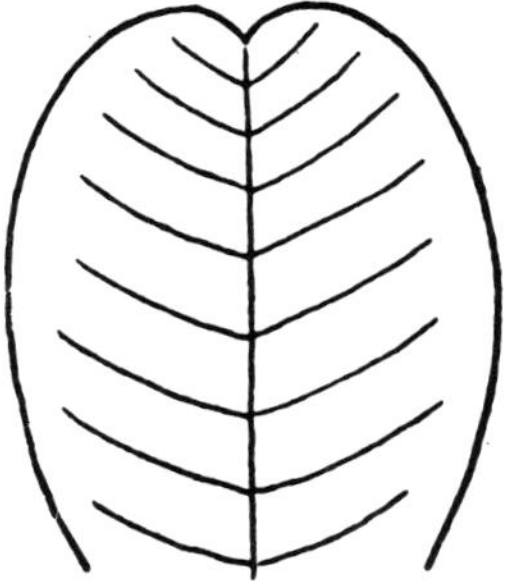

Emarginate apex

Trillium chloropetalum Naturalized Planting

THE WILD FLOWER GARDEN

Native plants may be divided into two artificial groups: those which require sun, and the ones that need shade. For the person who wants both sorts two separate gardens are recommended. The south side of a house pretty well meets the requirements of the first and the north side the other. A much more effective setting for the latter is under trees. These may be evergreen or deciduous. The fact that the deciduous trees loose their leaves in the winter is of little consequence as far as the health of most plants is concerned for at that time of the year the cooler weather is an adequate substitute for summer shade.

The needle bearing coniferous trees are constantly shedding their old leaves. They are often too acid and over a period of many years may have to be raked away. The broad leaves of deciduous trees should be removed each fall both for esthetic reasons and to keep evergreen wild plants from being damaged from lack of light, air, and too much moisture inducing rot.

Among the deciduous trees suitable for protecting the wild garden are elms, sycamores, some of the maples, many of the fruit trees, and alders. Beeches and oaks are particularly desirable while the willows, cottonwoods, poplars and other members of the willow family have their roots too close to the surface. Almost all trees have this root problem in varying degrees but the naturalized effect of wild flowers under trees offsets this moderate disadvantage. I have wild flowers growing under thirteen trees.

Most garden soils are suitable to some wild flowers but few have the composition necessary for the maximum number. In nature usually not many species of wild plants are found in any one location. One of the main purposes of the native plant garden is to establish a wide selection of flowers. Such a concentration, if carefully planned, can be marvelously beautiful over a longer span of time than anything that can be found in the wild. This calls for modifying the soil to create conditions agreeable to the maximum number of different species.

Many plants like to send their creeping roots wandering

just under the surface. Some of them are the Bleeding Hearts, *Dicentras;* the Wild Gingers, *Asarums;* the Oconee Bells, *Shortias,* and a host of others. This calls for a loose, humusy, moist surface soil. Most wild plants will benefit from permanent moisture, a cool root run, aeration, plenty of food and *good* drainage.

There are various ways of creating these conditions depending upon how much work one cares to do to approach the ideal. One of my beds, on the north side of the house, is as nearly perfect as can be obtained. I chose a strip about six feet wide and over 30 feet long – all the space that was available. I dug out the old soil to a depth of 18 inches and hauled it to the dump. I replaced it with 50 percent forest humus taken from under maples, willows and alders, 25 percent rich, black forest top soil, and 25 percent coarse sand. This ordeal kept two of us busy for two weeks. Removing the old soil was just plain hard work and buying the sand was no problem. But getting the humus and high quality top soil was another matter. First I had to find it – no easy job even in my forested country. Then arrangements had to be made with the owner. Finally we scraped away loose branches, undecayed leaves and other debris to get at the pure, clean humus. It was only two or three inches deep in some places and less in others. But between the roots of the stumps of large trees that had been logged off half a century ago we were able to collect considerable quantities of the thoroughly rotted material we wanted. On the uphill sides of half decomposed logs were other concentrations. Then it was simply a matter of scraping it into piles with a hoe, filling the five gallon buckets and taking them anywhere from 50 feet to 100 yards through the woods to the trailer. The top soil was obtained more readily from the same place. Humus, top soil and sand were thoroughly mixed and spread into the bed, three inches higher than I wanted the permanent level, to allow for settling.

Less arduous methods will also produce good results. The street cleaning departments of some of the larger cities will take orders in late summer for truck loads of leaves to be delivered free. This material can be composted, which takes about two years. Then it should be screened to remove foreign material such as broken glass, scrap metal, tree branches and other miscellaneous debris. Excellent humus can be produced in this way with a minimum of toil.

Rotten wood from old logs and stumps is also very good but can not be used alone as a rule. Some dealers can supply rotten sawdust. If this is half a century or more old, it may be mixed with sand and leaf mold. Fresh sawdust destroys soil nitrogen and needs replacing with commercial fertilizer.

Most animal droppings will burn or do not provide the loose material needed. Thoroughly rotted horse or cow manures are excellent. Fresh material has a higher nitrogen content but is too hot and should never be used. The source of animal manures can be important. One such load, guaranteed 'weed free' contained crab grass and I have been fighting this pest ever since.

Peat moss is a good soil conditioner. Its principal objection is the much higher cost compared with other materials that can be used instead. It has little or no food value but does wonders in loosening the soil. Garden debris can be composted and provides a steady supply and is the most convenient source of soil conditioners.

The safest way to get genuine top soil is to dig it yourself. It should come from the surface of the earth or close to it. It may vary from a few inches to several feet deep and is darker in color than the deeper earth. Usually an abrupt alteration in color marks the change from the upper material to the lower. Top soil contains a large amount of decayed vegetation and is rich in organic material of good fertility. Earth taken from below the true top soil may have little or no value for the purpose for which it is intended.

"Top soil" sold by dealers often comes from basement excavations and is the farthest thing imaginable from what it purports to be. It would be wise to go with the dealer and watch him load. If he refuses to let you do this you may have the wrong dealer. Other so-called "top soil" is taken from land leveling operations or from river banks. One such operation I observed was taken from a ten foot high bank and contained no top soil whatever. Material taken from large river beds and banks may contain very fine sand that will pack too solidly.

Coarse sand can be obtained from sand and gravel companies. Fine sand should be avoided as it does not keep the soil nearly as loose as it should. Sand from large rivers, lakes and oceans is usually too fine. Sand from small streams is often coarse. Rock crushers have what they call "screenings." This is the material left after they have sifted out all the rock down to the smallest salable – less than pea size. The residue is splendid and the cost is low. But the demand often exceeds the supply.

A good combination is one-third garden soil; one-third coarse sand; and one-third horse or cow manure or peat moss, humus, rotten wood or decayed sawdust. A top dressing two or three inches deep of the above material without the garden soil will help retain moisture and provide an easy root run for those plants which prefer this treatment. If rotten wood or sawdust is used instead of humus or animal fertilizers an addition of commercial fertilizer will help maintain the necessary fertility. This method is for those who do not care to undertake complete removal of the soil and its replacement as I did.

Forest soils contain a minimum of weeds. If this is a problem it can be controlled with a layer of bark dust, one to three inches deep. Weeds have more trouble getting through a heavy covering than a thin one. Bark dust helps retain moisture but has little food value. However it is the best material for the purpose I have ever discovered.

Once the bed has been completed the planting follows. Such flowers as *Dicentras* and some of the *Sedums* that like to wander too much can be confined to pots which are plunged into the soil until the rims are barely out of sight. Mice and other rodents devour certain bulbs. They can be protected by wire screen baskets, likewise sunk out of sight.

Nature abhors a straight line and wildlings should not be placed in orderly rows if you are attempting to create the illusion that yours are growing in the same way that you found them in the fields, forests and mountains. Some species appear to better advantage in clumps. *Erythroniums* and *Trilliums* are good examples. Others that flower profusely, such as some of the *Irises* should live in solitary splendour. Each should have ample room to display its charms of blossom, foliage, or both. Taller growing species are better for backgrounds.

Most wild flower gardens are planted on a hit or miss basis. This is a mistake and can seriously reduce the maximum beauty that can be achieved with the same number of plants. The wise method is to make a scale drawing of the garden, decide what species are wanted, how many of each and the space they should have. Then do the planting. This systematic approach will take less work and reduce the several years later self incrimination.

INDEX

Scientific names are in bold face
Common names are in ordinary type
Synonyms are in italics

N

RARE WILD FLOWERS
OF
NORTH AMERICA

First Edition Limited To One Thousand Copies

This is Number

532

Leonard Wiley